COSTA RICA
A Natural Destination

Fourth Edition

Ree Strange Sheck

John Muir Publications
Santa Fe, New Mexico

John Muir Publications, P.O. Box 613, Santa Fe, New Mexico 87504

Printed in the United States of America.
Fourth edition. First printing October 1996.

Library of Congress Cataloging-in-Publication Data
Sheck, Ree.
    Costa Rica : a natural destination / Ree Strange Sheck. -- 4th ed.
       p. cm.
    Includes bibliographical references and index.
    ISBN 1-56261-291-3
    1. Costa Rica--Guidebooks. 2. Natural parks and reserves--Costa
Rica--Guidebooks. 3. Outdoor recreation--Costa Rica--Guidebooks.
I. Title.
F1543.5.S52 1996
917.28604'5--dc20   96-7724
                                                    CIP

Editors: Dianna Delling, Peggy Schaefer, Chris Hayhurst
Production: Nikki Rooker, Janine Lehmann
Graphics: Sarah Horowitz, Joanne Jakub
Design: Susan Surprise
Typography: Marilyn Hager
Cover Photo: Ree Strange Sheck
Maps: Kathleen Sparks
Printer: Publishers Press

Distributed to the book trade by
Publishers Group West
Emeryville, California

Contents

Acknowledgments

I first came to Costa Rica in 1968. I came as a visitor to this country that has been my home now since 1990, when I finished the first edition of this book. For unfailing support during the research and writing of the book, from the first edition to the fourth, loving thoughts go to Ronald Sheck and to my daughter, Claren Boehler-Sheck. Continuing love and gratitude go to my son, Curt, whose death in 1984 was the beginning of a new journey for me, a journey that led me back to Costa Rica and to this book.

For this edition, special thanks goes to Nora Schofield, whose belief in me and loving assistance in countless ways have been invaluable as I struggled to meet deadlines; to Omar Coto for graciously stepping in to assist with research; to Chino Soto and Alex Segura for helping hands on dozens of occasions; and to Mary and Eston Rockwell of Monteverde for listening and for hugs.

My sister Ruth Hamilton traveled with me some during research for the past two editions—her presence and her spirit helped me remember to savor the adventure—thanks.

I express continuing appreciation to Yehudi Monestel, a longtime friend and fellow journalist, who has walked trails with me since 1968. Thanks also to his parents, Don Bolivar and Doña Elena, who opened their hearts and home to me.

To the naturalist guides I have been privileged to travel with and to learn from, to tour operators, to the owners of private nature reserves and hotels visited, thanks for gracious attention. Travels in national parks, reserves, and refuges have given me profound respect for those who protect them, who often live and work under difficult circumstances. Thanks to each one who has taken time to talk or walk with me.

I would like to thank the Costa Rican Tourism Institute (ICT) and the staff of Expotur, an international tourism wholesalers' and retailers' fair, for their help through the years.

Thanks to many readers of this book who have sent helpful suggestions and shared their own discoveries with me.

Finally, I express my appreciation to the people of Costa Rica for their generosity of spirit, those I know and those whose names I will never know—for smiles, for helping me get on the right bus or the right road, for walking with me to the corner to point out the street I needed, for reminding me that neighborliness transcends international boundaries. And I am forever grateful to those who have worked to preserve the extraordinary richness of Costa Rica's tropical ecosystems.

1

Why Costa Rica?

Costa Rica touches the heart and mind, not through elegant boulevards, towering cathedrals, or an imposing place in history but through its incredible natural beauty and a gracious people disposed to peace, kindness, and a generosity of spirit. No one feels a stranger here for long.

It is one of the most biologically diverse countries in the world—a treasure house of flora and fauna unequaled in so small an area. Casual tourist and dedicated nature traveler alike come under the spell of a natural wonderland studded with tropical forests, rushing rivers, exotic animals, uncrowded beaches, high mountains, and awesome volcanoes.

Struggling to explain why increasing numbers of people are making their way to this small Central American country, one observer finally said simply, "The greatest tourist attraction in Costa Rica is Costa Rica."

With more than 100 years of democracy under its belt in a region with a history of political strife, Costa Rica boasts "teachers, not soldiers." The country has had no army since 1948. It lays claim to one of the highest literacy rates in the world and a national health care system that covers all its citizens. The people's inclination toward modesty, simplicity, and friendliness, along with the country's commitment to peace, create a climate of trust for travelers.

And what a place to travel! Visitors can walk among rainforest giants, see green turtles nesting, get a ringside view of one of the most active volcanoes in the world, ogle the keel-billed toucan, and hear the howler monkey. Pristine beaches beckon on the Caribbean and Pacific. Trees alive with their own mini-forests of bromeliads, lichens, and mosses assume mysterious forms in the high cloud forests; orchids grow wild amid lush vegetation that tumbles down along road cuts. Miles of coffee *fincas* (farms), sugarcane fields, and pineapple and banana plantations bear witness to a rural heritage

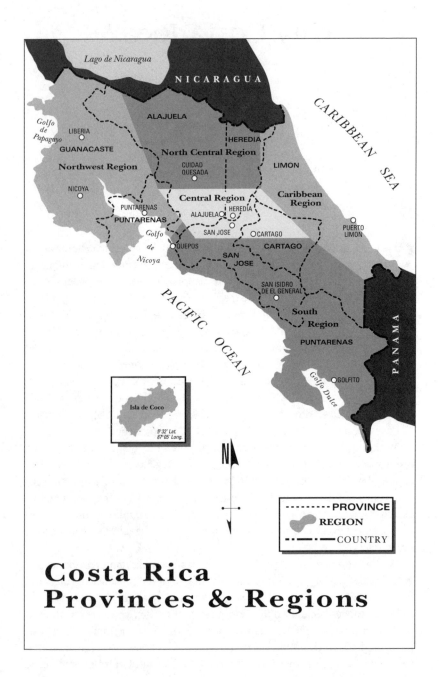

Costa Rica
Provinces & Regions

fields, and pineapple and banana plantations bear witness to a rural heritage and the influence of agriculture on the life of the country today.

Travelers can enjoy world-class white-water rafting, sunning on deserted beaches, bicycle touring, surfing, swimming, fishing, bird-watching, hiking, or shopping, or simply sit on the Plaza de la Cultura in the heart of San José and people-watch.

A small country, a little smaller than West Virginia or Nova Scotia, Costa Rica abounds with plant and animal species: North American, South American, and those native to the area.

It is possible to drive from Puntarenas on the Pacific to Port of Limón on the Atlantic in less than six hours, even allowing time to maneuver through the traffic in the capital city of San José en route.

Elevations go from sea level to 12,529 feet (3,819 m). In general, temperatures are moderate, varying more with altitude than time of year. San José's average high is 77°F (24.9°C); its low, 61°F (16.3°C). Lowland zones range from the 70s to the 90s (21°C to 37°C). Most people are surprised to learn that frost and ice can occur on some of the loftier peaks.

Costa Rica is known around the world for its national park system, now protecting about 12 percent of the land. With the aid of other reserves, about 30 percent of its territory is protected—an enviable record for any country, remarkable for a developing one. That commitment to conservation makes it possible for resident and tourist alike to encounter the natural world in a special way. An agouti and I once surprised each other on a park trail; a paca (called in Costa Rica by the marvelous name of *tepezcuintle*) amazed me by rushing from bushes to plunge into a pool at the base of a waterfall where I had just been swimming. Giant blue morpho butterflies can turn any ordinary day into a mystical experience. There is the chance that one will come face-to-face with a white-faced monkey or catch a glimpse of a scarlet macaw. Tropical trees towering to 150 feet and delicate, tiny flowers blooming in a high Andean-like climate open us to not only the magnificence of the universe but also the interrelationship of all living things.

This guide is offered as a companion for your journey in Costa Rica, to help you touch and be touched by the land and people on paths most comfortable for you. It includes information about the national parks and privately owned nature reserves, beaches, volcanoes, and towns. It also tells what you will find at the end of the trail: a private room and bath with hot water or a bunk in a dormitory atmosphere with a shared bath and cold water. It lets you know whether you can fly in or drive in, or whether access is by foot, boat, or horseback.

There is a nutshell version of the country's history, focusing on what makes Costa Rica stand out from its neighbors; tips on what to bring along and how to call home; and a few highlighted odds and ends—such as where and when you might see a quetzal; which beaches turtles lay their eggs on; water safety; and coffee from bean to harvest.

The book is intended to help you find your own adventure and sense the heartbeat of this special place, from the quiet rhythm of its rural landscape to busy San José. Your experience will be your own. Just bring an open heart to contain it.

Costa Rican waterfall (Ben Lidreth)

2

Marching to a Different Drummer

There's something different about Costa Rica. It is a country without an army in a world that counts tanks, missiles, and nuclear warheads as the measure of a nation's strength. The national hero is not a general but a young, barefoot *campesino* (farmer). Schoolchildren, not soldiers, parade on Independence Day. While other countries debate the issue, Costa Rica abolished the death penalty more than 100 years ago.

Located in a region where violence has too often been the order of the day, Costa Rica lives in peace. It has a literacy rate of 93 percent and a Social Security system that offers health care to all its people. Costa Ricans like to say they have gained through evolution what other countries try to attain through revolution.

Travelers often ask what has led this country on a path that sets it apart from its Central American neighbors. A brief look at Costa Rica's history, economy, and political and social systems will answer some of the questions visitors ask most.

Historical Highlights

When Christopher Columbus dropped anchor off Costa Rica in 1502, near the present-day Port of Limón, he still thought he had found a new route to the East and believed he was on the southeast coast of Asia, near Siam. Even today, some people confuse Costa Rica with another Caribbean locale: Puerto Rico.

Stories about great wealth to be found here began at that time. The Indians offered Columbus gifts of gold, and Spanish explorers began to refer to the area as *costa rica*, or "rich coast." Later expeditions touched along the Caribbean and then the Pacific coasts, but it was not until the 1560s that the first permanent European settlement took root. Cartago in the Central Valley became the capital of what would become a province under the Captaincy General of Guatemala.

The first Spanish inhabitants of this new land found neither mineral wealth nor a large indigenous population that could be used as forced labor. The Indians they did find were not keen on servitude. Resistance ranged from warfare to retreat into the forested back country. Colonizers were effectively reduced to small landholdings that they and their families could work themselves. Communication was hampered by rugged terrain and lack of roads, made more difficult by seasonally heavy rains. Efforts went into survival rather than commerce, with the agrarian society based on subsistence farming and ranching.

Throughout the colonial period, Costa Rica was a poor, neglected outpost of the Spanish empire. The poverty and isolation gave rise to a simple life, individualism, hospitality, and a spirit of equality that cut across social class lines, creating the beginnings of rural democracy.

Even the name Costa Ricans call themselves, *ticos*, is said by some to come from a colonial saying: "We are all *hermaniticos* [little brothers]." Diminutive endings of *-ito* and *-ico* are characteristic of everyday speech. For example, you may hear *pequeñito* for "small" rather than *pequeño*.

The Latin American wars for independence from Spain were far removed from this peaceful enclave. When victory finally came in 1821, Costa Rica received word about a month later. A popular story is that a messenger on a mule delivered the official letter. Costa Rica joined the Central American Federation for a time but declared itself an independent republic in 1848.

The war that did have an impact on the country came in 1856, when William Walker, a U.S. adventurer who had gained control of the armed forces of Nicaragua and dreamed of controlling all of Central America, invaded Costa Rica. The strong national identity forged during the colonial period of isolation brought volunteers from around the country to defend the nation. In a battle that lasted only a few minutes, the well-armed invading force was routed at Hacienda Santa Rosa in Guanacaste. (The site of the confrontation is now protected in Santa Rosa National Park. When you visit there, remember how remote it was at the time; the ragtag citizen army of 9,000 marched 12 days from San José to get there.) The army pursued Walker's forces into Nicaragua, where a second battle occurred. In the fighting at Rivas, a brave young campesino from Alajuela named Juan Santamaría volunteered to set fire to the Walker stronghold, losing his life in the act. He became the national hero for his part in this crucial battle. Walker's dream ended in 1860 before a firing squad in Honduras.

The first true popular elections came in 1889, which is why Costa Rica claims more than 100 years of democracy. The president at the time tried to cancel the promised vote to name his own successor, but the elections were held when peasants invaded San José and demanded their say. By this time, the exportation of coffee was ending Costa Rica's isolation. Soon, bananas thrust it further into international commerce. Population grew, frontiers expanded, and transportation routes carried produce out and the world in.

Costa Rica's own brief "revolution" came in 1948, when Congress annulled the presidential election to keep the opposition candidate from taking over. It was a short but savage civil war in which more than 2,000 people died. The leader of the revolt was José "Pepe" Figueres, who took control of an interim government for 18 months before the elected opposition candidate assumed office. Figueres abolished the army; military facilities were converted into schools, a prison, and the National Museum. The Constitution of 1949 set up a government of checks and balances.

Succeeding governments have spent money on roads, schools, hospitals, electricity, and running water instead of arms. Compromise and negotiation are the key words in resolution of conflict. Citizens do, however, take to the streets to protest or pressure the government for action.

Today, large landholdings exist alongside small farms; wealth exists alongside poverty. But there is still a genuine faith in peace as a force, in democracy, and in fundamental human dignity. Social, economic, and political mobility are possible. The national character is still tied to the land. Even in urban centers, Costa Ricans tell you their strength is in the hard-working, loyal campesino and the land. It will be interesting to see how this idealization of the past holds up as more and more campesinos become *peónes* (day laborers) and the pressures on the land increase. You can be sure of one thing: It will be a Costa Rican solution.

Political System

Governmental power is divided among executive, legislative, and judicial branches, with a Supreme Election Tribunal in charge of elections. The decentralized form of government reflects Costa Ricans' aversion to concentration of power.

A president is elected every four years by secret ballot and cannot be reelected. Two vice-presidents are elected at the same time. Numerous checks and balances were written into the 1949 constitution, under which the country is governed, to prevent abuse of power, especially by a strong president. The unicameral Legislative Assembly is considered to have more power than the president. Its 57 deputies are also elected every four years

Monument in Alajuela honoring Costa Rica's national hero, Juan
Santamaría (Ree Strange Sheck)

and may not serve consecutive terms. Seats are allocated according to population in each of the country's seven provinces.

Magistrates of the Supreme Court of Justice are named by the legislature for staggered eight-year terms. These magistrates name justices at the provincial level.

To safeguard against electoral fraud, a kind of fourth branch of government is set up as an autonomous body. This Supreme Election Tribunal oversees everything from voter registration to the actual counting of votes. It also oversees registration of political parties and keeps an eye on political campaigns for misconduct. As a further check, six months before the election, command of the Civil and Rural Guard, essentially police forces, passes from the president to the tribunal.

Campaigning can get dirty, but election day itself is a party. Even children turn out to help get people to the polls, wave party flags, and shout slogans. Organized travel tours come just to observe the process and join in the civic fiesta.

Do not, however, mistake fanfare for frivolity. Ticos take their voting seriously; turnouts are high. Women have the vote, as do 18-year-olds. Even those who cannot read and write are entitled to cast a ballot. Women have been elected to high office—both in the legislature and as vice-president.

Municipal elections take place at the same time as national elections. These are the two important levels of government.

Political parties come and go; the two principal ones today are the National Liberation party and the Social Christian Unity party. Factions split off and coalitions form. The Communist party is recognized but does not have much weight at the polls.

Costa Rica has a large bureaucracy. The government produces electricity, runs the telephone service and a national banking system, builds houses, and distills liquor, along with doing all the other things one expects a government to do. More than 15 percent of the country's workers on fixed salaries are employed in the public sector.

Social Welfare and Education

The Social Security system, referred to by ticos as the *Caja* and identified by the initials CCSS, was instituted in 1941 by the same president who helped enact a labor code that set minimum wages and guaranteed workers the right to organize. Though complaints about inefficiency and the level of care are common, no one denies the vital role Social Security has played in improving health care. Infant mortality rates are among the lowest in Latin America. Life expectancy at birth in the early part of the century was 40 years; today it is 76 years. When the system started, coverage was limited, but now practically all citizens have access to care.

Rural health-care programs geared to both prevention and treatment touch the lives of the poor even in remote corners of the country. Scenarios may include a medical center staffed by paramedics and visited regularly by doctors and nurses. I was once visiting a rural highland school when the doctor came for his scheduled community visit, using one room of the two-room school for consultations. In a coastal Caribbean village, a young mother told me the doctor came by boat once a month. Poor urban neighborhoods are also targeted.

As you travel around the country, you will see clinics in small towns and a growing number of regional hospitals. The Red Cross, or *Cruz Roja* as it is called in Spanish, is a strong, highly respected organization in Costa Rica with dedicated staff members and volunteers in many communities. It works closely with health care agencies and provides ambulance service.

Costa Rica and schools are practically synonymous. The country was one of the first in the world to mandate free, compulsory, tax-supported education. This 1869 constitutional provision preceded passage of such laws in the United States. About 18 percent of the national budget goes to education.

In a rural place, the schoolhouse may be one room, with six grades divided between morning and afternoon classes. Continuing on to secondary school can mean real commitment for students, for while primary schools are abundant, secondary schools are centered in areas with larger populations. Two young people who stopped to rest near me on a mountain road explained that they were on their way to the nearest bus stop for a 30-minute ride to school in Turrialba. The daily walk to and from the bus stop was 90 minutes each way, with the return trip after dark.

Costa Rica has four state universities in the Central Valley, with branches in outlying areas. University education is not free, but tuition—although increasing—is generally low, and scholarships are available. Technical and vocational schools outside the San José metropolitan area also put higher education within reach of more students as well as promote other regions in the hope of stemming the flow of people into the heavily populated Central Valley. There are a number of private institutions of higher learning.

Most visitors ask about the rationale behind school uniforms for primary and secondary students. This, too, harks back to egalitarian roots. The idea is to minimize differences between social classes. Private schools also have uniforms. Secondary schools may petition to have a uniform that differs from the traditional blue shirt and navy pants or skirt.

Debates on the quality of education, and even what constitutes an education, rage here as elsewhere. Resources are stretched thin, and urban areas have an advantage because of backup facilities such as libraries and easier access to educational support. It is sometimes difficult to retain teachers in small, isolated areas. The overall picture, however, looks positive. Schools are frequently the nucleus around which a sense of community forms. Dedicated teachers do exist, often working with few of the materials that teachers in the United States or Canada take for granted. Innovative projects include radio programs aimed at primary schoolchildren in rural areas, one of which focuses on environmental education. Bilingual materials in the six surviving Indian languages (Maleku, Cabecar, Térraba, Boruca, Guaymí, and Bribrí) are incorporated into the curriculum on Indian reserves, including history and legends that have passed down through oral tradition.

Housing, another focus of social programs, has been particularly emphasized in the last few years. Both urban and rural public projects have been implemented in an attempt to meet a serious housing shortage.

Economy

Starting from a base of subsistence agriculture in colonial times, Costa Rica moved into the world economy only in the latter half of the nineteenth century with the exportation of coffee to Europe. Exportation of bananas followed soon afterward. A Costa Rican journalist, lamenting his country's dependence on agricultural exports, once said to me, "What makes it worse is that the country produces *postres* [desserts]—coffee, bananas, sugar, and chocolate. When importing countries are in an economic bind, demand for these things drops first."

Some of Costa Rica's current economic problems have roots in the crisis from 1979 to 1982, when the country went through probably the worst economic crunch in its history. World prices for its traditional crops collapsed at the same time that petroleum costs soared. Since Costa Rica imports all its oil, the dynamics were devastating. The country had borrowed heavily from eager banks with the money used largely, as one Costa Rican put it, "to maintain our accustomed standard of living." It has been difficult to cut social programs citizens take as their due. National spending still outstrips income earned from exports and taxation, while juggling foreign debt payments demands enormous energy.

However, there is light on the horizon. Investment in nontraditional products to increase exports and cut dependence on the postres is starting to pay off. In 1988, for the first time, nontraditional exports edged past traditional ones in dollar value. Textiles, fresh flowers, ornamental plants, pineapples, frozen fish, macadamia nuts, and melons are among the items filling out the menu. Check the label of the next shirt or pair of pants you

Bananas—woven into the economic and social fabric since the 1880s
(Ree Strange Sheck)

buy. It could very well say, "Assembled in Costa Rica." The country has become one of the largest brassiere manufacturers in the world.

The nation's stability, a large and educated middle class that provides a stable work force, lower labor costs, and national and international incentives have drawn foreign firms into joint ventures with Costa Ricans. (Average per-capita income, by the way, is $2,546.) The U.S. Caribbean Basin Initiative, which provides preferential customs treatment to many products from the region, has been a stimulus; the United States is the country's biggest business partner, but multinational companies from Europe and the Far East are also setting up shop. Tourism has edged out coffee and bananas to become the country's number one foreign exchange earner. This is a result of both increasing numbers of visitors and decreasing income from those traditional crops because of falling prices, competition, and restrictive trade agreements.

Someone once observed that Costa Rica has a way of turning fatal flaws into saving graces. Perhaps the national debt is a case in point. "Debt-for-nature" swaps were used a few years ago to reduce the debt while providing money for in-country conservation projects. The plan worked like this:

Conservationists raised funds to buy a piece of the debt on the secondary market—usually in dollars—from a foreign bank or institution willing to sell for less than the face value. It was usually the Central Bank of Costa Rica that bought the debt from the conservation group through interest-bearing government bonds, in local currency. The conservation group had to use the money to finance environmental projects. The foreign bank got what it considered a bad debt off its books, Costa Rica lightened its burden, and money flowed into the preservation of natural resources. There is currently talk of renewing this strategy.

Natural Resources

Historically, Costa Rica's Indian population was small and dispersed, causing little human impact on the land. Spanish colonial settlement was also limited, both in size and location, being focused in the centers of San José, Cartago, Alajuela, and Heredia. As the limits of the frontier began to widen after independence from Spain, first around the Central Valley and then fanning out from transportation routes to the coasts and eventually to the north and south, occasional legislation began to appear to protect natural resources. Initial concerns seemed to be with wildlife and hunting or with prohibiting private ownership of certain tracts of land or a volcano crater. Precedents were set, though early enforcement was not terrific.

As time went on, foreign naturalists, who first began to arrive in the mid-nineteenth century, came in increasing numbers, drawn by the biological richness of the area. By the middle of this century, natives and foreigners alike began pressing for preservation. Unprotected, forests were obviously not going to last forever. Costa Rica began building a national park system that today protects nearly as many bird species as is found in all of North America and almost half its number of plant species. There are more butterflies in this tiny country than in the entire United States.

While preservation was the necessary initial step, the goal and challenge of protected areas today is not only conservation of biodiversity but also putting people into the conservation equation. Population pressures are increasing at a time when public land available for new settlement is practically gone.

Neighbors who receive some benefit from those protected lands will be more inclined to preserve them. New concepts go beyond promotion of the areas for scientific research, nature tourism, and environmental education, all of which, when carefully carried out, can benefit local people. In some protected areas, for example, local residents are being involved as rangers,

SOME CONSERVATION ORGANIZATIONS

Many small, nonprofit groups around Costa Rica are hard at work to protect the environment of this biologically rich country. All can use a helping hand. A few are listed here.

APREFLOFAS is a volunteer force that helps patrol protected zones to combat illegal hunting and lumbering and works to increase conservation awareness through environmental education. Apartado 917-2150, Moravia, telephone/fax 240-6087.

Friends of Lomas Barbudal (AMILOBA) is dedicated to the conservation of tropical dry forest, focusing on the Lomas Barbudal Biological Reserve in Guanacaste. An initial and continuing concern has been wildfires, one of the greatest dangers facing the reserve. Some are set by hunters to flush out game, some are the result of carelessness, some start accidentally from neighboring fields being cleared. Through the conservation group's efforts, fire prevention and control strategies are now in place. It also offers environmental education programs at the group's center in Bagaces, and operates a visitor center at the northern entrance to the reserve. Volunteers, *preferably Spanish speakers, are needed for special projects. In the United States, fax (510) 528-0346. In Costa Rica, Amigos de Lomas Barbudal, Bagaces, Guanacaste, telephone/fax 671-1029.*

ARBOFILIA has reforestation projects, organic farming, and wildlife conservation programs principally in rural communities around Carara Biological Reserve. A small center in El Sur de Turrubares is open to visitors, who can swim in clean rivers and explore the zone on horseback. The organization was founded by small farmers with a goal of economic and environmental restoration. Write to ARBOFILIA, Apartado 512-1100, Tibás, telephone/fax 240-7145, telephone 240-8832.

The Monteverde Conservation League owns and manages the first international children's rainforest and has programs in environmental education, habitat rehabilitation, research, and small-scale sustainable development projects. Some volunteer opportunities exist. Apartado 10581-1000, San José, telephone 645-5305 or 645-5003; fax 645-5104; e-mail: acmmcl@sol.racsa.co.cr.

The coffee bean brought Costa Rica into the world market
(Ree Strange Sheck)

teachers, caretakers, and even researchers. Their livelihoods come from conservation.

Throughout the country, the challenge is to teach people that they can make a living from natural resources without destroying them. This is a crucial concept since practically all forest reserves are in private hands, and about 12 percent of the parks are still privately owned. Sustainable development is the watchword. Managed harvesting of trees, plants, or seeds can bring more money than clearing the forest, and the resource survives. Carefully planned, responsible tourism can bring benefits to those who live around protected areas.

Government and private reforestation efforts are a long way from replacing what is cut every year, but they are growing. Research and plantings with native trees are under way. A project that encourages natural regeneration of a tropical dry forest could have implications for projects around the world.

Costa Rica has come a long way from its beginning, poor and forgotten by the world. Its accomplishments in health and literacy put it in the ranks of highly developed nations. In conservation and commitment to peace, it seems a giant.

3

Lay of the Land

Rising up between the Atlantic and the Pacific as part of the land bridge between North and South America, Costa Rica lies in a region unique in the world. The land is home to plants and animals from both North and South America as well as to species native to Costa Rica. The cultural mix is as rich as the biological one. Indigenous peoples, though small in number compared with their neighbors to the north and south, were influenced by the advanced civilizations of both Mesoamerica and South America.

The rugged terrain of this small Central American country, wedged between Nicaragua on the north and Panama on the south, springs surprises on those who come expecting the tropical temperatures always to be balmy. At some times of the year, ice forms at the highest elevations.

Topography

From sea to shining sea in Costa Rica can be as short a distance as 74 miles (119 km). However, where the country is narrowest, near Panama, it is also the most rugged and hardest to cross. The chain of mountains that forms a backbone down the length of the land becomes higher and wider as it curves from northwest to southeast.

In the north, near Nicaragua, the chain is known as the Guanacaste Cordillera (*cordillera* is the Spanish term for mountain range), giving way as it progresses southeast to the Tilarán Cordillera and Central Cordillera, all of which were formed as a result of volcanic activity. The Cordillera of Talamanca in the south is an uplifted mountain range that contains the country's highest peak: Chirripó, reaching 12,529 feet (3,819 m) above sea level.

You won't be in Costa Rica long before you hear people talking about the Meseta Central, or Central Valley. Since colonial times, this region has been the center of population. But it is not just the area around San José, as many visitors assume. In addition to the lower and larger valley of San José, where the capital is located, along with towns such as Heredía, Alajuela, Grecia, Naranjo, Atenas, and San Ramón, there is the higher, eastern valley of Cartago, which contains the colonial capital of Cartago as well as Paraíso and Turrialba.

Elevations in the Central Valley range from almost 2,000 to 5,000 feet (600 to 1,500 m). Separating the two depressions is the Continental Divide, which runs through the mountains known as La Carpintera at 5,085 feet (1,550 m) above sea level. The San José Valley drains toward the Pacific via the Virilla and Grande Rivers, tributaries of the Tarcoles River. The Cartago Valley is drained by the headwaters of the Reventazón River, which flows to the Caribbean.

VOLCANOES

Volcanoes are a hot topic. Some 112 craters, including the two on Cocos Island, mark the landscape of Costa Rica. They range from extinct to dormant to active and from a mere remnant rising 328 feet (100 m) above the Tortuguero Plains to majestic peaks more than 11,000 feet high (3,350 m) that still fuss and fume along the country's spine.

If you have never heard a volcano breathe, consider a visit to 5,358-foot (1,633-m) Arenal, one of the most active in the world. Hearing the huff of its breath one unforgettable morning made me one with primitive peoples; the mountain became a living being. When it hurled fiery blocks high in the air, not a doubt remained: Arenal was angry. It has been angry enough to kill people since it began its current phase of activity in 1968,

including a tourist who climbed up its slopes. Be prudent when you visit: keep a respectful distance from all active volcanoes.

Activity at 8,884-foot (2,708-m) Poás Volcano and 5,925-foot (1,806-m) Rincón de la Vieja has caused the national parks associated with them to close at times since 1989. The Volcanological and Seismological Observatory of Costa Rica at the National University in Heredia (telephone 237-4570) monitors Poás and other active sites. It has published a map that pinpoints the craters and gives the elevation and type of volcano.

Other volcanoes with some level of activity include Irazú at 11,260 feet (3,432 m), Miravalles at 6,653 feet (2,028 m), and Turrialba at 10,925 feet (3,330 m).

The third major intermountain basin, the General-Coto Brus Valley, is between the high Talamanca Range and the coastal mountains in the southwest. Elevations here are lower than in the Central Valley, ranging from about 330 to 3,200 feet (100 to 1,000 m). Significant population has spilled over into this rich region only in the last half of this century, with San Isidro de El General serving as a center for shopping and transportation in a largely rural landscape of dispersed settlements. Two tributaries of the great Térraba River—the General and Coto Brus—drain the basin toward the Pacific.

The spine of mountains that winds its way down the country separates two coastal regions that have noticeable differences. A number of hilly peninsulas jut out from the Pacific coastline (Santa Elena, Nicoya, Herradura, Osa, and Burica); there are two large gulfs (Nicoya and Dulce) and many small coves and bays. The two major commercial ports are Puntarenas and Puerto Caldera. For the most part, mountains come close to the sea on the Pacific side. The greatest expanse of flatlands in the Pacific lowlands is inland, centering around the Tempisque River drainage at the north end of the Gulf of Nicoya and narrowing northward to Nicaragua.

The Pacific coastline is almost 780 miles (1,254 km) long, while the Caribbean coast is only 132 miles (212 km) long and has a natural harbor only in the Moín-Limón area. The largest area of lowland plains in the country stretches back from the eastern coast: the Plains of Guatuso, San Carlos, Tortuguero, and Santa Clara form a wedge-shaped lowland reaching from the San Juan River, the border with Nicaragua, nearly to Limón. These *llanuras* make up about one-fifth of Costa Rica and generally have an elevation of less than 330 feet (100 m). There are small volcanoes even here, but the tallest rises less than 1,000 feet (300 m) above surrounding lands. This region contains the only rivers navigable for any distance inland. You will not see large ships, but the San Carlos and Sarapiquí rivers allow smaller-boat travel for about 30 miles (50 km) from where they flow into the San Juan River. These rivers were important early transportation routes.

Climate Patterns

Costa Rica lies in the tropics between 8 and 11 degrees north of the equator, about the same latitude as the southern tip of India. Because it is a small country without much latitude variation, one might expect the climate to be relatively uniform. Wrong. Climate can vary over short distances because of the rugged mountain chains that affect such factors as wind, rain, and temperature. The result is a series of microclimates where altitude is the key to change.

Mysterious pre-Columbian spheres (Ree Strange Sheck)

Microclimates make countrywide generalizations about rainfall and temperature misleading. What is helpful to the traveler are some rules of thumb for various regions, backed up with specifics for a few locations. We are going to hit the high spots; my apologies to climatologists for ignoring the intricacies.

Following are some average annual highs and lows at particular locations to illustrate the differences, along with median averages derived from the two (totals are rounded off). Elevations given are of the measurement sites.

Elevations and Average Temperatures

	Average High		Average Low		Median	
Place/Elevation	**°F**	**(C)**	**°F**	**(C)**	**°F**	**(C)**
San José 3,845 ft. (1,172 m)	77	(25)	61	(16)	70	(21)
Limón 10 ft. (3 m)	86	(30)	72	(22)	79	(26)
Puntarenas 10 ft. (3 m)	91	(33)	73	(23)	82	(28)
Liberia 279 ft. (85 m)	91	(33)	72	(22)	82	(28)
San Isidro de El General 2,306 ft. (703 m)	86	(30)	63	(17)	75	(24)
Golfito 49 ft. (15 m)	91	(33)	72	(22)	82	(28)
Tortuguero 16 ft. (5m)	88	(31)	70	(21)	79	(26)

Source: Instituto Meteorológico Nacional

Temperatures

Remember that temperature goes down as elevation goes up: it is cooler in the mountains than at sea level. Temperatures are generally higher on the Pacific side than on the Caribbean at the same elevation. (There are more clouds on the Caribbean watershed year-round than on the Pacific.) At sea level on either side, the annual average is always above 75°F (24°C).

Some of the highest peaks in the Central Mountain Range and Talamanca

Mountains average 54°F (12°C), though temperatures can fall below freezing. The lowest temperature yet recorded was in the Talamancas: 16°F (–9°C) at Chirripó, the highest mountain in the country.

Variation in temperature is much greater from night to day than from season to season. Differences between the hottest month and the coldest at a particular location average only 4°F to 5°F (2°C to 3°C), while the daily fluctuation averages 14°F to 18°F (8°C to 10°C). The greatest daily fluctuation occurs during the dry season, when cloudless skies permit lots of sunshine in the daytime and lots of heat radiation at night back into the clear sky. Add some wind, and it can be downright chilly.

From November to January, cold air from the north can funnel down through the mountains of North America. Though much weakened by the time they get to Costa Rica, the breezes bring a bite to the air. This is one of the few places in the world where polar air gets this close to the equator, so the coolest month anywhere in the country is probably going to be November, December, or January; the warmest, March, April, or May.

Rainfall and Seasons

While spring and fall have little meaning here, summer and winter are tied to rainfall. Ticos call the dry season summer (*verano*), which can stretch from December through April in some parts of the country. The winter designation (*invierno*) is reserved for rainy months, generally from May through November. It reverses the standard Northern Hemisphere understanding of which months are summer and which are winter, but it makes sense to ticos.

There are some rainfall rules of thumb, always keeping in mind microclimatic differences. On the Pacific side, particularly from the central to the northern area, the rainy season usually begins at the end of May and ends in November. The wettest months are September and October. However, the length of the wet season increases the farther south you go. January to March are the only dry months in some places, and by the time you reach the Golfo Dulce area, there may be practically no dry season. Rainfall amounts vary from less than 59 inches (1,500 mm) in the northwest and central part of the country to more than 190 inches (4,800 mm) in the south.

On the Atlantic side, the rainy season can begin in late April and end in January. The wettest months are usually December and January, while some areas have higher amounts in July as well. When it is rainy in the rest of the country in October, the Southern Caribbean can be sunny. Annual rainfall averages are higher on the Caribbean than on the Pacific side. The heaviest rainfall is inland, not along the coast; in some places on the eastern (windward) face of the northern mountains, it exceeds 355 inches (9,000 mm) per

Annual Precipitation	
Place	**Inches (mm)**
San José	74 (1,890)
Limón	139 (3,527)
Puntarenas	62 (1,570)
Liberia	61 (1,538)
San Isidro de El General	106 (2,697)
Golfito	193 (4,893)
Tortuguero	206 (5,232)

Source: Instituto Meteorológico Nacional

year. In the rest of the Caribbean lowlands, annual rainfall usually averages from 118 to around 200 inches (3,000 to 5,000 mm).

Throughout Costa Rica, less rain falls on valley bottoms, so places like San José and San Isidro de El General are drier than the surrounding slopes. The country's most prevalent rainfall pattern is in the range of 79 to 158 inches (2,000 to 4,000 mm). See the Annual Precipitation table for some specific locations and their average annual rainfall.

Precipitation can come in the form of a tropical downpour—a gully-washer complete with impressive lightning and thunder—or a steady rain. The downpour is called an *aguacero*; a continuous rain for several days is a *temporal*.

Other weather terms you may hear are *veranillo* (little summer), which refers to a brief dry period in July in the Pacific zone; *papagayos*, strong winds blowing inland from the Pacific; and *nortes*, the winds coming down inland from the north toward the Pacific. Both of these winds are very strong in Guanacaste from January through March. *Alisios* are the northeast trade winds, felt during the dry season over the Pacific slope, except in the south.

Do not imagine that rain is constant throughout the wet season. Sunshine can dominate several days in a row. When the rains come, they usually begin in early afternoon in the Central Valley and other highland areas and later in the afternoon in the Pacific lowlands. Rain can drum steadily at night in the Atlantic lowlands and valley bottoms.

Each season has its beauty and its particular cares. In wetter times, plant life is profuse, with a vibrant greenness that seeps into the soul. In the dry season, a subtler background is a perfect canvas for orchids, bougainvillea, and *reina de la noche* (queen of the night), with its large white or pink trumpet-shaped flowers, as well as for deciduous trees that flower only at that time.

Cataloging Costa Rica's species at the National Biodiversity Institute
(Ree Strange Sheck)

Biological Diversity

Costa Rica is species-rich. This small country, which covers less than three
ten-thousandths of the Earth's surface, is home to 5 percent of all the plant
and animal species known to exist. As a matter of fact, species are still being
discovered in the country's rich mix of tropical habitats. The National
Biodiversity Institute (INBio) has begun a multiyear project to discover and
catalog all plant and animal species found in the country. Here are some
numbers from INBio to give you an idea of what is known to exist: birds, 850
species; arthropods (insects, spiders, crabs with segmented bodies and jointed limbs), 366,000; plants, 13,021; mammals, 209; reptiles, 220; amphibians, 163; freshwater fish, 130. Some scientists believe that as many as a half-
million species exist in Costa Rica, with a number of them—five species of
mammals, six of birds, 41 amphibians, 24 reptiles, and 16 species of fresh-
water fish—not found anywhere else in the world.

As a land bridge between the continents, a bridge that dates back about
3 million years, Costa Rica became a corridor for the movement of plant and
animal species north and south. This interchange was slowed by the gradual
growth of humid tropical forests that became widespread in the last 2 million years. Today Costa Rica has flora and fauna from both North and South

23

America as well as some endemic species. They live in a variety of habitats: tropical dry and seasonally deciduous forests, rainforests, cloud forests, mangrove swamps, coral reefs, rivers, and *páramos* (high, cold, humid landscapes). Costa Rica is the northern limit for Andean páramo vegetation. You will find it above the tree line at Cerro de la Muerte and on Chirripó and other of the Talamancas' highest peaks.

Descriptions of Costa Rica often mention its 12 life zones. Defined by L. R. Holdridge, they classify vegetation based on temperature, rainfall, and their seasonal variation and distribution. Basically, the zones are tropical dry, moist, wet, and rainforests (with their premontane and lower montane versions), plus the tropical subalpine rain páramo.

The Tropical Science Center, a private nonprofit Costa Rican association that focuses on natural resources in the tropics, has a striking map of the country showing these zones in color. It is a vivid picture of variation over small distances—the microclimates mentioned earlier. The map is for sale at the center's office in San Pedro, 15 minutes by bus from the center of San José. It is 100 meters south of Servicentro El Higuerón and 125 meters east; open weekdays from 8:00 a.m. to noon and 1:00 to 5:00 p.m. Other interesting publications for the serious nature traveler are also available (telephone 225-2649, fax 253-3267). The Tropical Science Center also operates the Monteverde Cloud Forest Preserve and Santuario Los Cusingos, the farm of ornithologist Alexander Skutch, near San Isidro de El General.

Forest was the natural cover of this tropical land for about 2 million years, and until this century the forests continued to dominate. However, with commercial logging and the clearing of land for agriculture and settlement, less than one-third of the country remains forested, a substantial amount of it in protected lands. Though trees are still being cut, private and government efforts and national and international attention are focused on integrating conservation and sustainable development to preserve what remains. But private and public reforestation projects under way do not keep up with the number of trees cut every year.

Reforestation is tricky. Complex relationships between flora and fauna are not fully understood. What is understood points dramatically to the intricacies of nature. For instance, there are 65 species of fig trees in Costa Rica, adapted to a variety of habitats. Each of these species is pollinated by a different species of wasp. After the female wasp pollinates the fig, she lays her eggs inside the fruit. The wasp depends on the fig, and the fig depends on the wasp. Remove either and the cycle of survival is broken.

Animals are more important to seed dispersal of plants in tropical forests than in temperate ones, where wind is the primary agent. Maintaining the rich animal mix is crucial to maintaining the diverse plant species in a tropical forest.

Around the world, species are being lost before they have even been identified, much less studied for their importance to humanity. Plants are gone before their medicinal value is known. Disappearance of a species of fauna can cut a link in a food chain that affects several other species.

We are beginning to appreciate the necessity of maintaining natural forests. Replacing a primary forest of mixed species with one or two types of trees will not maintain the diversity: the fig wasp is not going to make it in a eucalyptus grove. While reforestation projects on already-cleared lands are essential—erosion control and watershed protection alone merit the effort—they are not going to replace what has been lost.

Costa Rica's creation of national parks, reserves, and refuges is a step toward preserving a biological diversity that is important far beyond its national boundaries. Maintaining them in the face of increasing economic and population pressures may have to be a shared responsibility.

Population Patterns

The Central Valley, home to most of the country's 3.3 million people, has been the center of population since colonial times. As was the pattern in other Central American countries, settlement centered in the highlands. Early Spanish colonists in Costa Rica shunned the hotter, rainier coastlands to settle in this mountain valley with rich volcanic soil. It was an enclave in the New World that continued in relative isolation until the nineteenth century. As late as 1700, Cartago, with a population of 2,535, was the country's only permanent urban center. In 1821, when Costa Rica gained independence from Spain, 60,000 people lived there, with 90 percent in the Central Valley. About 5 percent had ventured out toward Esparza and Bagaces to raise cattle, and another 5 percent were indigenous peoples living in dispersed settlements on their traditional lands in the north and south.

A small bean introduced into Costa Rica around the beginning of the nineteenth century ended up transforming the life of this agrarian society, pushing the frontier farther and farther away from the Central Valley. Coffee was its name. The export of coffee led to the opening of a road to Puntarenas, since the first loads went to Panama, then Chile, and finally to Europe via the Strait of Magellan. To transport the beans to the Port of Limón for more direct access to the European market, a railroad was built, which indirectly brought about the beginning of large banana plantations on the Caribbean. Blacks brought to work on the railroad and plantations, mainly from Jamaica, added another ethnic group and an English-speaking component. The

African American population today is about 3 percent. The estimated Indian population is about 1 percent; East Asian, mainly Chinese, is 3 percent.

As land values went up in the Central Valley, small farmers sought new territory. Satellite towns took shape around colonial centers, but Costa Rica still had an abundance of unoccupied land at the beginning of the twentieth century.

In 1938, banana activity moved to the southern Pacific coastal region from the Atlantic; roads followed, and so did settlement. With the opening of the Pan American Highway south of the Central Valley to San Isidro de El General in 1946, the trickle of pioneers who had braved Cerro de la Muerte on foot or horseback became a flood of immigrants looking for new land, following the transportation route as it made its way to Panama in the 1960s. (The Pan American Highway is called the Inter-American Highway in Costa Rica, as it is throughout Central America.)

Immigrants added to Costa Rica's population. Italians, for example, developed San Vito, and Quakers from the United States settled Monteverde. New transportation routes helped drain some of the population pressure in the central region. In 1956, Costa Rica had 1 million inhabitants; by 1976, 2 million. The limits of settlement extended to the Plains of San Carlos and Sarapiquí, to Guanacaste and Tilarán, to the Nicoya Peninsula, and to the San Isidro de El General and Coto Brus regions.

Today, for the first time in its history, Costa Rica is facing the pressures of a growing population with little remaining public land. Most of what

POPULATION

Costa Rica	3,301,210
Province	
San José	1,198,283
Alajuela	589,059
Cartago	371,091
Heredía	264,740
Guanacaste	261,611
Puntarenas	368,208
Limón	248,218

Source: Dirección General de Estádistica y Censos, January 1, 1995, census figures

exists is in Indian reserves, forest reserves, national parks, and wildlife refuges. Since one of the frontier legacies is a belief that every campesino has a right to a piece of land to work, pressure on this protected land is going to be enormous.

As you travel on the road to San Isidro de El General, remember that most settlement along here dates from the middle of this century. As you drive over the new road to Limón through Guapiles, look at what has developed in this decade. If you sense a frontier spirit as you get to know outlying areas, you will understand why.

La Fortuna (Ree Strange Sheck)

4

Ticket to Enjoyment: Planning the Journey

Entry Requirements

For citizens of the United States and Canada, entry requirements are simple: No visas are necessary. With a valid passport, you are on your way. In lieu of a passport, you can use a birth certificate or voter registration document along with photo identification, such as a driver's license, to buy a $2 tourist card when you check in at the ticket counter of the airline flying you to Costa Rica. You do not need a tourist card if you have a passport. Citizens of other countries can check with the nearest Costa Rican consulate or the Costa Rican Institute of Tourism for entry requirements.

From the date of entry, U.S. and Canadian citizens with passports can stay for 90 days; however, those who have no passport but enter with a tourist card are limited to 30 days. The law requires travelers to carry a passport or tourist card at all times while in the country. A photocopy of the passport will do, so you can leave the original in the hotel safety deposit box. Be sure to copy pages that show your name, photo, passport number, and date of entry into Costa Rica. (Copy machines abound—signs advertise *copias*.)

Allow me a plug for passports: Routinely accepted at banks when you change money and at hotels when you register, a passport simply makes travel easier. If you don't have a passport, consider applying for one.

Immunizations

No immunizations are required. But even when staying at home, it is wise to have inoculations up-to-date. Is your tetanus booster current?

Incidence of malaria increased a few years ago in some parts of Costa Rica with the influx of refugees from neighboring countries, but is now on the decrease. Mosquito eradication programs are used to control its spread.

Most cases have been in the northern border area and around Limón. Dengue, also carried by mosquitoes, has reappeared. Signs everywhere are evidence of a countrywide campaign to avoid the spread of cholera—which so far has been minimal. Both dengue and cholera cases are decreasing. Check with your physician or local health office for advisory information.

Exit Requirements

When leaving the country by air, all tourists must pay an airport tax, currently $15, as well as a few other small taxes that push the total past $16. You may pay that fee in the airport—airline personnel can advise you where—in either dollars or *colones* (NOT traveler's checks).

If you leave Costa Rica within the time permitted for your stay—either 30 days with a tourist card or 90 days on a U.S. or Canadian passport—you are not affected by new government regulations that tighten up on those who overstay. Before, travelers who entered with a passport could apply for an exit visa at the end of the 90 days and receive a de facto extension of another month. No more. Travelers have only five days in which to leave after the exit visa is issued or they risk deportation and limitation on re-entry. For anyone who stays beyond the legal limit, the airport tax jumps to what Costa Ricans pay, about $45.

Airlines

Time, distance, and political considerations lead most tourists from the United States and Canada to opt for air travel to Costa Rica, which means landing at Juan Santamaría International Airport, 20 minutes from San José. Don't be startled if you hear the pilot say the plane will touch down at Cocos International Airport; Cocos was the previous name. You are in the right country.

By the time you come, some international airlines and charters may be landing at the Daniel Oduber Quirós airport near Liberia, which will make it Costa Rica's second international airport. Liberia is a gateway to Guanacaste Province and its beautiful Pacific beaches, folklore towns, and a number of the country's spectacular national parks.

Various airlines fly into Costa Rica from the north, some direct, others with intermediate stops. Be sure to inquire if you want to minimize your ups and downs.

Commercial carriers include American, Continental, and United (U.S. carriers), Aero Costa Rica, SANSA, and LACSA (Costa Rica), Mexicana (Mexico), and TACA (El Salvador). Phone numbers for these airlines are listed in Practical Extras at the back of the book. Here are some departure points:

Atlanta: Aero Costa Rica

Chicago: Mexicana

Dallas: American

Denver: Mexicana

Houston: TACA, Continental

Los Angeles: American, LACSA, Mexicana, TACA, United

Miami: Aero Costa Rica, American, LACSA, Mexicana, TACA, United

New Orleans: LACSA, TACA

New York: LACSA, Mexicana, TACA, United

Orlando: Aero Costa Rica, LACSA

San Antonio: Mexicana

San Francisco: Aero Costa Rica, LACSA, Mexicana, TACA

Tampa: Aero Costa Rica, LACSA

Washington, D.C.: TACA

If possible, have your ticket written up as if issued by the airline with an office in San José. For example, if you fly from Atlanta to Miami on Delta and Miami to San José on American, be sure the ticket is written up on American stock. If you have to make a change for the return trip, American will help you if the ticket is on its stock; otherwise, you have to try to deal with Delta, which has no office in San José. I learned that the hard way.

From Canada, several companies have scheduled direct charter flights: Air Transat and Mirabelle out of Montreal and Quebec, Fiesta Holidays out of Toronto, and Fiesta West out of Vancouver, Calgary, and Edmonton. Their airfare/transportation packages are sometimes less expensive than airfare alone from the United States. KLM and Iberia, as well as charters, fly in from Europe.

Whichever airline you choose, it is best to reconfirm your return flight at least 24 hours before departure. Addresses and phone numbers of the airline offices in San José are listed in Practical Extras.

You will be told to be at the airport two hours early. It is good advice; check-in lines can be long, and you need time to pay the departure tax and change your remaining colones into dollars. The airport bank is open for dollar transactions only from 9:00 a.m. to 4:00 p.m. Monday through Friday.

Here's a tip to save possible embarrassment at the airport. Porters who carry your luggage from curbside will leave it as close as possible to the check-in counter. Many an unsuspecting tourist has followed his or her luggage, only to receive disapproving looks from fellow passengers for not going to the end of the line. Waiting your turn is a surviving piece of the "everyone is equal" mentality born in colonial times. No one is exempt. In fact, the more important a person is, the more essential it is that this tenet be respected. I observed this for myself one lunchtime when I noticed the Costa Rican president entering a downtown McDonald's. It was almost as if a ritual—understood by all the players—was being performed as he took his place in line and looked for an empty table. That president was Oscar Arias, winner of the Nobel Peace Prize.

The same decorum is expected when waiting for a bus or to be helped at a department store counter. (The sign that says *Haga Fila* means "get in line.")

What to Bring

Having read the Climate Patterns section in Chapter 3, you know that you can encounter everything from frost in the early morning on the high mountains to a hot midday sun on the coast. Even in San José, the nights can be chilly, so bring a sweater or sweatshirt and jacket. Light clothes that can be layered will serve you well.

Costa Ricans dress on the conservative side. In San José women do wear pants or jeans, and shorts are beginning to be seen, though much more on tourists than local men and women. In coastal areas or for sports, shorts are common. In a nice restaurant in the evening, men may wear a coat and tie or at least a dress shirt; women, a dress or skirt and blouse. Clothing is casual in resort areas and private reserves.

Cotton and polyester long pants are good. It takes forever and a day for jeans to dry in the rainy season, but they are good for horseback riding or hikes in chilly climes. A long-sleeved shirt or two is wise for protection from the sun—remember, its rays are direct at ten degrees from the equator—and from insects and scratches on narrow forest trails. Shorts are not recommended for hiking in rainforests. Bring your bathing suit; nudity on public beaches is not acceptable in this culture.

Many researchers and naturalist guides prefer tennis shoes to hiking boots for forays into the tropical world. Whichever you choose, be sure the footwear is comfortable and can get wet; even in the dry season, some trails lead through small streams. In rainy times, rubber boots are a joy, and they are available in Costa Rica for less than $10. (Some lodging places have a few pairs for their guests.) You can buy the boots, which are standard footwear for campesinos, in central markets and many shoe stores throughout the country. If you don't want the extra weight going home, make a gift of the boots to the last nature reserve you visit. If you have large feet, consider bringing a pair from home.

There is a lively debate on rain ponchos versus umbrellas for experiencing the rain in a tropical forest. Just remember, sweltering under a poncho can leave you just as wet from sweat as from the rain. I pack an umbrella and a lightweight, hooded poncho that opens up on both sides so I can drape it over my shoulders and let more air circulate. The poncho gives better protection to backpacks or fanny packs, binoculars, and cameras, and it is handy for boat rides or trips on horseback. The umbrella is great for town time and for when you are not carrying twenty other things on the trail. Bring an inexpensive one so that if you would rather stick an extra poster or gift in your bag when you leave, you can present the umbrella to the maid or bellboy, who will probably be your friend by now. Reasonably priced umbrellas are available in San José. In warmer areas, I suggest you try simply getting wet one time, especially on a forest walk. Experience the elements. Just protect your camera or binoculars (plastic bags) and go for it.

If you will be staying at hotels or nature reserves that have shared baths, consider a lightweight sweatsuit for trips to the shower. It can double as sleeping attire if the night is chillier than expected or as something comfortable to change into after a day of sightseeing or travel.

Here is a checklist of other items:

Wide-brimmed hat—for rain or sun.

Flashlight—for nighttime hikes, to get from your cabin to the dining room in the middle of the forest, and in case the power goes off in town or the generator is shut off before you are ready for bed at one of the remote reserves.

Sunscreen

Insect repellent

Pocket calculator—simplifies currency calculations.

Moist towelettes

Pocketknife

Small mirror—some rustic facilities lack a bedroom mirror.

Anti-itch ointment—an antihistamine cream for insect bites or even an antihistamine to take orally to reduce discomfort. If you do find yourself with bites and no ointment, juice from the stem of the impatiens (*china*) plant, abundant in many parts of Costa Rica, is an excellent natural remedy.

Antidiarrheal medicine—better to have the kind you are comfortable with, just in case.

Washcloth—most Costa Rican hotels do not supply them.

Reclosable plastic bags—small ones are ideal for keeping a passport or other important papers dry; a larger one is handy for packing a wet bathing suit, or even for your camera or extra lens.

Plastic water bottle—for some independence in what and where you drink. Bottled water is increasingly available in Costa Rica.

Rubber boots (*botas de hule*), standard gear for tropical trails
(Ree Strange Sheck)

Binoculars—to see the expression on the face of the sloth high in the tree. (You'll be sorry if you don't bring a pair.)

Antifogging agent for eyeglasses—especially during the rainy season, when putting binoculars or a camera to your glasses can result in one big blur. (If you are in the forest with Amos Bien of Rara Avis, he can show you a plant leaf that will do the trick, but otherwise bring your own stuff.)

Old tennies or sandals—for climbing over rocks at the beach to explore tide pools.

Tissues or toilet paper—many of the public rest rooms in Costa Rica may not have any.

Coin purse—to accommodate an ever-growing supply of change. (Unfortunately, only the small denominations seem to self-generate: coins of one or two colones.)

If you stay in the rustic facilities at some parks, you need to bring soap, towel, and sleeping bag or sheets.

Leave expensive jewelry at home. Much to Costa Ricans' dismay, thievery is on the upswing, especially in San José. I had a chain snatched from my neck on a downtown street at midday.

The electric current is 110 volts, the same as in the United States and Canada. Plugs and outlets are standard. Be aware, however, when packing electric razors, hair dryers, and such that travel in the boonies may put you in a room without an electric outlet. Some outlets do not accommodate the larger grounding plugs on new appliances, so you may need an adapter without the larger prong.

When packing your bags, remember that travel to a remote spot by small plane, boat, or jeep may limit what you can take. Some domestic airlines limit luggage to 26 pounds per person. You will generally be able to store your larger bags at the hotel until you return, so include a small bag with enough room to carry a change of clothes, swimsuit, toilet articles, another pair of shoes, umbrella or poncho, camera, and so on. A day pack also comes in handy, even for city sightseeing. You can stick in a jacket, camera, umbrella, and guidebook. Be sure it closes securely. To further foil the light-fingered in heavy street traffic or on crowded buses, put your fanny pack in front or move your day pack to your shoulder where you can control access to it. A water-resistant pack helps.

As for film, you can get Fuji, Kodak, Agfa, and other brands in San José and some outlying towns, but it is best to bring a few rolls just in case. Slide film is generally hard to find outside San José. You will not find the variety of ASA ratings and types of film you may be accustomed to. Don't forget spare camera batteries.

Imported goods are expensive, so if you run out of toilet items, consider local brands. Keep any medicines you require with you, not packed in luggage to be checked.

One item you should not bring along is impatience. Leave it at home. Who knows, after a time in Costa Rica without it, you may find you do not need to lug it around anywhere anymore.

Information on Costa Rica from Abroad

The Costa Rican Tourism Institute (ICT) has an 800 number accessible from the United States (at this writing, not from Canada). Call (800) 343-6332 between 8:00 a.m. and 4:00 p.m., and a bilingual operator (English and Spanish) will attend to your questions. ICT does not make reservations for callers.

A private initiative, INFOtur, has offices in Costa Rica and California. A large data base includes information on lodging, restaurants, bus schedules, embassies, museums, souvenir shops, and travel and car-rental agencies. INFOtur will make reservations for you. In California, call (800) 901-TICO; in the rest of the U.S. (800) 807-TICO. Fax (805) 929-7006.

Information on destinations accessible to the physically handicapped is being gathered by the Kosta Roda Foundation, telephone/fax 236-5185. Or you may write to Apartado 1312-1100, San Juan de Tibás. The person in charge is Monique Chabot.

If you cruise the electronic superhighway, several information sources are available via computer. Here are some via the World Wide Web (WWW): Costa Rica's TravelWEB has a growing list of hotels, tours, car rental agencies, language schools, and background info on the country; there is an on-line reservation service. The locator is http://www.magi.com/crica/. E-mail address is iiclayton@magi.com. Costa Rica's TravelNet has information on hotels, resorts, car rental, tours, and more. There is an on-line reservation service. The locator is http://www.centralamerica.com. E-mail address is calypso@centralamerica.com. *Tico Times*, the local English-language newspaper, has a shorter on-line version of the print edition. The locator is http://magi.com/crica/ttimes.html. E-mail address is ttimes@sol.racsa.co.cr. Green Arrow Guide to Central America includes ecotourism destinations as well as conservation and educational opportunities for travelers. E-mail address is camese@sol.racsa.co.cr. The National Chamber of Tourism "one-stop shop" is http://www.costarica.tourism.co.cr. Look for others as you surf the web.

Reservations

Reservations are highly recommended for visits from December to April and are increasingly advisable in the low season, now marketed as the Green Season. They are essential for Christmas time and Easter week. (Some hotels have higher rates at these times.) Think about reservations not only for hotels but also for lodging at the privately operated nature reserves, where the number of rooms is limited. Even hotels, with the exception of some in San José and a few beach resorts, tend to be small. I emphasize smaller hotels, many of them owner-operated, because I believe they give the traveler a better opportunity to taste the flavor of the country. Some hotels and reserves offer substantial discounts during off-season months, especially in beach areas. Phone numbers and faxes for hotels, private reserves, and tour companies are included in this book, but mailing addresses are not because service is slow and unreliable. Call once in the country to reconfirm reservations you made from home, and bring copies of your confirmation. Prices listed are valid for January 1996. However, rates do change. Use these as guidelines. I have not included taxes in rates unless specified.

Tourist attractions also feel the impact of Costa Rican vacationers during school vacation from December through February and during a two-week midyear break in July. Beaches and parks are prime destinations.

Chapter 4

Thoughts on Itineraries

The first-time visitor to Costa Rica can feel overwhelmed by the banquet of choices: tropical forests to explore, steaming volcanoes to photograph, beaches to comb, mountains to climb, rivers to raft, flowers to smell along the way. Hire a guide? Take a tour? Travel independently?

Here are some suggestions to help you get started. If it is your first trip, do not slight San José. It has crazy traffic and crowded sidewalks, but it also has museums and parks. It is the center of Costa Rican culture and government. Go with a naturalist guide to a park or reserve in the first day or two. (See Chapter 14 for some tour possibilities.) With a good introduction to the tropical world, your travels afterward will be richer.

On the guided day trip, you will generally get Costa Rica's history in a nutshell, learn something about current economic realities, and have a chance to ask questions about what you are seeing or want to see. A naturalist guide knows where the crocodiles hang out, what time the scarlet macaws fly over the trail, what tree the hummingbird nest is in, and which orchids are in bloom. You will get an early taste of what is out there waiting for you while you leave the driving to someone else. If you want to see a monkey, there is no reason to go home without having seen one.

But you don't want to limit your stay to San José. Costa Rica's essence is tied to its rural roots. Its people and its natural resources are the biggest part of what it has to offer. Several smaller towns now have adequate hotels, restaurants, and transportation to serve as bases for travel to nearby areas of interest. Traditional destinations are Limón, Puntarenas, and coastal resorts, but think about staying in such places as Turrialba, San Isidro, or Liberia. See Chapters 6–11 for some possibilities. Chapter 14 is a rundown of several privately operated nature reserves that cater to ecotourists; one will have the level of comfort and adventure just right for you. Chapter 12 guides you to the national parks. Chapter 5 suggests ways to move around the country.

All prices given are in U.S. dollars. Hotel rates were given to me as valid for the 1996 high tourist season, but prices go up in Costa Rica as everywhere else. Taxes are not included in hotel rates, except where specified. Bus and plane schedules change, so check once you arrive at one of the places listed under Tourist Information in Chapter 5.

Vacations have to do with moving you beyond the ordinary. Let your dreams come true in Costa Rica: sail a yacht, raft down a river, sit on a beach, walk in a cloud forest, hike in a jungle miles from nowhere, visit a banana plantation, see birds and animals you know only from *National Geographic* specials, bathe under a waterfall. Meet a warm and gracious people. Walk softly, aware of your own impact on the culture and environment.

5

Bienvenidos: Welcome to Costa Rica

Bienvenidos means "welcome." This chapter is intended to help you feel more comfortable as you move about city and *campo* (countryside). Here are details about money, calling home, where to find out what is going on, and how to get to where you want to go. You'll find health and safety tips, with a special focus on nature travel, a list of holidays to plan around, and typical foods and drinks to try.

Language

Spanish is the official language of Costa Rica. However, major hotels have bilingual receptionists, and some restaurants have menus in English and Spanish. (The English translations can be delightful.) English is taught in some public schools, so you will come across ticos who want to speak English with you or will try to help out if you do not speak Spanish. Do not, though, expect to find people who speak English wherever you go. Your taxi driver may not speak English, and no one at the bus station may understand a word you say. However, Costa Ricans are genuinely nice people on the whole, and they will try hard to help as long as you are polite.

Ticos are delighted when you try out whatever Spanish you know, so learn a few words and phrases—at least *por favor* (pronounced por fah-VOR) and *gracias* (GRAH-see-ahs), "please" and "thank you." You will soon be saying *buenos días* (boo-EN-nos DEE-ahs), "good morning," with the best of them.

At the Airport

One of the first welcomes you can look for after you make your way past *migracion* (immigration) and *aduana* (customs) is at the Costa Rica

Tourism Institute's airport information office (ICT), open from 9:00 a.m. to 5:00 p.m. daily except holidays (listed at the end of this chapter). ICT staff, aided by student interns studying tourism, can answer your questions, help you make hotel reservations, and give you a road map of Costa Rica. You can pick up brochures put out by ICT as well as by hotels and tour companies. If there is no time to stop at the airport tourist booth, you can get information at the ICT office in San José.

COSTA RICA ODDS AND ENDS

Population: 3.3 million

Area: 19,730 square miles (51,100 sq km)

Capital: San José population: 318,765 in the cantón of San José; greater metropolitan area contains half of the country's population

Elevation: 3,809 feet (1,161 m)

Official language: Spanish

Official religion: Roman Catholic (80 percent of the population)

Government: Constitutional, democratic republic; elections every four years

Currency: Colón

Time: Central standard, no daylight savings time

Electric current: 110 volts

Telephone country code: 506

Highest point: Mount Chirripó, 12,529 feet (3,819 m)

Seasons: rainy—May to November; dry—December to April

The bank at the airport is open for dollar transactions from 9:00 a.m. to 4:00 p.m. Monday through Friday. It is across from the ticket counters on the ground floor.

A taxi ride for the 11 miles (18 km) into San José is about $10 U.S. If you share a microbus with other travelers, ask the person assigning the taxis what your share will be. Fare on the frequent public buses is less than 50 cents, but there are no luggage racks, so if you have big bags, forget that option. You would also still have to get to your hotel from the bus terminal at Avenida 2, Calles 12/14.

Outside the front door of the terminal are the offices of several rental car agencies, but be sure to read the section on transportation in this chapter before you rush out and rent a car.

Money Matters

The monetary unit is the *colón* (co-LONE). Its symbol is ¢. Take time to look at the coins—some are *colones* (co-LONE-ess) and some are *céntimos* (SEN-tea-mos). Each is clearly marked, but it pays to recognize that the coin marked "20" is 20 colones, not 20 céntimos. Bills come in denominations of 50, 100, 500, 1,000, and 5,000. Pretty 5- and 10-colón notes are rarely used now, though you can buy them as souvenirs. Coins are 10, 25, and 50 centimos, and 1, 2, 5, 10, and 20 colones, though few of the céntimos are around now.

The colón floats in relation to the U.S. dollar; as of August 1996, the exchange rate was nearly 209 to the dollar. Continuing mini-devaluations will change this rate.

From my experience, you can expect to pay a premium for colones in a departure airport, so change a minimum or wait until you get to Costa Rica. You may change money legally at banks or at your hotel. It is certainly more convenient at the hotel, but sometimes the cash drawer is low, so do not wait until the last minute to ask. You will find accommodating people who offer to change dollars as you walk around San José, especially on Avenida Central near the Central Bank. This is illegal; both buyer and seller can be prosecuted. The difference in the legal and black-market rate is only a few colones, and you risk receiving counterfeit money or being otherwise shortchanged or robbed.

Western Union has offices at Calle 9, Avenidas 2/4 if you need to transfer cash. Telephone 257-115 or 257-1312. Another office is in San Pedro, telephone 283-6336.

Hotels and banks usually charge a small amount for changing traveler's checks or give a lower exchange rate. Ask. Some have a minimum service charge whether you change $50 or $500 worth of checks. Do not assume that all hotels will accept credit cards, especially outside San José. Be sure to inquire when you make your reservation. Also, some establishments add a surcharge for use of credit cards.

Do not take off for the countryside with only 5,000-colón notes, because small restaurants or shops may not have change; keep some smaller bills with you.

Banks

Hours vary, but except on holidays and weekends, banks are open at least from 9:00 a.m. to 3:00 p.m. Two with longer hours, open weekdays, are Banco de San José (on Calle Central between Avenidas 3 and 5), open from 8:15 a.m. to 7:00 p.m., and Banco Metropolitano (Avenida 2 between Calle Central and Calle 1), open from 8:15 a.m. to 4:30 p.m. The process, especially at the latter, is generally painless. There is a charge for changing traveler's checks. Just tell the guard at the door of any bank that you want to change dollars (that much English everybody understands), and he will point you in the right direction.

Before you take a place in any bank line, ask again to be sure you are in the right one. You sometimes must hand over your identification documents (passport, tourist card) at one window and complete the transaction at another. It can be a happy five-minute experience, or it can take 30 minutes or more, depending on the lines.

Remember that banks are closed on holidays. (See the list at the end of this chapter.)

Credit Cards

The number of establishments accepting credit cards is increasing, but check before you spend if you are depending on plastic.

With an American Express card, you can generally write a personal check to buy traveler's checks in dollars. You can do this at Banco de San José across from the Hotel Europa on Calle Central between Avenidas 3 and 5. Regular hours are 8:15 a.m. to 4:15 p.m., but you can get cash advances or change traveler's checks until 7:00 p.m. weekdays. Telephone 221-9911.

With VISA and MasterCard, there are more options. You can get cash advances in colones or dollars. A handful of hotels provide this service for guests: ask at yours. Automatic teller machines with 24-hour service, some for Plus and some for Cirrus, are increasingly available. There is a charge for cash advances. The Banco de San José also works with VISA and MasterCard. A Credomatic office across from that bank can help you with card services. The San Pedro Credomatic office may be able to help you with cash advances on Saturday from 9:00 a.m. to 1:00 p.m.—call to check, 253-2155. Address is Avenida Central, Calles 31/33, second floor, above a Banco de San José branch that can also give cash advances on weekdays.

If that seems too far to walk, use this as an opportunity to try the city bus system. Take a bus marked San Pedro, which starts east of the National Theater on Avenida 2, and watch the street signs. Get off at the bus stop (*parada*) near Kentucky Fried Chicken on Calle 31; Credomatic is half a block east of the Colonel.

For VISA, I have also used the Banco Crédito Agrícola de Cartago, Avenida 4, Calle 2, near the Metropolitan Cathedral, open from 9:00 a.m.

to 3:00 p.m. Decals on bank windows indicate which credit cards can be used there. You will need to show your passport or tourist card for any transaction.

Some establishments add a surcharge of about 6 percent for use of a credit card. You may want to ask when you make your hotel reservation.

Tourist Information

In addition to the office at the airport mentioned earlier, ICT has an office in the heart of downtown San José, underneath the Plaza de la Cultura. Go down the stairs facing Calle 5, between Avenida Central and Avenida 2, and you will find some very kind people who can answer questions in English as well as Spanish about attractions, services, and transportation. You can get a free ICT road map and lists of hotels, restaurants, buses, museums, galleries, and such. Hours are 9:00 a.m. to 5:00 p.m. weekdays. You may call there for information: 222-1090. If you need help when that office is closed, call the airport office at 442-1820.

INFOtur is a computerized service that offers information on lodging, restaurants, bus schedules, embassies, museums, souvenir shops, and travel and car rental agencies. The bus list is a marvel, with departure times, addresses, and telephone numbers. The office is at Calle 5, Avenida 2. Hours are 9:00 a.m. to 5:30 p.m. Monday through Friday. Personnel there speak English, Spanish, German, and Italian. Telephone 223-4481, fax 223-4476. INFOtur will make reservations for you.

For information before you come, see Chapter 4 and Practical Extras.

Communications

Mail

Some hotels sell postage stamps and will mail cards and letters for guests. However, it is fairly painless to do it yourself at the local post office, and Spanish usually is not necessary. Just hand the card to the person at the window, who will sell you beautifully colored stamps; insert the card or letter in the slot marked *Exterior* (foreign). There may be a slot specifically for the United States and Canada. The line moves quickly at the Central Post Office in San José, Calle 2, Avenidas 1/3. Hours of window service are 7:00 a.m. to 9:00 p.m. weekdays, 8:00 a.m. to noon on Saturday.

The first automated stamp machines were introduced in 1993 at several locations in San José, two being the Central Post Office and Gran Hotel Costa Rica (Avenida 2, Calle 3). Instructions are in English and Spanish.

Telephones

International calls are easy, once you have access to a phone. From a private phone, you can dial direct, using the appropriate country code (001 for the United States and Canada), followed by the area code and the number. You can call person-to-person collect, or charge a call to your credit card by dialing 09, the country code (1 for the U.S. and Canada), area code, and phone number. An operator will come on the line for billing and person-to-person specifics. You can also dial 116 for the international operator, but service is quicker and cheaper using the 09 service. At most hotels, you must go through the switchboard, and there may be a fee. Ask.

Radiográfica Costarricense in downtown San José, Avenida 5, Calle 3 is open from 8:00 a.m. to 10:00 p.m. weekdays and 8:00 a.m. to 8:00 p.m. weekends; Comunicaciones Internacionales on Avenida 2 just west of the Gran Hotel Costa Rica and Plaza de la Cultura is open daily from 7:00 a.m. to 10:00 p.m. Both have phones where you can call the United States and Canada and pay on the spot (or call collect or use a telephone credit card). Comunicaciones Internacionales also has an office in Puntarenas.

From any phone in the country, you can contact an operator in Canada or the United States to place collect or credit card calls.

United States	Canada
AT&T: 0-800-0114-114	0-800-015-1161
MCI: 0-800-0122-222	
Sprint: 0-800-0130-123	

To make a local call from a public telephone, have a supply of 5-, 10-, or 20-colón coins (look on the phone to see which it accepts). Place the coin in the slot; if the phone is working properly, it will drop only when your call goes through. Sometimes a series of beeps at the beginning makes conversation impossible, but persevere. If the phone starts beeping after you have talked awhile, feed it another coin or you will be cut off. When calling a friend, give the person the number you are calling from (posted near the phone) so she or he can call you back and avoid the problem. To call within the country, just dial the number; there is no long-distance code. Even on in-town calls, charges are based on time used, which is one reason most businesses do not let the public use their private phones. It costs them.

Some hotels, groceries, and department stores have public phones that are quieter than those on the street. Public phones do not have phone books. Calls from your hotel can be expensive.

Notice the many public telephone signs as you travel around the country.

Often they are in the local grocery or sometimes even in a private home. To call from one of these, give the person in charge of the phone the number to be dialed. Time is metered, and you pay when you finish.

NOTE: As of April 1, 1994, it's a whole new ball game with telephone numbers in Costa Rica. Every number in the country went from six digits to seven. Tourist literature giving six-digit numbers is still around, but calling those numbers will get you nowhere. Numbers change regularly. If repeated calls to a hotel or lodge get no answer, assume the number has changed.

Telex and Fax
If your hotel does not offer this service, go to Radiográfica or Comunicaciones Internacionales in San José, where you can both send and receive telexes and faxes. Most post offices have telegraph services. Western Union has an office at Calle 9, Avenidas 2/4.

Taxes and Tipping

At press time, the sales tax is 15 percent, with a drop to 13 percent scheduled for 1997. I have not included taxes in rates listed except where specified because the tax rate seems to change more often than the editions of my book. Until it is changed again, you will pay the 15 percent sales tax at hotels and lodges as well as a 3 percent tourism tax, similar to a lodger's tax, for a total of 18.45 percent. (How? The 15 percent tax is also levied on the 3 percent). At restaurants, you pay the 15 percent sales tax and a 10 percent service charge that is automatically added to your bill. Tipping beyond that service charge is at your discretion.

Tipping for services is a personal matter depending on one's own philosophy and economic realities. If you like to leave extra and are in the dark as to amounts, here are suggestions to guide you.

Taxi drivers appreciate but do not expect tips. If they load and unload your luggage or provide extra-special service, you may want to tip.

People who carry luggage generally get at least $1. Some give up to $1 per bag. Do not forget the housekeeping staff or the cook at the private reserve who turned out those good meals. Consider 50 cents to $1 a person per day.

Naturalist guides and river guides expect tips. The range could be from $3 to $5 per day, depending on level of service. Local guides without naturalist training usually get less, maybe $3. If your tour has been by bus, give something to the driver as well, perhaps $2 or $3 per person per day—the same for river captains.

Some people prefer to tip individually, others like to combine tips from everyone in the group.

Business Hours

We have already covered banking hours, which are at least 9:00 a.m. to 3:00 p.m. Government and professional offices are usually open from 8:00 a.m. to 5:00 p.m., though some government offices close at 4:00 p.m. Shops are generally open from 9:00 a.m. to 7:00 p.m., though some still observe the long lunch hour—closing from noon to 2:00 p.m. Downtown San José used to close up at midday Saturday and reopen on Monday. These days, more stores observe weekday hours on Saturday, and a few are open on Sunday. Some restaurants close on Sunday, some on Monday; check before you charge off in a cab.

A note on daylight hours. Since Costa Rica is near the equator, it does not have the seasonal variations in daylight hours as lands to the north have. If you get up with the sun, you will be getting up between 5:00 and 5:30 a.m. Darkness falls between 5:30 and 6:30 p.m. year-round.

Transportation

You have options for getting around that you may not have considered. In San José, taxis and buses abound. To get out into the countryside, taxis, buses, planes, boats, bicycles, and rental cars are available.

The miles of paved roads grow yearly; Costa Ricans tell you the increase is always greatest the year before a presidential election. But highway construction and maintenance are expensive in this mountainous, rainy nation, to say nothing of the havoc wreaked by hurricanes and earth tremors. I traveled over the newly paved road between San Isidro de El General and Dominical in southern Costa Rica in 1987, just after it was finished, marveling at what an easy, quick trip it was through a spectacular landscape. Six months and Hurricane Joan later, the landscape was still spectacular, but some of it had shifted onto the roadbed, and potholes required full driver attention. To be honest, quality control in construction has also been lacking. As you travel, you will encounter superb highways, potholes, unpaved gutbusters, and charming country roads, and even the most recent road map cannot keep up with all the changes.

Taxis

Taxis are supposed to use meters, called *marías*, for distances of up to 7.5 miles (12 km). Do not be embarrassed to ask the driver before you get in if his maría works, or look below the front dash to see if it is on. The meter will start with a minimum charge (at press time, 125 colones for the first kilometer), and it goes up 62 colones for each additional kilometer in metropolitan areas; 67 in rural areas. From 10:00 p.m. to 5:00 a.m., 20 percent is added. If you phone for a taxi, the driver can turn on his meter where he got the call. A driver who does not use his maría can be fined if the passenger files a complaint at the Ministry of Public Works and Transport. If you want to do this, be sure to get the taxi's number and driver registration number, and note the time.

Licensed taxis are painted red except for the orange airport vehicles. Take an unlicensed taxi at your own risk.

Taxis will slow down beside you when you don't need one, but they are, of course, impossible to catch when you are running late on a rainy day. Drivers are generally courteous, though some will refuse to take you if they consider the distance too short or the traffic too fierce. Do not be surprised if this happens to you at the taxi stand on Avenida 2 in front of Gran Hotel Costa Rica. It gets my vote for the greatest percentage of surly drivers.

Drivers can be incredibly kind as well. One picked me up as I ran down a dark suburban street, carrying a backpack, to meet a 5:00 a.m. downtown departure for Tortuguero. Though he could not take me all the way because he was going off duty, he dropped me at the nearest bus stop without charging me a single colón and admonished me for being out alone: "*Es peligroso, señora.*" (It is dangerous).

You can hire a taxi to go practically anywhere there is some kind of road. In outlying areas, taxis are often four-wheel-drive jeep types. Drivers have remarkable skill. If you do not fancy going on an organized tour to a particular location or do not want to take a bus or drive, you could hire a taxi. The fare will be based on distance and time, more if the trip is over bad roads. If you do not want to arrange it yourself, ask your hotel to call and get the fare and reserve the taxi. The advantage is that the driver will stop wherever you want to take a picture or have an extra moment to soak up the scenery; the disadvantage is that he may not speak English. (Airport drivers usually speak some English, but their rates are higher.) There are a number of taxi companies. (See Practical Extras for a few numbers.)

Buses
Bus service in Costa Rica is reliable and inexpensive. It offers a good opportunity to mix with the people, perhaps in closer quarters than we of automobile-prone societies are accustomed to. You may actually have to rub shoulders with someone, but you will sense the nature of those people by the time the trip is over. And they might have a glimpse of yours.

My bus travels have revealed a genuinely courteous people—helpful, friendly, good-humored, dignified. No pigs and chickens in these buses. The vehicles are usually clean (unfortunately, some carry a sign advising passengers to throw trash out the window rather than litter the bus!), and so are the Costa Ricans who use them. I have encountered some foreign tourists in Costa Rica who must have thought that "back to nature" in the tropics meant going without a bath. Not so for Costa Ricans: for them, cleanliness is truly next to godliness.

Let's talk first about intercity bus travel, leaving San José and the greater metropolitan area for last. You can take a bus from the capital to any destination in the country that has bus service for less than $10 one way. For that reason, I do not include exact fares with bus information in later chapters. I know some of us have to count pennies when we travel, but just allow $10 per ride and you will come out OK. (Departure points in San José for various towns are listed in Practical Extras.)

Sometimes seats can be reserved with advance ticket purchase. If not, go to the bus stop at least an hour early. If the bus line has an office there, buy your ticket and get in line. If there is no office, you will buy your ticket from the driver or his assistant. Get in line, but be sure to ask if you are in the right one. Verify that it's the right bus when you get on. Some buses carry only the number of passengers for whom there are seats; on others, if you can get on or hang on, you can go. Check to see if your ticket gives you an assigned seat.

Some buses have compartments underneath for luggage; some have overhead luggage racks that usually are too small for anything but a sack or tote bag. Some have nothing but a small space toward the front where bags can be piled. Do not take any more luggage than you would be prepared to hold on your lap or put under your feet during the trip, and you will be OK. Some of the newer long-distance buses have adequate leg room, while some of the old ones bring back memories of riding on a school bus: The seats are the same, but you are bigger.

I include length of trip with bus information for specific destinations (see Practical Extras), so you can judge whether it appeals to you. Remember that the country is small. By the Inter-American Highway, it takes only six hours to get to Nicaragua from San José, eight to get to Panama.

On longer trips, there is a short rest stop. I usually carry juice or fruit; your plastic water bottle will come in handy. Do not expect a restroom on board.

Tell the driver where your destination is, and he will generally let you off as close as possible. If you need to catch a taxi, they usually wait where buses stop in towns.

Watch your belongings. If you end up standing in a crowded bus, watch your pockets. Even with those courteous, helpful, friendly, dignified people around you, a bad apple may be on board. Be especially careful with checked luggage. Get off the bus quickly to claim it at your destination. I usually try to watch at intermediate stops to see that no one else claims my bag. If you put a bag on an overhead rack, keep your eye on it as well.

I look forward to bus trips off the major highways. They are so human. The driver may stop to chat a minute with the driver in the bus you meet or be flagged down by a housewife asking him to pick up something in town and drop it off on the return trip. These buses are a lifeline in rural areas. Once while I was on a trip from Monteverde, the bus stopped so the driver's assistant could move a piece of milled lumber to the side of the road. A few bumps later, another piece and another stop. Then another. Soon everyone on the bus was craning to see the next piece, laughing about the truck ahead that would arrive without its cargo, telling the driver to keep the pieces and add a room to his house. Even non-Spanish-speakers were caught up in the fun of it.

Some ability in Spanish makes bus travel easier, but with politeness, persistence, and imagination, someone who does not speak the language can manage. Carry a map and point to destinations, or write the destination down and show it when asking for guidance. *Bus* is spelled the same in Spanish but is pronounced "boos."

Thousands of people ride buses in San José every day. You can, too. City fares and even fares to other towns in the greater metropolitan area are minimal. You can take a bus to the airport or Alajuela for less than 50 cents, or to some of San Pedro's good restaurants or the art museum at La Sabana Park for less than 15 cents. You do not need correct change. Hotel staff members or the ICT office can tell you where stops are. Wait your turn in line and pay as you enter; the fare may be posted on the front window.

If there is no vacant seat, hang on. Men and women passengers relinquish their seats to pregnant women; parents with a small child or two in tow; the handicapped; and frail, elderly persons. It is not uncommon for men to surrender seats to females in any form, but that is strictly by choice. I have sometimes felt I was given a seat because I was a foreigner—a nice feeling after traveling in some other parts of the world. Microbuses cost more but are quicker, and you are guaranteed a seat.

Again, watch your money and passports. My coin purse was lifted so skillfully on a Sabana–Estadio bus that I have yet to figure out how it was done. But I have ridden the bus hundreds of times in Costa Rica and have had that happen only once. Buses are great for people-watching, eavesdropping, and catching glimpses of people's everyday lives.

When it is time to get off, push a button, pull a cord, or yell "*parada*," and the driver will stop at the next scheduled place.

For those who like bus travel but want the option of more individualized service, Pura Natura is an option. The company picks up passengers at their hotels and delivers them to their next destination, direct to the doorstep, in air-conditioned vehicles. Seven interlinked routes are available, encompassing many of the country's top destinations (see Practical Extras for itineraries). For example, if you want to go to the Arenal area, you can stay at a lodge or hotel in Fortuna or around the lake and, with a reservation the night before, move to another location via Pura Natura with options of Monteverde, heading east to the Sarapiquí area and the Caribbean, or going west to Liberia and Pacific beach destinations. The company also has a travel agency that can help with hotel reservations. Rates range from $5 to $59. Telephone 233-9709, fax 223-9200. The office is in downtown San José on the second floor of Edificio Cristal, Avenida 1, Calles 1/3. Open Monday through Saturday 7:00 a.m. to 6:00 p.m., Sunday 1:00 to 6:00 p.m.

Planes

SANSA is the national domestic airline, with scheduled service from San José to Quepos, Palmar Sur, Puerto Jiménez, Golfito, Coto 47, Barra del Colorado, Liberia, Tamarindo, Nosara, Sámara (Carrillo), and Tambor. One-way rates range from $30 to $50. Tickets are available at the SANSA office, north of the corner of Calle 24 and Paseo Colón, and some hotels and tourist agencies. Flights leave from Juan Santamaría Airport, but SANSA offers free van service between its main office and the airport. Telephone 233-0397, 233-5330, or 233-3258; fax 255-2176.

Travelair has daily scheduled flights to Barra del Colorado, Tortuguero, Golfito, Puerto Jiménez, Nosara, Carrillo, Tambor, Punta Islita, Liberia, Palmar Sur, Quepos, and Tamarindo. One-way fares range from $45 to $80. San José departures are from Tobias Bolaños Airport in Pavas. Telephone 220-3054, or 232-7883, fax 220-0413.

Schedules for both of these airlines are in Practical Extras at the end of the book. Baggage is limited to 26 pounds (12 kilos) on each. Store your extra luggage at your hotel. Flights are generally less than one hour. Because planes are small, it is advisable to reserve as far in advance as possible, especially in high season.

Several charter companies provide air service. Three are Aeronaves de America (232-1413), VEASA (232-1010), and Aero Costa Sol (441-1444; in the U.S. and Canada, 800-245-8420). Look in the phone book under "Aviación" for other possibilities.

Alas Anphibias, a seaplane operation, opens up new possibilities for getting around in Costa Rica, especially to more remote places. Some destina-

Small planes get to remote spots (Ree Strange Sheck)

tions include Drake Bay, Cocos Island, Lake Arenal, and Playa Flamingo. Telephone/fax 232-9567 or 290-0167.

Helisa Helicópteros Internacionales does sightseeing tours as well as transport by helicopter. Telephone 222-9219.

Do not schedule yourself too tightly, and be aware that flights can be canceled because of bad weather, more of a threat in the rainy season. Once, on a charter flight from Marenco, humidity and temperature led the pilot to ferry two passengers and luggage to Palmar Sur, returning for the other three of us. From Palmar Sur we flew to San José together. Standing on the short grass runway at Marenco with ocean on one side and rainforest-covered mountains on the other, not one of us questioned the pilot's decision.

Trains

The famous Jungle Train from San José to Limón is no more. It came to an end in 1991, when passenger service between the Central Valley and the Caribbean shut down. The Puntarenas passenger service was also discontinued that year. In 1995, all rail service in Costa Rica came to an end.

Ferries

On the Pacific side, car/passenger ferries cross the Gulf of Nicoya from the mainland to the Nicoya Peninsula. The Puntarenas–Playa Naranjo ferry operates from 3:30 a.m. to 9:00 p.m. The charge for a standard car with driver is less than $11; passengers pay about $1.50 each. The trip is about an hour.

The ferry across the Tempisque River operates hourly between Puerto Níspero and Puerto Moreno from 5:00 a.m. to 7:00 p.m., starting from the mainland side. The rate for a standard car with driver is less than $3; passengers pay a pittance for the 30-minute trip.

A passenger launch makes the trip from Puntarenas to Paquera on the southern end of the Nicoya Peninsula for those heading from there to Montezuma. It leaves from behind the Municipal Market in Puntarenas three times a day. The cost is less than $2 for the 90-minute trip. A car/passenger ferry makes the same trip four times a day; vehicle $2.75; passengers $2 each, or $4.25 first class.

A passenger launch also operates between Golfito and Puerto Jiménez, crossing the Golfo Dulce for a sea link between the mainland and the Osa Peninsula. It runs once a day. The voyage is about 90 minutes. See Practical Extras for departure times and telephone numbers.

Car Rental

To rent a car, you need a valid driver's license, passport, and credit card. The minimum age is usually from 21 to 25 depending on the company. All major car rental agencies have offices in Costa Rica, and there are several local companies as well. Offices are at Juan Santamariá International Airport and in San José either at major hotels or concentrated in the Paseo Colón area. Several beach hotels now offer car rentals, and there are agencies in Limón, Quepos, Liberia, Golfito, and others.

Shop around. Some companies require purchase of insurance; others do not. Deductibles can be high. Weekly rates are discounted, and travelers in the low season, from May to November, may pay as much as 20 percent less. You may get better rates by reserving your car before you come, through international reservations. A ballpark figure for a small car, based on current quoted rates, is $125 for three days, $230 for one week, including insurance and taxes. There is usually a $600–$800 damage deposit.

Some agencies also rent coolers, surfboards, beach chairs, and tents. You can even rent a driver for your rental car if you like. Ask for a handout sheet on basic Costa Rican traffic regulations.

Gasoline is sold by the liter. Regular and diesel fuels are available, and some stations have lead-free fuel, called "Super." All petroleum is imported and refined in Costa Rica by RECOPE, the national refinery. Current prices per gallon are $1.68 for regular, $1.73 for super, and $1.18 for diesel. In rural areas, watch the gas gauge. You will not find a service station at every intersection. While round-the-clock service is available in San José, service stations in other areas may open at 6:00 a.m. and close at 6:00 p.m.

Speed limits are posted. Remember that the speedometer usually indicates kilometers, not miles, per hour. Speeders are subject to heavy fines, as are people in the front seat who do not buckle up.

Be sure to check the car over for dents, scratches, or other damage before you accept it, and have those noted in writing by the agent. It could save you some problems. Also be sure to check the spare and jack and such details as brake fluid, oil, water, and lights.

Before you rent a car, please read the Traffic Hazards section of this chapter. Just know what you are in for. If you do rent, do not leave belongings visible even in a locked car, and do not leave luggage in the trunk at night or even unattended during the day. In fact, do not leave anything of value in an unattended car.

Because of road conditions, driving times are usually longer than expected. (See "Intercity Buses" in Practical Extras for some idea of driving times.)

Bicycles

Bicycle tourism is beginning here. If you are going to do it on your own, remember that bike lanes do not exist. If it is your first trip to Costa Rica, you might consult one of the tour companies before you set off; there are roads you should avoid.

Hitchhiking

Hitchhiking on major roads is not common since bus fare is so cheap. However, local people wait by the road for a ride in rural areas where bus service is nonexistent or infrequent. Tourists do not generally hitchhike in Costa Rica except in an emergency. For example, when my return flight from Golfito fell through and I had to be in San José the next day for an appointment—and all the buses were sold out—I hitchhiked for the first time in my life. At the end of the seven-hour trip, the charming young man who had rescued me said, "Ree, you should not do this any more. Not everyone is good." He delivered me right to my door.

Traffic Hazards

For a tourist, there are easier ways to get around San José than by rental car. Parking space is limited, and traffic is fierce. I would suggest you walk or take a taxi or bus.

In the countryside, roads are for cars, buses, trucks, cows, dogs, chickens, people, and landslides. Be careful out there. Some specific driving habits to look out for are passing on curves, use of climbing lanes by cars going downhill, and driving on whichever side of the road has the best pavement or fewer rocks or ruts. Tailgating is a national pastime.

Watch out for two-lane roads that feed suddenly into one-lane bridges; for lethal *huecos* (WAY-kos), holes in the pavement, which can knock passengers and vehicle for a loop; and for tree branches laid across the road that warn of trouble ahead. Geography and climate team up to create landslides big and small.

Fog is a permanent possibility on the highest section of the Inter-American Highway south of San José toward San Isidro de El General—the range known as Cerro de la Muerte. The earlier you get through that section, the better. The scenery is magnificent. The same advice goes for the new road to Limón through Braulio Carrillo National Park, though at least the road is wider there. It is prone to landslides as well.

On the miles of the San José-Puntarenas highway that have yet to be widened, you may find yourself in a string of cars, buses, and trucks belching diesel fumes on a narrow, winding road. Adrenaline flows as vehicles jockey for position without a clue as to what may be approaching just around the curve. I would avoid that road on weekends and after dark. In fact, for safety's sake, I would avoid driving at night in general.

Even with road map in hand, you will need to ask directions when traveling off main roads. Additional signs are going up along main tourism routes, but choices to be made outnumber signs, especially on dirt roads. In the rainy season, always ask about the condition of the roads you plan to take before setting out each day.

Traffic police equipped with radar are on major roads. Watch the posted speed limit and buckle up. When an oncoming car flashes its headlights, it usually means "police ahead," an accident, or some other danger. Slow down. Rental cars, marked by their license plates, are targets for some transit police. If you are stopped and cited, fines must be paid to a bank, or the rental agency will handle it for you. You should not pay the officer—if he says you should, take down his number and report him.

Safety

Theft is a worldwide phenomenon. Use common sense: do not wear expensive-looking jewelry, do not flash lots of cash, and watch your belongings. Do not leave cameras or binoculars lying unattended on the beach. Watch your pockets and purse on crowded buses and streets. Use a sensible purse, one that closes securely; choose a bag that can be carried with a strap over the shoulder, held tightly between arm and body. Travel stores now carry all kinds of hidden pockets and pouches to wear on practically any part of the body; investigate which serves your purposes. Keep your passport separate from your money. Better yet, carry a photocopy of your passport (the photo and entry date pages) and leave the original in the hotel safety deposit box, along with your airline ticket. Carry only the credit cards you need.

Be alert on the street if approached by an overly friendly person who claims to have met you somewhere. There are expert pickpockets around. I lost a watch while trying to explain to a man that I did not believe I knew him. I would know him now.

One of the most dangerous things facing a traveler in Costa Rica is crossing a downtown San José street. Your job as a pedestrian is to keep out of a driver's way, whatever he or she may decide to do. The tico's gentle nature seems to give way to rampant individualism once behind the wheel. Cars turning right do not yield to pedestrians even though the traffic law requires it. Expect no mercy if the light change finds you in the middle of the street. To meet the challenge, I get beside a Costa Rican woman who is hanging onto at least two small children. When she goes, I go. By watching the natives, I have also learned that if I do not see the light turn green at a wide street like Avenida 2, the safest thing to do is wait a full cycle and be ready to sprint across when it next turns green. You do not want to be in front of four lanes, or more, of cars gunning their engines when they get the signal to go.

One other word of caution: back up on corners where buses make turns on narrow streets; you could actually be hit by the bus while standing on the sidewalk.

The pedestrian walkway along Avenida Central between the Central Bank and the Plaza de la Cultura is a delight. You can walk right down the middle of the street. Lots of people crowd the narrow sidewalks; a study revealed that at one corner of the Central Market, an average of 65,000 people a day pass by.

If you do run into trouble and need assistance, you can call the ICT security line for help and information: (800) 012-3456.

Staying Healthy

Costa Rica feels like a healthy place to travel, but some precautions make travel anywhere healthier. Give your body a break: keep to a diet it can recognize at first, adding a few new things each day. Get plenty of rest. If you would not eat in a "greasy spoon" or buy food from a street vendor at home, why risk it elsewhere in the world?

Food and Drink

I used to say it was OK to drink the tap water in San José and most other cities in the Central Valley. Then in 1991, a study revealed that only 50 percent of the country had water not contaminated by fecal material. Costa Ricans demanded action by government officials to remedy the situation, so it continues to improve (confirmed by a more recent study). I tend to exercise more caution in coastal areas and try to follow the saying, "When in doubt, don't." When you stay at a hotel or reserve in a rural area, you have every right to ask what the source of water is. Bottled water is available almost everywhere, as are bottled carbonated drinks, beer, and packaged fruit juices. Contaminated ice continues to be a problem, mainly from the poor hygiene of those who handle it.

A good substitute for water on a hot day on the coast is the liquid from a *pipa*, a green coconut. And remember, if you don't trust the water as safe to drink, do not brush your teeth with it either.

You can get *té de manzanilla* (chamomile tea) practically anywhere, with water that most likely has been boiled. Several companies offer a variety of delicious, packaged herbal teas. Buy a box to carry with you in case the restaurant does not offer herbal tea. Some of the private reserves at low and medium altitudes have lemongrass (*zacate de limón*) in the garden. If you ask, the kitchen staff is usually delighted to brew a tea from it. It is not only delicious but also used as a remedy for gastrointestinal problems and colds. You can always get fine coffee.

The two largest dairy product companies are Dos Pinos and Borden; both are reliable and offer pasteurized products. Even laser-treated milk that does not have to be refrigerated until opened is available.

Raw fruits and vegetables that can be peeled are safer. (That is one reason you carry a pocketknife.) Be sure to try the *mamón chino* (an exotic-looking red, spiny fruit with a succulent white flesh inside that you suck off a large seed), several varieties of mangoes, pineapples, bananas with the taste of the sun still in them, and *cas* (wonderful in juice or ice cream). Be careful with the colorful cashew fruit (*marañón*)—it causes an allergic reaction in some people.

If you hike, raft, or engage in a lot of physical exertion, remember that the salt content of sweat goes up with rising temperatures. Drink plenty of fluids and add salt to your food if you are sweating heavily.

Nature Travel Tips

Insects and snakes come with the tropics. Try to observe them on your terms. Plants can offer some surprises, so look before you grab hold of a tree along a steep or slick trail. It could have a protective coat of spines. If you choose to experience the jungle at night, take along a good light and go with a guide.

Remember that rivers can rise substantially with rain upstream; the river you waded across in the sunshine can look quite forbidding under a leaden sky. When you plan to hike along the beach, inquire about tides. Some beaches disappear at high tide, which also can make the mouth of a river dangerous to cross.

Remember, too, that the sun's rays are more vertical than you may be used to, so you can sunburn more easily. Be especially careful of the midday sun. Wear a hat with a brim large enough to protect your face and lips, and use sunscreen. If tanning is a goal, limit yourself to brief exposures in the early morning or late afternoon, increasing the time gradually.

Long sleeves and long pants protect you from sun, insects, and scratches whether you are in open grassland or forest. Leave the shorts for leisure time at the beach. Loose-fitting clothes are cooler, and baggy pants legs can get the first full dose of venom in the unlikely case of a snakebite.

Insects

I am well acquainted with two insects in particular: chiggers (*coloradillas*—co-lo-rah-DEE-lyahs) and ticks (*garrapatas*—gahr-rah-PAH-tahs). Chiggers are actually mite larvae and live in grassy, bushy areas waiting to climb up the legs of passersby. Their bites itch like crazy, and the red bumps get worse if you scratch them. To discourage chiggers, dust sulfur powder on socks, feet, ankles, and lower calves before you walk in the grass. Put some on your pants legs. Mosquito repellents are not effective. For bites, Caladryl or Eurax cream helps; some people take an antihistamine for severe itching. The effect of the bites can last for weeks.

Ticks hang out especially where horses and cattle are found. You may notice some itching, but you also may feel nothing and then discover their reddish black bodies under your skin when you undress. Be careful not to leave the biting end embedded (a tick doesn't really have a head) because it can fester and cause infection. Apply alcohol, gasoline, or kerosene to the bite or hold a lighted match or cigarette close to the tick to get it to let go and come out. Squeeze gently to help it along. Ticks can carry disease, so if you get a fever after being bitten, see a doctor.

In an area where mosquitoes are bothersome, use repellent and wear protective clothing. (A tip: don't forget to apply repellent on your hands—especially the skin between thumb and index finger—and, when wearing sandals, on the arches of your feet. The insects will get you there every time.) Some places provide mosquito netting for beds; if not, inexpensive mosquito coils, or "spirals" as they are known in Costa Rica, keep the population down. Buy them in groceries. The smoke from the end of the lighted spiral does the trick, but you also breathe that smoke. I would not recommend putting it next to your bed.

Ants in a wonderful assortment of sizes and colors will bite or sting if you are where they do not want you to be. Try not to stand still without first checking out the area. Sounds easy, but the advice is hard to remember when you freeze in place to observe a great green macaw or a coati. Be alert in innocent-looking grass. A group of us waiting for a plane on a grass airfield were bitten by ferocious fire ants, and when we landed back in San José, we had to do battle again with the swarms that had infiltrated our luggage. For hikes and trail rides, hats and long-sleeved shirts give some protection against ants that live in trees you may brush against.

If you are bitten by no-see-ums, the gnats known as *purrujas* in Costa Rica, use an antibiotic salve. You will not only be in more agony if you scratch the bites, but also risk infection. They live near the coast, but you can visit the coast many times and never encounter them; they prefer areas near salt marshes. Repellents are not too effective; protective clothing works best.

African (killer) bees arrived in Costa Rica in 1982, and you would do well to assume that all bee colonies are now Africanized. Keep your distance from hives or swarms. The stings of Africanized bees are no more venomous than those of your garden variety bee, but these insects are aggressive and attack with less provocation. The cumulative effect of many bee stings is dangerous. If attacked, move in a zigzag motion; you can probably outrun them. Head for water if any is nearby, and cover your head. If someone with you is attacked and cannot move, cover both of you with something light in color and get the person to safety. Remove stingers with a knife or fingernails, being careful not to squeeze more of the stinger's venom into the bite. Apply ice or cold water, and, if badly bitten, see a doctor.

I routinely shake out boots or shoes before I put them on, and shake and inspect my clothes. Having been bitten once by a scorpion when I did not, I rarely forget.

Snakes

Running on a path to catch a bus, I once came face-to-face with a snake racing to catch a gigantic frog. I had turned my head to glance at the frog as it leaped by and looked forward again to see a spectacular black snake with a luminous bright green stripe the length of its long body about four feet in front of me. The top half of that body was reared in the air, the head at about the level of my thighs. Startled, we stopped in our tracks and stared at each other for a timeless moment. Then in one graceful move, it melted to the ground and slid off into the leaves at the side of the trail. The lesson: if a giant frog passes you with incredible leaps and bounds, consider the possibility that something is in hot pursuit, headed your way.

Although seeing a snake in the tropical forest can be thrilling, be respectful and keep your distance. Minimize unpleasant surprises. First, running is not a good idea. Take time to look around. Never sit on or step over a log or rock without checking out the other side. Some snakes live in trees, with protective coloration, so watch where you put your hands and your head. Most bites, however, occur below the knees, so consider high boots.

The spiny pochote tree (Ree Strange Sheck)

Two pairs of eyes are better than one, so walk with a friend. At night, carry a strong light. If you want to familiarize yourself with which of Costa Rica's 135 species of snakes are poisonous (18 species are) and which are not, visit the Serpentarium in San José (Avenida 1, Calles 9/11), open daily from 9:00 a.m. to 6:00 p.m., or visit the Clodomiro Picado Institute in Dulce Nombre de Coronado, about 30 minutes from downtown San José, open to visitors only on Friday at 2:00 p.m. Ask for directions at the ICT information office. A poster about poisonous snakes is for sale at gift shops and the Serpentarium. Fewer than 500 snakebites—mostly of farmworkers—are reported each year, with fewer than 15 fatalities. The fer-de-lance, or *terciopelo*, accounts for almost half the bites.

Most naturalist guides carry antivenin kits. Ask. All Social Security hospitals, Red Cross stations, and National Guard posts have antivenin available. Bite marks of venomous and nonvenomous snakes differ, so if someone is bitten, look to see whether there are fang marks. There also may be small marks made by teeth. The bite of a nonpoisonous snake shows two rows of teeth marks but no fang marks. If the bite was from a poisonous snake, keep the victim still (especially the affected part), and squeeze out as much venom as possible with your mouth or hands within the first ten minutes after the bite. (Tourniquets and incisions are not recommended for amateurs.) Get medical attention as quickly as possible. A description of the snake is helpful. There is an anticoral serum and a polivalent serum for use against all other venomous Central American snakes.

Swimming

Fungus infections, especially in the ears, from swimming in pools or rivers is not uncommon. To prevent infection, clean out your ears with rubbing alcohol and a cotton swab after swimming. If you are swimming in a river, check the water for visible pollutants before getting in, and bathe with soap and water afterward. Read the information on water safety in this chapter before you swim in the ocean.

Medical Care

Costa Rica has good doctors and modern medical facilities, in both private clinics and its public health care system. (Tourists have access to treatment in the Social Security hospitals and clinics in case of accident or sudden illness.) One of the largest private hospitals is Clínica Bíblica: telephone 257-5252. Most hotels will contact a doctor for you, or the ICT information office in San José can help. (U.S. and Canadian Embassy addresses and phone numbers are listed in Practical Extras.) There is

WATER SAFETY

The beaches in Costa Rica are no more dangerous than those in southern California, according to Donald Melton of Quepos, who has pushed lifesaving efforts in coastal areas for many years.

Basic rules apply whenever you swim in coastal waters: Do not swim alone, on a full stomach, or while intoxicated. Do not swim at the mouth of a river, where currents can be treacherous. For the same reason, be careful around rocky points. Look before you leap. How deep is the water? Are people standing? Is the slope gradual or is there a steep drop-off?

According to Donald, about 80 percent of the 200 people who drown each year in Costa Rica are victims of riptides. Some rips are called permanent because they are always in the same place. Ask local people how safe the water is. In other areas, rips can come and go. Some telltale signs are discoloration of the water—brown spots where turbulence is kicking up sand—and areas where breakers do not return directly to the surf but run parallel to the beach for a bit. Take a few minutes to watch the action of the sea before you go in.

If you are caught in a rip, remember that it will only take you out, not drag you under. Panic is a factor in drownings. Do not fight the current. See if you can use the energy of a big wave to push you toward the beach. Motion to shore for help, but while it is coming, swim parallel to the beach, and then as the current weakens, swim at a 45-degree angle toward shore. Never try to swim directly toward the beach. If you cannot swim, float; keep your legs and body close to the surface. If you can walk when you feel yourself being pulled out, also go parallel to the shore as fast as you can to try to get out of it.

Some dangerous beaches are Playa Bonita near Limón; near the entrance to Cahuita National Park; Doña Ana and Playa Barranca near Puntarenas; Jacó; and south Espadilla Beach at Manuel Antonio.

a private air ambulance service with a 24-hour emergency number: Ambulancia Aérea, 225-2500. Pharmacists often diagnose ailments and prescribe remedies. In addition to patent medicines, some medicines requiring prescriptions in the U.S. may be sold over the counter in Costa Rica.

Typical Fare

Gallo pinto is the staple of the Costa Rican diet: black beans and rice. Try to eat it somewhere other than a first-class hotel. A *gallo* is something with a tortilla wrapped around it, such as beef, cheese, beans, chicken, or pork. When faced with an unfamiliar menu in the countryside, you usually cannot go wrong ordering one of the rice dishes such as *arroz con pollo* (chicken and rice) or a *casado*, which often comes with beef, chicken, or pork and vegetables such as *yuca* (cassava, a tuber similar to a potato), plantain, or squash with the ever-present rice and black beans. A vegetarian casado may also be available. *Olla de carne* is a soup of beef and vegetables—chunks of yuca, squash, potato, corn on the cob, plantain, or whatever is the house recipe for olla de carne.

Tico tamales, traditional at Christmas, are wrapped in banana leaves rather than cornhusks, with a filling of pork most common, though it can be chicken. Try a *tortilla de queso*, a substantial tortilla with cheese mixed in the cornmeal. *Pupusas* are, I believe, of Salvadoran origin, but they have found their way into typical restaurant menus in Costa Rica. Basically they are two tortillas fried with cheese inside—tasty and greasy.

Sea bass (*corvina*), prawns (*langostinos*), and lobster (*langosto*) are among the fresh seafood available. An appetizer of *ceviche*, certain types of raw seafood "cooked" in lime or lemon juice and mixed with onion and coriander leaves, can serve as a good light lunch.

The big bunches of bright red or orange fruit you see for sale along roadsides are *pejibayes*, a palm fruit that has been harvested for food since Indian times. When boiled, it is often served as an hors d'oeuvre with a dollop of mayonnaise on top. Try it. You may not like it. The flesh is quite dense and on the dry side. Most ticos love them. Another product of the pejibaye palm is *palmito*, or heart of palm, served cooked or fresh. Some palm species do not resprout when cut for the "heart." The pejibaye does, and commercial plantations now supply the market. So you do not have to worry that your heart of palm salad cost a forest tree its life. Natives also make a fermented drink from the sap when a tree is cut. Have a guide point out the tree, a stately palm with hairy spines on the trunk.

Naturales, or natural fruit drinks, may come mixed with milk, in which case they will be listed as *en leche*, or with water (*en agua*). Popular fruits for the naturales include *mora* (a berry), *piña* (pineapple), papaya, mango, and cas. Let your surroundings guide you as to which is safest, or stick to bottled drinks. I often order *agua dulce* in the campo, a hot drink made of boiling water and brown sugar. You can also have it mixed with milk, *con leche*. It is especially good in the mountains when there is a chill in the air. Cane-based *guaro* is the national liquor.

For sweets, try a dessert (*postre*, POS-tray) of flan, a sweet custard, or *tres leches*, a moist cake. *Cajeta* is similar to fudge.

Current Happenings

The *Tico Times* is an English-language newspaper published every Friday. It is an excellent source of information on what is going on in Costa Rica and is widely available in downtown San José.

Costa Rica Today comes out every Thursday. It is distributed free at many hotels and other tourist-related businesses throughout the country. It has a restaurant section and articles on health, language, hotels, and tours, plus a calendar of events and delightful natural history pieces.

Radio 2 at 99.5 FM has English-language programming with music from the 1960s to the '90s (including a request line), news, weather, and a Friday-morning segment devoted to tourist information. Telephone 224-7272.

Holidays

Gaily decorated trucks carrying costumed children brightened the dusty road. We discovered it was the day of San Isidro, patron saint of the farmer, celebrated in the area we were passing through with a local fair and the blessing of animals and carts and other vehicles. Many such religious or civic festivals occur throughout the year. Ask at the ICT Information Office where festivals will occur during your visit.

On official national holidays, most businesses, including banks, close. Holidays are listed here so you can plan around them.

January 1—New Year's Day

Holy Week—Maundy Thursday and Good Friday rival Easter in importance. Banks and businesses close, some of them all week.

April 11—Day of Juan Santamariá, national boy-hero in the battle against William Walker and his filibusterers in 1856

May 1—Labor Day

July 25—Annexation of the Province of Guanacaste, formerly part of Nicaragua

August 2—Day of the Virgin de Los Angeles (Our Lady of the Angels), patron saint of Costa Rica

August 15—Mother's Day

September 15—Independence Day (independence from Spain)

October 12—Day of the Cultures (Discovery of America)

December 25—Christmas (many businesses close from Christmas to New Year's Day)

6

What to See and Do: San José and Environs

If you have not guessed by now, I should tell you straight out that I love Costa Rica. My only reason for writing this book is to help other travelers discover the beauty it has to offer. The six "What to See and Do" chapters present an overview of what awaits you in different parts of the country: the towns, parks and wildlife refuges, privately owned nature reserves, hotels, beaches, rivers, and good places to try typical food. You also will find out about some of the country's important agricultural crops.

Not so long ago, most visitors used San José as a base for one-day trips into the countryside. Other towns now offer adequate hotels and services, opening up the option of staying in an area to explore it rather than returning to the capital every night. Places such Turrialba, Liberia, Golfito, and San Isidro de El General are not crowded with tourists; to experience the day-to-day rhythm of life in these areas puts you more in touch with the rural roots of Costa Rica than dodging traffic on San José's Central Avenue. Many small hotels and lodges in outlying areas offer tours for their guests, so you can visit a forest or a beach from a base in the countryside. Consider spending a few nights on nature reserves, either public or privately operated, to hear the birds as they greet the day, to have time on a forest trail, and to sit quietly after supper and visit with the owner, the guide, the cook, or the ranger.

As for accommodations, I emphasize smaller lodges and hotels when possible because I believe they give the traveler a sense of place and are more in keeping with the wonderful smallness and variety of the country itself. The connection, both with people and nature, is easier to make. I have tried to cover a range of price possibilities. Information on tour options from lodges and hotels is mentioned.

There are some excellent nature-oriented package tours to places mentioned in each region. Some companies feature naturalist guides and offer day trips customized to fit the wishes of as few as two people. Details on what some companies offer and price information are in Chapter 14. How to get to the national parks and reserves on your own is included in Chapter 12 with a discussion of what each has to offer the tourist. The privately owned nature reserves described in detail in Chapter 13 are mentioned here; some of them offer one-day as well as multi-day visits. We already talked in Chapter 5 about the options of travel by public transportation, renting a car, and hiring a taxi or van with a driver.

Costa Rica is a country of the unexpected. You may spot a sloth in a tree as you pass along a busy highway, round a bend to discover a herd of cows meandering along the road, watch monkeys swing from tree to tree on shore as you swim in warm ocean waters, or spot a flock of parrots in downtown San José. It is a place to try things you have never done before: go rafting or kayaking, be pampered on a cruise, tramp along trails in a tropical forest, ford rivers with water to the hood of the car, stay up all night trying to photograph a volcanic eruption, or take off on horseback to explore the countryside. The following pages guide you to the level of adventure you choose.

Getting Your Bearings

Like most cities, San José (founded in 1737) has its good and bad sides. It is the center of government, theater, and art, as well as of air pollution and congestion. It has beautiful parks and museums, along with a few beggars on the streets. It is big and often noisy, but even from its crowded downtown streets, one can manage a view of surrounding mountains, green against the sky. I find it a friendly, interesting city. Increased theft, however, is a reality. Be alert, and be careful.

With all the traffic, it is hard to realize that the era of the automobile began here only in the 1950s. It is not uncommon to see carts scattered among the cars even now, though they are generally pulled by a person rather than oxen or a horse, as you may still encounter in the countryside. Walk along Avenida 1 to the area around the Central Market, Calles 6/8, or Borbón Market, Avenida 3, Calles 8/10, in the early morning to see carts being loaded and unloaded.

Avenida? Calle? These are words to add to your vocabulary. *Avenida* (pronounced ah-vay-NEE-dah) means "avenue." Avenidas run east and west in the city. *Calle* (CAHL-lyay) means "street," and calles—you got it—run north and south. It helps if you can get your bearings early, because when you stop to ask for directions, the answer probably will be in terms of so many meters to the north, east, south, or west. A city block is about a

San Jose

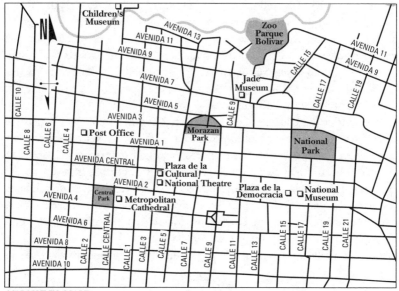

Children's Museum
AVENIDA 13
AVENIDA 11
AVENIDA 9
Zoo Parque Bolivar
AVENIDA 11
AVENIDA 9
AVENIDA 7
Jade Museum
AVENIDA 5
AVENIDA 3
Post Office
Morazan Park
AVENIDA 1
National Park
AVENIDA CENTRAL
Plaza de la Cultural
National Theatre
AVENIDA 2
Plaza de la Democracia
National Museum
Central Park
Metropolitan Cathedral
AVENIDA 4
AVENIDA 6
AVENIDA 8
AVENIDA 10

MAP NOT TO SCALE

hundred meters long, so a helpful person will tell you to go "*200 metros al norte,*" two blocks north. *Metros* is pronounced "MAY-tros."

About the hardest thing you will do in San José is keep the street numbering systems straight. Calle numbers originate from Calle Central, with odd-numbered streets running parallel to the east of it, even-numbered streets west. Avenida numbers originate from Avenida Central; odd numbers are north of it and even numbers south. Thus, if you go north from Avenida Central, you cross in succession Avenida 1, Avenida 3, Avenida 5. Walking west from Calle Central, you encounter Calle 2, Calle 4, Calle 6. Few buildings have numbers, so a typical address is Calle 1, Avenidas 2/4. This means the place is on Calle 1 in the block between Avenida 2 and Avenida 4. Look at the map of central San José to fix the system in your mind.

Street and avenue numbers are posted on buildings at some intersections. Keep looking as you walk, and you will eventually find one. Fortunately, more street signs are going up. The Costa Rica Tourism Institute (ICT) map of the country has a city map on the back. Get one and carry it with you.

The Plaza de la Cultura, (Avenida Central, Calles 3/5), above the downtown ICT office, is a good place to people-watch. A mime, juggler, marimba band, magician, or storyteller may be performing for whatever is collected when the hat is passed. Civic functions, book fairs, or a visiting music group from the Andes draw clusters of onlookers. Artisans display their wares. The adjacent open-air terrace of the Gran Hotel Costa Rica is a popular place to have refreshments or a meal while watching the activity or listening to the music.

On the Avenida 2 side of the plaza is a source of pride for ticos, the National Theater. Inaugurated in 1897, the building was paid for by coffee growers through a voluntary tax on every bag of coffee exported. The reason? A famous European opera star appearing in Guatemala had refused to perform in Costa Rica for lack of an adequate theater. National honor in this case resulted in a work of art. Perhaps you can attend a performance there. The theater is open for tours Monday through Saturday from 9:00 a.m. to 5:00 p.m., with an admission fee of less than $2.50.

Museums and Such

San José museums can be a good way to get a feel for the country before you take to the road. Most have reduced or free admission for children and students (with identification card).

National Museum (Avenida, Central/2, Calles 15/17). An exhibit on modern history joins pre-Columbian art, natural history, and religious art in this nineteenth-century building, which was converted from a military fortress after the army was abolished. The Plaza de la Democracia next door, dedicated in 1989, commemorates one hundred years of democracy in Costa Rica. The museum is open from 8:30 a.m. to 5:00 p.m., except Monday. The admission charge is about $5. The museum has a good gift shop, with copies of Indian artifacts and ceramics. Telephone 257-1433.

Museum of Costa Rican Art (Calle 42, where Paseo Colón comes to La Sabana Park). La Sabana Park was until 1955 the international airport (Charles Lindbergh landed here), and the museum is in the old terminal building. After looking over the art exhibits downstairs, climb to the second floor to see the Golden Room, whose embossed walls depict the country's history. It is open 10:00 a.m. to 4:00 p.m., except Monday. Admission is less than $3. The Sabana-Cementerio bus will get you from Calle 7, Avenida Central to the museum. A delightful restaurant operated by Café Britt looks out on Sabana Park. Telephone 222-7155.

Jade Museum (Avenida 7, Calle 9). The museum is on the 11th floor of the Instituto Nacional de Seguros (National Insurance Institute) building. In addition to the marvelous collection of jade objects, there are pre-Columbian ceramic and stone works as well as displays with archaeological and ethnographic information. You also get some good views of the city from this height, and the rest rooms are clean. (Public rest rooms are in short supply.)

Morazán Park, a peaceful piece of green downtown (Ree Strange Sheck)

The museum is open from 8:30 a.m. to 4:30 p.m. weekdays, except holidays. Admission is $2. Telephone 287-6034.

Gold Museum (Calle 5, Avenidas Central/2). Located underneath the Plaza de la Cultura, this spectacular collection of indigenous gold art belongs to the Central Bank of Costa Rica. It is open Tuesday through Sunday from 10:00 a.m. to 4:30 p.m. Admission is about $5. Telephone 257-0987.

Museo del Niño (Children's Museum). It may be for children, but this museum will delight adults as well with its hands-on exhibits (biology, astronomy, electricity, natural history), television and radio studio, art galleries, and mechanical talking figures (astronaut Franklin Chang of Costa Rica, Clodomiro Picado, and writer Carmen Lyra, who tells some of her stories to children who sit enraptured in a small gazebo). The only children's museum in Central America is housed in the old prison, the building itself worth a visit. Signs in English will be coming, but language is not a barrier to enjoying this special space. Open 8:00 a.m. to 1:00 p.m. Tuesday to Friday; 10:00 a.m. to 5:00 p.m. Saturday and Sunday. Admission less than $3 for adults, $1.50 for students, about $1 for children. To get to the museum, take Calle 4 past Avenida 9 until you get to the castle. You're there.

Museum of Natural Sciences (Colegio La Salle) across from the southwest corner of La Sabana Park. Though some of the specimens appear a bit moth-eaten, exhibits show many of the mammals and birds to be found in Costa Rica. It may be your only chance to see the harpy eagle, an endangered species, even if it is stuffed. Some signs are in English and Spanish; some are only in Spanish, with Latin names. (See Practical Extras for a list of some of the more common animals in Costa Rica, with their English and Spanish names.) Do not overlook the butterfly collection above the shells. A few crocodiles and caymans live on a small island on the patio. Take the Sabana-Estadio bus from near the Cathedral on Avenida 2 and ask the driver to let you off at Colegio La Salle for the Museo de Ciencias Naturales. The museum is down a tree-lined drive, near the Ministry of Agriculture. It is open Sunday through Friday from 8:00 a.m. to 4:00 p.m., 8:00 a.m. to noon Saturday. Admission is about $1. Telephone 232-1306.

Insect Museum (University of Costa Rica campus in San Pedro). This small museum in the basement of the Music Arts Building (Facultad de Artes Musicales) has a dazzling display of butterflies. There are also bee specimens, exotic-looking beetles and walking sticks, poisonous spiders, the large bala ant found in the Atlantic zone, and a 162-pound wasp nest from near San Isidro de El General. Another display shows how animals protect themselves by mimicry and coloration. The entrance, at the bottom of the stairs, may be locked. Ring the bell. Hours are from 1:00 to 5:00 p.m. weekdays; admission is about $1.50. The easiest way to find it is to go by taxi. Buses to San Pedro, leaving across from the National Theater on Avenida 2, will get you to within a ten- to 15-minute walk. Get off at the church in San Pedro and follow the street in front of it as it curves around to the north side of the campus. Watch for the "Facultad de Artes Musicales" and "Museo de Insectos" signs. It is a pretty campus, and students are extremely helpful when you ask directions. Telephone 207-5318.

Serpentarium (Avenida 1, Calles 9/11). You may not encounter a single snake during your forays into the natural world, so here is a good chance to see some of what lies hidden there: the boa constrictor, coral snake, brightly colored tree viper, and fer-de-lance. More than 45 species of reptiles and amphibians (including the tiny poison dart frogs) are here, and there is also a nice photographic exhibit of Costa Rican wildlife. Most signs are in English and Spanish. Take time to look at the illustrations showing how to distinguish between venomous and nonvenomous snakes. You can also buy posters, T-shirts, postcards, nature books, and slides. A bilingual biologist is on hand. The Serpentarium is open from 9:00 a.m. to 6:00 p.m. daily; admission is less than $3. There is a sign at the entrance on the street, but the Serpentarium is upstairs. Telephone 255-4210.

Clodomiro Picado Institute (Dulce Nombre de Coronado). Snakes are "milked" at this snake "farm" for the production of serum to be used against Central American snakes, including most coral species. The low fatality rate from snakebites in Costa Rica is attributed to the widespread availability of antivenins, which the lab also exports. The institute is about 30 minutes from

San José. It is open to visitors Friday at 2:00 p.m. for a program that includes a slide show and a demonstration of how venom is extracted. Admission is free. Take a taxi or the bus to Moravia (from Avenida 3, Calle 3). Telephone 229-3135.

Parque Bolívar—the zoo (Avenida 13, Calles 7/11). The zoo tends to be jammed with local folks on weekends. Most of its wildlife is from Costa Rica, but an African lion, Bengal tiger, and assorted other foreign species round out the picture. The facilities themselves are improving, and the setting is beautiful. There is a new entrance and gift shop. Bolívar once again has a tapir, and a new herpetological aquarium displays all five of Costa Rica's colorful poison dart frogs. The zoo is open from 8:00 a.m. to 3:30 p.m. Monday through Friday; 9:00 a.m. to 4:30 p.m. Saturday, Sunday, and holidays. Admission is about $1. Telephone 233-6701.

Zoo Ave (La Garita de Alajuela). More than 1,000 birds and a few species of mammals (including all four species of Costa Rica's monkeys) await the visitor on the spacious grounds of this former coffee plantation. You can see the king vulture, toucans, parrots, scarlet macaws, green macaws, and many other species that are so elusive in the rain forest. There are 84 species of birds here, 66 of them native. Signs give English and Spanish names. Owners Dennis and Susan Janik operate Zoo Ave not only as a bird zoo but reproduction center for endangered species. Hours are 9:00 a.m. to 5:00 p.m. daily. Admission is about $8 for adults and less than $1 for children. From Alajuela, you can take a La Garita or Dulce Nombre bus, which passes in front, or go by taxi for about $3. Telephone 433-8989.

Walk in a world of butterflies—I recommend it. In the San José area, several possibilities exist.

The Butterfly Farm in La Guácima de Alajuela has a garden of native plants that are home to 70 species with about a thousand breeding butterflies. Visitors can see all stages of the butterfly life cycle. Joris and María Brinkerhoff have created a beautiful opportunity to observe and to learn and to photograph butterflies and tropical flowers. The two-hour guided tour touches on butterfly defense mechanisms, predators, host plants, and reproduction, along with a film and a visit to the breeding facilities. Admission for the butterfly tour is $10 for adults, $5 for children; a package including transportation from San José is $19. The Butterfly Farm is open daily from 9:00 a.m. to 5:00 p.m., with the last tour beginning at 3:00 p.m. The Blue-Crowned Motmot Restaurant is open from 7:00 a.m. to 5:00 p.m. Call 438-0400 for reservations, bus information, or instructions on driving there.

Butterfly Paradise in San Joaquín de Flores, 7 miles (14 km) from San José, features hundreds of butterflies, representing 30 species, in a tropical garden with some 50 species of host plants, plus a botanical exhibit. Visitors can spend the day if they like. The fee of about $6 for adults and $3 for children includes a walk through the laboratory (cocoons are exported), gardens, and a small museum. Visitors receive a printed guide with photos of principal species they will see. A new circular path is suited for the handicapped. Butterfly Paradise is open from 9:00 a.m. to 3:30 p.m. Call 265-6694 for information.

Not far from the heart of San José is Spirogyra, a smaller garden that nevertheless showcases hundreds of butterflies of some 30 species. Visitors learn about the whole process from egg to metamorphosis to feeding habits and defense systems via a video and self-guided tour. The garden is open daily from 8:00 a.m. to 3:00 p.m. Admission is $5 for adults and $2 for children. Spirogyra is in the Guadalupe district, about 1 block east and 1½ blocks south of El Pueblo Shopping Center. Telephone 222-2937.

Madame Butterfly Garden and Gaspar Fish Observatory has a 1,200-square-meter observation dome in which both wet and dry ecosystems are represented. Some 220 species of plants and 41 species of butterflies create a beautiful tropical garden on a terraced hillside. Each tour includes a presentation on the life cycle of the butterfly, the different species, and butterfly conservation. Two pools are home to the gaspar fish, considered a living fossil because it has existed some 180 million years. There is a cafeteria. Hours are 8:00 a.m. to 4:00 p.m., and the guided tour is $8 (free to children up to 12); with transportation from San José, cost is $18. The garden, owned by Mitur Agency, a travel company, is northwest of San José past La Guácima and the Los Reyes Country Club. Call for instructions on driving there. Telephone 255-2031, 255-2262.

Jewels of the Rain Forest (Joyas del Trópico Húmedo) is museum where you will see butterflies and beetles (spectacular scarabs) along with spiders, centipedes, and crustaceans, all mounted in artistic displays. Margaret and Richard Whitten share this collection of arthropods of the world—more than 1,000 exhibits—along with information focused on the importance of saving the habitats where these creatures live. Open Monday through Saturday from 9:00 a.m. to 5:00 p.m., opening Sunday at 10:00 a.m. The museum is in Santo Domingo de Heredía, across from the cemetery. Admission $5. Telephone/fax 244-5006.

Pueblo Antiguo in Parque de Diversiones recreates the ambiance of an earlier Costa Rica, from 1880 to 1930, portraying the history and life of the city, the country, and the coasts. You will find a market, a replica of the building the legislature met in, reconstructed rural houses, a milking barn, a train station, a traditional *trapiche* (for extraction of cane juice), a replica of the Tortuguero canals, a reforestation project, an aquarium, and a mini-plantation of banana and cacao (along with a demonstration of how chocolate is produced). It is open Monday through Thursday from 9:00 a.m. to 5:00 p.m., Friday through Sunday from 9:00 a.m. to 9:00 p.m. Admission for adults or children is about $7, which entitles one to entrance and games. Entrance alone is $5. Telephone 296-2212. The park is about a mile (2 km) west of Hospital Mexico.

Souvenir Shops

You can buy a wide variety of quality products in San José: jewelry, wooden items, furniture, T-shirts, leather goods, and artwork. Many of the shops also sell park posters, postcards, and slides; most accept credit cards.

La Casona (Calle Central, Avenidas Central/1). Two floors of shops, open from 9:30 a.m. to 6:00 p.m. except Sunday.

Mercado Nacional de Artesanía (Calle 11, Avenidas 4/6). This is behind La Soledad Church, which offers a quiet place for reflection in this busy city and impressive stations of the cross. The artisan center is open weekdays from 9:00 a.m. to 6:00 p.m., Saturday from 9:00 a.m. to 5:00 p.m. Telephone 221-5012.

Travelers' Store, Costa Rica Expeditions (Calle Central, Avenida 3). Attention bird-watchers: You can get a locational checklist of birds of Costa Rica here. It is open from 9:00 a.m. to 6:00 p.m. Monday through Saturday. Telephone 257-9886.

Annemarie's Boutique, Hotel Don Carlos (Calle 9, Avenidas 7/9). There is lots of artwork along with one of the most complete selections of handcrafts around—something for every budget and taste. Shopping here gives those not lucky enough to stay in this hotel an excuse to see it. The shop is open from 9:00 a.m. to 7:00 p.m. every day. Telephone 221-6707.

Suraska Gallery (Avenida 3, Calle 5) and La Galería (Calle 1, Avenidas Central/1) show off handcrafts and elegant jewelry like the works of art that they are. Do not fail to go upstairs in each. They are open weekdays from 9:00 a.m. to 6:00 p.m., Saturday from 9:00 a.m. to 1:00 p.m. Telephone 223-2110.

Central Market (Avenidas Central/1, Calles 6/8). Handcrafts are sold here along with rubber boots, fish, flour, herbal remedies, shirts, and pots and pans. Be ready for crowds and watch your belongings.

Do not miss Atmósfera on Calle 5 between Avenidas 1 and 3. Art and handcrafts are beautifully displayed on three floors in a lovely old building itself worth the visit. Atmósfera is open Monday through Saturday from 8:30 a.m. to 6:00 p.m., Sunday 10:00 a.m. to 4:00 p.m. Telephone 222-4322.

The nearby town of Moravia, which is famous for its leather goods, also has shops offering a variety of other gifts. It is an easy bus trip to do on your own or about 10 minutes by taxi from downtown San José. In addition to the many small shops, an artisan mall has thirty shops—ask for Mercado de Artesanía Las Garzas. You can find everything from jewelry and clothing to Costa Rican coffee.

The International Market of Arts and Crafts in Curridabat, about 20 minutes east of San José, has some 130 stands of arts, crafts, and food from Costa Rica, Honduras, Mexico, Colombia, Nicaragua, Ecuador, Peru, and El Salvador. You'll find Guaymí Indian paintings on bark; bows and arrows of the Boruca Indians; mirrors, furniture, sculptures, wooden trunks; pottery, hand-painted tiles, glass animals, reproductions of pre-Columbian gold jewelry, and more. Open Tuesday through Thursday and Sunday from 9:00 a.m. to 6:00 p.m., Friday and Saturday until 9:00 p.m., closed Monday. Telephone 253-3613.

In downtown San José, you will find arts and crafts stands at various locations—try the daily fair at Calle 5, Avenida 4, which is for independent artisans, as well as near the Plaza de la Democracia in front of the National Museum, Calle 15 between Avenida Central and 2, active Monday through Saturday.

General Shopping

Head west from the Plaza de la Cultura on Avenida Central to find Librería Lehmann (Calles 1/3) for books and magazines, Librería Universal (Calles Central/1) for books, posters, maps, film, photo developing, and department store items, and La Gloria department store (Calles 4/6).

Next to the Avenida 1 "back door" of Librería Universal is a photo shop (look for the Fuji sign), where you can get film and same-day print developing. Credit cards are accepted. An IFSA photo shop is at Avenida Central, Calle 5.

Casa Amón, formerly The Bookshop (Avenida 11, Calles 3/3b), has English-language books, newspapers, and magazines, and also has an art gallery and a great selection of Costa Rican handcrafts. The bookshop is open daily from 9:00 a.m. to 6:00 p.m.; the café is open from 11:00 a.m. to 5:00 p.m.

Chispas bookstore at Calle 7 between Avenida 1 and Avenida Central has a marvelous selection of natural history books along with interesting history, science, cultural studies, and fiction volumes. You'll find magazines, newspapers, and new and used books. Open 9:00 a.m. to 6:00 p.m. daily. Telephone 256-8251.

Two other downtown stores that have new and used books are Book Traders (book exchange also) at Avenida 1, Calles 5/7, and Shakespeare Books, Avenidas 5/7, Calle 3.

If disaster strikes with your camera, do not despair. Try Equipos Fotográficos Canon, Avenida 3, Calles 3/5. They also have camera equipment. Open Monday through Saturday from 9:00 a.m. to noon and 2:00 to 7:00 p.m. Telephone 223-1146.

The supermarket closest to the Plaza de la Cultura is La Gran Via, just west of the plaza; other large ones downtown are Mas x Menos (Avenida Central, Calle 13), and Automercado (Avenida 3, Calle 3). Pharmacies (*farmacias*) abound, but there is a very complete drugstore/pharmacy about 7 blocks from the Plaza de la Cultura on Calle Central, Avenidas 8/10. Look for the Botica Mario Jiménez sign. Another is in Fischel at Avenida 2 and Calle 3. Remember, some stores require that you check packages when you enter, and you sometimes pay for a purchase at one counter or window (*caja*) and receive it at another (*empaque*).

Restaurants

San José and surrounding towns have many fine restaurants serving typical fare as well as French, Italian, Chinese, German, and Japanese cuisine. Look in the English-language weekly newspapers, *Tico Times* and *Costa Rica Today*. American food chains are here: Pizza Hut, Mr. Pizza, Kentucky Fried Chicken, McDonald's, Burger King, Hardee's. A 15-percent sales tax is included in your restaurant bill, along with a 10-percent service charge (tip).

If you want a light meal, look for a *soda*. San José also has good ice cream shops, such as Pops, two of which are near the plaza, and Monpik. Churrería Manolo (Avenida Central, Calles 9/11) has a typical Costa Rican breakfast for less than $4. Churros are those long, thin doughnut-like pastries for sale at the front. Warning: They are habit-forming. A larger Manolo's is at Avenida 1, Calles Central/2.

Some hotels with excellent international cuisine are Amstel Morazán (Avenida 1, Calle 7), Fleur de Lys (Calle 13, Avenidas 2/6), Villa Tournón (Barrio Tournón), the Camino Real (between Escazú and Santa Ana), and the Hotel Bougainvillea (in Santo Domingo de Heredía). Try the breakfast buffet at the Hotel del Rey (Avenida 1, Calle 9) and the unusual fare at the Hotel Grano de Oro (Calle 30, Avenidas 2/4). At El Pueblo Commercial Center, you can have typical food at La Cocina de Leña or seafood, with good service, at Rías Bajas. For a typical Costa Rican midday meal, try the third-floor restaurant at the Hotel La Gran Vía (Avenida Central, Calles

1/3)—it is inexpensive and tasty. San Remo (Calle 2, Avenidas 3/5) also has good inexpensive *platos del día* (daily specials) and pastas. Other eateries worth returning to are Ambrosia (vegetarian dishes and good crepes) in San Pedro; excellent El Balcón de Europa (Calle 9, Avenidas Central/1); Peperoni La Corte, Italian of course (Avenida 8, Calles 15/17); and La Galeria in Los Yoses, German food and classical music.

A favorite of mine is La Hacienda—nice atmosphere, good food, and friendly staff. Nils and the other waiters will do their best to make sure you enjoy your meal (Calle 7, Avenidas Central/2). The *flan de coco* is yummy for dessert. Another favorite is Angus Steakhouse, on Calle 41, 2½ blocks north of Avenida Central. Diners can eat inside or on a covered patio next to a lovely garden. In addition to beef, there are also fish and chicken dishes, good salads, and a marvelous pastry tray.

Any of the Café Ruiseñors are a delight with quiches, extraordinary sandwiches, memorable pastries, and cappuccino. Here are two locations: in the National Theater next to the Plaza de la Cultura, and in the Museum of Costa Rican Art (a beautiful setting with dining in a semicircular room featuring glass and wrought-iron walls with views of La Sabana Park). For Chinese and Thai food, try Restaurante Tin-jo, Calle 11, Avenidas 6/8. Restaurante El Chicote, on the north side of Sabana Park has excellent beef and seafood—you'll see well-dressed businesspeople at lunch time. Barbecue Los Anonos is a charming/rustic restaurant near the Los Anonos bridge (taxis know). They serve good barbecued meat; closed Monday. La Esquina del Café, a souvenir and coffee shop, has gourmet coffee to serve and to sell as well as *empanadas*, cakes, and gifts (Avenida 9, Calle 3b). For pastries and chocolates, Giacomín is at Calle 2, Avenidas 3/5.

Las Orquídeas, about 7 miles (12 km) north of San José on the road to Braulio Carrillo National Park, has a nice atmosphere, good food, and good service. Few people can resist the ambiance of the outdoor terrace at the Gran Hotel Costa Rica next to the National Theater and Plaza de la Cultura. At happy hour, music from inside mingles with the sounds of a city getting ready to go home.

When I cannot stand the thought of one more meal in a restaurant, I drop by Spoon at Avenida Central, Calles 5/7, and choose among wonderful pastries, sandwiches, and desserts for a carryout lunch; you can get natural fruit-juice drinks to go, too. Morazán and España parks are a few blocks away on Avenida 3, a place to join ticos eating their sack lunches, and watch playing schoolchildren and the park's birds—blue-gray tanagers, a few parrots, a woodpecker or two. The metallic school building you see nearby was built in the 1890s, the plates designed by Alexandre Gustave Eiffel of Eiffel Tower fame and shipped from Belgium by boat to be assembled here.

The National Park, farther down Avenida 3 at Calle 15, is another good place to escape the crowds.

Hotels

This is not a comprehensive list of hotels, but it represents a range of prices, with more of an emphasis on smaller places. I do not list any that I would not stay in myself, depending on my pocketbook at the time. The approved rates should be posted in the rooms.

Rates listed here do not include tax, unless so specified. If you arrive without a reservation, the ICT airport office will help you, but reservations are recommended. When calling from outside Costa Rica, use the country code, 506, before the number. Because mail service can be slow and unreliable, it is better to phone or fax for reservations.

I use the term "shower-head hot water" throughout the book to indicate that hot water is from a thermoelectric device on the shower head—in which case you probably will not have hot water from the bathroom sink faucet.

Cost Rica has a youth hostel association, with offices at Avenide Central, Calles 29/31. The Costa Rican Network of Youth Hostels offers its members lodging at Toruma, its own facility in San José, and reduced rates at a growing number of other sites, including Rara Avis and Islas del Río in Sarapiquí, Santa Clara Lodge in Guanacaste, Rincón de la Vieja Mountain Lodge, San Isidro Hotel and Club in Puntarenas, and Hotel Marparaiso in Jacó. For information, telephone/fax 224-4085.

The Costa Rican Bed and Breakfast and Country Inn Association Costa Rica has a youth hostel association, with offices at Avenida Central, involves

KEEP IN MIND

Rates quoted are those given to me for the 1996 high season, which generally runs from December until April. Prices do change with time, however, so take these as guidelines. Rates for the Green Season, or rainy months, may be considerably lower, *especially in beach areas. At press time, taxes are 15 percent and are NOT included in the rates quoted except when specified. The 15 percent sales tax will drop to 13 percent in 1997, and the 3 percent lodgers tax may be eliminated by your arrival.*

more than 35 establishments in practically every part of the country. Call 289-8401 for information and reservations, or fax 289-8729.

The following hotels are in the San José greater metropolitan area. Look also at the Central section for others with easy access to San José, close to the airport.

If your tastes run to larger hotels, here are a few you can contact, all with the amenities you would expect from a full-service hotel: air conditioning, restaurants, shops, cable TV, casino, etc.

Sheraton Herradura Hotel & Spa. The least expensive single is $100, double $110; suites start at $230. It is five minutes from the airport, 20 minutes from San José. Telephone 239-0033, or in the U.S. (800) 245-8420; fax 239-2292.

Aurola Holiday Inn. Rooms start at $128 for a single, $139 for a double. Avenida 5, Calle 5. Telephone 233-7233, or in the U.S. (800) HOLIDAY; fax 255-1036.

San José Palacio. Rooms start at $130 for a single, $135 for a double; $185 for suites. On the highway in from the airport, ten minutes from downtown. Telephone 220-2034, fax 220-2036 or 231-1990.

Corobicí Hotel and Spa. The least expensive single is $115, double $120; suites are from $140 to $425. Near La Sabana Park close to Paseo Colón. Telephone 232-8122 or 231-6512, or in the U.S. (800) 227-4274; fax 231-5834.

Hotel Europa Zurquí. Rooms start at $110 for a single, $120 for a double. Junior suites are $140. Follow Calle 3 north past Avenida 13 to Barrio Tournon—the hotel is beside *La República* newspaper office. Telephone 257-3257, fax 221-3976.

Tara Resort Hotel Spa and Conference Center is centered around an antebellum three-story mansion in San Antonio de Escazú above San José. Single is $90, suites range from $125 to $190; a bungalow is $200; continental breakfast included. There's a Scarlett suite, a Twelve Oaks suite, and Rhett's Boca Bar, along with the Atlanta Dining Gallery. Scarlett's Fountain of Youth Spa offers a full range of treatments, from body cocoons, massages, facials, reflexology, and private specialty baths to nutritional consultation and fitness classes. A two-day, three-night package is $369 each, double occupancy, including some meals, lodging, and specified spa treatments and services. Ask about other packages. Credit cards accepted. Telephone 228-6992, fax 228-9651.

Hotel Irazú. Rooms start at $80 for up to three persons. It is 15 minutes from downtown and has a daily bus to its sister hotel at Jacó Beach. Telephone 220-1441; in the U.S. (800) 272-6654; in Canada (800) 463-6654; fax 232-3159.

The hotels and inns that follow are smaller, arranged according to price range. Many are in what were once lovely old homes in residential areas whose use has changed as the city grew. It is a nice trend.

Hotel Amstel Amón is in the historic Barrio Amón section. The four-story, 90-room hotel has souvenir shops, a restaurant, bar, beauty shop, casino, spa, gym, travel agency, conference center, and underground parking. Rooms for single or double are $105, junior suites, $123; other suites from $155. Credit cards are accepted. Telephone 257-0191, fax 257-0284. Avenida 11, Calle 3b.

Hotel L'Ambiance was one of the first to take the charm of a historic building and turn it into a hotel that feels like an elegant home. Six rooms plus a suite open onto an interior courtyard and the large entry hall, or *zaguán*, typical of Spanish colonial construction. Antiques collected by owner William Parker are throughout. Polished wooden floors in rooms contrast with original tile in the hallways. Sounds of water in the fountain mix with soft classical music in an intimate dining room, also open to the public, which specializes in fine French cuisine. Rooms are air-conditioned and have cable TV. The concierge can arrange a private car with a driver. A single is $70, a double $90, a suite $140. Credit cards are not accepted. Calle 13, Avenidas 9/11 in Barrio Amón. Telephone 222-6702, fax 223-0481.

Hotel Le Bergerac in pretty Los Yoses is roses on the table, balconies and gardens, a sun terrace, fountains; Monet prints on the walls, spacious rooms, and personalized service. The French Canadian owners pay attention to detail. The two-story establishment, with the flavor of a fine French inn, has 18 airy rooms—in three buildings connected by gardens and archways. Framed, padded headboards match the soft tones of the bed coverings, and each room has ceiling fans, cable TV (including the French and German channels), hardwood floors and baths with dark forest-green fixtures. The standard room for one or two people is $68 ($88 with a garden or balcony), including a continental breakfast. The restaurant next to the central garden, for guests only, also serves drinks and bocas in the afternoon and evenings, and dinner. Telephone 234-7850, fax 225-9103. Le Bergerac is half a block south of Avenida Central on Calle 35.

The Britannia Hotel is at Avenida 11 and Calle 3 in a 1910 mansion I have long admired. Great care has been taken in its restoration and conversion into a 24-room hotel. The entrance is grand, giving one the feeling of having arrived somewhere special. Even the standard rooms are large: $73 for a single, $85 for a double. Deluxe rooms are $84 for a single, $96 for a double; suites are $108 for two. Included is a breakfast buffet served in a former patio. Rooms have hardwood or carpeted floors, tiled baths with tubs and showers (hair dryers in suites), cable TV, writing desks, pretty comforters with matching window treatment, and wallpaper wainscoting; some have king-size beds. There is a gift shop, parking, restaurant, conference room, and bar. Telephone 223-6667, fax 223-6411.

Hotel Rosa de Paseo is in a restored century-old residence on Paseo Colón, the boulevard that brings you into San José from the airport. The 20-room hotel has some beautiful antique pieces—chests, benches, wardrobes—painted stenciled friezes at ceiling level in some rooms, charming alcoves and bay windows on the front, some beautiful painted tile floors, and stained glass. Rooms have high ceilings (how long since you stayed in a room with a transom?), matching drapes and bedspreads, a wardrobe, desk, and large baths with bathtubs. A lovely two-story addition in keeping with the older house shares a pretty garden. Nice sitting areas have attractive wicker furniture. A single is $60, a double $70, suites (some with Jacuzzi) start at $75 for two; a tropical breakfast is included. Credit cards are accepted. The gift shop has fine jewelry, paintings, and other artwork. The restaurant serves light meals. Telephone 257-3213 or 257-3225; fax 223-2776.

Hotel Milvia is past San Pedro on the way to Tres Ríos, only 15 to 20 minutes by bus from downtown San José. The wooden residence, built more than fifty years ago, has been renovated as a five-room hotel surrounded by a lovely garden. Rooms are large, with antique furniture, cable TV, telephone, mini-bar, hair dryers, and private baths with hand-painted tiles. There is a boutique, library, terrace, and parking. A single is $55, a double $60. Credit cards are accepted. Telephone/fax 225-4543.

Hotel Grano de Oro is a personal favorite—I am partial to bathtubs, and these are spotless and large in charming blue and white bathrooms with brass and porcelain fixtures. Cushions in white wicker chairs match comforters on the beds in restful rooms. Each has a writing desk, TV, and wardrobe closet; non-smoking rooms are available. Starting out in a gracious turn-of-the-century mansion, the hotel has expanded next door—with 36 rooms in all. Inner patios and courtyards with fountains connect the old and new. By day, one can see volcanoes from the rooftop terrace where there is a Jacuzzi and bar; at night, city lights sparkle. If you cannot stay here, come try the creative *bocas*—the restaurant is open to the public—as well as delicacies such as chicken and mushroom lasagna, enchilada pie, beautiful salads, or stuffed palm heart pie. There is a gift shop and parking. Standard doubles are $70, superior $82, deluxe $92, and suites from $120—depending on room size and type of beds. Credit cards are accepted, but there is a service charge. Hotel Grano de Oro is on Calle 30, Avenidas 2/4, just 1½ blocks south of Paseo Colón. Telephone 255-3322, fax 221-2782.

Quiet breakfast at Hotel Grano del Oro (Ree Strange Sheck)

La Casa Verde is another of the lovely Barrio Amón mansions that has been renovated as an exclusive small hotel. The green Victorian house at Avenida 9 and Calle 7, La Casa Verde has five rooms and two suites, with king- or queen-size beds, cable TV, ceiling fans, and private baths (I saw one with a claw-foot tub). The loving restoration was supervised by owner Carl Stanley. The upstairs Victorian lounge, with its 110-year-old German-made baby grand piano, wicker furniture, and polished wooden floors, is stunning. You could get lost in one of the enormous suites. Artwork for sale on the walls gives the hotel the air of a gallery. A complimentary breakfast buffet is served on a garden patio. The coffee shop is for guests only. Deluxe rooms are $72 to $86, suites from $86 to $126. Credit cards are accepted. Telephone/fax 223-0969.

The Fleur de Lys Hotel is about a block from the Plaza de la Democracia at Calle 13, Avenidas 2/6. The renovated three-story house, built more than sixty years ago, has 20 unique rooms, each named for a flower and all taste-fully furnished. They offer cable TV and private baths. Some of the original tile and hardwood floors remain; rooms are carpeted. Fresh flowers brighten comfortable sitting alcoves. Skylights bring the sunshine in. Singles are $65, doubles $78; suites start at $85, breakfast included. There is a tour agency (the hotel belongs to the same company as Aventuras Naturales, which specializes in rafting, mountain biking, and nature tourism) and a fine restaurant specializing in Swiss-Italian cuisine. Dishes are a visual as well as gastronomic delight. A superb executive lunch is served from noon to 2:00 p.m. Service is superb, and the setting is intimate. If you cannot stay at the Fleur de Lys, try to eat there. Telephone 222-4391 or 257-2621; fax 257-3637. Credit cards are accepted.

Hotel Presidente has grown to 80 rooms with suites and junior suites. Some are carpeted, some have rich tones of parquet; carved doors set a nice tone. Standardized new rooms are nice, but the older ones, in various shapes and sizes, also have appeal. Amenities include satellite TV, Jacuzzi, sauna, small gymnasium, solarium, air conditioning, and concierge. There is a piano bar, restaurant (Italian and international cuisine), and parking. New rooms have a special glass to shut out street noise. Singles are $60, doubles $70, suites from $90 to $125 for two. Credit cards are accepted. Avenida Central, Calle 7. Telephone 222-3022, or in the U.S. and part of Canada, (800) 972-0515; fax 221-1205. There is free pickup at the airport for guests who reserve via the 800 number.

A restored 1926 mansion awaits at Casa de Finca, about 15 minutes east of San José, past the suburb of San José. Built by the owner of a coffee plantation, the ten-room country house is still surrounded by coffee fields and tropical gardens. From the polished patterned tile of the gallery entrance to the large, distinctive rooms with king-size beds and private baths with hot water, Casa de Finca is quiet elegance. Single $59, double $69, including a full breakfast and welcome cocktail. Gourmet lunches and dinners prepared upon request. There is a library and a bar. Tours are arranged. Telephone/fax 225-6169.

Gran Hotel Costa Rica, in the very heart of San José next to the Plaza de la Cultura and the National Theater, has been a meeting place since it opened in 1930. The terrace café is open 24 hours a day; daytime diners are treated to marimba music. The 108 pleasant, carpeted rooms have satellite TV and writing desks. The single rate is $54, double $71; suites are from $81 to $127 for two. Credit cards are accepted. There is also a casino and parking. Avenida 2, Calle 3. Telephone 221-0796, fax 221-3501.

Hotel del Rey is an appealing and comfortable hotel of 104 rooms right downtown at Avenida 1, Calle 9. The large gracious lobby with tropical plants and cushioned wicker furniture groupings says welcome. The six-floor Neoclassical structure has a skylight-covered central atrium that washes the building with light. Rooms are carpeted and have soft-colored quilted bedspreads, cable TV, direct-dial telephones, private baths with tubs, and washcloths! The hand-carved wooden doors to each room depict quetzals, butterflies, iguanas, a coffee picker, and other Costa Rican motifs—real works of art. The hotel has a travel agency, gift shop, street-side bar, casino, car rental, parking, and restaurants. Standard singles are

$55, standard doubles $68; deluxe rooms are $75, single or double. Master suites, which can include as many as three bedrooms, begin at $125 for two people. Credit cards are accepted. Telephone 221-7272 or 255-3232; fax 221-0096.

Hotel Vesuvio is a 20-room, owner-operated hotel on Avenida 11, Calles 13/15 in a residential setting. The carpeted rooms are decorated in soft colors (the print in the comforter matches the curtains), each with ceiling fan, desk, and TV. There is a bar and a restaurant featuring Italian specialties. Parking is available. Singles are $40, doubles $50, junior suites $97, continental breakfast included. Credit cards are accepted. Telephone 221-7586; telephone/fax 221-8325, or 256-1616.

Hotel Santo Tomás, with 20 rooms, is in a renovated mansion that dates back to the turn of the century. Each room is different, but all have high ceilings and reproduction Louis XV furniture. Persian rugs decorate hardwood floors. Corridors and some other areas have handmade tile floors. Some bathrooms have tubs. There is cable TV in the comfortable parlor area, along with reading material. Staff members help arrange tailored tours. Parking is nearby at a discount. Standard rooms are $55; superior $65; deluxe $75. Continental breakfast is included. Credit cards are not accepted. Avenida 7, Calles 3/5. Telephone 255-0448, fax 222-3950.

The Hotel Europa Centro on Calle Central, Avenida 5 has 72 carpeted rooms and a pretty outdoor swimming pool surrounded by plants right in the heart of town. Good-sized carpeted rooms have cable TV, air conditioning, large closets, and a writing desk—and some rooms have balconies. A few baths have tubs. Singles are $55, doubles $65, deluxe singles $65, deluxe doubles $70; suites from $77 to $96 for two. Credit cards are accepted. There is a restaurant, a cozy downstairs bar, meeting rooms, an art gallery, and a gift shop. Telephone 222-1222, fax 221-3976.

Hotel La Gran Vía is on Avenida Central, Calles 1/3, just ½ block from the Plaza de la Cultura. The 32 carpeted rooms are nicely furnished in soft colors, lace curtains, and drapes. The avenida is closed to through traffic here, so car noise is reduced. The upstairs restaurant serves simple, inexpensive, flavorful food. A single is $45, a double $55. Credit cards are accepted. Telephone 222-7737, fax 222-7205.

Hotel Torremolinos, at Calle 40 and Avenida 5, is 2 blocks from Centro Colón near La Sabana Park. It has 72 rooms and suites, each carpeted and with cable TV and either air conditioning or ceiling fans. There is a pool in a garden area by the restaurant, a Jacuzzi, sauna, and parking. Rooms are $50 for a single, $60 for a double, $80 for a junior suite, and $90 for a suite. Telephone 222-9129 or 222-5266; fax 255-3167.

Hotel Edelweiss is in a remodeled 45-year-old house on Avenida 9 between Calles 13 and 15. Each of the 16 rooms has distinctive wallpaper, custom handmade furniture (the fold-out writing desk is a gem), a ceiling fan, and private bath with hot water. The bar is in a covered patio enhanced with many orchids and other tropical plants. The dining room specializes in cuisine from Austria and Germany (the birthplaces of two of the four owner-managers). Singles start at $45, doubles at $65, including continental breakfast. Credit cards are accepted. Telephone 221-9702, telephone/fax 222-1241.

Casa Morazán in Barrio Amón was the home of a former president; now it is a stylish 11-room hotel. Rooms have restful green and rose carpeting, air conditioning, high ceilings, cable TV, telephones, and large private baths with tubs; some rooms have king-size beds. Lovely watercolors hung throughout are for sale. The dining room opens onto a patio and there is a comfortable sitting area. Guests can enjoy a quiet dinner, with selections such as lasagna, crepes, and stroganoff, for about $10. The Costa Rican owner-operators are happy to help arrange tours. Parking is available. Singles are $50, doubles $65, and suites $70; continental breakfast is included. Credit cards are accepted. English and French also are spoken. Telephone 257-4187, fax 257-4175. Casa Morazán is at Calle 7 and Avenida 9, about 2 blocks from Morazán Park.

A fine collection of modern art, personalized service, and an unimpeded view of the Central Valley and downtown San José are amenities at Posada El Quijote Inn in the hills of Bello Horizonte de Escazú. Owners Gordon and Lucy Finwall cater to guests' needs, whims, and desires, making travel and tour arrangements and even taking care of theater and concert tickets. Eight spacious rooms have cable TV, private phones, king or queen beds, and large bathrooms with hot water. Standard rooms are $58 for a single, $68 for a double, including a full breakfast. Deluxe rooms with private terraces are $5 more— expansive views. Credit cards accepted but subject to a surcharge. Telephone 289-8401, or toll free (800) 570-6750, extension 8401; fax 289-8729. Call for directions.

Hotel Dunn Inn is centered in a tastefully renovated 1924 home at Avenida 11, Calle 5 in Barrio Amón. The two-story house had an interior courtyard that owner Pat Dunn turned into a tropical garden restaurant. Lovely exposed brick walls are a perfect backdrop for original art. Each of the 27 rooms—including a newer addition—carries a Bribrí name. Striking stained glass uncovered in the restoration is the focus of a small sitting area. Rooms are carpeted and well-lighted, with pretty comforters and reading chairs. There is also cable TV, ceiling fans, and arranged parking (with the hotel paying part). A single or double is $45, and a suite $89. Credit cards are accepted. Telephone 222-3232 or 222-3426; fax 221-4596.

Hotel Petit Victoria is a two-story Victorian house, more than 70 years old, near the Sala Garbo theater off Paseo Colón (Calle 28, Avenida 2a). It has elaborate tile floors in the reception area, wood floors in some of the high-ceilinged rooms, and a carpeted upstairs. Pretty quilted bedspreads brighten the rooms, some with king-size beds and cable TV. Singles are from $35, doubles from $45 to $55 in the 15 rooms with private baths. Seven rooms with shared baths are $40 each for doubles. Taxes are included. A complimentary continental breakfast is served on the patio. Telephone 233-1813; telephone/fax 233-1812. Swedish and English also are spoken.

Hotel Royal Dutch is on Calle 4, Avenidas Central/2. This 26-room hotel has carpeted, air-conditioned rooms, but local TV only. There is a pleasant second-floor restaurant. Parking is available. Singles are $41, doubles $54, breakfast included; some suites have very large rooms. Credit cards are accepted. Telephone 222-1414, fax 233-3927.

Hotel Don Carlos in Barrio Amón (Calle 9, Avenidas 7/9) has character: patios with fountains, lots of plants, walls covered with artwork, rooms stuck away here and there, and a two-story shop (Boutique Annemarie) loaded with gifts. The 25 comfortable rooms range from $48 to $54 for singles and $60 to $66 for doubles, including complimentary continental breakfast and taxes. Suites are $71 for two. Some rooms have patios; all have cable TV. The hotel has its own tour company that offers rafting and trips to Tortuguero and volcanoes with a bilingual naturalist guide, and it also books for Travelair and SANSA. Credit cards are accepted. The restaurant serves light meals, offering such things as ceviche, tamales, chicken and rice, or gallo pinto. Its staff is multilingual. Annemarie's is open from 9:00 a.m. to 6:00 p.m. daily—it is great for one-stop shopping even if you are not staying at the Don Carlos. Telephone 221-6707, fax 255-0828. Credit cards are accepted.

Hotel Hemingway is in a Spanish-style house built in 1930. Each of the 17 rooms is named for a twentieth-century author—you could be in the Steinbeck, Faulkner, or T. Williams room. Shoulder-high wooden wainscoting, hardwood floors, and high ceilings predominate. Rooms have private baths with shower-head hot water and cable TV. There is a hot tub, music, plants, and Costa Rican and South American wall hangings. The complimentary continental breakfast, including exotic fruits along with the standard fare, is served in an interior courtyard. Singles are $39, doubles $49. Credit cards are accepted. Telephone/fax 221-1804. The architecturally distinctive two-story hotel is at Avenida 9, Calle 9 in Barrio Amón.

Diana's Inn is next to Morazán Park at Calle 5 and Avenida 3. The nine rooms in the three-story wooden building (no elevator), which once was home to a former president of the country, are different shapes and sizes, each with air conditioning, telephone, local TV, and private bath with hot water. The Costa Rican owners offer a family atmosphere, and the staff is helpful. Singles are $36, doubles $45; continental breakfast is included. VISA and MasterCard are accepted. There is no smoking in rooms. Telephone 223-6542, fax 233-0495.

Pico Blanco Inn is located on 12 acres (5 ha) above San Antonio de Escazú, about 20 minutes from San José at an elevation of 5,000 feet (1,524 m). The 22 pleasant rooms have private balconies with breathtaking views of the Central Valley below and nice baths with central hot water. Most rooms have queen-size beds. A single is $35, a double $45–$50. Two-room suites are $55 to $65. A fireplace in the restaurant area, which also has good views and is open to the public, is welcome—nights can be chilly. You can hike on nearby trails, rent horses, choose from hotel tours, or swim in the pool. A new terrace bar on this edge-of-the-mountain place is spectacular. Owners John and Flor are gracious hosts and proud caretakers of free-flying macaws, four scarlet and one great green. Telephone 289-6197, fax 289-5189.

Costa Verde Inn in Escazú, 20 minutes by car from downtown San José or the airport is a country home with 15 charming rooms surrounded by quiet gardens. Swimming pool, Jacuzzi, lighted tennis court, sun deck, king-size beds, and a fireplace in the lounge area are only a few of the extras. Standard single is $35, standard double $50; superiors are $50 for a single, $60 for a double. A one-bedroom apartment with balcony is $85. Rates include breakfast. Credit cards accepted. It's a typical Costa Rican direction: 100 meters west and 300 south of the Escazú cemetery. Telephone 228-4080, fax 289-8591. The Costa Verde Inn is associated with the Costa Verde Hotel at Manuel Antonio.

Also in Escazú is Amstel Country Inn, a pretty, 14-room, two-suite inn with pool and gardens. A standard room is $45 and suites are $75 for up to two people, including continental breakfast. It is part of the Amstel chain. Telephone 228-1764, fax 228-0620.

Hotel Ave del Paraíso in San Pedro is a 21-room bed and breakfast in a quiet area near the University of Costa Rica. Owners Marek and Kattia Adamski are attentive hosts—they can also speak to guests in English, French, Polish, German, or Russian. It is a friendly place. There are sitting rooms, the upstairs one opening onto a balcony. Rooms are carpeted and have big windows, pretty oval mirrors with wooden frames, telephones, and TV (local stations only). Private tiled baths have hot water, some shower-head, some tank. There is an outdoor area for the full breakfast included in the price: $35 for singles, $45 for doubles. A new mini-apartment is $70 for two. Credit cards are accepted. Telephone/fax 225-8515, 253-5138,

283-6017. Ave del Paraíso is 350 meters north of Hispanidad Fountain; watch for the sign.

Hotel Plaza is a six-story building right downtown on Avenida Central, Calles 2/4. The size of the 40 simple rooms varies; some are quite small, but all have in-room phones, TV with local stations, ceiling fans, and private baths with central hot water. The pleasant street-level restaurant looks out on the pedestrian boulevard in front. Singles are $35, doubles $45. Credit cards are accepted. Telephone 257-1896, 222-5533; fax 222-2641.

Hotel Rey Amón is in the pink building at Avenida 7 and Calle 9. The 13 rooms are light, carpeted, with high ceilings, cable TV, and private baths with shower-head hot water. Notice the 100-year-old floor tile in the large lobby and reception area. A single is $35, a double $50, with continental breakfast included. There is also free parking and a tour desk. Telephone 233-3819, telephone/fax 233-1769.

The Garden Court Hotel is also a favorite of mine. Rooms are quiet, beds comfortable, and yes, the bath has a tub. There is an outdoor swimming pool next to the breezy open-air restaurant, a tour company, and free parking. Rooms are carpeted and air-conditioned. The only drawback is that the neighborhood is risky, but friendly staff members will call a taxi for you. Singles are $33, doubles $45, with a buffet breakfast included. Telephone 220-1441 or 222-3674; fax 232-3159. In the U.S. (800) 272-6654; in Canada (800) 463-6654.

Hotel Joluva is an eight-room bed and breakfast on Calle 3b between Avenidas 9 and 11 in the Barrio Amón district. The single-story building with a row of pretty *palo verde* trees in front has high ceilings, some with gold motifs. Some rooms are carpeted; others have hardwood floors. Six have private baths, and the shared bath also has hot water. Room sizes vary. The complimentary breakfast is served on a former patio. Rooms with private baths are $$35 to $45, depending on room size; with shared bath they are $25. Credit cards are accepted. Small group tours are offered. Telephone/fax 223-7961.

Hotel Belmundo reminds me of New Orleans' French Quarter architecture. There is definitely Southern hospitality inside from India and David Norman, who own the place, and their three children. Each of the 27 rooms is different; some on the second floor have small porches that look out on city roofs and the mountains beyond. All rooms have a private bath with windows and hot water. Pretty comforters brighten the rooms. Singles are $25, doubles from $30 to $49. There is a dormitory-style room with five single beds and a private bath for $20 per person. Credit cards are accepted. Rates cover a hearty natural food breakfast. The outdoor dining room serves delightful home-cooked dinners every night, for guests only. There is a TV area, small gymnasium, and tour desk. Telephone 222-9624, fax 257-0816. The Belmundo is at Calle 20 and Avenida 9, a short walk from Paseo Colón.

Hotel Galilea on Avenida Central, Calles 11/13, has 23 rooms, all on the second and third floors (no elevator). The captain and staff befriend guests—making it a home away from home. There is cable TV in the small lobby and coffee 24 hours a day. Rooms are simply furnished, comfortable, and clean, with telephones, reading lamps, and desks. Private baths have central hot water. A single is $25, a double $30, taxes included. Credit cards are not accepted. Telephone 233-6925, fax 223-1689.

Hotel La Amistad Inn is a German-owned and -operated bed and breakfast at Avenida 11 and Calle 15, a ten-minute walk to the Plaza de la Cultura. The 22 rooms have private tiled baths with hot water, cable TV, ceiling fans, and orthopedic mattresses. Singles are $25, doubles $35, with suites at $50; all include a German-style breakfast and taxes. Credit cards are accepted. Telephone 221-1597, fax 221-1409.

Hotel San José Colonial is right downtown, near the back of the Metropolitan Cathedral. Rooms are on the second floor, with the restaurant on the ground floor. Each of the 11 simply furnished rooms is a bit different, but each has hardwood floors, a fan, and private bath with shower-head hot water. Guests can watch cable TV in the small lounge. Single is $30, double $35, including breakfast and taxes. Credit cards accepted. Telephone/fax 221-7595.

Hotel Diplomat, with 29 rooms, is on Calle Central, Avenidas Central/2. Rooms are bright, clean, and generally small, though closets are large. The upstairs restaurant has a nice atmosphere. Singles are $22, doubles $29 to $31, taxes included. MasterCard and VISA are accepted. Telephone 221-8133, fax 233-7474.

Hotel Aranjuez, in one of the oldest districts of San José, has 23 rooms with the flavor of a Costa Rican home. Rooms have bright, typically Costa Rican bedspreads and bamboo chairs with bright cushions. Rooms with private baths have cable TV. Local calls are free, as is parking. All baths have hot water. Rooms with shared baths are $17 for a single, $20 for a double; with private baths, singles are $25, doubles $30. Rates include a breakfast buffet. Telephone 223-3559, 256-1825; fax 223-3528. The Aranjuez is on Calle 19 between Avenidas 11 and 13. English, German, and French also spoken.

Hotel Kekoldi in Barrio Amón is color, from bed coverings to a multicolored balustrade and murals that bring sea views right into San José—you can almost feel the breeze. The 14 large rooms have telephones, king-size beds, and private baths with hot water. Wicker furniture provides accents. The house itself, in this historic district, is more than 80 years old, but it now has a young spirit. First-floor rooms are $22 for a single, $35 for a double; second-floor rooms are $32 for a single, $45 for a double. Breakfast is served. VISA and MasterCard accepted. Telephone 223-3244, fax 257-5476.

Toruma Youth Hostel has been remodeled so that guests now have more security and privacy. The 19 rooms have 105 beds. Nonmembers pay $12 per person, members $8, in shared rooms. Private rooms are $28 for nonmembers, $26 for members, double occupancy, with a shared bath. A small restaurant is open to the public and has very reasonable prices. Guests have use of a washing machine and iron. Toruma stores luggage and has safety deposit boxes. Telephone 234-8186, fax 224-4085. The hostel is at Avenida Central, Calles 29/31.

One-Day Package Tours from San José

Because of the country's small size and San José's central location, the traveler who wants to use the capital as a base can touch many parts of Costa Rica in one-day excursions.

National parklands with easy access are Irazú and Poás volcanoes and Braulio Carrillo. Package tours by air bring Tortuguero and Barra de Colorado National Parks into the picture. Guayabo National Monument, the only archaeological park, and the Tapantí National Wildlife Refuge are also good road trips. A cruise in the Gulf of Nicoya or a tour to Carara Biological Reserve takes you to the Pacific. Exploring the historical and biological treasures of the Central Valley is possible with tours to the Orosi Valley, Lankester Garden (for orchids), the colonial capital of Cartago with its religious shrine, and the handcraft city of Sarchí. One-day tours take you rafting or kayaking on the country's waterways and hiking on Barva Volcano.

If, after all this physical activity, you could use a relaxing massage when you return to San José, it's about $18 at Integree. Marine mud wraps and oil and herb steam baths are also available. An incredible three-hour "tune-up," for $79, is a treat you owe yourself. Manager Nazira Naranjo and her staff are qualified professionals, and the facilities are pleasing. Telephone 233-3839. Integree is on Avenida 14, Calles 1/3, and is open Monday through Friday from 8:00 a.m. to 6:00 p.m.

7

What to See and Do: Central Costa Rica

The four colonial cities of Costa Rica were San José, Cartago, Alajuela, and Heredia. Each had its own character and strong sense of identity. That is still true today. When a man tells you he is from Alajuela, he has centuries of pride in his voice.

As you travel to or through these places, remember that this land was once covered with forest. Try to imagine what travel must have been like on foot or horseback up and down these mountains and across the rivers now spanned by bridges. Life here was hard; it forged the national character.

Beauty, not hardship, is the sensation one experiences when traveling through this land today. Patches of protected forest remain, but the landscape is largely one of coffee fields, sugarcane, small farms, picturesque villages, and pastures for dairy cows. Each rural house has its flowers, a porch to sit on when the work is done, a few banana and coffee plants, some fruit trees, and perhaps some beans, squash, and corn—a link back to agrarian self-sufficiency.

Alajuela

Alajuela (population 48,645) was the home of Juan Santamaría, the country's national hero. He is honored here with a statue and the Juan Santamaría Cultural and Historical Museum, open every day except Monday from 10:00 a.m. to 6:00 p.m. Telephone 441-4775, free admission. The Central Park is a veritable orchard of mango trees. Blue-gray tanagers are among the birds that flock to eat the ripe fruit when it falls on the ground. In July, the Festival of Mangoes brings nine days of music, parades, farmers' markets, and an arts and crafts fair. Alajuela can be a stop on your way to Sarchí and Poás Volcano, or you can take a half-hour bus ride from San José (leaving

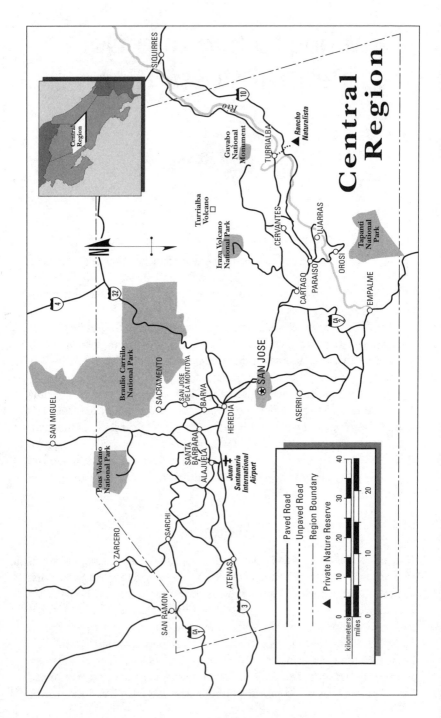

88

from Avenida 2, Calles 12/14) to explore the town. This is the capital of the province of Alajuela.

Since Alajuela is five minutes from Juan Santamaría International Airport, some travelers choose to stay here or nearby. You can ask about possibilities at the ICT airport office. Here are a few:

The Hampton Inn, only two minutes from the Juan Santamaría Airport, is a 100-room hotel with spacious, comfortable rooms (smoking and non-smoking), king-size or two double beds, air conditioning, free in-room movie channel, outdoor pool, and free local calls. Baths have shower and tubs, with central hot water. Windows are double-glazed to minimize noise. Single $59, double $65, including a continental breakfast. Some are accessible for wheelchairs. Kids and third and fourth adults sharing the same room are free. A shuttle provides service to and from the airport. There is a restaurant, bar, a small travel agency, and a casino. Credit cards accepted. Telephone 443-0043, fax 442-9532. In the U.S. (800) HAMPTON. E-mail Hampton @sol.racsa.co.cr.

Hotel Aeropuerto is 2.5 miles (4 km) from the airport on the road to Puntarenas. Its 24 pleasant, air-conditioned rooms have TV (local channels), in-room telephones, and private hot-water baths with tubs. Single $55, double $65. It has a pool, tour service, car rental, a restaurant (buffet and a la carte), and bar. Airport transfers available. Credit cards accepted. Telephone 441-2555, fax 441-5922.

Apartotel El Erizo in Alajuela has eight apartments with kitchenettes and four rooms. All have cable TV, ceiling fans or air conditioning, private baths with hot water, and telephones. Two-bedroom apartments are $84, one-bedroom apartments $72, rooms $54. Credit cards are accepted. Telephone/fax 441-2840, telephone 442-6879.

Just 10 minutes north of Alajuela on the road to Poás is Las Orquídeas Inn, a charming inn in a lovely garden setting. Eighteen ample rooms have arched windows that let in lots of light, colorful bedspreads, fresh flowers (orchids, of course), and private baths. Note the glass-topped tables on old Singer sewing machine bases. Owners Fred and Darlys McCloud serve up Buffalo-style chicken wings in the Marilyn Monroe Bar as complimentary bocas—you can get your popcorn fix here. Guitarist, composer, singer Rolando and daughter Leidy give a great evening performance most weekends. There is a large gift shop, a pretty swimming pool, and paths to walk on and admire the tropical plants on this 5-acre (2-ha) estate. Keep your eyes open for the sloths that drop by.

Las Orquídeas can fix you up with a van and driver for custom tours (Poás and waterfall, $60 for two people for half a day; Sarchí $40), and the McClouds offer a mystery trip to a destination off the beaten path. The inn is also beside a road to Sarchí and is only 20 minutes from San José. The hotel's van and a driver will take guests anywhere for $100 per day—up to nine persons. Singles with fans are $55, doubles $65, $5 more for air conditioning. VISA and MasterCard are accepted. Two large suites are also available. New on the scene is a geodesic dome suite ($120 for up to four) with two rooms and a loft. A marvelous breakfast is included in all prices. You will probably share it in the company of the free-flying toucans who have made Las Orquídeas home (watch your bare toes—toucans seem to like them). No children under 13 are permitted. Telephone 433-9346, fax 433-9740.

For something a bit different, try Tuetal Lodge, less than 2 miles (3 km) north of Alajuela in Tuetal Norte. Don and Janet Caldwell and their daughters offer campsites, cabins, or treehouses. Yes, treehouses. You can sleep in a bamboo structure built among the branches, sharing bath facilities with the campers—washrooms, solar-heated showers. Campsites are about $7 for two (you can also rent the tents), and the treehouse is about $12. Six cabins have private baths with solar hot water; ones with kitchenettes are $40 for two, without kitchenettes $30. Terraces look out on pretty tropical gardens. A pleasant restaurant (Canadian chef) serves full breakfast, lunch, and a choice of three to four main dishes in the evening. No credit cards. Telephone/fax 442-1804.

Hotel Buena Vista is a 25-room Mediterranean-style, mountain hotel 3 miles (5 km) north off Alajuela just off the road to Poás Volcano (in Pilas de San Isidro). With a 360-degree view of farmlands, settlements, and volcanoes (Poás, Barva, and Irazú), Buena Vista does indeed have spectacular views. Spacious, carpeted rooms have two queen-size beds, cable TV, desk, big bathrooms with central hot water, and private balconies. Singles $65, doubles $70. Landscaped grounds include a pool and pleasant patios where you can sit and enjoy the surroundings. The restaurant features international dishes; breakfast $5, lunch $8, and dinner $10. Credit cards accepted. Telephone/fax 443-2214.

Sarchí

Sarchí is an artisan center where even the trash cans and bus stops are decorated with colorful paintings. The most famous product is the painted oxcart. Oxcarts played a vital transportation role in earlier times, carrying coffee from the highlands down to the Pacific for export. Carts, painted and unpainted, still transport produce. Farmers are usually pleased to stop to let you photograph their carts and oxen when you encounter them on a rural road. At Sarchí, you find the genuine item as well as replicas turned into bars, napkin holders, and miniatures, complete with a few beans of coffee stuck on. There are salad bowls, wooden fruit, lamps, furniture, jewelry, and more. At the Joaquín Chaverri store and factory, watch artisans paint the delicate designs freehand.

Plaza de la Artesanía has more than 30 stores exhibiting arts and crafts of Costa Rica as well as other countries: pottery, sculpture, paintings, jewelry, leather goods, glassware, textiles, and wood and bamboo furniture. The shopping center offers parking, an ice cream shop, restaurants, and restrooms.

The bus to Sarchí leaves Alajuela every half-hour. Some tours to the magnificent Poás Volcano National Park stop here. (See Chapter 12 for further information about Poás.)

Toward Poás

Near Poás is another natural destination: La Providencia Ecological Reserve, a private reserve on a farm that has 395 acres (160 ha) of primary forest. Denizens of this forest include the resplendent quetzal, ocelots, coyotes, armadillos, emerald toucanets, peccaries, hummingbirds, and tayras. Giant ferns abound; there is the huge-leafed *sombrilla del pobre* (poor man's umbrella) and magnificent oak forests, one of which is white because of acid rain from the volcano.

The panorama from La Providencia when the weather is clear is impressive: the Central Valley, the Pacific, lakes in Nicaragua, and Arenal Volcano. The elevation is 8,200 feet (2,500 m). Visitors are welcome for both day tours and overnight stays. The reserve has five rustic wooden cabins with private baths. (Electricity from a generator gives hot water.) A short distance away is a small restaurant where meals are cooked on a wood stove. Nighttime brings candlelight meals.

A three-hour horseback ride takes visitors on the slopes of the volcano through primary and secondary forest (including the "white" oaks) and to waterfalls, páramo, and view points, in the company of a biologist guide. The cost is $25 including breakfast, $30 with lunch. The rooms for two are $38. A *casita* for ten people is $10 per person; there is also a four-person house for $50. Meals are $6 for breakfast, $10 for lunch and dinner. Bring warm clothes and rain gear. Telephone 232-2498, fax 231-2204 (mark faxes "for Amalia").

The black shade cloths covering fields on the way to Poás Volcano are sheltering ornamental plants and flowers, a growing nontraditional export. Strawberries grow there as well, and you can often buy them at roadside stands.

Also north of Alajuela toward Poás via San Pedro de Poás and San Juan is Las Fresas Restaurant and Hotel. The mountain restaurant is a favorite with local folks out for a country drive. Owner Ruggero Scola is an excellent host, attentive to guests. Food and service are excellent. It is a varied menu with Italian specialties—homemade pastas. You will probably find orchids on the table—it is a cloth napkin place. Big windows in the beautiful old building look out on gardens and forest and a fire in the fireplace adds coziness on cool, rainy days.

Behind the restaurant are six pleasant rooms in a hexagonal building. Private baths have central hot water, $30 for a double. VISA and MasterCard accepted. Telephone 448-5567.

Heredia

Heredia (population 29,173) is the gateway to another volcano, Barva. It is also the home of the National University and a church built in 1796. The tower of an old fort remains in pretty gardens near the church. See Practical Extras for bus schedules from San José. The 25-minute trip has stops in Tibás and Santo Domingo. Microbuses also come directly. Heredia is the capital of the province by that name.

Right downtown is Hotel America, a pretty four-story hotel only 20 minutes from the international airport and 15 minutes from downtown San José. The 36 rooms and four junior suites have private baths with solar hot water, in-room telephones, and TV (local channels). Singles are $35, doubles $45, suites $65 for two persons. On the first floor is the Restaurante Nuevo Vienna, beauty shop, jewelry store, and souvenir shop. A conference center is on the fourth floor. Owner Carlos O'Campo is proud of Heredia and his hotel. Tours are arranged to volcanoes, rivers, and parks. Credit cards accepted. Hotel America is half a block from Heredia's Central Park. Telephone 260-9292, fax 260-9293.

Other lodging possibilities in the Heredia area are especially appealing for nature travelers. Bougainvillea Santo Domingo Hotel in Santo Domingo de Heredia is located on 6 acres (2.4 ha) of gardens. The 44 nicely furnished, carpeted rooms are spacious, with a separate sitting area, cable TV, and private baths (tub and shower). Each opens onto a balcony. Sculpture and paintings by Costa Rican artists are scattered throughout the hotel. Facilities include tennis courts, a solar-heated swimming pool, sauna, and jogging trail. The fine restaurant is known for its cuisine and its service. There is hourly free shuttle service to San José, about 15 minutes away. Singles cost $70, doubles $80. Credit cards are accepted. Telephone 244-1414, fax 244-1313. E-mail bougainvillea@centralamerica.com.

Finca Rosa Blanca Country Inn is outside Santa Barbara de Heredia, 30

Finca Rosa Blanca near Santa Barbara de Heredia (Finca Rosa Blanca)

minutes from San José. It is exquisite. The building seems to soar above surrounding coffee plantations, with great views of the Central Valley and Irazú
Volcano through enormous windows. Inside, interesting architectural details
abound. Beautiful tropical hardwoods gleam in floors and walls—the wood
was salvaged from a road-widening project. Each of the eight rooms is
unique; one has a mural by artists from nearby Barva that flows from a large
window and continues the landscape on the wall. Bathrooms are unique.

There is a walking trail where butterflies await, 200 fruit trees on the
grounds to attract birds, and a river. The spring-fed swimming pool is as
unusual as the building. Rooms range from $125 to $208 for two people,
$106 to $187 for singles, including a full breakfast. Two villas, each with two
bedrooms, a central lounge and kitchen area and a deck, are in keeping with
the main house, also with murals and hand-painted tiles. They can sleep up

to six persons each. An organic garden supplies produce for the restaurant, which is for guests only. Tours that focus on Costa Rica's natural beauty are arranged for guests. Telephone 269-9392, fax 269-9555.

North of Heredia is Hotel Chalet Tirol, 30 to 45 minutes from San José. Located at about 5,900 feet (1,800 m), the main lodge, ten chalets, and 14 suites are in a cloud-forest setting. Paths through the forest allow guests to see trogons, motmots, hummingbirds, and trees and ferns typical of this altitude. You can play tennis or go trout fishing, horseback riding, or bicycling. Chalet Tirol offers a number of tours, including visits to Barva Volcano and coffee farms, and hikes in the cloud forest. The hotel's fine French restaurant is well-known. Lodging includes options such as fireplaces, TV, bathtubs, telephones, and hair dryers. Rooms and chalets are $80 for two; suites are from $110 to $150, including continental breakfast. Dinner theater and concerts are in the Salzburg Café Concert, and there is a pizzería and gourmet cooking school at Tirol. Telephone 267-7371, fax 267-7050.

Barva Volcano is in Braulio Carrillo National Park. The resplendent quetzal and a variety of other birds can be seen here. To get to Barva Volcano, take the Paso Llano bus from the Central Market in Heredia. A walking trail then leads you about 4 miles (6 km) to the park entrance. The lagoon is about 2.5 miles (4 km) farther on. (See Chapter 12 for details.) There are two or three buses a day. Check with ICT for the times.

On the road between Heredia and the jumping-off place for the volcano at Sacramento is the historic town of Barva, with its large church and tiled-roof adobe houses. Farther along, in the area of San José de la Montaña, are three hotels that offer a chance to hike, bird-watch, and spend the night in this chilly clime. Bring a coat; it is cold at night and brisk in the early morning, and I have wished for my long johns to sleep in.

Hotel Cypresal has a swimming pool, sauna, gift shop, conference rooms, restaurant, and a bar with a fireplace. Rooms have a private bath with hot water, color TV, and telephone. The larger unit has a separate bedroom and sitting room and a private terrace. The smaller rooms have a sitting area in front of the fireplace. A single costs $40, a double $50. You can rent horses, and airport pickup can be arranged. Telephone 237-4466, 237-0509; fax 237-7232. Cypresal is about 13 miles (20 km) from San José.

Within walking distance up the road is the 18-room El Pórtico, which has a Jacuzzi, sauna, pool, and restaurant. The mountain lodge has polished brick floors, fireplaces, and heaters in the rooms. Rooms have private baths and hot water, $60 for a single, $70 for a double, including breakfast and taxes. Credit cards are accepted. The pretty dining room looks out on bright tropical flowers in a landscaped garden. Guests can walk on a beautiful river trail in back of the lodge. Telephone 260-6000, 237-6022; fax 260-6002.

Further up the road past Sacramento is Sacramento Lodge, practically at the doorstep of the Barva sector of Braulio Carrillo National Park. The rustic dining room has a big fireplace at one end, brick floors, lots of flowers, checkered tablecloths, and an open view of the farms, forest patches, and towns in the valley below. Cooking is over a wood stove. The five rooms, some for two people, larger ones for up to seven, have the same rustic look—lots of wood, colorful quilts, sheepskins on beds, tree-trunk stools. Each has a private bath—hot water when you give enough notice to light the fire that heats the water. Rates are $34 for singles, $46 doubles. Breakfast is $5.50, lunch or dinner $9. The Castro family, who manage the lodge, will graciously see to your needs. Horseback tours are offered, $70, as well as park tours. Horses are $12 for half a day, and a guide charges $10 a day. No credit cards. Telephone 237-2116 or 237-2441; fax 237-1976.

Atenas Area

The town of Atenas southeast of Alajuela is also easily reached from the international airport for those who prefer to stay outside of cities. Delightful El Cafetal Inn is just 20 minutes from the airport, turning right in Atenas for Santa Eulalia de Atenas. Signs point the way. The spectacular two-story house with rounded, glass corner alcoves overlooks the Colorado River Valley and fields of coffee and sugarcane, with views of Alajuela, part of Heredia, and Poás, Barva, and Irazú volcanoes. Lee and Romy Rodríguez greet you at the door and treat you as an honored guest throughout your stay.

It is a classy place—shining marble floors, a soothing waterfall in the two-story atrium that is a lovely lounge area, light and airy rooms, deep cushions on wicker furniture, lots of floor to ceiling windows. Each of the ten doubles has a private bath with central hot water—big turquoise and rose towels and washcloths. Meals are a treat—nothing ordinary about the cuisine here—Romy dons the chef's hat and cooks with a flair. Guests can savor cappuccino at the coffee bar and try coffee from the Atenas area or that grown on the farm. Down a garden path through coffee plants is a large pool and a rancho where a Sunday brunch is served.

From El Cafetal Inn, guests can choose tours to Poás Volcano; to orchid, butterfly, and coffee farms; to the Las Musas Waterfall; to Sarchí, Jacó beach, Tortuga Island, and the Carara park; to San José for a city tour; and to Alajuela for a night mariachi tour. A single is $45, a double is $55; corner tower rooms are $65. Credit cards accepted. Telephone 446-5785, fax 446-5140. El Cafetal Inn can also be reached from the Inter-American Highway going toward Puntarenas. Watch for the sign after the Grecia-Sarchí intersection—turn left before the bridge.

COFFEE

Coffee was Costa Rica's number-one export from the middle of the last century until this decade, when bananas edged it into second place. Today it is the third-largest foreign exchange earner, after bananas and tourism. Its cultivation and export brought the country into the world market and initiated a cash economy in a land previously tied to subsistence agriculture. But the instability of world market prices for coffee brings good years and bad years, and even though Costa Rica is working hard to diversify its economy through nontraditional exports, a drop in the price of coffee still sends a shudder through the country.

Coffee, which originated in Ethiopia and Arabia, was brought to the New World by the French, Spanish, and Portuguese. Seeds were first planted in Costa Rica around the beginning of the nineteenth century, but coffee did not become a substantial export until 1840. Most is sold to Germany, the United States, and Great Britain.

The best flavor comes from coffee grown above 4,000 feet (1,200 m) on land where temperatures average between 59°F and 82°F (15°C and 28°C). A definite dry season helps because plants then flower evenly once the rains start, and fruit will mature over a few months, creating a short harvest period. Coffee is picked by hand. Since all the berries, even on a single plant, do not ripen at the same time, much labor is involved. Reducing that labor-intensive period is economically important to the grower.

Coffee plants are grown in nurseries until they are about one year old, then transplanted to the field. After two years, they begin to bear commercially. Some growers harvest from coffee trees for 15 to 20 years and then prune them way back for 20 more years of production before replacing the plant. (Coffee wood is highly prized for cooking because it burns slowly and produces little smoke.)

In some fields, bananas or citrus trees are planted to shade the coffee, reducing the need to add nutrients to the soil. Legumes, such as the poró, add nitrogen to the soil.

Coffee is planted in May and June. Harvest time depends on the elevation: October to January in the Central Valley, June to October or November in Turrialba and Coto Brus. Pickers are paid by the cajuela (basket), they fill. A good picker can earn about $10 a day. All ages take to the fields for the harvest. Each berry, which turns from green to red when ripe, contains two seeds: the coffee beans. The pulp of the fruit must be removed and the beans dried before they can be roasted or exported.

Cartago and Turrialba

On the other side of San José across the Continental Divide lies Cartago (population 31,413). Once the colonial capital, it now is the capital of the province of Cartago. As you travel the Bernardo Soto highway for the 13 miles (21 km) between San José and Cartago, you have a chance to use the country's first automated tollbooth—throw exact change into the basket and breeze through (60 colones at this writing, but check the sign just before the booth: *vehículo liviano*). For those who haven't yet figured out the money, do not have correct change, or freeze up in automated situations, there are alternate lanes where human hands and hearts can help you out.

If you like markets, stop by the one here (downtown on Avenida 4), which has gorgeous vegetables. A few blocks away on Avenida 2, Calle 2 are reminders of the city's colonial roots. The ruins of a stone church (Ruinas de la Parroquia) now surround a peaceful garden. This first parish church in Cartago was founded in 1575. During the colonial period it was reconstructed several times, having been almost totally destroyed by an earthquake in 1841. But it was the May 4, 1910, earthquake that brought the last rebuilding efforts to a halt. In front of the ruins is a sample of cobblestone streets from the colonial era.

The most famous church in Cartago—in the entire country for that matter—is the Basílica de Nuestra Señora de los Angeles, built in honor of La Negrita, Costa Rica's patron saint. The church is built over the rock where the tiny stone image of a black Virgin first appeared to Juana Pereira, a young woodgatherer, in 1635. Descend stairs in the room to the left of the altar to see the rock where she appeared. The Virgin is above the altar. Cases along walls in the anteroom contain thousands of tokens celebrating miracles attributed to her. Outside, behind the basilica, the faithful and the hopeful come to the holy water that flows from a spring. On August 2, all roads lead to Cartago, as some half a million pilgrims gather at the shrine for the Day of Our Lady of the Angels, many having come on foot over long distances. The public bus to Cartago from San José leaves every ten minutes between 5:00 a.m. and 7:00 p.m., with less frequent runs after that. Catch it at Avenida 10, Calle 5.

Cartago has felt the effects of not only earthquakes but also Irazú Volcano, now a national park (see Chapter 12). The drive to the volcano offers spectacular views of the valley. Farmers tend fields of potatoes, onions, and cabbages. Milk cows move along the road. When we stopped once to photograph a young man forking hay into an ancient-looking barn, he insisted on taking us inside to see his bull.

A public bus goes from San José to Irazú Volcano National Park on

Basílica de Nuestra Señora de los Angeles in Cartago (Ree Strange Sheck)

Saturday and Sunday only, leaving for the 90-minute trip at 8:00 a.m., returning at 1:00 p.m. Catch it at Avenida 2, Calles 1/3 in front of the Gran Hotel Costa Rica. That bus stops at 8:30 a.m. in Cartago beside the church ruins mentioned above to pick up passengers. Many agencies offer tours to Irazú.

Off the road to Irazú is a lodge between Irazú and Turrialba volcanoes: Volcán Turrialba Lodge. This small lodge, located at an elevation of 9,186 feet (2,800 m), offers the nature traveler hiking, horseback, and biking—magnificent ways to see Turrialba's old lava beds, hot springs (on the slopes of Irazú Volcano), and the crater of Turrialba Volcano. The crater is less than 4 miles (6 km) from the lodge. Another flora and fauna tour is in a 208-acre (84-ha) primary forest on the farm where ocelots, river otters, quetzals, porcupines, coyotes, and kinkajous live. This is a place I have not yet visited; perhaps you will see it before I do. Owner Tony Lachner converted an old milking house into a comfortable, rustic lodge with nine rooms, each with private bath and hot water. Lodging and three meals a day are $55 for singles, $95 for doubles. The road is accessible only by four-wheel-drive vehicles, but transportation is provided from San José; cost depends on the number of passengers. The activities at the lodge are also open to day visitors. A one-day tour from San José is $60. Packages are available, including a two-night, three-day trip that includes transportation, lodging, meals, taxes, and tours to the lava beds, Turrialba Volcano, and hot springs and fumaroles for $195. Credit cards are accepted. Telephone/fax 273-4335.

Only about 2.5 miles (4 km) from Cartago toward Paraíso is beautiful Lankester Botanical Garden. Begun in the 1950s by English naturalist Charles Lankester to preserve local epiphytes, the garden was bought in 1973 by the North American Society of Orchideology and the Stanley Smith Foundation of England and donated to the University of Costa Rica. Most of the thousands who have walked these paths have come to see the orchids—more than 800 species of local and foreign orchids, from tiny miniatures to flowers with stalks more than 15 feet high (5 m). Though the greenhouse of miniatures is not often open, a staff member is usually happy to let you have a look if you ask. Though peak months for orchids to bloom are February through May, you are guaranteed to see enough in flower to dazzle you any time of the year.

Well-maintained trails through part of the 26-acre (10.7-ha) botanical garden lead over brooks, under arbors, to greenhouses, through a breathtaking display of flowers and trees that attract more than 100 species of birds. You may be surprised to find a cactus and succulent garden here. Though most cacti in Costa Rica grow in the tropical dry forest, some live as epiphytes in the rain forest. Palms bromeliads, bamboo (40 varieties), and heliconias (35 varieties), gingers, aroids, and ferns abound. The secondary forest is in the premontane life zone. Research and education go hand in hand with plant production at Lankester Botanical Garden. Though there are currently no guided walks, some descriptive signs are in place and a written guide for the self-guided tour may be available by your arrival. Open daily from 9:00 a.m. to 3:30 p.m., visitors admitted every half hour. Closed January 1, Thursday and Friday of Easter Week, and December 25. Admission is less than $3, children 25 cents. To arrive by bus, go first to Cartago (25 minutes) and catch the bus to Paraíso, telling the driver to let you off at the entrance to Jardín Botánico Lankester. Follow the signs for a ½-mile walk to the building. If you are driving from Cartago, watch for the entrance on the right just past Casa Vieja Restaurant and next to Campo Ayala. A taxi from Cartago is about $5. Allow one to two hours to enjoy the garden and the gift shop, where you can get T-shirts, books, and a video about the garden. Bring insect repellent in rainy season. Telephone 551-9877 or 552-3151; fax 552-3247. Apartado 1031-7050, Cartago.

From Paraíso, roads go east and south for magnificent views of the Orosí Valley, Reventazón River, and the lake formed by the Cachí Dam. The east road leads to ruins of the seventeenth-century church of Ujarrás. Archaeological digs show that the colonial town that once surrounded it lies over pre-Columbian roads. There is a restaurant at the view point (*mirador* in Spanish) overlooking Ujarrás. Ten minutes away by car is Charrarra, a recreation park on the lake, with swimming pool, restaurant, picnic areas, horseback riding and bicycling, and trails (closed Monday). The distinctive call of the oropendola, a large dark bird with yellow tail feathers, resounds through the trees. Crowded on weekends, the park is peaceful on other days. The road continues on to the dam.

The road south of Paraíso goes to the town of Orosí and its eighteenth-century church. Beside the church is a small historical museum, open daily (signs in Spanish only). A mirador before you reach Orosí offers glorious views. Just beyond the town is Hotel Río Palomo, on the Palomo River, with its popular restaurant, open 8:30 a.m. to 5:00 p.m. Cabins of various sizes rent for $10 per person. There is a large swimming pool by the restaurant. Telephone 533-3128, 533-3057.

The Tapantí National Park is about 6 miles (10 km) from Orosí. Tours combine some of these sites near Cartago in day trips from San José. Public buses from Cartago go to Orosí and Ujarrás (ask at ICT), with a taxi extension for Tapantí. Or you can get a taxi from Cartago or Paraíso, where they are more plentiful. If you are driving, you can make a loop from Ujarrás around the lake, but the unpaved section from the dam to Orosí is bumpy (and dusty in the dry season).

The road from Cartago to Turrialba is spectacular as it winds up and over the mountains. This was the route to Limón before the shorter highway from San José to Guapiles opened. When you get to the town of Cervantes, watch on the left for La Posada de la Luna restaurant. I am unable to pass this place without stopping for a scrumptious, freshly made *tortilla de queso* (cheese tortilla) and a glass of hot *agua dulce con leche*. Some people swear that the best *gallo pinto* (beans and rice) in the country is served here. The main room is now nonsmoking. Showcases hold bits of history, from Indian artifacts to old telephones, radios, and flatirons. La Luna is quite a place, and service is with a smile. It is open from 8:00 a.m. to 8:00 p.m., except Monday.

The agricultural lands around Juan Viñas are among the most beautiful in Costa Rica. Fields of sugarcane wave across this top-of-the-world setting. Then comes the winding descent into the Turrialba Valley.

Only 40 miles (64 km) from San José, Turrialba, with 31,455 people, is the center of a rich agricultural region and is increasingly a destination for tourists. Kayakers and white-water rafters use the town as a base for forays on the mighty Reventazón and Pacuare rivers. Its location makes it ideal for travelers interested in archaeology, agriculture, and nature. From here you can visit Guayabo National Monument 11 miles (18 km) away (Chapter 12), Turrialba Volcano, plantations of coffee, macadamia nuts, cardamom, sugarcane, and bananas, and tour CATIE, a tropical agricultural research and education center.

Hotel Wagelia in Turrialba has two locations. The 18-room downtown hotel offers parking and a restaurant with good food and a pleasant atmosphere. Rooms open onto terraces around a courtyard. Five of the rooms are air-conditioned, the rest have ceiling fans; private baths have hot water. Rooms are simple but comfortable, with tile floors, reading lamps, and dressers. Five have refrigerator and TV. The 17-room annex, with private baths, showers, and hot water, is on a quiet street backed by coffee fields at the edge of town. It has a swimming pool. Rates at either are $30 for a single, $45 for a double, and $50 for doubles with air conditioning, refrigerator, and TV. Credit cards accepted. The hotel arranges tours through local agencies to Guayabo, Turrialba Volcano, and CATIE as well as rafting trips. Telephone 556-1566, fax 556-1596, annex telephone 556-1142.

Hotel Turrialba is another downtown hotel, private baths with hot water, fans, television in some rooms. Singles about $15, and doubles $22 including tax. It is above the store Superdigrasa. Telephone 556-6654 or 556-6396.

Do not plan to sleep late anywhere in town. Its peaceful air will be broken by three strong blasts of the town's fire alarm announcing 6:00 a.m.

You can get from San José to Turrialba by express bus. (See Practical Extras.) If you have a car, there is a back door to Turrialba that winds through San Isidro de Coronado and Rancho Redondo, dairy country, and oak forests often shrouded in mist. The last time I was on this road was a Corpus Christi Sunday. Flowers strewn in the road marked the path of religious processions in village after village. In one, a milk cow stood in the middle of the road eating the flower petals while worshipers sang in a nearby church. Past Llano Grande is the turnoff for Irazú Volcano. Continue on to Cot and Pacayas for Santa Cruz, watching for waterfalls on the skirts of Turrialba Volcano. At Santa Cruz, turn to Turrialba. This road is passable even in the rainy season. From Santa Cruz, a jolting road—which is supposed to be surfaced some time soon—goes on to Guayabo and the national monument.

From Turrialba, Guayabo is 12 miles (19 km) northeast. Guayabo National Monument is an archeological site under the national park system, well worth a visit not only for the special energy of this Indian site but also for the forest it protects (see Chapter 12). Closest lodging to the park is a ten-minute-walk away at a small mountain lodge called La Calzada. The lodge has four doubles (two single beds in each), shared bath, and a common lounge area. From the balcony on three sides of the wood building, one sees the small lake with its reflections of eucalyptus trees and an expansive

SUGARCANE

Sugarcane was brought to the New World by Columbus and introduced into Costa Rica in 1530. Though it is grown in most of the country, the major cane-producing regions are the Central Valley around Atenas and Grecia; the Turrialba and Juan Viñas area of the Central Valley; Guanacaste; San Carlos; and Pérez Zeledón and Parrita to the south. Some 101,200 acres (42,000 ha) are in production.

At 3,280 feet (1,000 m) or less, cane takes 12 to 18 months to reach harvest; above that elevation, it takes 24 months. Almost all the cane is cut by hand except in Guanacaste, where machines are used because there is insufficient labor. In Costa Rica, most cane is burned first to make the cutting easier. A worker can cut two to three tons of unburned cane per day compared with three to six tons of cane that has been burned. The harvest season is from January to May, though in higher regions around Juan Viñas, it can last until August. Large sugar mills are called ingenios, and

companies often provide a school and housing for workers. Small trapiches, *where juice is extracted by ox power, can still be found.*

More than 4,500 people have cane operations, ranging from a few acres to 7,400 acres (3,000 ha). Some 60,000 workers and their families depend on cane production. In some places, especially in the Central Valley, the cane harvest alternates with the coffee harvest.

The United States is the biggest buyer of Costa Rican sugar and has been since 1963 when it stopped buying from Cuba. Nicaragua and Trinidad also buy tico sugar. Some cane is used to produce alcohol for fuel, which is also exported to the United States, at distilleries in Cañas and Liberia.

The price of cane is fixed by the government, and the Sugarcane Agricultural and Industrial League (LAICA) regulates buying and selling and conducts research to improve production. Costa Rica is third in the world in production per hectare.

view of sky and mountains. It is peaceful. Owners José Miguel and Grettel García, terrific hosts, say what they offer is tranquillity and good food. The thatched open-air restaurant serves typical fare. The lodge and restaurant are open from January to July; call for reservations in other months, though the restaurant is always open on weekends. The cost is $15 for a room for one or two persons, VISA accepted. Telephone 556-0465, fax 556-0427. The bus from Turrialba to Guayabo passes in front of La Calzada.

Another side trip out of Turrialba is to CATIE, continuing east on what was the main road to Limón until the new highway through Braulio Carrillo was built. CATIE, is an agricultural education, extension, and research center. Studies have focused on dairy and beef livestock as well as cacao, coffee, plantains, spices, fruit trees, and *pejibaye* (peach palm). Some 1,200 students from 34 nations hold master's degrees from its graduate studies program in agriculture and natural resources. Day visitors, welcome Monday through Friday, may choose from among options such as the forest walk (about an hour), bird observation, agroforestry systems, the arboretum, plant collection, seed bank, or the lake for the half-day visit. Cost is $5 per person, and staff recommends arriving early in the morning or right after lunch for the tour. Call 556-6431, extension 254, to make arrangements; fax 556-6431. E-mail pbaltoda@catie.ac.cr.

Just 3 miles (5 km) from Turrialba on this same road, past CATIE, is the turnoff to La Suiza and Casa Turire, a splendid country house on the Atirro Hacienda. Situated in a curve of the Reventazón River, Casa Turire reigns over nearby forest as well as fields of sugarcane, coffee, and macadamia nuts. The hacienda belongs to the Rojas family, who extended their enterprises to include tourism in 1991. The 12-room, four-suite grand "plantation house" sits amid formal gardens, with a pool, Jacuzzi, and tennis court. Rooms are elegant, furnished in soft tones, with two full beds in each. They have satellite TV, shower with tub, ceiling fan, hair dryer, and direct-dial telephone. Each room has a stunning view of the mountains from a private balcony. Floor-to-ceiling windows welcome light that shines on polished hardwood floors. Singles are $95, doubles $110, suites from $130. No children under 12 are permitted; building not equipped for the handicapped.

Guests at Casa Turire can choose from mountain biking, rainforest tours, horseback riding, or kayaking and white-water rafting on the Reventazón. There are tours to Irazú Volcano, Guayabo, the Lankester Botanical Garden, and one- or two-day tours to Tortuguero National Park. On the hacienda, guests can visit processing plants for cane, coffee, and macadamia nuts. The restaurant is open to the public for lunch and dinner, reservations please. Credit cards accepted. Telephone 531-1111, fax 531-1075.

The privately owned nature reserve Rancho Naturalista, a favorite with bird and butterfly enthusiasts, is near Turrialba, southeast through La Suiza (see Chapter 13).

Further along the road to Limón are two small mountain lodges: Turrialtico and Pochotel. Turrialtico is about 4 miles (7 km) from Turrialba. Its 12 rooms with private baths (shower-head hot water) are above the lodge's locally popular restaurant, which has a dynamite view of the valley. Pleasant rooms, brightened by Guatemalan bedspreads, open onto a common space with two appealing sitting areas. Run by owners Hector Lezama and Lucrecia Garcia, the lodge offers trips to a nearby serpentarium, to Guayabo park, to Turrialba Volcano, rafting, horseback riding, and hiking. Camping is permitted on the property. There is a small gift shop and a big paperback library where guests can buy or borrow. Single $25, double $30. VISA accepted. Telephone 556-1575. Telephone/fax 556-1111.

Pochotel is 7 miles (11 km) from Turrialba. From its mirador on a clear day, you can see not only the Reventazón Valley but also Cerro de la Muerte, Chirripó, Irazú and Turrialba volcanoes, and the Caribbean coast. The eight rooms are simply furnished, and the ones in the more secluded bungalows along the edge of the forest have rustic charm. The restaurant has a wood-burning stove (*cocina de leña*, in the dining room so guests can be a part of this traditional way of cooking). Owner Oscar Garcia will arrange rafting tours; a visit to the Lagunas de San Joaquín, where you can fish, hike, or horseback ride in the forest; a helicopter ride; or a trip to Tortuguero, where he has cabins. Rooms are $35 for two (tax included), $10 per person extra. VISA accepted. Telephone 284-7292 or 556-0111; fax 556-6222. Staff speak mainly Spanish at both Turraltico and Pochotel, but people of many languages find their way here.

Just 400 meters past the turnoff for Pochotel is Viborana, a small serpentarium that also has a natural butterfly garden. Admission is less than $2 for adults, less than $1 for children. Fax 556-0427.

8

What to See and Do: North Central Costa Rica

Mountains, plains, volcanoes, lakes, rivers, forests, fruit farms, and cattle ranches form a colorful and diverse mosaic in this region of Costa Rica. Several routes take the traveler into the north-central area from San José. To get to the La Fortuna-Arenal-Tilarán areas from the Inter-American High-way west of San José, you can go north through Naranjo, Zarcero, and Ciudad Quesada; or San Ramón and Chachagua. (Don't forget to have change ready for the toll booth [*peaje*] before the airport if you are driving— 60 colones at this writing.) Westbound travelers do not pay at the peaje near kilometer 40; eastbound, it's 120 colones.

Travelers can also go northwest out of San José through Varablanca and San Miguel and either head west for Lake Arenal or Caño Negro, or go east to the Puerto Viejo area. (There are several towns named Puerto Viejo in Costa Rica; this one is Puerto Viejo de Sarapiquí.) The road northeast out of San José through Braulio Carrillo National Park toward Limón is another gateway to Puerto Viejo, turning north before Guapiles and going through Las Horquetas.

If you are in Guanacaste in the northwest region, you can visit the north-central section by either heading northeast at Cañas for Tilarán and the Arenal area or taking the mostly unpaved road from La Cruz near Nicaragua to Upala. The western entrance to Caño Negro National Wildlife Refuge is accessible via an unpaved road from Upala. (Many visitors arrive on the eastern side via a paved road to Los Chiles, a stone's throw from Nicaragua.)

Buses run throughout this area. (Check the Bus section in Practical Extras at the end of the book.) Direct buses from San José go to Ciudad Quesada, Puerto Viejo de Sarapiquí, Braulio Carrillo Park, and Tilarán, with connections to other destinations. For instance, there are two buses a day each way between Ciudad Quesada and Tilarán for access to Lake Arenal.

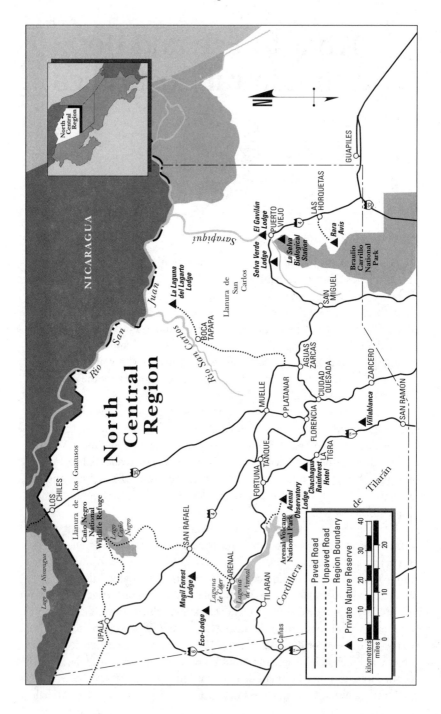

San Ramón-Chachagua Route

Let's begin with the route through San Ramón. If you are driving, watch for killer speed bumps near San Ramón—the signs say *"Reductor de velocidad."* Part of the magnificent primary forest along this road is in the Alberto Manuel Brenes Biological Reserve, and some of it is Bosque Eterno de los Niños, the first international children's rain forest.

About 12 miles (19 km) north of San Ramón is a private nature reserve called Villablanca. Guests stay in a replica of a colonial village nestled next to a cloud forest (see Chapter 13).

A few miles north of the turnoff to Villablanca is Valle Escondido Lodge, where you can combine treks in fantastic forest with walks through acres of ornamental plants grown for export, while enjoying very nice quarters. The lodge itself has 25 rooms, each opening onto a covered gallery with a magical view of a valley and green, green mountains that appear and disappear according to the mists. Large frogs convene on the porch in the evenings. Rooms are large and bright, with beautiful polished hardwood furniture, including an ample writing desk. Bathrooms have big lighted mirrors and come with bidets, not common in Costa Rica. Singles are $55, doubles $66. Credit cards are accepted.

The restaurant, a short walk downhill from the rooms, offers an international menu with Italian specialties. Food is a feast for the eyes as well as the palate. Don't forget to take your binoculars to the dining room to enjoy the birds in the garden at the back while you eat. The restaurant is open to the public and is only a five-minute drive from the highway turnoff.

Owner Marco Hidalgo exports the more than 20 species of ornamental plants grown here to Italy, the Netherlands, and Belgium. Guests can also visit the greenhouses and packing sheds.

The farm includes about 150 acres (60 ha) of forest and an abundance of mountain streams. The understory of the tall forest is a natural tropical greenhouse with a variety of heliconias and fascinating tree roots. I watched as one masked tityra fed another. An aracari, a member of the toucan family, frustrated my attempts to photograph him but allowed wonderful glimpses. Near one trail is a huge tree with enormous buttresses where bats live. The wide forest trails begin and end at the plantation. The lodge offers a tour—on foot, horseback, or mountain bike—to the San Lorenzo River, where you can swim in a natural pool. Or you can hike to a three-tiered waterfall. A guided tour of the ornamental plant farm combined with a hike in the forest is $12; a trail hike without guide is $5 (free to hotel guests). Horses cost $6 per hour, and mountain bikes $3. Boots are also for rent.

The elevation is about 2,000 feet (600 m), and the temperature ranges from 68°F to 86°F (20°C to 30°C). Valle Escondido Lodge is 21 miles (33 km) from San Ramón and 56 miles (90 km) from San José. English and Italian also are spoken here. Telephone 231-0906, fax 232-9591. Day visitors welcome. The lodge can arrange transportation, or you can take the public bus to San Ramón and a taxi from there or continue by public bus to the turnoff.

As you continue on the main road north, you will see the magnificent forest-covered mountains between La Tigra and La Fortuna. This is Bosque Eterno de los Niños, a forest protected with gifts from children and adults around the world. The Monteverde Conservation League owns and manages this valuable resource, which reaches all the way over the Tilarán Mountains to Monteverde. It has a small office along the highway at the entrance to San José de La Tigra. Stop by for information, to browse in the small gift shop, and to leave a donation if you are touched by this special project.

Chachagua Rain Forest Hotel is on a private nature reserve that borders the children's forest. It offers an unforgettable experience within a tropical paradise. See Chapter 13 for a description.

Naranjo-Ciudad Quesada Route

The route through Naranjo, which turns off of the Inter-American after kilometer 44, heads north on a narrow mountain road through coffee plantations and small communities. As it climbs higher, dairy cattle paint the landscape. If you get out early, you will see the country wake up. By 6:00 or 6:30 a.m., things are in full swing—students, workers waiting for buses, farmers in the fields. Views as the road climbs are stupendous, but better wait until the El Mirador restaurant to pull off for photos; narrow road, curves, and no shoulders make roadside stops dangerous.

Zarcero, 15 miles (24 km) from the turnoff, is a mountain town famous for its animals—that is, animals sculpted from plants, topiary art. The fantastic gardens in front of the church hold an evergreen elephant, bull, and rabbit, plus dozens of other forms. Roadside stands offer fruits, *cajeta*, delicious cheeses, and other specialties of this rural center of some 3,566 people. The food known as *palmito* is not made from heart of palm, as some visitors deduce from its name. It is a layered ball of white cheese.

Across the street from the church and gardens is Hotel Don Beto. Flory Salazar and her son Luis offer their guests the comfort of their home. Eight shining-clean rooms, some with beautiful parquet floors, are tucked here and there, off of sitting rooms and balconies and down halls in the two-story house. Rooms with shared bath are $20 for a double;

with private baths (shower-head hot water), $27, taxes included. A furnished apartment is also $27. A charming sitting room off of a flowered garden has cushioned bamboo furniture. Breakfast is served in the next room if guests tell Flory ahead of time. She is enthusiastic about the natural beauty around Zarcero and can tell you about nearby waterfalls, miradors, and parks. Ask her to point out the India Dormida (Sleeping Indian Maiden) mountain. She or Luis will accompany you in your car if you want a guide or, as she says, "charge a little for gasoline" if you want to go in their car. VISA accepted. Telephone/fax 463-3137.

Before you begin to drop down into San Carlos, you will see signs at small communities indicating elevations around 6,000 feet (1,840 m). If it is a clear day as you begin the descent, you will see the vast Plains of San Carlos before you, somewhat surprising to those who think of Costa Rica as all rugged terrain.

Ciudad Quesada (population 31,256) is a center of this rich agricultural area. Located on the edge of the San Carlos Plains about 60 miles (95 km) from the capital, it is often referred to as San Carlos. As you come into town, watch on the left for CATUZON, the tourism office for the northern zone. It is open Monday through Saturday from 8:00 a.m. to 12:30 p.m. and 1:30 to 5:00 p.m. You can buy a map of the area for about $2 and pick up brochures and pamphlets.

Signs for Hotel Conquistador are nearby. The 46-room, two-story hotel, simply furnished and clean, has private baths, most with central hot water, and a restaurant. Single $11, double $19, taxes included. VISA accepted. Telephone/fax 460-0546.

Downtown is Hotel & Casino Central. The 48-room hotel, three-story hotel has pleasant rooms with comforters, reading lamps, fans, and private baths with hot water. Some have balconies. Rooms start at $20, up to $40 for a king-size bed. Credit cards accepted. A guided tour to Arenal Volcano is $45, to Caño Negro $65. Telephone 460-0301, fax 460-0391.

Ask at Hotel Central about its Río San Carlos Lodge, 20 miles (33 km) north at Boca de Arenal. Between the main road to Los Chiles and the banks of the San Carlos River, a former country house offers five rooms and a big living area and outdoor terrace. Rooms have private baths with hot water and fans or air conditioning. Grounds around the pool have fruit trees you may be unfamiliar with—*caimito, mamón chino,* and *manzana de agua* (water apple). Single $45, double $55, including breakfast. Credit cards accepted. From here, the Arenal Volcano trip is $35 and Caño Negro $55.

In 1992, a national park named Juan Castro Blanco was created east of Ciudad Quesada, but it has no developed facilities for visitors.

Five miles (8 km) northeast of Ciudad Quesada on the road to Aguas

Zarcas is lovely Hotel El Tucano Resort and Spa, a country inn set among the trees, complete with a restaurant featuring Italian food. It has tennis courts, swimming pools, paths through a primary forest, a natural sauna whose steam comes from hot springs, and two Jacuzzis supplied by thermal water. Guests can also bathe at the base of a small waterfall in the cold river water and choose the temperature they like best by their distance from the hot springs along the shore.

The thermal waters here have long been said to be effective for treatment of arthritis, skin and kidney disorders, rheumatism, and sinus problems. They have been tested by El Tucano; based on the results, a new clinic with doctors from Romania offers treatments with the thermal water, mud baths, and therapeutic massage. The impressive spa and natural medicine facility has dry and humid saunas, Jacuzzis, a gymnasium, and separate areas for men and women. Contact the hotel for prices and packages.

In the hotel, fresh flowers grace the desks in the 90 spacious, carpeted rooms, which have both showers and bathtubs. Singles are $65, doubles $75; suites begin at $95. One mile (1.5 km) of trails wind through the hotel's forest, and more are being added. Perhaps the exercise area in the jungle will be finished by your arrival. Guests can ride horseback in the forest or along the road, and trips are arranged to local attractions such as Arenal Volcano, Caño Negro, and Venado Caves. Transportation from San José can be arranged. Telephone 233-8936 or 460-3152; fax 221-9095 or 460-1692.

A pretty park next door to the entrance to Hotel El Tucano is a public nature reserve known locally as El Tucanito. A ½-mile (1-km) trail, partly through beautiful forest, leads to the river where you can bathe in hot springs water as it mixes with the cooler river water. Entrance fee is $2, open 6:00 a.m. to 6:00 p.m. The landscaped park has covered picnic areas. It is about a 15-minute taxi ride from Ciudad Quesada.

Just a piece farther down the road toward Aguas Zarcas is La Marina zoo, which has 40 species of birds and 60 of mammals and reptiles, including toucans, a crested eagle, a king vulture, an ocelot, jaguars, white-tailed deer, tapirs (named Clarisa, Chepa, and Toñio), and peccaries (including one albino). Alba María Alfaro, the owner, says most of the animals were brought to La Marina because they were sick or wounded or had been abandoned either by former owners or in the wild. The small zoo is open daily from 8:00 a.m. to 4:30 p.m.; admission is $1.50 for adults, 75 cents for children. Donations are gladly accepted. A gift shop at the entrance has handcrafts, T-shirts, machetes, and ice cream and cold drinks.

North of Ciudad Quesada at Platanar, between Florence and Muelle, is the attractive Hotel La Garza, built along the Platanar River with a view of Arenal Volcano. The 12 rooms are in bungalows with ample windows and

Oxcarts still add color to the Costa Rican landscape (Ree Strange Sheck)

French doors that open onto porches looking out to the river and landscaped grounds. There are telephones in the rooms, hardwood floors, a modern bath with shower-head hot water, and ceiling fans. The restaurant and bar are in what was the gracious main house of the Hacienda Platanar. Polished wood floors inside continue out onto the wide veranda where there are also tables and bamboo and cane chairs. The place exudes tranquillity. Access to the restaurant and a swimming pool and Jacuzzi area is across a hanging foot bridge over the river.

Garza means egret or heron, and the hotel's name hints of the abundant bird life to be seen here. Some 740 acres (300 ha) of rainforest have trails open to overnight guests and day visitors. La Garza is also a working dairy and cattle ranch. Guests may take three-hour horseback rides led by a bilingual naturalist guide for $30. Guided birding tours are also available, and tours are arranged to Caño Negro, the volcano, Venado Caves, or Tabacón. Hot-air balloon rides are an option. The charge for a day visit is about $2 per person. A single room is $65 and a double $75, including breakfast. Credit cards accepted. Telephone 475-5222 or 222-7355; fax 475-5015 or 222-0869.

Muelle, 14 miles (22 km) north of Ciudad Quesada, is a crossroads where the north-south route from Ciudad Quesada to Los Chiles crosses with a kind of east-west route that can join the Sarapiquí area and Aguas Zarcas with La Fortuna or Guatuso and Upala. Gas stations are here.

About 4 miles (6 km) east of Muelle at Palmera is Complejo Turístico Huetar Norte. You will notice the distinctive, towering thatched roofs of the restaurant, open 11:00 a.m. to midnight. The menu lists soups, sandwiches, typical rice dishes, fish, meat, chicken, and casados. Signs point to a lagoon in back where you can see crocodiles. By the time you arrive, cabins and a pool may be finished. Credit cards accepted, and there is a public telephone. Telephone 474-4497.

Just west of the Muelle intersection is the Tilajari Resort Hotel, located on the banks of the San Carlos River in sight of Arenal Volcano. Facilities include pools, three lighted tennis courts, racquetball courts, sauna, restaurant, and bar. The restaurant, open to the public, is a favorite with guests because of the bird-feeding stations close by. Bring your camera. You are sure to see scarlet-rumped tanagers.

The newest addition is a butterfly garden with a pretty fountain and flowering plants; a rancho alongside has educational displays. The gardens of the hotel itself contain more than 600 species of plants—you can go on a self-guided tour with a written guide.

Tours operated from the hotel include visits to the Caño Negro refuge (a full day, with a drive to Los Chiles and a boat trip on the Río Frío to the refuge, is $48); Venado Caves; Fortuna waterfall ($45 each for two persons); Arenal Volcano (a late afternoon/night tour that allows time at the Tabacón hot springs); and a safari float on the Peñas Blancas River ($50). Tours of the Tilajari rain forest are either by horse or tractor-drawn cart to the forest's edge for a hike on foot ($10). Guides for the trips are trained and bilingual. I was fortunate to travel to Caño Negro with one of them, who was excellent at spotting species along the road and from the boat and also knowledgeable about local history and geography.

Rates for the 81 rooms are $69 for singles, $70 for doubles. Suites have a living room, terrace, TV, and refrigerator, $100. All have air conditioning, ceiling fan, telephone, and private bath with hot water. Credit cards accepted. Lodging quarters are quiet, located apart from the sports areas, restaurant, and pools. They are surrounded by manicured lawns and gardens. The large rooms open onto covered terraces where you can enjoy a variety of birds. Crocodiles amble along the river bank. In low trees near the restaurant are keel-billed and chestnut-mandibled toucans who were raised here and have decided to stay—their wings are not clipped. They seem to enjoy posing for photos. Owners Jaime Hamilton and Ricardo Araya hope that a great green macaw added to the menagerie will do the same. I saw a young sloth curled up in one of the many fruit trees that supply produce for the restaurant. You may want to investigate travel packages that include round-trip transportation from San José. The Tilajari is 73 miles (117 km) from San José. Telephone 469-9091 or 469-9092; fax 469-9095.

West of Muelle, about 4 miles (6 km) from La Fortuna, is Hotel Rancho Corcovado. Arenal Volcano looms in the distance. The 23 rooms are in buildings facing a pretty swimming pool, rather like a motel. Rooms are spacious, with telephones, central hot water, and a tiled porch that runs the length of each building. The restaurant and bar are in a large open-sided structure overlooking a small lake, where you may spot a caiman or two. Birds abound—at least 90 species, including violaceous trogons, kingfishers, and four types of toucans. Egrets sleep here at night. Notice the gourd tree near the restaurant. Tours can be arranged to Caño Negro ($35), to Arenal and Tabacón, to the Fortuna waterfall ($15), and an all-day getting-to-know-the-area trip. A one-day or multi-day trip to Nicaragua can be arranged. Singles $35, doubles $50. Credit cards accepted. Telephone 479-9300, telephone/fax 479-9090.

Another nearby lodging possibility is at Las Cabañitas Resort. It looks like a tiny village with its cluster of 30 individual cabañas, swimming pool, restaurant, gift shop, and snack bar. The delightful rooms have vaulted wooden ceilings, polished wood floors, some king-size beds, ceiling fans, and a bathroom with a large shower, some bathtubs. Guests enjoy the individual porches. Handicap accessible. Transportation can be provided in the resort's mini-bus from practically anywhere. English, Italian, and French also spoken. Tours are arranged throughout the northern zone. Singles $60, doubles $73; credit cards accepted. Telephone 479-9343, fax 479-9408.

A couple of private nature reserves accessible from this area offer opportunities to experience the region's variety of natural beauty. (See Chapter 13.) The rustic Magil Forest Lodge is west and north of Muelle, 12 miles (19 km) from San Rafael de Guatuso, on a line between Lake Arenal and Caño Negro on the map. It is on the skirts of Tenorio Volcano. La Laguna del Lagarto is east and north of Muelle, through Pital, an extremely pleasant town, and Boca Tapada. Yes, there are *lagartos* (caimans) there, and monkeys and colorful frogs.

See Chapter 12 for information on Caño Negro Wildlife Refuge. Many tours from this area enter the refuge from Los Chiles, but refuge headquarters are at the town of Caño Negro, which is accessible through San Rafael de Guatuso as well as Upala, paved roads to each of these towns but gravel on to Caño Negro. If you enter through Upala and need a place to stay, Cabinas Maleku has six clean basic rooms with ceiling fans and private baths (no hot water), $6 per person. Six more are being built, one to have air conditioning. Owner Zoraida Villalobos and her children are friendly and

helpful. The restaurant is open to the public. It is just a couple of blocks
from the bus station. Telephone 470-0142.

In Caño Negro, Cabinas El Querque has six rooms for up to 15 people,
shared baths, no hot water, $6 per person. Rustic is the key word. The view
from the two-story building across the garden is of Lake Caño Negro, with
the birds that have made it famous. Owner Don Alvaro offers a boat tour,
price depends on number of persons. Although there is no restaurant, two
sodas are nearby. Call the public phone at 460-4164 and leave a message.
Lodging is sometimes available at the Caño Negro refuge headquarters,
as well.

La Fortuna-Arenal-Tilarán Route

La Fortuna (population 6,570) is the eastern gateway to the Lake Arenal
region. Arenal Volcano is a presence in this small place—it dominates the
horizon. Local tour agencies offer trips to it and to Lake Arenal, to Caño
Negro wildlife refuge, to the waterfall just south of town (very steep trail),
Venado Caves, to hot springs, and to the Guatuso area. Three tour and information companies you can contact are Sunset Tours (telephone 479-9199,
telephone/fax 479-9099); Aventuras Arenal (telephone/fax 479-9133); and
Aventuras con Gabino (telephone 479-9350, fax 479-9178). Aventuras con
Gabino offers two-day canoe trips to Caño Negro, entering through Guatuso
and leaving through Los Chiles ($100 per person), as well as a tour to the
beautiful Río Celeste. Gabino's aviary and ecological project for endangered
animals should be open by your arrival. His office shares a building with a
vegetarian restaurant El Liro y la Luna (The Lily and the Moon). The
restaurant is open Monday through Saturday from 7:00 a.m. to 7:00 p.m.,
serving homemade bread, muffins, veggieburgers, pocket bread, and more.
It is located on the main street through town, across from the church. The
Rancho Restaurant, next door to Sunset Tours, is open from 6:00 a.m. to
11:00 p.m. daily. Another good eating place is El Jardín, typical Costa Rican
offerings, also open from 6:00 a.m. to 11:00 p.m.

Signs have sprouted everywhere advertising new cabinas and small hotels.
Two you might check out downtown are Hotel San Bosco and Hotel La
Colinas.

To get to Hotel San Bosco, turn north at the Plaza—it is 1½ blocks off
main street. Celso, Flor, and their family have created a pretty place to stay.
Not all of the 28 rooms have volcano views, but not to worry. A covered
open-air volcano-viewing room on the third floor has chairs and tables
where you can watch to your heart's content. Porches, verandas, orthopedic
mattresses, architectural accents of river stone, reading lamps, and private

baths with central hot water are some of what you will find. The 16 air-conditioned rooms in the two-story portion are $40 for a single, $46 for a double; the 11 with fans in the original structure (recently refurbished) are $25 for a single and $30 for a double, tax included. VISA and MasterCard accepted. Tour arrangements are through Sunset Tours across the street. The Rancho Restaurant is handy for meals. Guarded parking. Telephone 479-9050, fax 479-9109.

Friendly Hotel La Colinas, just a block south of main street, has 17 spacious, plainly furnished but very clean rooms, each with a private bath and shower-head hot water. Rates range from $12 to $34, depending on the number of people. MasterCard and VISA are accepted. Rooms on the front have Arenal Volcano out the windows. Telephone/fax 479-9107.

Fortuna has a bank and gasoline stations, the last you will see for a while if you are heading west. The 10 miles (16 km) to the turnoff to Arenal Volcano National Park skirt the slopes of the volcano and its forested slopes give way to ash and fumaroles as you approach its western face. Remember that lava flows are visible usually only on the western side, though the sound and the eruptions are impressive from La Fortuna and environs. Not until the turnoff to the park do you begin to see the lava flow down the side.

A marvelous spot for viewing the volcano from a different perspective is at Jungla y Senderos Los Lagos, about 2.5 miles (4 km) from Fortuna heading for Arenal. Near the entrance is a multilevel swimming pool with a water slide; at the top, water flows out of cone-shaped replica of the volcano. A large rancho-style restaurant and eight rooms in four bungalows were being constructed when I visited. Nice touches in the rooms were evident—a mixture of white stucco, wood, and river stone on the outside. Pitched ceilings, private baths with hot water inside. You can see how they turned out ($50 for up to three persons). A 15-minute drive from the entrance takes you down to a placid lake with reflections of the forest around it, the sound and maybe sight of the chestnut-mandibled toucan, and a sky dominated by Arenal Volcano. It is special. Picnic areas are scattered along one side of the lake, and a tent camp has been added. Each tent is on a base and has its own bath, a closet you can lock, and electricity, $27 per tent. You can walk on forest trails, paddle on the lake, or go horseback riding. Admission for day visitors is about $3, which entitles you to swim in the pools or lake and hike the trails. A guided horseback tour, $11, takes you through primary forest, over an old lava flow, to a mirador with a view of Arenal, Tenorio, and Miravalles volcanoes. Telephone 479-9126.

Back on the main highway west, Cabañas Arenal Paraíso has eight individual cabañas with the volcano practically in the front yard. Single or double is $36, one with a small refrigerator is $50, and a furnished house for up to nine persons is $65. No credit cards. Pretty white-tile bathrooms in the cabañas, central hot water, have blue accents and a mirror with a lovely painted flower border. Rooms have ceiling fans and good mattresses. Guests may enjoy the Jacuzzi in the front and there is a tour to Los Lagos and to the Fortuna waterfall. Restaurant serves breakfast only. Telephone/fax 479-9006.

Montaña de Fuego Inn, practically next door, has 12 rooms with private baths and central hot water. Each attractive wooden cabin contains two units, and the glassed-in front porch looks right out on Arenal. Guests can hike on 1 mile (2 km) of trails in the forest and go horseback riding. Single or double is $37. Credit cards accepted. Telephone/fax 479-9106.

Next comes Tabacón Resort at the base of Arenal Volcano. The complex offers four pools with thermal waters and one with cold water. The beautiful landscaped grounds center on paths along the river and a waterfall of hot water that steams against the greenery. The water from the hot springs is more than 126°F (52°C).

The admission charge of $10 for adults and $4 for children covers use of pools, range from 80°F to 102°F (27°C to 39°C) the gardens, bar, a Jacuzzi, the river, and a ½-mile (1 km) trail along the forest to a small volcanic lake. Visitors may eat in the restaurant overlooking the gardens (Italian and Costa Rican food) without paying the admission fee. It is open from 10:00 a.m. to 10:00 p.m. Telephone 222-1072, telephone/fax 479-9033; fax 221-3075.

Across the road is another, less expensive, no-frills opportunity to bathe in hot springs waters.

About 10 miles (16 km) west of Fortuna is the turnoff to Arenal Volcano National Park and several lodges. Stop by park headquarters for information (see Chapter 12). Arenal is one of the world's most active volcanoes, thundering and blowing now since 1968. Signs along the dirt road here caution visitors about viewing the fiery colossus at a safe distance. Climbing to the crater would be hazardous to your health; in fact, it could be fatal. It is best to respect the warning signs.

Three lodges with good volcano views are past the park entrance—lots of signs to guide you. The road to Arenal Volcano Observatory (5.6 miles or 9 km from the highway turnoff) is quite tame now—bridges over the rivers and everything. No more standing at the rushing water's edge in rainy season with a thumping heart, wondering if the jeep and you will make it through. Find a description of this very special private nature reserve in Chapter 13.

Signs before the lodge point to two other options on a road off to the right where you may still get your tires a little wet: Linda Vista del Norte and Arenal Vista Lodge.

Linda Vista del Norte is 5 miles (8.5 km) in from the highway. High on a hilltop, the ten-room lodge has simple furnishings and gorgeous views of forested mountains, Lake Arenal, and the volcano. The glassed-in dining room and its outdoor terrace have the best vantage point for volcano viewing, though it can also be seen from the terrace off of back rooms. Ones on the front face the lake. Tiled rooms have a wooden wardrobe, ceiling fan, and an interesting bathroom arrangement: the sink is in the room and the toilet and large shower (central hot water) have their own little rooms. Breakfast is $5 and lunch or dinner $6. Single $47, double $65, VISA and MasterCard accepted. A horseback ride to the volcano is $20, and a tour on the 494-acre (200-ha) farm, which has cattle, forest, and waterfall, is $12. A horseback trip to San Gerardo Abajo near Monteverde can be arranged. Guests can hike the trails on the farm—lots of birds. Telephone/fax 479-9263—message is radioed to the lodge.

Arenal Vista Lodge is an unbridged river down the road, but it probably will be spanned by your arrival. If not, just keep to the right going through the water. Each of the 25 rooms, terraced up a hillside, has a view of the lake and volcano and there is an open-air mirador with tables and chairs for those who want to view in community. Each spacious room has its own balcony, reading lights, pitched ceiling, private bath with central hot water, and a walk-in closet with plenty of room for luggage and clothing. Single $60, double $70. VISA and MasterCard accepted. Meals are served buffet style in the large dining room (coffee always on): $6 breakfast, $8 lunch, $10 dinner. To one side of the dining room is a theater-type setting for lectures and videos. The forest comes right up to the buildings, with three marked, self-guided trails available to guests. You will hear howler monkeys in the morning and owls at night and see some of the 200 resident bird species found in this area, or perhaps neotropical migrants. Watch for toucans at the papaya trees. Horseback tours of the forest ($10) and volcano ($15), and boat trips on the lake for fishing or bird-watching are available. Make reservations by calling 220-2121, fax 232-3321. A cellular telephone/fax is available for emergencies at the hotel, 381-1428.

Less than a mile from the turnoff to Arenal Volcano park is Lake Arenal. Archaeological studies show that Indians had small settlements around Lake Arenal, near the volcano, as long ago as 2000 B.C. Today the lake has been greatly enlarged by a dam, completed in 1979, built to provide hydroelectric energy. Twenty-four miles (39 km) long, Lake Arenal is a favorite for fishing and water sports such as windsurfing and kayaking. The road around the northeast side takes you over the dam and on to Nuevo Arenal and Tilarán.

If you are driving around the north side of the lake, be alert for one-lane bridges that seem to be mostly on curves. And be aware that the road is more potholes than pavement in some places, and the pavement ends altogether at Nuevo Arenal for about a 6-mile (9-km) stretch going east—slow going. While paving seems imminent, I hesitate to predict it will be done by your arrival. (I said this in the previous edition, too.)

Just past the dam and up a paving-stone road through a macadamia nut farm is the very pleasant Arenal Lodge. Rooms in the front at the main lodge have impressive views of the volcano, while those in back are around a covered brick courtyard graced with orchids. The 12 view rooms are junior suites, with a king size and single bed, upholstered bamboo couch and chairs, private balconies, and baths with shower and tub. Single $85, double $100. The six standard rooms, with showers only, are $65 for a single, $77 a double. Breakfast is included. Ten nice suites with kitchenettes are in buildings up from the lodge, large rooms with balconies, $135. Credit cards accepted. The lounge area has a large fireplace. There is a Jacuzzi, a billiard table, and a small library. Guests will probably see howler monkeys in the forested area at the edge of the lodge and may even spot a tayra or anteater. Hummingbird feeders and platforms for fruit bring a variety of birds to the gardens. The lodge offers lake fishing and tours to Caño Negro and also to Venado Caves, the hot springs, the base of the volcano, and the La Fortuna waterfall. Owner Woodson Brown wrote a handy driving guide for guests covering routes to San José. Telephone 228-3189, fax 289-6798.

For a taste of Switzerland, check out Los Héroes back on the main road around the north side of Lake Arenal. You can't miss the imposing chalet-style structure. Eleven carpeted rooms, some with balconies, have private baths with central hot water, some with bathtubs. Prices range from $56 and $68 for a double to $75 for a suite, including full breakfast. Two apartments for up to six people are $106 each. Credit cards are not accepted. There is a nice pool and Jacuzzi with a lake and volcano view. The restaurant, with decor right out of the Swiss Alps—big cowbells, red-and-white-checkered curtains—is open to the public. If you are tired of rice and beans, you can choose from a menu that includes meat and cheese fondue, *roesti* (a delicious potato dish), spaghetti, and sausages. Entrées range from $4 to $10. Telephone 228-1472 or 441-4193; fax 233-1772.

Marina Club Hotel has 12 split-level rooms in bungalows facing Lake Arenal. Two couches and cushioned wicker chairs next to a writing table are on the lower level (plus a stereo radio), with beds and a pretty wardrobe on the upper. Through swinging barroom-type doors is a bath with decorative tile and hot water showers, $75 each, VISA accepted. Water flows from a big clay pot (*tinaja* in Spanish) into a swimming pool in a garden of colorful shrubs and flowering plants. The restaurant is open to the public. There is a day trip to Venado Caves, horseback rides around the lake, and a tour to

Arenal Botanical Gardens. Free use of canoes on the lake. English, French, Italian, German, and Dutch spoken. Fax 479-9178.

About an hour from La Fortuna and 2 miles (6 km) before the town of Arenal is the sign for La Ceiba, a bed and breakfast with four bright and airy rooms that open off a tiled terrace with a panoramic view of Lake Arenal. Rooms are $20 per person with breakfast. Owners Ursula and Julio are artists; their paintings are displayed in the rooms. Private baths have central hot water. The house is on a working cattle and goat farm. Guests may see three kinds of toucans, howler monkeys, or sloths on paths in the forest. The owners, who also speak German and English, will serve evening meals featuring produce from their organic garden. A sailboat tour for up to four people ($30) can include a visit to islands in the lake, a close-up view of the volcano, or fishing. For those who do not come by car, the hosts arrange tours to the volcano or Venado Caves, costing $30 for two people. If you come by bus, have the driver honk when he lets you off at the highway so Ursula or Julio can pick you up and save you the uphill walk. Fax 695-5387.

Heliconias, begonias, orchids, tree ferns, gingers, anthuriums, euphorbias—2,000 varieties of plants from around the world thrive in the Arenal Botanical Gardens, including many that are native to Costa Rica. Owner Michael LeMay, who has collected plants for 17 years, began to convert degraded pastureland into a breathtaking garden in 1991, and opened it to the public in 1993. Easy trails weave through dazzling displays that were laid out to look like a natural forest but with groupings that permit the visitor to stand in one area and see varieties in the same genera or family. There are 200 kinds of bromeliads, 200 varieties of orchids, and more than 100 types of palms and ferns. Visitors take self-guided walks; booklets available in English, Spanish, and German. Entrance fee is $4. In addition, there is a trail through a natural forest that can take up to an hour. Flowers attract butterflies and birds, including six species of hummingbirds. In addition to seeing butterflies throughout the garden, you can visit Michael's butterfly farm, and perhaps by the time you arrive, an unusual serpentarium will be in place—the snakes will be in glass enclosures scattered around the gardens. Open 9:00 a.m. to 5:00 p.m. daily. Telephone 694-4273, fax 694-4086.

Michael, who can tell you where he got each plant, set up the garden to preserve native species of plants, create a habitat for birds, insects, and other wildlife, and provide a living classroom for the study of plants. (He is also a whiz at opening a locked Toyota for a certain writer who left her keys in the car. Thanks, Michael.) Arenal Botanical Gardens is 2.5 miles (4 km) east of the town of Nuevo Arenal.

Just about a mile further (2 km) is lovely Villa Decary, where you will be more than just a name on the register. Owners Jeff and Bill are innkeepers in

Decary, an inn above Lake Arenal (Ree Strange Sheck)

the finest tradition. They tell guests about local fairs, even go with them if they like, and advise on local restaurants and sightseeing. Each of the tastefully decorated rooms has orthopedic mattresses (with real mattress pads—not so common in Costa Rica), reading lamp, central hot water in the bath, a balcony set up for bird-watching with convenient benches. Washcloths and big towels in the bathroom, $45 for a double including a full breakfast. No credit cards accepted. A separate bungalow for up to four persons has an equipped kitchen. Take time to enjoy the orchids in the garden and a path around some of the 7-acre (2.8-ha) former fruit and coffee farm. Howler monkeys cross the yard to eat in the papaya trees. The pretty dining room opens onto deck through two sets of double doors. With notice, lunch or dinner can be served. Fax 694-4132.

The town of Nuevo Arenal (with a population of 2,362) was built by the Costa Rican Electrical Institute to replace house by house the old Arenal, which was flooded because of the dam put in for the hydroelectric project. There are cabinas and places to eat here. One restuarant you do not want to miss is Pizzaría e Ristorante Tramonti. Gianni and Adriana serve 16 types of pizza in the $4 to $6 range, along with homemade pasta: lasagna, fettucine, and spaghetti. They use Italian cheese and oil and serve Italian wine. The pretty dining room is open to the garden. Open 11:30 a.m. to 3:00 p.m. and

5:00 to 10:00 p.m., closed Monday in low season. VISA accepted. Telephone 694-4282.

Just down the road is Chalet Nicholas, a small bed and breakfast with a front-porch view of Arenal Volcano. The three rooms with private bath are $39 for a double. No smoking. Credit cards are not accepted. Guests can hike in a nearby protected forest, and the Nicholases can arrange horseback riding. Catherine has a small orchid garden, a walk-in aviary of toucanets and parrots, and is starting a plant nursery. Telephone/fax 694-4041.

Past the town of Arenal near Lake Coter is a private nature reserve called the Eco-Lodge. It has marvelous nature trails through its biologically rich forest. (See Chapter 13.)

La Rana de Arenal, at kilometer 45, has five rooms with pretty decorator sheets, windows with delicate lace curtains and drapes, reading lamps, ceiling fans, and private baths with hot water. Single $25, double $40, including breakfast. Two apartments are also available. VISA accepted. A spacious upstairs dining room/bar, open to the public, has a lake-view balcony, offering an option for outdoor dining. The pool may be in by the time you arrive. Area tours are offered, and La Rana has car rental. Telephone 694-4032; telephone/fax 694-4031.

An inviting white portal on the main road around the lake marks the entrance to Albergue Club Alturas de Arenal, a small, two-story, 12-room hotel with a pleasant dining area open to landscaped grounds that slope toward Lake Arenal. It is open December through July only. The carpeted rooms are small but pleasant, with a large mirror; a double is $40. Credit cards are accepted. The hot tub sits amid tropical flowers, and a pool is in the works. The hotel is on an 82-acre (44-ha) farm where coffee, macadamia nuts, ornamental plants, and fruit trees are cultivated. It includes 25 acres (20 ha) of forest. Trails lead into a habitat where white-faced and howler monkeys live and where you may see birds such as a collared aracari, a chachalaca, or an oropendola. Night tours to Arenal Volcano from the lake side are $30 a person, and the hotel has a boat. Telephone/fax 694-4039.

Not far down the road at kilometer 40 is Rock River Lodge, with rooms terraced above and behind a main building that houses the bar, dining room, and a small library. Most nights find a fire going in the big fireplace at the far end of the open-air dining room. There are views of the lake and the volcano. Rooms are wood-paneled and cozy; each has a lighted mirror in the private bath, shower-head hot water, and windows onto a terrace facing the lake. Single or double $35. Eight newer bungalows have a definite southwestern U.S. flair, with built-in *bancos*, a rounded wall on one corner giving it the feel of an adobe, and inside walls with the look of being hand-plastered. Very attractive. See the unusual bathtub for yourself. Bungalows are $55. Credit cards are not accepted. The restaurant is open to the public—Norman's breakfasts are famous. You can go windsurfing or bicycling (Rock River's two specialties), as well as raft on the Corobicí River, ride horseback, fish, or bird-watch. Telephone/fax 695-5644.

Mist, hills, lake, volcano—it is a mystical place and hence its name, Mystica Resort. On a rainy night it was a haven for this traveler. I was welcomed by the warm fire in the fireplace, calmed by the soft music, and tempted by the smells of pizza and pasta from the Italian kitchen. Owners Barbara Moglia and Francesco Carullo serve 12 kinds of pizza and nine kinds of pasta, most in the $4 to $7 price range. Pizzas are cooked in a big brick oven. The pasta with Gorgonzola sauce is terrific. Six large, comfortable rooms up a path from the restaurant through the garden have private baths with big hot-water showers and bathmats (bathmats are not a common feature in Costa Rica). Each sleeps four in a double and bunk beds. Coverlets like patchwork quilts, and the wooden chairs and desk have a Shaker flavor. Animal cutouts on the wooden lampshades create interesting effects. A common veranda with chairs affords lake viewing. Single $35, double $50, breakfast and taxes included. No credit cards. Italian, English, and French also spoken. Windsurfing, mountain biking, and horseback rides can be arranged. Cellular phone 284-3841, fax 695-5387.

Near the northeastern edge of Lake Arenal is the Hotel Tilawa and its WindSurf Center. The imposing two-story building sits on the slope above the lake. Every room has large windows looking out on either the lake or attractive gardens, two queen-size beds with orthopedic mattresses, a writing desk, and bathrooms with both a tub and a shower. Colorful Guatemalan bedspreads brighten the rooms. There are 24 standard rooms (a single is $50, a double $63, breakfast included) and four junior suites with sitting area and furnished kitchenette for $125, taxes included. Credit cards are accepted. Color, in fact, is the word in this building, whose architecture is reminiscent of the Palace of Knossos: you see it in custom-designed floors, painted designs on walls, dining room tablecloths, room decorations. The restaurant is open to the public and there is a poolside bar.

Trails take off in the forest next to the swimming pool—howler monkeys were calling when I was there, and you have a good chance of seeing keel-billed toucans. Guided tours to the volcano are available by either boat or car, as are trips to the Corobicí River, Venado Caves, and the hot springs at Tabacón. There also is tennis, sailing, horseback riding, and rental of mountain bikes and cars. The strong suit at Tilawa, however, is windsurfing. Lake Arenal is gaining a reputation as one of the top areas for this sport, and the lakeside WindSurf Center offers equipment for rent and lessons for adults and children.

Hotel Tilawa offers airport pickup in San José, $110 one way for up to four people; transport via hydroplane can be arranged. Packages for seven days and seven nights, double occupancy, are $328 for sailors (with unlimited use of equipment) and $148 for non-sailors. Taxes are not included. Telephone (800) 851-8929 in the United States, or 695-5050; fax 695-5766 in Costa Rica.

From the hotel property on clear days, you can see not only Arenal Volcano and three others: Rincón de la Vieja, Miravalles, and Tenorio. These majestic peaks are also visible from the road between Tilarán and the lake.

Tilarán (population 8,842), about 2 miles (3 km) from Lake Arenal, is a pleasant town laid out around the traditional square. Across the street from the south side of the cathedral is the Hotel Naralit. The 17 pleasant rooms have ceiling fans and reading lamps, and most have private baths with hot water. Furnishings are eclectic—the base of an old Ideal sewing machine is an attractive table; some have cable TV. Upstairs rooms are larger, while some downstairs rooms have glassed-in porches with chairs. Single $14, double $18, taxes included. Rooms with shared baths are less. VISA is accepted. The staff will arrange lake fishing and boat trips to the volcano. Telephone/fax 695-5393.

If you are in Tilarán about mealtime, you may want to check out the Restaurante Catalá around the corner from the Hotel Naralit. The food is very tasty. If you have yet to try the typical casado, here is your chance to enjoy a good one. Hours are 6:30 a.m. to 10:00 p.m. There is also a pleasant bar open to a pretty garden, with access to the Hotel Naralit.

Just north of the park is Cabinas El Sueño, a second-floor, 12-room hotel with most rooms around an open courtyard with a fountain in the middle. The carpeted rooms are pleasant and have ceiling fans; all have private baths with shower-head hot water. Singles are $10, doubles $16, taxes included. VISA, MasterCard are accepted. Staff members will arrange full-day or night tours to the volcano and trips to Venado Caves, Tabacón, and La Fortuna waterfall, as well as horseback riding with a guide or mountain biking. There is a supermarket below. Telephone 695-5347.

Hotel y Restaurant Mary is on the south side of the park downtown. The hotel's 16 rooms above the restaurant are simple but very clean, and the staff is attentive. Rooms with shared bath have no hot water, while private baths have central hot water. No credit cards. A single is about $6, a double about $18. Telephone 695-5479.

From Tilarán you can take the back road to Monteverde through Quebrada Grande (unpaved) or continue on the main paved road to Cañas. From there you can head in to Palo Verde National Park, or stay on the Inter-American highway to head north into Guanacaste, south to the Tempisque

Ferry that crosses over to the Nicoya Peninsula, or continue to Puntarenas. Buses run from Tilarán to San José, to Cañas, and to Monteverde (see Practical Extras).

Poás-Varablanca-Sarapiquí Route

The route from San José to the north-central region through Varablanca is spectacular, with Barva Volcano and Cacho Negro on one side and Poás Volcano and Cerro Congo on the other. Just before Varablanca is a turnoff to Poás Volcano. On a clear day from the heights, you can see the plains stretching to the coast. The winding descent passes gorgeous waterfalls—the most photographed being the Peace Waterfall. The river that feeds the waterfall rises in the forests of Poás.

Near the turnoff is charming Poás Volcano Lodge, only 10 miles (16 km) from the volcano and an invigorating 6,234 feet (1,900 m) high. The lodge is a large farmhouse built by an English family, and it has somewhat the flavor of a manor. A sunny sitting room is off of a large foyer with a sunken conversation area and fireplace. Two rooms with shared bath and a master suite with private bath, king-size bed, and double glass doors opening onto a terrace are in the main building. Six rooms in two other buildings hint of English or Welsh cottages, private baths with hot water. Each room is different, with creative use of wood and rock walls, but all of the windows open to a landscaped garden featuring shrubs, impatiens, and hydrangeas—even poor man's umbrella plants. Poás dominates the horizon. Rooms with shared bath $55, private bath $65, and master suite $80, including a country breakfast. Light lunches or dinners served on request. Guests can take guided bird-watching walks in the forest patches in the large farm, with a chance to observe such species as the golden-browed chlorophonia, black-faced solitaires, hummingbirds, even the quetzal. Horseback riding is available, and the lodge is only ten minutes from the Peace Waterfall. VISA and Master-Card accepted. Telephone/fax 482-2194.

Restaurante Vara Blanca at the intersection to Poás is a typical Costa Rican countryside meeting and eating place. Staff have become accustomed to foreign tourists dropping in and are delighted to help you order. There is a public telephone here.

Just over a mile (2 km) further toward San Miguel is Juanbo Mountain Restaurant and Cabins, a delightful stopping off place. The mountain view is spectacular, the dining room warm and cozy and full of good smells. The two cabinas are charming—with polished wood floors, brightly upholstered bamboo furniture and big windows and closets. Each has a private bath with central hot water. A double is $60, including breakfast. Telephone 482-2099.

Between here and Cariblanco you pass a big El Angel plant, and there is a store where you can buy some of their food products at a 25 percent discount: juices, condensed milk, raisins, jellies. Open 6:15 a.m. to 2:30 p.m. Monday through Saturday. It is a big local employer, so watch for workers walking along the narrow road on their way to and from work.

The road to San Miguel is winding and narrow all the way. At the little town of San Miguel, where there is a large sawmill, a popular eating spot is Señor Tortugas, open from 11:30 a.m. to 10:00 p.m., closed Monday. It is on the main road, before the sawmill. There's a bank and a terrific grocery store that sells cold bottled water—Coopesarapiquí. You have choices to make at San Miguel: roads west and north take you to Aguas Zarcas and Ciudad Quesada, destinations already discussed. To continue to Puerto Viejo, head northeast.

In La Virgen de Sarapiquí, about 8 miles (13 km) from San Miguel, is Rancho Leona. The unexpected lives here—a workshop where Tiffany-style stained glass is created. Visitors are welcome to watch artisans at work. There are kayak jungle tours; a restaurant catering to vegetarians (homemade brown bread, eggplant parmesan, French onion soup, banana splits); rain forest jewelry; and a geodesic dome to bunk in. Actually Rancho Leona is the stepping-off place for the dome, which is in a 198-acre (80-ha) protected forest. For $80, you are transported to the site, which has 11 bunkbeds and kitchen facilities, candles, and lanterns. You can stay for two nights. If the bed is not needed by someone else, you can stay longer at no extra cost. There is a composting outhouse and a beautiful swimming hole in the Peje River for bathing. Camping is also allowed here. Proceeds from the stained glass work and the kayak tours have helped purchase this forest. Kayak tours are $75, including equipment, guide, picnic lunch, and two nights at the Rancho Leona hostel in La Virgin. If the hostel's rustic rooms are not being used by kayakers, they are rented for $9 per person, shared baths. There's also a sauna. The two creative people who keep all of this going are Ken and Leona. Telephone/fax 761-1019. If that doesn't work, try 269-9410.

Just 3 miles (5 km) from La Virgen is La Quinta de Sarapiquí, a quintessential country inn. Situated in a curve along the Sardinal River, the inn has 11 rooms in bungalows surrounded by a tropical garden rich in heliconias (more than 24 species), gingers, palms, flowering trees. The brilliant flash of hummingbirds feeding along heliconia-lined paths in the morning sun is dazzling. Each room opens onto a shaded porch with chairs so you can enjoy the flowers and birds (almost 100 species identified so far).

Inviting, large rooms have white tile floors, dusky rose bed coverings—good mattresses, green and rose drapes, ceiling fans. Private baths have central hot water and king-size bath towels. The bar and lounge area next to the dining room have comfortable cushioned bamboo furniture. Food is delicious and nicely served. You may get some delicacies from the garden itself— here is where I finally got to taste fried breadfruit. Thanks, Leonardo.

Leonardo and Beatriz are caring owners and hosts who help guests with trips: rafting or a wildlife boating trip on the Sarapiquí, a day trip to the La Selva Biological Station, guided nature walks at Selva Verde, or the aerial tram. Right on the farm, guests can swim in the Sardinal (an *anhinga* was perched on a log over the clear waters when I took the path to the river) or go horseback riding or mountain biking—no extra charge. A game room has ping pong and table games. A small swimming pool may be a reality by your arrival. Some groups help with a reforestation project in former pastures. Singles $35, doubles $45. Breakfast is $5, lunch or dinner $7. Credit cards accepted. Signs at the road point the way—La Quinta is about half a mile (1 km) of unpaved road in from the highway across an unforgettable bridge. Telephone/fax 761-1052.

Islas del Río near Chilamate has 30 rooms. A double is from $39 to $50 with shared bath, $57 with private bath and shower-head hot water, meals included. No credit cards. Guests have access to four small forested islands in the Sarapiquí River and a nature trail behind the lodge where river otters, armadillos, monkeys, anteaters, and sloths may be seen. Rooms are simple but comfortably furnished, large, and airy, with fans. Typical meals are served in the pleasant, open-air dining room on the banks of the river. Inner tubes are available for $10, horse rental is $10, and rafting or kayaking is $45. A two-hour wildlife boating trip is $20. A bilingual guide is available for night walks and the island walk ($12 each) or a visit to La Selva. Telephone/fax 710-6898.

Just a mile further in Chilamate is a hotel with its own forest reserve: Selva Verde. See Chapter 13 for a description of the attractive lodge and its beautiful gardens, forest reserve, and tours. Its restaurant along the river (buffet-style meals) is open to the public, though reservations are preferred: breakfast 6:00 to 7:00 a.m. ($6), lunch noon to 1:00 p.m. ($8), and dinner 6:00 to 7:00 p.m. ($10). A nice gift shop is downstairs from the dining room.

Also open to the public is Selva Verde's botanical and butterfly garden, $5 per person, pay at the reception desk. A self-guided tour with a booklet that includes plant names and some of their medicinal uses carries you through the rich colors of the garden, where you will see many birds and free-flying butterflies. The butterfly enclosure has benches where you can sit and admire these ethereal creatures—a photographer's delight. Perhaps you will feel the light kiss of a butterfly on your hand.

Continuing on to the town of Puerto Viejo (population 7,132), you enter an area where large banana plantations have developed in recent years.

Self-service cable car to island trails at Islas del Rio near Chilamate
(Ree Strange Sheck)

Unfortunately, primary forest sometimes fell to make way for the bananas. Downtown you will find a bank, Pops ice cream (a welcome addition), and a medical clinic. Puerto Viejo is on the banks of the Puerto Viejo River, which flows into the Sarapiquí.

El Bambú is an 11-room downtown hotel with private baths, shower-head hot water, and ceiling fans. Rooms for up to two people are $55, including continental breakfast. VISA and MasterCard are accepted. Bamboo furniture decorates the pleasant rooms. A restaurant and bar are on the ground floor, open on one side to the greenery outside. The hotel offers trips on the San Juan River to Tortuguero and Barro del Colorado as well as bird-watching trips, boat rides, and visits to La Selva. Telephone 253-2308, fax 225-8860.

Mi Lindo Sarapiquí is a modest hotel next to the soccer field right downtown. Six simple, clean rooms above the restaurant have ceiling fans and private baths with shower-head hot water. A single is $10, a double $17, taxes included. VISA, MasterCard accepted. Staff members will arrange tours in the area and to Tortuguero. Telephone/fax 766-6281.

Travel companies and hotels in the area offer river trips—rafting, kayaking, or wildlife tours. Waters from the Sarapiquí make their way to the San Juan River, which forms the boundary between Nicaragua and Costa Rica. Though the San Juan is actually Nicaraguan territory, Costa Rica has a perpetual treaty right to use it. In the days before roads, when waterways were the area's main transportation routes, some of the Forty-Niners made their way from the East Coast of the U.S. to California by traveling on the San Juan River through Lake Nicaragua to the Pacific. Today some travelers embark on a river trip to Barro del Colorado or Tortuguero from Puerto Viejo de Sarapiquí.

Just outside Puerto Viejo between the Sucio and Puerto Viejo rivers is El Gavilán Lodge. Turn south at the intersection coming into town where the rural guard checkpoint is. Four rooms in a two-story building adjacent to the dining room look out on an outdoor Jacuzzi in the gardens. Ten more rooms are in comfortable, simply furnished two-room bungalows across the garden. All but two of the rooms have private baths, and all have either central or shower-head hot water and ceiling fans. Orchids decorate the spacious grounds, along with coconut palms, fruit trees, heliconias, heliotrope, and other flowering tropical plants. A thatched rancho is furnished with hammocks and chairs for reading or bird-watching, and there is a small open-air conference center. Green coconuts, called *pipas* in Spanish, are served as natural refreshment, along with drinks from other fruits that grow here: starfruit, oranges, guayabas, passionfruit, mangos, and pineapples. *Cas* is a favorite of mine.

Guests can choose from a variety of activities. Paths along the river lead to three tree decks terrific for bird-watching. A short distance away is Gavilan's almost 300-acre (120 ha) forest reserve, which you can visit on foot or by horseback. On my most recent boat trip there I saw crocodiles, sloths, turtles, iguanas, howler monkeys, long-nosed bats, kingfishers, parrots, a laughing falcon, an anhinga, mangrove swallows, and several species of heron. It is always an interesting trip. The plant life along the banks includes fragrant heliotrope, colorful heliconias, and vines trailing into the water.

Rates for bed and breakfast are $34 per person. Credit cards accepted if you pay in San José. Lunch and dinner are $8 each. Boat trips include the Sarapiquí ($20), San Juan ($60), and Tortuguero ($85). Horseback riding is $15 for three hours. Packages include transportation, meals, bilingual guide, boat rides, and hiking. The one-day trip coming through Braulio Carrillo park is $75 including a boat trip on the Sarapiquí, $85 with the boat trip to the San Juan River. A two-day, one-night trip takes in Poás Volcano, hiking or horseback riding, and a trip to the San Juan River, $185. Telephone 234-9507, fax 253-6556.

Just a little more than a mile (2 km) past the El Gavilán turnoff is the entrance on the right to La Selva Biological Station, a research facility and private nature reserve operated by the Organization for Tropical Studies. Visitors can walk on the excellent trails during a day visit: there is lodging for overnight stays when facilities are not occupied by researchers. See Chapter 13 for details.

Less than a kilometer south of the La Selva turnoff is Centro Ecoturístico Lapa Verde, a restaurant you cannot miss. Two tall thatched roofs shelter an open-air restaurant/bar that serves typical food, 11:00 a.m. to 11:00 p.m., closed Wednesday. If you are looking for La Selva and you get to the restaurant, turn around—you have gone too far.

Braulio Carrillo-Las Horquetas Route

You may also enter the north-central region through Braulio Carrillo National Park. As you drop down toward the lowlands, still inside the park, you'll see the joining of the Hondura River with the Sucio, which looks dirty because of mineral content carried from its origins on Irazú. The interplay of the blue and brown waters as they flow together is fascinating. If you want to take a photo, there is a place to park after you cross the bridge, but be alert. Unfortunately there have been robberies of both people and cars along this highway. Travel on the Río Frio–Puerto Viejo de Sarapiquí bus will also let you see the joining of the rivers and will take you to some of the sites described in the Poás, Varablanca, Sarapiquí section, providing a nice loop.

Just 2 miles (3 km) after the bridge over the Hondura and Sucio rivers is the entrance to El Tapir. The high, conical thatched roof of the open-air restaurant is stunning against the backdrop of the forest. El Tapir is a 250-acre (100 ha) reserve borders Braulio Carrillo and the Sucio River at an elevation of 1,476 feet (450 m). Day visitors can enjoy hiking on three trails, each about 1 mile (.6 km), in a premontane rain-forest habitat. Tree ferns, orchids, gingers, peccaries, deer, monkeys, crested guans, trogons, manakins, parrots, poison dart frogs, and a wealth of other tropical species live here. Yes, the tapir does roam these parts—footprints are common. Some of the trails are fairly flat, more accessible to those who cannot manage steep paths. If you do not see enough butterflies on the trail, you can visit the Heliconia Butterfly Farm, where the educational tour focuses on symbiosis, and enjoy the botanical garden. Entrance is $5. Open 8:00 a.m. to 4:00 p.m. The Guapiles or Río Frío bus from San José can let you off right in front. Overnight lodging may be available by the time you arrive.

About 1.5 miles further (2 km) is the entrance on the right to the Rain Forest Aerial Tram, in Spanish called the *teléferico*. Bringing ski-lift technology to the rain forest, the tram passes through what founder Donald Perry calls the hanging gardens of Central America, the forest canopy where it is believed two-thirds of the species of the forest live. As you move slowly along a 1.6-mile (2.6-km), 90-minute round trip, with brief automated pauses during the ride, you have a chance to see the plants whose flowers you find when walking on trails. Perhaps you'll see monkeys and some of the more than 300 species of birds in this area—or, as I did, an anteater making his way through upper branches. Guides in each of the four-to-five-passenger "aerial chariots" radio finds to other cars. "Look for the sloth in the upper branches of the tall tree to the right of station such and such." The highest part of the ride is on the return trip, 100 feet (30 m) above the ground. At each end of the tram are short circular trails where your guide can point out the colorful rufous-winged woodpecker, a *canfín* tree that exudes a flammable liquid, sleeping bats, and other forest treasures. A beautiful *bocaracá* (eyelash viper) rested in foliage near the restaurant when I was there, and the lovely *flor de un día* shared its one-day flower.

An open-air restaurant serves breakfast and lunch, $7.50 each. Rainforest mud pie is on the menu. In the information center, a video presents an introduction to canopy exploration and details on construction of the tram, which involved a Sandinista helicopter as well as banana-plantation technology. Entrance to the Rain Forest Aerial Tram is 32 miles (52 km) from San José. Entrance fee is $47.50 for adults and $23.75 for children ages 5 to 18. Children under 5 enter free, though they are not permitted to ride the tram. The fee entitles visitors to the tram ride, guided walks, and information center activities. The tram opens at 6:30 a.m. and the last one leaves at 3:30 p.m. Public buses pass in front and the aerial tram has a shuttle— $17.50 round trip. Cars are left at the entrance, with transportation provided almost a mile in (1.5 km) to the information center, riding in a truck bed except for a short walk over a suspension bridge and through a bit of forest. Allow at least four hours for the visit. Bring your binoculars. The San José office is at Avenida 7, Calle 7. Telephone 257-5961, fax 257-6053.

Continuing down the highway toward Limón, watch for the road north to Puerto Viejo de Sarapiquí; the turnoff is before Guapiles. This paved road passes by Las Horquetas, which is the jumping-off place for a visit to one of the first nature-adventure lodges in Costa Rica, Rara Avis. See Chapter 13 for details about this one-of-a-kind adventure to a glorious forest and an awe-inspiring waterfall.

Past Las Horquetas going toward Puerto Viejo, you will see *pejibaye* palm, grown commercially for its fruit, which Costa Ricans love, and the heart (*palmito*). Try a palmito salad while in Costa Rica. Near Puerto Viejo are entrances to La Selva Biological Station and El Gavilán Lodge of the Organization for Tropical Studies. These and Puerto Viejo de Sarapiquí are all described above in the "Poás–Varablanca–Sarapiquí Route" section.

9
What to See and Do: Northwest Costa Rica

Cloud forests, cattle ranches, miles of long beaches, deciduous dry forests—the area defined here as the northwest region contains national parks, reserves, and refuges; privately owned reserves catering to the ecotourist; and more beach resorts than any other section. This is the area with access from the Inter-American Highway north of Puntarenas, plus the Nicoya Peninsula. It is a big region, so these subsections deal with areas along transportation routes that I hope seem as logical to you as they do to me: Puntarenas–Montezuma Route, Inter-American to Liberia and Points North, Monteverde Area, and Pacific Northwest Beaches and Upper Nicoya Peninsula.

Buses go to Puntarenas, all the way north to Nicaragua, and down into the peninsula; ferries cross the Gulf of Nicoya; scheduled domestic flights go to Tamarindo, Sámara, Nosara, Carrillo, Punta Islita, Tambor, and Liberia; and taxis in many small towns fill in the blanks. (See Practical Extras for transportation possibilities.)

Though the Inter-American Highway opens the biggest door, some travelers slip in the back way through the north-central region after a visit to the Arenal area, or from the south after a visit to southern beaches.

From San José, the Inter-American Highway passes through pretty highland mountains and valleys of coffee, cows, and cane on the way to the warmer lowlands. Remember to be prepared for tollbooths before the airport and near Naranjo. A favorite stop of mine is just past the turnoff to San Ramón at a restaurant on the right called La Colina. The *gallo de picadillo de papa* (tortilla with a potato filling) or *gallo de arracache* is great for a snack, even for breakfast. The *torta de yuca* is a treat. Try *agua dulce con leche*, and do not miss the coconut *cajeta*—pure sugar and yummy. Open 7:00 a.m. to 10:00 p.m. daily. It is also fun to stop at roadside stands in Esparza to stretch

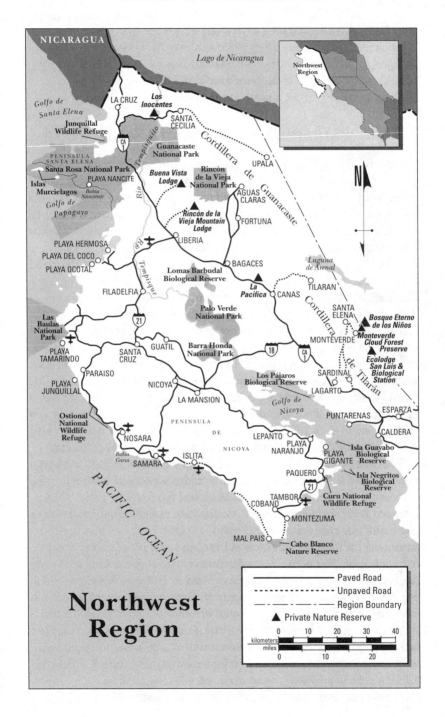

NICARAGUA

Lago de Nicaragua

Northwest Region

Golfo de Santa Elena

LA CRUZ

Los Inocentes

SANTA CECILIA

Junquillal Wildlife Refuge

CA 1

Río Tempisquito

Guanacaste National Park

Cordillera de Guanacaste

UPALA

PENINSULA SANTA ELENA

Santa Rosa National Park

PLAYA NANCITE

Buena Vista Lodge

Rincón de la Vieja National Park

AGUAS CLARAS

Islas Murcielagos

Bahía Nanciente

Golfo de Papagayo

Rincón de la Vieja Mountain Lodge

FORTUNA

PLAYA HERMOSA

PLAYA DEL COCO

PLAYA OCOTAL

Río Tempisque

LIBERIA

BAGACES

Laguna de Arenal

Lomas Barbudal Biological Reserve

La Pacífica

TILARAN

FILADELFIA

Palo Verde National Park

CANAS

Cordillera de Tilarán

Las Baulas National Park

21

SANTA CRUZ

GUATIL

Barra Honda National Park

18

CA 1

SANTA ELENA

Bosque Eterno de los Niños

Monteverde Cloud Forest Preserve

PLAYA TAMARINDO

MONTEVERDE

Ecolodge San Luis & Biological Station

PARAISO

NICOYA

Los Pájaros Biological Reserve

SARDINAL

PLAYA JUNQUILLAL

LA MANSION

LAGARTO

Ostional National Wildlife Refuge

PENINSULA DE NICOYA

Golfo de Nicoya

ESPARZA

NOSARA

LEPANTO

PUNTARENAS

CALDERA

Bahía Garza

SAMARA

ISLITA

PLAYA NARANJO

PLAYA GIGANTE

Isla Guayabo Biological Reserve

PACIFIC OCEAN

PAQUERO

Isla Negritos Biological Reserve

21

TAMBOR

Curu National Wildlife Refuge

COBANO

MONTEZUMA

MAL PAIS

Cabo Blanco Nature Reserve

Northwest Region

	Paved Road
	Unpaved Road
	Region Boundary
▲	Private Nature Reserve

0   10   20   30   40
kilometers

0   10   20
miles

your legs and give thanks for safely getting over the hair-raising stretch of winding road south of San Ramón that has yet to be widened. You will probably see some fruits you do not recognize, along with watermelons, pineapples, and avocados. The Restaurante Mirador Enis, on the western edge of Esparza, has a view of the coast, good food, and clean restrooms.

Puntarenas–Montezuma Route

Puntarenas (population 40,706) is built on a narrow piece of land with an estuary on one side and the Gulf of Nicoya on the other. Its economy is based largely on fishing and tourism. Travelers who have never been to Costa Rica sometimes choose Puntarenas for their beach experience. This is the closest beach area to San José (80 miles, 130 km, to the city center—less than a two-hour drive), but it has had bad press because of polluted water and dirty beaches. However, the town has rolled up its sleeves and improved things—even buying a machine that regularly cleans the beaches. The waste treatment plant you see on the way into town has helped, as has a new aqueduct. Tests indicate that the water between the pier and the point is now OK. Whether you swim in the ocean or not, you can go to Puntarenas to experience a laid-back coastal lifestyle, walk along the oceanfront promenade, swim in a pretty hotel pool under a warm blue sky, and watch people, ships anchored offshore, and sunsets. Drop by the small museum downtown, the Museo Histórico Marino at Avenida Central, Calles 3/5, for a look at the history of the town of Puntarenas. A picture of the culture of this port city emerges through exhibits, terrific old photos, a video, and artifacts. Admission is $1, hours 9:00 a.m. to 5:00 p.m. Tuesday through Sunday.

The Pearl of the Pacific will take on a new luster with the Puntarenas Forever project that encompasses parks and a new dock for large cruise ships; a plaza where traditional arts, crafts, and foods will be sold; an aquarium; and beautification of streets. Projected date of completion is 1997, so you should see changes when you visit.

Among the most popular tours in the country are those offering a day on a yacht out of Puntarenas—cruising around islands in the Gulf of Nicoya (including the Guayabo, Pajaritos, and Negritos biological reserves); eating well; and swimming and snorkeling in the clear waters off the island selected for a lunch stop. Packages can include transportation from San José.

There are hotels for every budget. The generally cheaper rates in the low season, now called the Green Season, may be even lower in beach areas. Puntarenas is popular with San Joséfinos on weekends but is less crowded for midweek visits. The following are hotels you might consider.

Hotel Fiesta is the largest, with 310 rooms and suites. Rooms range from

Traffic on the road to Palo Verde National Park (Ree Strange Sheck)

$95 for a standard single or double to $250 for the master suite. Credit cards are accepted. Spacious rooms, some with ocean views, have air conditioning and satellite TV. The hotel has two tour agencies, a casino, restaurants and bars, car rental, lighted tennis courts, a Jacuzzi, pools, volleyball courts, and a gym. It is located outside Puntarenas. Telephone 663-0185, or in the U.S. (800) 662-2990 or (800) 228-5050; fax 663-1516.

Hotel Yadrán is in town on the tip of the peninsula at the end of Paseo de las Turistas. It has 43 air-conditioned rooms, some carpeted and some tile, with satellite TV. Modern baths have central hot water, showers, and tubs. Standard singles are $75, doubles $85; ocean-view rooms are $10 more. Credit cards are accepted. There is a pool, restaurants, bicycle and car rental, cable TV, and on-street guarded parking. Telephone 661-2662, fax 661-1944.

Hotel Porto Bello is along the estuary off the road from San José close to the yacht club, not right downtown. The 35 rooms have air conditioning and fans, local TV, in-room telephones, a large dressing table, and private baths with hot water (most with bathtubs). Each has a view of pretty tropical gardens. A single is $41, a double $55, including breakfast. Credit cards are accepted. There is a pool, and the restaurant has a terrace for dining beside the estuary as well as a large dining room open to the gardens. The hotel arranges excursions in the Gulf of Nicoya. Telephone 661-1322 or 661-2122; fax 661-0036.

Next door is Hotel Colonial, with 56 rooms. Carpeted rooms have either a terrace or balcony, air conditioning, optional TV, large closets, and private baths—some with tubs, some with shower-head hot water. A single is $35, a double $48; taxes included. Credit cards are accepted. There are pools, parking, a private dock, bar, restaurant, and disco bar. Telephone 661-1833 or 661-1834; fax 661-2969.

Hotel Tioga is downtown across the street from the palm-lined promenade and beach. (Beach umbrellas are gratis.) The 46 rooms have air conditioning and private baths. Older rooms built around an interior courtyard with a pool do not have hot water but otherwise have the same decor. Singles $30, doubles $37. Rates for newer, larger, rooms with hot water are $40 for a single, $50 for a double. Rooms with private balconies are $45 for a single, $55 for a double; breakfast and taxes included. Credit cards accepted. There is a wonderful selection of old photos in the hallways. The second-floor terrace café looks out on the ocean, the staff is friendly, and the on-street parking is guarded. Telephone 661-0271 or 255-3115; fax 661-0127 or 255-1006.

The two-story downtown Las Brisas Hotel has 19 air-conditioned rooms and a small restaurant that serves excellent spaghetti along with salads (including a Greek salad), sandwiches, and other dishes—try the bouillabaisse. Bright rooms are in an L-shaped building around the pool. There is no garden to speak of, but the promenade and beach are just across the street. A single is $40, a double $50. Credit cards are accepted. Private baths have solar and shower-head hot water. English, Italian, French, Greek, and Arabic also are spoken by the owners, the Saals. Telephone 661-4040, fax 661-2120.

San Isidro Hotel and Club, a block off the boulevard into town before you get to the narrow peninsula, near the hospital, has a variety of lodging possibilities. Five pleasant, bright rooms have TV and private baths with tubs (hot water): $42 with air conditioning, $32 with fan. Twenty-six six-person cabins have two bedrooms, kitchenette, private bath, and ceiling fans, $58. Cabins for four and nine persons also have equipped kitchenettes and fans, from $42 to $74. A hostel section with shared baths is $10 per person, including a continental breakfast. Seven swimming pools are located on the grounds, and the large, open-air restaurant is next to the beach. Day visits are about $5. Credit cards accepted. The hotel rents bicycles, kayaks, and horses; it arranges boat trips and car rental. San Isidro is popular with Costa Rican families. Telephone 233-5027 or 223-0843; fax 221-6822.

Hotel Las Hamacas, downtown across from the beach, is more basic but clean and friendly. Singles are $14, doubles $24, including taxes. The 27 rooms have fans (about $2 more if you want an air conditioner) and private baths—no hot water. VISA accepted. A small restaurant/bar is on the first floor, a lounge on the third floor, and small pools for adults and children next to the street. Telephone 661-0398.

Check out Casa Dulia east of El Jorón, in front of Parque Lobo. The five-room bed and breakfast has large rooms, one with private bath (no hot water), and kitchen privileges. The $25 double rate includes breakfast. Telephone/fax 661-1292.

To cross the Gulf of Nicoya to destinations from Playa Naranjo to Montezuma, there are three options: a car/passenger ferry to Playa Naranjo, the Tambor car/passenger ferry, and the passenger launch from Puntarenas to Paquera. See Practical Extras for schedules.

In Playa Naranjo is Oasis del Pacifico, a small resort and marina not far from the dock. Hotel transportation meets each ferry. The 36 rooms have ceiling fans and private baths with hot water. They face the hotel's gardens on 12 acres (5 ha) and the Gulf of Nicoya. Singles are $35, doubles $45, tax included. Credit cards are accepted. The restaurant is surely one of the few in Costa Rica where you can get biscuits and country gravy for breakfast and eat it to the sounds of pet macaws and parrots.

Ranchitos with hammocks by the water and swimming pools are conducive to staying right at the hotel, but you can also rent horses ($20 for the first hour, $10 after that); charter a boat; or go on a fishing trip ($350 a day for up to three people, including tackle, food, and drinks). Oasis de Pacífico has its own 260-foot (80-m) pier. Half-day kayak trips to San Lucas Island, a former penal colony, are $40. Day trips in the Gulf of Nicoya are tailored to what people want, according to owners Lucky and Agie, two of the world's truly nice people. They also own the Piano Blanco Bar next to the Hotel Balmoral in San José, and you can sometimes find Lucky there. Telephone or fax Oasis del Pacífico at 661-1555. For those who want to cross on the ferry but have no time to go farther, a day-rate at the hotel lets visitors use the pool and showers.

The road from Playa Naranjo to Cabo Blanco (paved to Tambor) goes up and down through the hills, with lots of birds and occasional magnificent views of the coastline.

Hotel Bahia Gigante sits on a bluff above the bay of the same name. It can arrange pickup service at the ferry 5.5 miles (9 km) away and will arrange transportation from San José. It is a friendly place. The large, pleasant dining room, open to the public, is screened and has a pitched thatched roof. You can dine on typical dishes, catch-of-the-day, cracker-crusted fried chicken, fresh vegetables, pasta, smoked barbecued pork chops, and specialty sandwiches. Rooms are large, and most face the pool. There are private baths but no hot water yet. Furnishings are simple. A single/double is $35.

The hotel owns a chunk of surrounding property with 5 miles (8 km) of road and numerous trails through forests and along the beach. As many as 256 species of birds and many butterfly species have been counted. You may see howler or capuchin monkeys, armadillos, and deer as you hike. There is an estuary for bird watching, tours to the Gitana, San Lucas, Tortuga, and Negritos Islands, and a guided horseback adventure for $5 an hour to a waterfall with three large pools and a natural water slide. Scuba, snorkeling, and sportfishing equipment is arranged. There is a dock on the beach, and Bahia Gigante has supplies, fuel, and fresh water for yachts. Telephone/fax 661-2442.

The ferry and launch from Puntarenas come in at Paquera (see Practical Extras). A bus waits for the launch to take passengers as far as Montezuma. There are no bus connections for ferry passengers.

South of Paquera is Curú National Wildlife Refuge, but access is through private property and you will need arrangements and directions beforehand. (See Chapter 13.)

Bahia Ballena, which means Whale Bay, is down the road a piece. Waters lap on a long, curved beach with a very gentle slope. At sunset one July evening, two dogs and I were the only ones on the beach near the town of Tambor. A roseate spoonbill perched in a tree at the mouth of a stream, kingfishers darted back and forth, and howler monkeys sounded just out of sight. The 400-room Playa Tambor Hotel, opened in 1993, reduces the chances of you, the dogs, and the wildlife having the beach to yourself, but the last time I was there, it was still a tranquil setting.

The luxury resort complex built by the Barcelo hotel chain has helped focus the debate in Costa Rica about the impact of tourism on the physical and social environment. What kind of tourism does the country want? What is its market? What can it support? How can environmental safeguards be enforced? And what tradeoffs are acceptable? As a visitor, your vote counts. You can write to ICT. (Address in Practical Extras.)

The focus of this book is on smaller hotels, but if your taste runs to large, full-service beach resorts, Hotel Playa Tambor's telephone number is 661-1915 or 661-2039; fax 661-2069. Rooms are $170, including lodging, meals, bocas, and national drinks. There are restaurants, bars, shops, tennis courts, pools, and equipment for water sports. Rooms have satellite TV and are air-conditioned.

Tambor Tropical is a delightful destination on Tambor beach. Ten rooms are in five hexagonal structures made of 15 varieties of wood. The hand-crafting does not stop on the outside. It continues in the breakfast bar, chairs, stools, beautiful cabinets in a blue-tiled bathroom, and even in details such as lamps. These are 1,000-square-foot, open rooms with a well-equipped kitchen (same rich blue tile in the countertop) set off by a breakfast bar, a living area furnished with cushioned bamboo sofa and chairs, and a raised sleeping area with a queen-size bed.

Each of the rooms, whether upstairs or down, has a beach view out the front, as well as a pretty pool and Jacuzzi. Adults only. Rates are from $125 to $150, double occupancy, including continental breakfast. Credit cards accepted. A small restaurant serves reasonably priced light meals, with choices such as cheeseburgers, chicken nuggets, and burritos. Fishing, snorkeling, horseback riding, and kayaking are arranged. Telephone 381-0491 (cellular), in the U.S. (503) 363-7084.

Hotel Dos Lagartos is also on the beach in the town of Tambor. The 23 rooms are neat and simple with ceiling fans. Six have private baths, $25. For those who share, there are about three rooms per bath, from $17 to $20. No hot water. VISA is accepted. The small dining room serves breakfast; two restaurants are nearby. Dos Lagartos arranges horseback rides and boat tours. Telephone/fax 683-0236.

Hotel Tango Mar past Tambor offers the traveler deluxe surroundings and a full range of activities including horseback riding, snorkeling, fishing, kayaking, scuba diving, golfing, tennis, and a range of tours. A day trip goes to Tortuga Island for snorkeling, to Curú for a guided hike, and through a mangrove estuary ($70). A visit to Montezuma and its waterfalls is $35, and a sunset champagne cruise or sunset bird watching. Turtles come ashore to nest on the beach in front of the hotel, with largest arrivals in October and November, rainy months. There is a pool with natural mineral water, a restaurant, a gift shop, a ten-hole golf course, and tennis courts. The hotel rents equipment for tennis, golf, diving, and fishing, and you can get a massage. The 125-acre (50-ha) complex includes pastures, primary forest, and beachfront. A 40-foot (12-m) waterfall graces one end of the property, and at low tide, there is a great natural pool at the bottom for swimming.

Large, elegantly simple rooms have cool floors of reddish-brown polished tiles, two queen-size beds (two rooms have a king-size bed), rattan furniture, including a desk and long benches, folk art and original paintings, fresh flowers, satellite TV, reading lamps, ceiling fans, and an ample closet area with space for luggage. Baths have central hot water—and big towels. Each room opens onto a private balcony facing the sea. For the 16 rooms, singles are $137, doubles $150. Fourteen tropical suites have hand-carved four-post canopy beds, in-room Jacuzzis, and come with a golf cart. All have ocean views, but most are not on the beach. Single $120, double $130. Two-bedroom villas with kitchenettes start at $195. The Presidential Mansion by the golf course has four suites, a pool, Jacuzzis, ocean views, personal maid, and a fully equipped kitchen. The mansion is $1,000 a day; individual suites are from $199 to $395. All rates include continental breakfast. Credit cards are accepted. Food is excellent in the open-air restaurant surrounded by lush tropical plants. Guests may arrive by sea, air, or water—ask for details and about packages. Telephone 222-3503 or 223-1864; fax 221-6551. Telephone/fax at the hotel is 661-2798. Tango Mar is about 2 miles (3 km) from Tambor.

At Cóbano, turn left (dirt road all the way) toward Montezuma. Just 2.5 miles (4 km) past Cóbano is the sign for Finca Los Caballos, which has a small inn on a ranch. The eight rooms in the Spanish ranch-style structure (only five minutes from the beach) have private baths and terraces. An outdoor patio dining room has a marvelous view overlooking the swimming pool. Owner Barbara MacGregor serves three healthy meals a day, with homemade bread, jams, and sauces featured. She can set you up for daytime or overnight horseback rides on beaches, through hills, and along jungle trails. She can also arrange day hikes, excursions to Cabo Blanco, boat trips to Tortuga Island, birding ventures, bicycling, and beach trips. A double is $39. Telephone/fax 642-0124.

About 2 miles further (3 km) is the interesting little beach town of Montezuma. In the past, it could not seem to decide whether to dress up and go for big-time tourism or just hang out and take what came. Now some in the community have organized to combat some of the problems that did come, such as unregulated camping anywhere someone decided to pitch a tent. Now there is a specified camping area with latrines and water. You can pitch in and help on Saturday beach cleanups. New small hotels are going in, and older ones are being spruced up. The beaches are spectacular—some to the north have loads of gorgeous shells. You can go horseback riding, hike to a waterfall, snorkel, visit the Cabo Blanco reserve farther down the road, bird-watch, or just hang out.

Travelers to Montezuma now have another transportation option with the SIMBA water service. A forty-passenger, 52-foot boat with a lounge area, two bathrooms, kitchen (refreshments served), and deck area sails daily from Puntarenas, leaving at 10:00 a.m. The return trips leaves Montezuma at 1:00 p.m. The voyage is about 2½ hours, passing by Isla Tortuga and other Gulf of Nicoya islands, by deserted beaches, with a chance to see turtles, dolphins, and jumping fish, $15 per person. For information or advance ticket purchase in Puntarenas, go by the Polar Pizza Restaurant, Avenida Central and Calle 4, or call 661-0344 and ask for SIMBA. Currently SIMBA operates only from December to April, so check for other months.

Monte Aventuras is a tour and information center in Montezuma with a helpful, friendly staff. See the bulletin boards for interesting tidbits. Here is a sample of some of the day tours: boat trip to Cabo Blanco and Cabuya, enjoying sunset at Malpais ($15); land trip to Malpais for sunset ($30); horseback riding to El Chorro ($25); Tortuga Island and snorkeling ($25); and transportation to Cabo Blanco. Now here's a bargain: a three-day adventure that starts in Montezuma and ends in Puntarenas, taking in Curú and Caño Negro wildlife refuges, La Fortuna, Arenal, and a horseback ride from there to Monteverde. The price of $189 covers lodging and transport, but not meals. Telephone/fax 642-0025.

The Sano Banano, a macrobiotic restaurant, serves delicious food with a flair. It has not only a frozen yogurt machine but also a slush machine and serves fresh popcorn, too. Open 6:00 a.m. to 10:00 p.m. Lenny and Patricia Iacona, the owners, also show nightly movies on a large screen. The Iaconas also have Cabinas El Sano Banano—a combination of seven romantic bungalows tucked into the forest near the beach and six pleasant rooms in a two-story unit, also with ocean views. Some have kitchenettes, all have private baths. Rates range from $45 to $70. Credit cards accepted but there is a surcharge. Telephone/fax 642-0068, telephone 642-0272.

Hotel El Jardín has ten very clean rooms with refrigerators, floor or ceiling fans, and private tiled baths, most with hot water. From the upstairs balcony, there is a view of the sea—the beach is less than a four-minute walk away. An outside shower lets guests rinse off beach sand before going in their rooms. A room for up to two is $45 without hot water, $50 with. There is a restaurant, tourist office, and store. Telephone 642-0074, fax 642-0025.

Hotel Los Mangos is past the town center on the way to Cabo Blanco, across the road from the sea. More than 200 mango trees shade the grounds, their fruit drawing birds and animals. Anteaters have been known to visit. Pleasant, raised, thatched bungalows with pyramid ceilings have private baths with central hot water, lots of windows, ceiling fans, a full-length mirror, and rockers on the porches. The cost is $75 for up to three people. Some older rooms do not have private baths, from $20 to $50. VISA is accepted. A pretty pool with a view of the ocean and forest is next to the restaurant/bar, which is open to the public and specializes in Italian food. English, Greek, Italian, and Polish also are spoken.

Los Mangos rents horses, bicycles, and motorcycles and offers tours on a catamaran—for example, a one-day trip to Tortuga or Malpais or three days around the area. Forest covers the hillside behind the hotel; you are likely to hear the sounds of the howlers and perhaps spot white-face monkeys. Telephone 642-0259, fax 642-0036.

Hotel Montezuma Pacífico has nine rooms, some with both air conditioning and fans. All have private baths, some have shower-head hot water. Rooms are $19 for two. Telephone/fax 642-0204.

The Amor de Mar is family-oriented: owners Doris and Richard Stocker welcome children. Eight of the rooms have private baths, some with shower-head hot water, at $35 to $45 for a double. Rooms with shared baths are $30. English, German, and French also are spoken. The two-story hotel has the sea in front and the river on one side. Hammocks are strategically placed in the pretty, grassy garden. The restaurant serves full breakfasts all day—marvelous homemade bread and natural fruit juices—and snacks, even milk shakes. Telephone/fax 642-0262.

Hotel Montezuma, downtown on the beach, has rooms with shared baths from $8 single to $11 double; with private bath, $13 for a single and $18 for a double, tax included. There are ceiling fans but no hot water. Rooms across the street from the restaurant are quieter. The hotel rents bicycles, motorcycles, and horses, and offers boat trips to Cabo Blanco and Tortuga Island. Telephone/fax 642-0058.

Hotel Aurora has eight rooms and private baths (no hot water) in a three-story house. Each is cooled by a fan and has mosquito netting. An open lounge on the second floor is a gathering place for guests; some take advantage of an exercise corner. Doubles are $20 to $30, VISA accepted. There is a living/dining area, and a refrigerator where guests may keep things. Coffee, tea, and natural drinks are always on hand as a courtesy to guests. Angela, an owner and hostess, is an articulate proponent of Montezuma's special natural attractions—she can steer you to activities suited to your interests. Telephone 642-0051, fax 642-0025.

Before coming down the hill to Montezuma, you will see a sign saying "Juan's." This is short for Hermanos y Hermanas de la Madre Tierra, which offers rustic lodging on 250 acres (100 ha) of regenerating pastures and primary and secondary forest. The restaurant focuses on vegetarian food, using produce from its organic garden, but you will find dishes with Thai, Spanish, Indian, and Mexican flavors. Guides can take you on forest trails to waterfalls, springs, and the river, either walking or on horseback. Basic accommodations run the gamut from three rooms with private baths to dormitory-style sleeping with communal toilets and baths in a separate building, no hot water. Rates range from $15 to $35. Howlers come every morning; morphos drift by. Telephone 642-0291. Actually, the "Juan's" sign is for owner Juan Cielo. Local people call it "Juan's place."

The village of Mal Pais is another option on the Pacific side near the tip of the Nicoya Peninsula. Access is from Cóbano via a dirt road. Mar Azul offers simple lodging and an area for camping. Some of the 13 rooms have private baths. Now that electricity has arrived, all have fans. Owners Otto and Jeannette are your hosts. They explain that while there is no hot water, neither is it cold. Rates range from $15 to $25. The restaurant serves seafood and typical meals. Telephone/fax 642-0298.

The Cabo Blanco Strict Nature Reserve is worth the trip. The road eventually narrows to a one-lane track that can be quite muddy in the rainy season. There is one large river to cross. When I got out of the car to photograph a thatched house with a television antenna atop a bamboo pole, a small child ran up to advise me not to venture too close to the water. "There are crocodiles in there," she said. Spiny pochote trees and gumbo-limbo trees, in Spanish called *indio desnudo* (naked Indian), with their peeling reddish bark, form living fences along the road. A huge strangler fig stands at the road's edge. (See Chapter 12 for information about the reserve, including days it is open to the public.)

Inter-American to Liberia and Points North

If you are continuing on to the northwest, you will note vegetation changes as the Inter-American Highway winds between the coastal zone and the mountains to the east. At kilometer 125 is Garabito Restaurant, a pleasant stop where you can order *ceviche*, fried yuca, shrimp, fish, and lots more. The covered fields a few miles farther are a nursery—lots of orchids.

If you are taking a side trip to Monteverde, watch for signs at either route, through Sardinal about kilometer 134 or before the Lagarto River about kilometer 149 (see Monteverde Area, the following section). Eleven miles (18 km) past the Lagarto River bridge is the turnoff to the left to the Tempisque ferry, which carries cars and passengers to the Nicoya Peninsula.

At Cañas (population 23,542), the next major town on the Inter-American, travelers can find gasoline stations, banks, a clinic, pharmacies, and small restaurants. Hotel El Corral on the highway has 26 rooms with private baths, some with hot water, $35 for a single; double $45. Rooms are clean, with air conditioning. VISA and MasterCard accepted. Many of its customers are businesspeople. Telephone 669-0367, fax 668-0309. A paved highway from Tilarán to Cañas facilitates travel between the Arenal area and the north-central sector with destinations up and down the Inter-American highway.

Just past Cañas at kilometer 191 is Capazuri Bed and Breakfast, where the Gamboas will give you a warm greeting. They have four bright, pleasant rooms with bamboo furniture, private baths but no hot water. Single $15, double $30 to $40. Camping is permitted, $3 per person, with access to a toilet and shower and to the large rancho in the garden. Breakfast for campers is $3. The Gamboas keep lots of good information on hand for their guests—maps, pamphlets—and they can offer helpful tips on your travels. Many fruit trees on the grounds. No credit cards. Telephone/fax 669-0580.

Now in drier Guanacaste Province, the question may not be "When will the rains stop?" but "When will they start?" In the dry season, flowering red, white, pink, and yellow trees decorate a brown landscape. In any season, the national tree, the *guanacaste*, spreads its branches out like a great fan. Horses and cattle seek shade under its mimosalike leaves in pasturelands.

The big ditches you see as you proceed are part of the government's ambitious Arenal-Tempisque irrigation project (SENARA) to supply Guanacaste farms with water. By the time the water gets to the lowlands, it already has generated electricity three times: at the Arenal, Corobicí, and Sandillal hydroelectric plants. The project benefits more than 1,000 farm families, providing water to almost 45,000 acres (18,000 ha) that otherwise would be dry for half the year.

Watch for Safaris Corobicí on the right, which offers a bird-watcher's special on the Corobicí: $35 for a two-hour float trip, $43 for three hours to the Catalina entrance of Palo Verde. There is also a five-hour family float trip for $60 per person. Children under 14 accompanied by an adult are half-price on all trips. A half-day salt-water estuary trip for $50 takes you by boat to the border of Palo Verde, into the Tempisque River. Telephone or fax 669-1091.

On the same side road as Safaris Corobicí is Las Pumas, an animal sanctuary run for many years by Werner and Lily Hagenauer, on their farm. Here are all six species of cats found in Costa Rica: jaguar, puma, margay, jaguarundi, ocelot, and *oncilla* (little spotted cat), along with peccaries and other assorted animals that have been brought to the Hagenauers. Open from 8:00 a.m. to 5:00 p.m. daily, no charge but donations needed and gladly accepted. To help finance the care of the cats, they also raise parakeets to sell. Telephone 669-0444.

Just next door is La Pacífica, a working farm with a private nature reserve, which offers a marvelous chance to explore tropical dry forest and learn about how La Pacífica combines hotel, hacienda, and nature as sustainable development strategies. See Chapter 13 for specifics. Day visitors are welcome.

On the banks of the Corobicí River, just 2.5 miles (4 km) north of Cañas, is Restaurant Rincón Coribicí, a delightful pause in the journey, another of my favorites. Whether you are dining indoors or on the open terrace, the view of the river and Tenorio Volcano is fabulous. Take your binoculars in with you, and you will appreciate why birders like this area. Food is good here—get a side order of fried yuca if you have not yet tried it. Pleasant restrooms; public phone outside. The gift shop is loaded with handcrafted items, books, cards, jewelry. Open 8:00 a.m. to 10:00 p.m., generally closed in September or October. Telephone 669-0303.

You may see river rafters on the Corobicí River—it is one that offers a white-water and natural history combination.

Another grand river trip is offered by Cata Tours on the Bebedero, to Palo Verde and the Tempisque River. You will see crocodiles and birds galore, and probably monkeys, too. Three hours on the river with a bilingual guide is $45 from Cañas, $75 from San José. Telephone 296-2133, fax 296-2730, telephone/fax 669-1026.

The next town of any size along the Inter-American is Bagaces (population 7,860). Turn west here for Palo Verde National Park, 17 miles (28 km) away; a bit farther north is the road to Lomas Barbudal Biological Reserve. Both of these are wonderful natural history destinations (see Chapter 12). As a matter of fact, there is a back road that connects the park and the reserve, basically unmarked. I tried it, and the beginning was marvelous: roseate spoonbills dotted the rice fields. Farther along, however, as night approached and the muddy ruts got deeper on what became little more than a track through isolated fields, I kept thinking, "This cannot be the road to Lomas Barbudal," and it wasn't. I had missed a turn. Perhaps you follow directions better than I do.

For good directions and information on either Palo Verde, Lomas Barbudal, or Barra Honda National Park, stop at the office of the Tempisque Conservation Area in Bagaces, in a white house on the highway next to the gasoline station, just across from the road to Palo Verde. You can also call or fax the office for information, 671-1062.

Albergue Bagaces right on the highway offers 13 clean rooms with private tiled baths (shower-head hot water) built around a large lounge and TV room (local channels). Each has a desk, reading lamps, high wood ceilings, and fans. Single $23, double $26, VISA accepted. It is a modest place, but it does offer a convenient base for side trips in the area. The rooms are back of a large restaurant, which is open 8:00 a.m. to 9:00 p.m. Telephone 671-1267, fax 666-2021.

A road northeast out of Bagaces leads to the Miravalles Geothermal Project and to the Santa María sector of Rincón de la Vieja National Park. Follow the Miravalles signs, passing through Fortuna. There is a small gate in the fence along the road for public entrance to the bubbling mudpots, small geysers in grey pools, steam, and the powerful natural energy found here. The sign is also small, so keep asking if you do not find it (ask for *las hornillas*). Signs also advise that you should not leave valuables unprotected in your car, but the thermal site is not far from the road (on a trail through open grassy ground). Perhaps you can take turns if your car is loaded. Taxis would be available from Bagaces. It is an awesome place, with the underground forces rising to the surface in front of you and majestic Miravalles Volcano reigning on the horizon.

Continuing on this same route takes you to Aguas Claras, Colonia

Blanca, and Santa María Volcano Lodge, a fantastically beautiful drive in a land of volcanoes. Santa María Volcano Lodge is a small place at the edge of a tiny town, at the base of a big mountain. Its wooden A-frame cabins somehow look like playhouses from the outside, though inside they have plenty of room for beds, closet, table and stools, and a full bath with shower-head hot water. Some have a sleeping loft, some have walls of river stone in the bathroom, all have a porch. Rates are $43, including room, meals, and laundry service; no credit cards. Two rooms with private bath are in the main house, which also contains a family-style restaurant where fruits of the land are enjoyed—trees in the garden include papaya, starfruit, grapefruit, *guanabana*, passionfruit, and macadamia. There is also palmito (for heart of palm) and banana. All this fruit brings birds—one visitor counted 20 species in the same tree. Owner Rosalba de Vargas says guests can see the milking if they like. A small rustic bar offers a quiet drink before supper.

Activities to choose from include a day trip to Rincón de la Vieja by horseback (about 9 miles or 15 km), a 2.5-mile (4-km) trek to hot springs and fumaroles, a visit to a nearby hacienda to swim in the Negro River, or a trip to neighboring Miravalles Volcano. Local guides are available for $25 per tour, and horses are $20 to $30, depending on length of tour. The lodge is not in the forest, but the forest is nearby; howler monkeys are neighbors. Bring your frontier spirit and you will discover the charm of this simple, out-of-the-way place. It is not so out of the way, however, that it cannot be reached by intrepid Costa Rican buses. Those for Colonia Blanca leave Liberia at 6:30 a.m. and 1:30 p.m., and the trip takes about 2½ hours. By car, Santa María Volcano Lodge is about 90 minutes from Bagaces. Telephone 666-2911, 666-1948, 235-0642; fax 666-2313.

Back on the Inter-American at Bagaces, continuing northward toward Liberia, watch for the sign on the left to Lomas Barbudal Biological Reserve about 6.8 miles (11 km) further along. The reserve is 4 miles (6 km) from the highway turnoff.

Liberia, capital of the Province of Guanacaste, is 16 miles (26 km) north of Bagaces, 154 miles (248 km) from San José. Two of the volcanoes in the Guanacaste range break the horizon: Miravalles and Rincón de la Vieja. It is sometimes referred to as the White City because the early adobe houses got a coating of the area's abundant lime. Note the unusual architectural feature of old houses that have two doors on their northeast corners, with views of the rising sun and twilight, giving long hours of natural daylight inside. An information center at El Sabanero Museum, Casa de la Cultura, is in a house with these *puertas del sol*. Signs will direct you to the 150-year-old building three blocks from the park. It is open Monday through Saturday from 8:00 a.m. to noon and 1:00 to 4:00 p.m. The small museum contains mem-

Mudpots at Miravalles Volcano north of Bagaces (Ree Strange Sheck)

orabilia related to the cowboy (or *sabanero*) and early life in this "Wild West" region. Friendly staff members can make reservations for you, and they have photos of many of the hotels and lodges in the area. Telephone/fax 666-1606.

With a population of 32,493, Liberia is the commercial center and a transportation hub for the area. Scheduled in-country flights now land at Daniel Oduber Quirós International Airport west of town at Llano Grande. Some international airlines and charters have announced plans to land there. By the way, the airport previously has been called El Llano and Tomás Guardia—you may still hear people use those names. Airport telephone 666-0695. From Liberia there is a highway to the Nicoya Peninsula and beach resorts on the northern Pacific coast. Direct San José–Liberia buses run about every two hours during the day and take four hours.

Not far from downtown on the road to the airport, close to the Guanacaste Regional campus of the University of Costa Rica, is a cooperative artisan workshop and store. Stop by any day from 8:00 a.m. to 7:00 p.m. Signs are in English. You can find handcrafts in bamboo and wood, macramé, gourds, paintings, ceramics, and pottery, and you can see local artisans at work. It is called Centro y Tienda Artesanal. The project received help from the Peace Corps. It is nonprofit, with funds going directly to the artists.

Day trips to Santa Rosa, Rincón de la Vieja, Las Baulas, and Palo Verde National Parks are possible from Liberia, as well as visits to beaches such as Ocotal, Hermosa, Coco, and Tamarindo. Here is a sample of hotels near the Inter-American:

Hotel Las Espuelas has 44 rooms with private baths and hot water. Singles are $60, doubles $80. Polished floor tiles gleam along covered walkways leading from the lobby and restaurant/bar areas through landscaped grounds to wings of rooms named for nearby parks and reserves. Rooms are bright and air-conditioned, with satellite TV. There is a large pool in the garden, and tennis courts. Telephone 666-0144; in the U.S. and Canada (800) 245-8420; fax 225-3987. Las Espuelas is now part of Costa Sol International. It is about a mile (2 km) south of Liberia.

Hotel El Sitio has 52 large, attractive rooms opening onto landscaped grounds and courtyard, and an open-air restaurant that serves both international and Costa Rican food. It has a pool, gift shop, exercise room, parking, children's playground, and thatched bar. Most rooms have air conditioning (single $50, double $65); some have ceiling fans (single $45, double $50); all have private baths with central hot water, satellite TV, and a large desk/dressing table. French, Italian, German, and English are also spoken. El Sitio rents bicycles, cars, and horses, and offers riding lessons. A real sabanero leads a guided horseback tour on 12 acres (5 ha) of the property, or guests can explore it on foot or mountain bike. Credit cards accepted. Telephone 666-1211, fax 666-2059.

The Nuevo Hotel Boyeros has 68 air-conditioned rooms built around a courtyard, adult and children's pools, a rancho-style bar, and a restaurant open 24 hours a day. Upstairs rooms have balconies, downstairs have small verandas. Private baths have central hot water. Single $29, double $40, including taxes. Credit cards accepted. Telephone 666-0995, 666-0722; fax 666-2529.

Just north of the main intersection into town is Hotel del Aserradero, built in what was a lumber mill. The 22 rooms have private baths with central hot water in large showers. Matching comforters and curtains are a nice touch—there's a trundle bed under the double. Rooms open onto extra-wide verandas with rocking chairs. Singles $23, doubles $29, tax included. VISA and MasterCard accepted. Telephone 666-1939, fax 666-0475.

Right at the junction of the Inter-American with the road to the beaches is El Bramadero, a 23-room hotel with a restaurant that is popular with locals as well as travelers. Rooms with private baths (shower-head hot water) surround two courtyards, one with a pool. El Bramadero offers car rental. Rooms with fans are $25 for up to two people; with air conditioning, they are $36, taxes included. Telephone 666-0371, fax 666-0203.

Fourteen miles (23 km) up the road from Liberia to the headquarters of Rincón de la Vieja National Park is a turnoff to Rinconcito Lodge, a small, rustic overnight option for visitors to the park. As my trustworthy 1977 Toyota and I lurched down the steep, incredibly rocky incline, I said to myself again, "This cannot be the road." But it was. The 1.8-mile (3-km) stretch is definitely four-wheel-drive. Better yet, let the owners transport you from Liberia for $30—an unqualified bargain considering the road. Five double rooms and two basic baths, without hot water, are in a house in a large clearing. No-frills rooms are $10 per person. Credit cards are not accepted. Lighting is by kerosene lamp, but a small hydro plant is planned. The small dining room down the hill serves typical Costa Rican food. (Breakfast is $4, lunch and dinner $6.) A horseback trip to the park is $7. There is a river pool for swimming, a tree where keel-billed toucans hang out, and a chance to join in ranch activities. The lodge is also about 5 miles (8 km) from Miravalles Volcano. Telephone 666-0636, 666-1889.

Just a little more than a mile (2 km) past the turnoff to Rinconcito is the ranger station for Rincón de la Vieja National Park. The drive from Liberia to the park entrance takes about 60 to 90 minutes. (See Chapter 12 for what you will find there as well as at the entrance off the Inter-American Highway on the other side of Liberia, going through Curubandé.)

See Chapter 13 for a description of a lodging possibility on the road between Curubandé and the entrance to the Las Pailas sector of Rincon: Rincón de la Vieja Mountain Lodge. It borders the park and has its own forest. At the gate into the Hacienda Guachipelín, you will be charged a fee because the road is private.

Another park neighbor with a private reserve and lodging is the delightful Buena Vista Lodge, about 20 miles (31 km) from Liberia, turning off the Inter-American at Cañas Dulces. (See Chapter 13.)

Santa Rosa and Guanacaste National Parks are farther north. A paved road goes all the way to Santa Rosa headquarters and the historical La Casona. Guanacaste National Park has overnight facilities. (See Chapter 12.) Visits to both are offered by nature tour companies and through hotels and private nature reserves in the area.

Near Cuajiniquil, which is off the Inter-American at the northern end of Santa Rosa, is Junquillal National Wildlife refuge—see Chapter 12 for details. You can contact the Guanacaste Conservation Area for information about Santa Rosa, Guanacaste, and Junquillal.

La Cruz (population 8,238) is the last town of any size before the Nicaraguan border. Several lodging options are in this pleasant place, which is on the hills overlooking beautiful Salinas Bay and Bolaños Island.

Amalia's Inn has seven comfortable rooms with private baths and central hot water. The third floor of the pretty house designed by Lester Bounds and managed by him and his wife, Amalia, has larger rooms for families. Each room has a fan. The second-floor balcony and the patio area by the swimming pool afford top-of-the-mountain views of the coastline—a place where you look down on birds in flight. Singles $20, double $35, and breakfast is $5 per person. Credit cards accepted. No smoking here. Amalia can tell you a lot about the area because of the history of her family and their big ranch you see below. She and Lester praise the unspoiled, little visited beaches here—places with names like Rajada and Jobo. Telephone/fax 679-9181.

Hostal de Julia was just opening when I dropped by. Twelve rooms with private baths and shower-head hot water (a solar heating system coming) are on two floors. Brick floors and nice use of wood in wardrobes, desks, and bathroom accessories make the rooms inviting. Single $30, double $35. Credit cards accepted. Julia arranges kayak and boat trips and horseback riding, telephone/fax 679-9084.

You may want to stop by the mirador, a cliffside viewpoint in town where you find Restaurante Ehecatl, open 10:00 a.m. to 10:00 p.m., a popular place. Dishes include ceviche, heart of palm, Mexican carnitas, *patacones* (fried plantains), even octopus and lobster along with the more usual rice dishes and sandwiches. VISA accepted. Telephone 679-9104.

One of the more delightful private nature reserves is Los Inocentes (see

Chapter 13) east of La Cruz. You can continue past Los Inocentes to Santa Cecilia and on to Upala to get to Caño Negro and the north-central part of Costa Rica.

Continuing north from La Cruz toward the Nicaraguan border, watch for Hotel Colinas del Norte on the left, about 4 miles (6 km). The dining room in the main building is pretty, with large glass windows looking out on the countryside. A pool with forest as a backdrop and thatched ranchos around it put one immediately in the tropics. The 618-acre (250-ha) property offers guests opportunities to hike or go horseback riding in primary forest, where there are toucans, 31 species of butterflies, and 50 species of mammals, including bats, of course. Guided walks available. Colinas del Norte also offers trips into Nicaragua and tours to Santa Rosa (the lesser-visited Murciélago sector) and Rincón de la Vieja. Rooms in the two-story wooden building have ceiling fans and private baths with hot water, $52 for doubles. Credit cards accepted. Italian, English, and French also spoken. Telephone/fax 679-9132. The bus from San José to Peñas Blancas will get you to the turnoff, a short distance from the hotel.

From here it is only 9 miles (15 km) to Peñas Blancas and the Nicaraguan border. There are a number of checkpoints along the way, but if you just want to go have a look, tell the guards and they will wave you through until you get to the border.

Monteverde Area

First let me explain that Monteverde is not only the name of a small town but the name is also used to describe the whole zone. There are three communities in the "urban area": Santa Elena is the largest, with a bank, shops, and the local high school; then next along the road is Cerro Plano, and finally, Monteverde.

There are two routes to the Monteverde area off of the Inter-American. The one near kilometer 134 goes through Sardinal (paved for a short distance), and the other begins near kilometer 149 just before the bridge over the Río Lagarto. The two join near Guacimal for the final climb. Count on 90 minutes for either route. The bumpy road gives occasional breathtaking views of the lowlands below as you climb on roads that seem to hang by grace along the edge of the mountains. As you wind through thin clouds, cows across deep valleys look like brown or white dots scattered on the steep pastures. The slow going gives you plenty of time to enjoy.

About 5 miles (8 km) after the Sardinal-Lagarto intersection is an orange bus stop and the road down into the beautiful San Luis Valley and a private nature reserve. The Ecolodge San Luis and Biological Station offers a chance

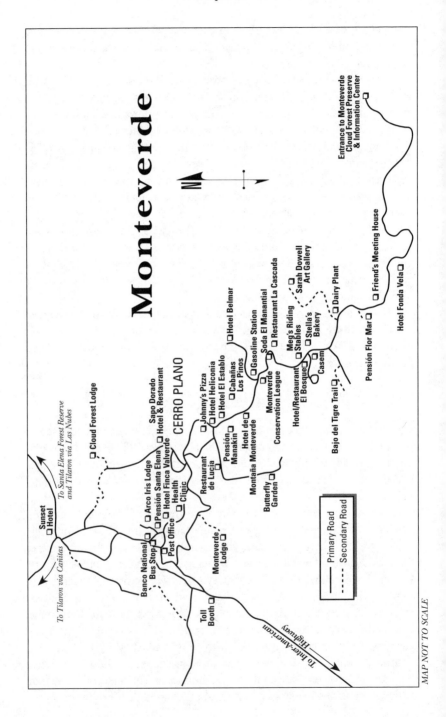

Monteverde

CERRO PLANO

Entrance to Monteverde
Cloud Forest Preserve
& Information Center

Cloud Forest Lodge

Sapo Dorado
Hotel & Restaurant

Johnny's Pizza
Hotel Heliconia
Hotel El Establo
Cabañas
Los Pinos

Hotel Belmar

Gasoline Station

Soda El Manantial
Restaurant La Cascada

Meg's Riding
Stables
Stella's
Bakery

Sarah Dowell
Art Gallery

Dairy Plant

Friend's Meeting House

Pensión
Manakin

Hotel de

Monteverde
Conservation League

Hotel/Restaurant
El Bosque

Casem

Pensión Flor Mar

Hotel Fonda Vela

Restaurant
de Lucía

Montaña Monteverde

Bajo del Tigre Trail

Butterfly
Garden

Arco Iris Lodge
Pensión Santa Elena
Hotel Finca Valverde
Health
Clinic

Sunset
Hotel

*To Santa Elena Forest Reserve
and Tilarán via Las Nubes*

Banco National
Bus Stop
Post Office

Monteverde
Lodge

To Tilarán via Cañitas

Toll
Booth

To Inter-American Highway

Primary Road
- - - - - Secondary Road

MAP NOT TO SCALE

INTERNATIONAL CHILDREN'S RAINFOREST

Once upon a time, there was a teacher from the United States who came to Monteverde, Costa Rica, to do biological research. Her enthusiasm for the rainforest and her concern about its destruction found its way into a small primary school far away in rural Sweden. There, a class of 9 year-olds wondered if there were something they could do to save the trees, the waterfalls, and the many animals who made their homes in the tropical forest. With their teacher, they decided there was. They wrote a play and presented it for their parents; they drew cards and sold them; they gave from their allowances. That money was sent to the Monteverde Conservation League, a group working hard to protect the threatened rainforest. It was enough to buy 15 acres (6 ha).

The idea of a rainforest saved by children for children spread to schools in Sweden, to Maine where the biology teacher lived, to schools in England and Germany. Now, children in other European countries, in Japan, and in Africa—more than 44 countries in all—are lending a hand. These children ask for donations instead of birthday presents, they collect materials for recycling, and they sponsor "green days." The result is Bosque Eterno de los Niños (Children's Eternal Forest), the first international children's rainforest.

Since it began in 1989, the children's rainforest has grown to cover thousands of acres of virgin forest. Living in this lush vegetation are quetzals, monkeys, bare-necked umbrella birds, ocelots, jaguars, and tapirs. Long vines trail to the forest floor. Many species have yet to be identified.

As children learn about this forest in Costa Rica, they begin to think in a new way about their own environment. Often, their parents join in the campaign. One day, an educational center in Bosque Eterno de los Niños will bring together children from around the world to learn more about natural history and each other. Research stations, where people learn about the tropical forest, are open already.

You can become a Rain Forest Partner with Bosque Eterno de los Niños. Long-term protection of the rain forest is more than buying land. It means patrols by forest guards, environmental programs in neighboring schools and communities, planting trees. Donations of any size can help. For $100, partners receive a certificate. Send contributions to: Monteverde Conservation League Apartado 10581-1000 San José, Costa Rica, 645-5003, fax 645-5104, e-mail acmmcl@sol.racsa.co.cr to rub elbows with researchers, explore beautiful forest, and meet local people. See Chapter 13 for details.

Besides the natural beauty of the place, the tiny, progressive community of Monteverde is itself worth a visit. Quakers from North America came here in 1951, drawn by Costa Rica's disarmed environment. They set up a business that now makes some the finest cheeses in the country. The Quakers bought milk from neighboring farmers and invited them to become share-holders—today there are about 430, including milk producers, employees, and neighbors. You can visit the modern dairy plant, La Lechería, Monday through Saturday from 7:30 a.m. to 4:00 p.m.; on Sunday, it closes at 12:30 p.m. Visitors may watch cheesemakers through a glass partition beside the sales room.

The CASEM gift shop sells locally handcrafted items, many with intri-cate embroidery or weaving. Save some of your souvenir shopping for here; the hand-painted cards and stationery make beautiful, easy-to-carry gifts. Designs used on the textiles and paper goods are drawn from the area's rich biological diversity: quetzals, bellbirds, golden toads. The craft cooperative, whose sales directly benefit local residents, is open from 8:00 a.m. to 5:00 p.m. Monday through Saturday year around, and 10:00 a.m. to 4:00 p.m. on Sunday from November through April. Next door is Coope Santa Elena's coffee-roasting operation; stop in and try Café Monteverde.

The Monteverde Conservation League is a nonprofit organization founded in 1986. It works in land acquisition, forest protection, habitat rehabilitation, research, small-scale sustainable development projects, con-servation of flora and fauna, and education. One of its most exciting projects is Bosque Eterno de los Niños, the first international children's rainforest. The league office, across from the gasoline station, is open from 8:00 a.m. to noon and 1:00 to 5:00 p.m. weekdays, 8:00 a.m. to noon on Saturday, but the league's information center is at Bajo del Tigre, which is part of the chil-dren's rainforest. Open from 8:00 a.m. to 5:00 p.m. daily, the trail goes through forest and around a beginning arboretum in an old pasture. The haunting notes of the long-tailed manakin and the raucous sounds of the bellbird sometimes predominate, and monkeys and coatis live here, too. At the entrance get material on league programs and gift items for sale. Ask about visiting other sectors of Bosque Eterno de los Niños.

There are a growing number of options for the nature traveler in the Monteverde area. See Chapter 13 for information about the Monteverde Cloud Forest Preserve, a private biological reserve that has attracted visitors since 1972. A newer kid on the block is the Santa Elena Forest Reserve, which is also cloud forest habitat. It has about 8 miles (12 km) of trails at an elevation of 5,600 feet (1,700 m). Arenal Volcano, some 7 miles (14 km) away, can be seen from the Sendero del Bajo and Sendero Youth Challenge—when the weather cooperates. Two of the trails are self-guided; booklets cost less than $1. Guided walks are available, and you can rent rubber boots and ponchos. There is a small café at the entrance. The visitor center has a gift shop; exhibits made by students of the local high school, which administers the reserve; and a room for free slides shows on natural history, which are offered at set hours. Visitation is limited to 80 persons at a time, so it is best to make reservations, especially in high season. Call the high school at 645-5014 between 7:00 a.m. and 8:00 p.m. The reserve, 3 miles (5 km) northeast of Santa Elena, is open from 7:00 a.m. to 4:00 p.m. daily. Admission is $5, free for children under 12. For those inclined to tent, there is a camping area available for visitors.

Volunteers are needed at the Santa Elena Reserve—minimum age 16. Housing is provided, but volunteers pay for meals and must work at least three days. Write for an application form to Santa Elena High School Cloud Forest Reserve, Apartado 90-5655, Santa Elena, Monteverde, Puntarenas, or call or fax 645-5014.

By the time you arrive, Aerial Trails should be open, a trail with six hanging bridges, some more than 135 feet (42 m) above the ground. A guided tour is $25. A trail walk along the river is $5. Open 7:00 a.m. to 3:00 p.m. daily. Telephone 645-5109, fax 645-5007. Aerial Trails is located just before the Santa Elena Reserve.

For a glorious experience with butterflies, visit the Monteverde Butterfly Garden. The entrance fee of $5 for adults and $3 for children entitles you to a walk with well-trained guides through three botanical gardens that provide different habitats for breathtaking butterflies: forest understory habitat, mid-elevation habitat, and highland forest-edge habitat. Afterward, you can have as much time as you want to walk along the paths or sit alone to watch or photograph the free-flying butterflies. It is a magical place. Owner Jim Wolfe, a biologist, has lived in the area for years and is glad to share fascinating tidbits about insects, plants, and their relationships. The nature center includes displays of butterflies and other insects—you can even look at butterfly wings under a microscope. You may get to see a butterfly emerge from its pupal case. A small reference library and a video are available to visitors, along with a colorful pamphlet chock full of butterfly ecology—feeding, defense, migration, life cycle ($1.30). Ask for the plant guide, which gives scientific and family names of labeled plants in the gardens and on the trail, along with brief information about them. A new addition to the garden is the inside view of an active leaf-cutter ant nest. You must see how Jim and the ants created this marvel. One of the prettiest small gift shops in the country is here, with its melodious fountain, stained glass window, and mural. The shirts with the elegant butterfly designs are the work of Marta Iris, the other half of the ownership. The garden is open from 9:30 a.m. to 4:00 p.m. daily.

Some hotels and private guides offer night walks in the reserves. A 7:30 p.m. walk at the Monteverde Cloud Forest Preserve costs $12. Call 645-5118 or 645-5311. The experience is dramatically different from daytime walks: nocturnal animals, glowing mushrooms, rain frogs, and a world of insects. Perhaps you will see the endemic golden-kneed tarantula, a beauty.

Gift shops, restaurants, pensions, and hotels are located in and around Monteverde and Santa Elena, strung along the road all the way to the Monteverde Cloud Forest Preserve. Art galleries include Sarah Dowell's studio (up the hill from the cheese plant) and the Hummingbird Gallery at the preserve. The Hummingbird is a favorite with tourists. The gallery displays spectacular photographs by Michael and Patricia Fogden, and the hummers put on a show-stopping performance as they zoom in to the many feeders in the garden. Open 8:30 a.m. to 4:30 p.m. Monday through Saturday, 10:00 a.m. to 2:30 p.m. on Sunday. Telephone 645-5030.

Chunches in Santa Elena has books, a small laundromat, and a coffee shop where you can get light meals and good desserts.

Santa Elena has a variety of lodging options. Just outside town is the Monteverde Lodge. The hotel has a 15-person Jacuzzi, a huge wood-burning fireplace in the bar/restaurant area, chandeliers, bathtubs, a good gift shop, and views of the surrounding forest through large windows. The gardens were designed to attract hummingbirds and other wildlife. Nature slide shows are presented several nights each week in a small auditorium ($5). The hotel offers transportation to the reserve and bus service from San José on specified days. Rubber boots are available for your walks in the cloud forest. The 27 forest-view rooms are bright and comfortably furnished. Singles are $67, doubles $78. Credit cards are accepted. Meal plans are available. Ask about packages; for example, a two-night tour is $366 per person (double occupancy) including lodging, meals, transportation, and guided walks in the reserve. Monteverde Lodge is owned by Costa Rica Expeditions. Telephone 257-0766 or 222-0333; fax 257-1665.

A bit more than a mile (2 km) on the other side of Santa Elena is the Cloud Forest Lodge, 18 rooms on a 70-acre (28-ha) farm. The two rooms in each house are separated by a concrete wall to cut sound between them. Each has a good-sized tile bath with high windows for nice natural lighting. Rooms have natural-tone tile floors, a private terrace, and high wooden ceilings. The large, separate dining room/lounge area, made of wood and stone, has a grand balcony with a view of the Gulf of Nicoya and surrounding forest. There are about 2 miles (3 km) of forest trails—with no charge for ponchos and boots. Guests can climb in the forest canopy for $35. No smoking is allowed in buildings or on trails. Room rates are: single, $45, double, $55. VISA accepted. Telephone 225-1073, fax 234-1676; in the U.S., telephone (415) 949-1064, fax (415) 949-1068.

Hotel Finca Valverde in Santa Elena has two-room wooden cabins set on a forested hillside, close to town but looking for all the world if they are remote. Each of the ten pleasing rooms has a loft so it can comfortably sleep up to four—a very open feeling. Private baths have showers and tubs. Singles are $45, doubles $50. Credit cards are accepted. The restaurant/bar is open to the public. On a short forest trail on the property, one naturalist saw 60 species of birds in two days. A serpentarium is next door, open 9:00 a.m. to 4:00 p.m., $3. Guests can even help pick coffee at harvest time—it is a farm, after all. The Valverdes offer tours to the Santa Elena reserve and will arrange transportation anywhere in the country. Five Valverde brothers and one sister have a hand in the operation, which is on the farm where they were raised. Telephone 645-5216, fax 645-5157.

Arco Iris Lodge, on one of Santa Elena's hills, must surely have good views of some of the spectacular rainbows (*arco iris* means "rainbow") that grace this high land. Owner Haymo Heyder is working to make the lodge a model of ecologically sound development. He uses natural concoctions rather than insecticides, separates garbage, and is developing an organic garden with his wife, Susanna, to supply produce for the small restaurant. The six rooms are in various buildings—one in a cabin at the edge of the forest and a small stream is called either the honeymoon or presidential cabin. It is special—windows on three sides and a porch facing the forest. All rooms have private baths with hot water, big towels, and ample windows. Prices range from $10 per person for bunk beds in one cabin to $35–$45 for a double. Credit cards not accepted. English, German, Dutch, and Italian also are spoken. Same-day laundry service. Telephone 645-5067, fax 645-5022.

Pensión Santa Elena is in downtown Santa Elena near the bank. Eight of the 11 simple rooms have private baths with hot water. A small information center is off the front porch, and this is the base for the Toruma bus from San José. Vegetarian dishes are available in the restaurant, which is open to the public. Single $15, double $20, including breakfast. Mireya, the owner, can arrange horseback tours, including a one- or two-day trip to San Gerardo Abajo, which has a view of Arenal Volcano. Telephone 645-5051, 645-5298; fax 645-5147.

The Sunset Hotel is about a mile (1.6 km) from Santa Elena off the road to the Santa Elena Reserve. Seven comfortable rooms have private baths with hot water and wonderful views of the Gulf of Nicoya and Chira Island. The dining room, with its pretty tablecloths, has windows on three sides to look out on the manicured garden and, of course, the spectacular sunsets. Carmen and Vitalis Mengel and their children orient you for area tours and rent horses for trips on their farm. A forest trail is open to guests. Doubles are $36, breakfast and taxes included. No credit cards. Telephone/fax 645-5048. The restaurant is open to the public for dinner, reservation required—go early for the splendor in the western sky.

Just out of Santa Elena on the road toward Monteverde is El Sapo Dorado. Its 20 charming rooms in ten bungalows are tucked among fruit trees and gardens in a clearing surrounded by forest. Each room has a quiet, spacious feel to it, with a pretty table and chairs and two queen-size beds. Classic suites have corner fireplaces, with wood provided. Sunset terrace suites have dynamite views of the Gulf of Nicoya, stained glass window panels, and a small refrigerator. The restaurant, open to the public, offers gourmet dining (better to have a reservation in high season). Daily specials may include sailfish Nicoise, beef in peppercorn sauce, or chicken in olive sauce. A vegetarian dish is always available. Desserts are scrumptious. Classic doubles are $65, sunset terrace doubles, $75. El Sapo Dorado does not accept credit cards. Telephone 645-5010, fax 645-5180.

The Cerro Plano area between Santa Elena and Monteverde has several hotels. Hotel Heliconia started out as a small pensión, but its growth to 22 rooms has not diminished its friendly atmosphere. Curtains hand-painted with designs of local flora and fauna grace each room. The large downstairs lobby and lounge area has lots of comfortable couches for conversations before or after dinner. The pleasant rooms are carpeted; private baths have tubs and showers. A single is $50, a double $60. Credit cards are accepted. Floor-to-ceiling glass in the Jacuzzi room gives it a forest setting. There is a small conference room, and the dining room/bar is open to the public, by reservation. The Heliconia has an organic garden project going with a local school, growing vegetables served in the restaurant. The Heliconia runs afternoon and evening tours to Arenal Volcano for $80 per person. Transportation can be provided to or from anywhere in the country. Telephone 645-5109, fax 645-5007.

Next door is El Establo, a 19-room, two-story hotel with its own stables. Carpeted rooms have pretty comforters on beds with orthopedic mattresses, two stylized dressing tables with mirrors, lots of windows, and tiled baths with central hot water. A single is $36, a double $44. Credit cards are accepted. The restaurant is for guests only. Wonderful photos of the early Quaker settlement in Monteverde are in a comfortable downstairs lounge area with a fireplace. Telephone 645-5110, 645-5033 or 225-0569; fax 645-5041.

Hotel de Montaña Monteverde has 31 rooms and a small conference room. It has an indoor Jacuzzi with a great view of forested mountains and the Gulf of Nicoya, a TV room, a lounge area with balcony and rocking chairs, and a bar with a gulf view. Doors to the rooms are decorated with painted butterflies and birds, and each room opens onto a terrace and pretty gardens with flowering plants. A single is $42, a double $62. The honeymoon suite ($95) has its own Jacuzzi and balcony. The dining room is open to the public. The hotel has a nature trail to a small lagoon, rents horses, has guided tours to the reserve, and offers transportation to and from San José. Credit cards accepted. Telephone 645-5046, 224-3050; fax 645-5320, 222-6184.

The Pensión Manakin has 11 rooms, three with private tiled bath and hot water. Windows make rooms bright, and they are very clean. There is a family atmosphere: Mario and Yolanda and their four children are caring hosts. Good typical food is served in the dining room. A single is $6, a double $12 for shared baths, $20 for two persons with private bath. VISA accepted. Telephone/fax 645-5080.

Cabañas Los Pinos' three cabins have kitchenettes equipped with refrigerator, hot plate, and dishes, all spotlessly clean. The one-bedroom cabin costs $35, the two-bedroom $65, the three-bedroom $90. Private baths have central hot water. VISA accepted. The sound of the wind in the pines pervades the grounds; each cabin is very private, set among the trees. Guests are free to explore the forest and the farm. Don Jovino, the owner, offers a horseback tour to the Santa Elena Reserve and to a viewpoint overlooking Arenal. He rents horses and helps arrange transportation. Telephone 645-5252, telephone/fax 645-5005.

Farther along is the Hotel Belmar, up the road next to the gasoline station. The 34 rooms are in two Swiss chalet-type buildings with a commanding view of the slopes of the Tilarán Mountains going down to the Gulf of Nicoya. Guests have reported seeing monkeys and even a quetzal from the balconies. Rooms are large and tastefully furnished, with matching comforters and upholstered armchairs. Many have private balconies; all have private baths with central hot water. Singles are $45, doubles $55. No credit cards are accepted, but personal checks are. There is a lounge area in each building. Meals are served family-style in a large dining room. The hotel arranges transportation, horseback riding, and guided tours to the forest (with rubber boots for rent). Telephone 645-5201, fax 645-5135.

El Bosque Hotel and Restaurant is in Monteverde near the CASEM gift shop. The 22 rooms are in buildings curved around a clearing off the main road, surrounded by trees. Each opens onto a covered porch and has tile floors, rough white-plaster walls, a high wooden ceiling, and a private bath with hot water. Bright bedspreads add color. Singles are $22, doubles $30;

VISA and MasterCard are accepted. The hotel has a small conference room and its own short nature trail. Guests get a 10 percent discount in the Bosque Restaurant, which has been a favorite in Monteverde for years. The Vargas family will treat you well. Telephone/fax 645-5129.

Past the main Monteverde community going toward the Monteverde Cloud Forest Preserve is the Fonda Vela, on the 25-acre (10-ha) Smith farm. The 28 rooms are in buildings situated to give maximum privacy. The surrounding forest offers ample opportunity for bird-watching without leaving the hotel—more than 60 species have been noted. Guests can go on hiking trails through forest on the farm and on guided horseback rides ($8 an hour). Rooms are lovely, with several floor plans. Most are spacious and have gleaming wood floors with area rugs and nice bedspreads. Artwork by Paul Smith is on the walls and in the gallery. Single standard rooms are $50, doubles $59. Junior suites start at $69, double occupancy, suites at $74. Credit cards are accepted. A big open dining room and bar have lots of glass— a small stage offers opportunities for musical presentations. This is the site of the music festival in January–February, and guests are often treated to other musical performances. Telephone 257-1413, 223-1083, 645-5125, or 257-1416; telephone/fax 645-5119; fax 257-1416.

As for eating, Johnny's Pizza serves pizza and more—good food—located in Cerro Plano between Santa Elena and Monteverde. A welcome addition for fine dining is Restaurant De Lucia on the road to the Butterfly Farm. Nice atmosphere, delicious food nicely served, candlelight at dinner, wines. José and Lucia are attentive hosts. Open daily from noon to 9:30 p.m. (reservations best in high season, 645-5337). The Daiquiri in downtown Santa Elena has good food at a reasonable price. A number of small sodas along the road between Santa Elena and Monteverde serve good, inexpensive food: The Cerro Verde across from the gasoline station is one possibility. The Cascada restaurant has a varied menu (it is popular with locals on weekends, and has floor space for dancing), and it and El Bosque have both indoor and outdoor dining. Stella's Bakery and Coffee Shop is across from CASEM.

Travelers can also reach Monteverde from Tilarán on a mostly unpaved road that goes through Quebrada Grande (21 miles, 33 kilometers, from there to Santa Elena). At Cabeceras you can choose to come through Las Nubes or Cañitas—ask which road is better. Between Las Nubes and Santa Elena is Monte de los Olivos, a small community working together in an ecotourist project with the help of the Arenal Conservation Area. There are four cabins with private baths and five cabins with shared baths and hot water. Rates range from $26 for a single to $36 for a double. You can hike on trails in cloud forest with a local guide, see Arenal Volcano, ride horses, enjoy the small lagoon, and get to know the community, many of whom share the last name of Barquero. The restaurant is open to the public. Telephone 645-5059, fax 645-5131.

Two companies give direct bus service to Monteverde, one departing San José from the Coca Cola district and one from Toruma Youth Hostel. See Practical Extras. The Toruma bus will deliver you to your hotel, while the other lets you off on the main road. If you arrive at night, have your flashlight handy. Both stop in Santa Elena before proceeding to Monteverde. Some hotels will pick up from the bus with advance notice. Public buses from Puntarenas and Tilarán go to Santa Elena, and taxis are available there to get you to hotels elsewhere.

Pacific Northwest Beaches and Upper Nicoya Peninsula

Access to popular beach and natural history destinations in this area by land is principally through two routes off of the Inter-American Highway: across the Tempisque River by ferry to the Nicoya Peninsula or west from Liberia, which gives the option of the Nicoya Peninsula as well as northwest Pacific beaches. Travelers may also cross the Gulf of Nicoya from Puntarenas to Playa Naranjo and head northwest on the Nicoya Peninsula, but that is slow going and hinges on ferry crossings (see the preceding Puntarenas–Montezuma Route section). Scheduled airline service from San José on Travelair or SANSA quickly moves travelers to Liberia or to Tamarindo, Nosara, Sámara (Carrillo), and Punta Islita. Practical Extras at the end of the book gives bus, ferry, and airline schedules.

Let us begin with the route from Liberia. As you drive out of town, remember to look on the left for the Centro y Tienda Artesanal, the artisan cooperative mentioned under the earlier Inter-American to Liberia and Points North section. The Daniel Oduber Quirós airport is farther up the road, on the right.

An increasing number of road signs now make travel in this area less by guess and by golly, and hotel advertisements also help direct drivers. The first cluster of beach hotels in the northwest Pacific is on a road that heads west just south of Comunidad, and the quicker land route is through Liberia rather than crossing the Tempisque.

To reach the ambitious government-directed Gulf of Papagayo project, take the road toward Playa Hermosa at the junction before Playa del Coco and follow the signs. At press time, two new Papagayo hotels are open—Costa Smeralda and Malinche Real; others may be by the time you arrive. In the works since 1974, the Papagayo project encompasses 17 beaches, mainly on Culebra Bay, and almost 5,000 acres (2,000 ha). The plan projects thousands of hotel rooms, a marina, a golf course, vacation homes, and shopping centers on land leased to developers. The project has been

Putting thatch on a rancho by the sea (Ree Strange Sheck)

considered a measuring stick for the government's commitment to environmentally responsible tourism.

Costa Smeralda has a spectacular Mediterranean-style reception area, dining room, conference center, and gift shop in the main building. It has 64 rooms in buildings terraced on the gentle hills that front Playa Buena. The bright white walls and red roofs of the resort hotel accent the landscaped lawn and beautiful plantings of palms, crotons, and other colorful tropical vegetation. The multilevel main building is arches and wide verandas and pretty railings on terraces and stairways. Its views are of the artistically curved adult pool and children's pool below, a large thatched rancho that houses a snack bar, a sprinkling of small ranchos for lounge areas, and then the blue of the Pacific and hills across the bay. The broad, curved staircases leading to the pool and paths to the rooms seem to lend celebrity status to those who walk them. The large, glass-fronted rooms open onto individual tiled porches. Each has a telephone and remote-controlled air conditioning that allows one to set the temperature and the time to turn on and shut off. Each room has satellite TV, colorful matching print drapes and bed coverings (some with king-size beds), reading lamps, big closets, and nice watercolors on the wall. Big bathrooms have a separate toilet area, large dressing area, hair dryer, big towels, and lighted mirrors. The four suites are bilevel, with the bedroom area above the sitting room. Emerald fixtures in the bathroom complement the jade-green tile; each has a Jacuzzi and bidet. Rooms are $140 for up to two persons, suites $240. Meal plans are available, as is room service. The restaurant specializes in international cuisine with Italian and French specialties, and it is open to the public as well, reservations preferred. English, Italian, French, and German spoken. The tour desk can arrange snorkeling, diving (with training in the pool), rafting, bird-watching, and horseback riding, with trips to Playa Grande, Rincón de la Vieja, Los Inocentes, and other destinations. Car rental available. Small patches of forest remain around the hotel, so howlers are present, along with iguanas, raccoons, coatis, hummingbirds, and many other bird species. Transportation is available from the Liberia or San José airport. Credit cards accepted. Telephone 670-0044 or 670-0032; fax 670-0379.

Malinche Real Beach Resort breaks new ground in Costa Rica. It has a full-service hotel and four restaurants (including a macrobiotic one with healthy drinks and snacks). It has a health club with indoor and outdoor Jacuzzis, sauna, lap pool, wave-resistance pool, exercise machines, aerobic classes, massage, and weights. About 60 acres (24 ha) of the 100-acre (40-ha) development are in forest, where guests can enjoy guided walks on five trails. There is horseback riding along the beach and in the forest as well as snorkeling and kayaking. Two-person sailboats, mountain bikes, water bikes, diving, and tennis are available.

From the entry gate at the top of the hill, the complex spreads out on the sloping land down to the beach. Attractive bungalow-type buildings hold 100 rooms, each with its own deck for enjoying spectacular ocean sunsets. Each room has a small refrigerator, telephone, cable TV, air conditioning and ceiling fan, king- or two queen-size beds, and matching drapes and comforters. Baths have dressing areas, bathtubs and showers, and big lighted mirrors. Singles are $211, doubles $271, including meals, all drinks, nonmotor sports, and health club and fitness facilities. Dinner at Da Vinci's Italian Restaurant is formal, by reservation only. The other restaurants offer more casual dining (one is poolside), and room service is available. Three pools in a tiered arrangement offer a shallow area for children and well as a deeper pool and the one with the in-pool bar. Programs for children include swimming and tennis lessons, skin diving, guided nature hike, art classes, table games, and storytime. There is a gift shop, a fine jewelry store, and a beauty shop. The tour desk helps guests with trips outside of the resort, and car rental is available. Credit cards accepted. English, Italian, German, and French spoken. Telephone 233-8566 or 670-0033; fax 221-0739 or 670-0300.

The next beach area south is Playa Hermosa, where it is not uncommon to see dolphins in the bay or howler monkeys moving through the trees, especially in the dry season. There is a daily express bus from San José.

At Hotel Condovac La Costa, a single or double room is $110 in high season. There are 54 rooms with air conditioning and fans, and 101 air-conditioned villas with bedroom, living room, bath, kitchenette, and terrace overlooking the bay, $140. Credit cards are accepted. The hotel also has pools, tennis, a restaurant, disco, mini-market, tour agency, poolside bars, and beachfront. Motorized carts take guests around the hillside resort complex. Also available is transportation to parks and from San José, scuba diving (including classes), snorkeling, sport fishing, jet-skiing, waterskiing, sailboating, and boat tours, plus kayaking, windsurfing, tennis, and hiking. The hotel has a day trip to a secluded beach where guests can swim, explore, and enjoy a barbecue. Telephone 221-8949 or 233-1862; fax 222-5637.

Hotel de Playa El Velero, owned and operated by Canadians, has 13 rooms. Velero means sailboat, and the hotel has one of its own for a variety of activities: a sailing trip with a box lunch is $55. Scuba and snorkeling excursions are arranged, as is a sunset cruise. Rooms are light and airy, with nice closet space, tile floors, ceiling fans, and hot water in private baths. The restaurant is open to the public, and there is a bar at poolside in a garden setting. A single or double is $69, air conditioning extra. Credit cards are accepted. Coming from the south, El Velero is off the second entrance to Playa Hermosa. Staff is helpful. Telephone 670-0330, telephone/ fax 670-0310.

Playa Hermosa Inn has nine rooms with fans plus two air-conditioned apartments with two bedrooms, kitchenette, and balcony. A single or double is $55, including full breakfast and private baths with hot water. The apartment is $100 for two. Credit cards are accepted. There is an air of quiet relaxation from the moment one enters the reception area with its comfortable furniture and view of the garden and beach beyond. A covered pavilion by the water has hammocks and chairs, and there is a grill where guests can cook their catch of the day. Only breakfast is served, but restaurants are nearby. Car rental arranged; secure parking. Since the owner, Pioneer Tours, also has Pioneer Raft, rafting tours are easily arranged. There are also kayak and snorkeling tours and visits to nearby parks. Telephone/fax 670-0163, or in the U.S. and Canada (800) 288-2107.

Cabinas Playa Hermosa is a quiet, laid-back place that has 22 rooms with private baths and shower-head hot water. The rooms are basic but clean, with tile floors and screened windows. A white-faced monkey and a pair of coatis roam the gardens, offering good photo opportunities. A single is $30, double is $40, including taxes. Credit cards are not accepted. The restaurant is open to the public and specializes in Italian food. A small boat for up to seven people is available for fishing or tours. Horse rental is $10 per hour, with a trip possible to a nearby farm with tropical dry forest where you may see monkeys and trogons. Tours can be arranged to area parks. Telephone/fax 670-0136.

Villa del Sueño, off of the road into the first entrance to Playa Hermosa, is a "house of dreams" (referring to its Spanish name) created by owners Claude, Silvia, and Robert. Travelers enter across a broad expanse of green lawn with inviting shade trees to receive a warm welcome in the large, open area that is both comfortable lounge (with cushioned wicker furniture) and dining room. The 20 rooms are large, some on the ground floor and some with hot water. All have private baths, rocking chairs, ceiling fans, shuttered windows, and pretty bedspreads; $45 for a double. Small children not encouraged. The beach is about 200 meters away; the sparkling pool, a few steps from the veranda.

Meals are a highlight, from a breakfast that can be crepes, French toast, fresh fruit, or eggs in various forms to lunch with something Italian generally included. The dinner menu has three choices of main dishes, with soup, salad, and appetizers such as calamari offered, along with desserts. The restaurant is open to the public also, but reservations are a good idea, especially in high season. Owners offer trip planning for anywhere in the country and can arrange local tours. English, French, German, and Italian also spoken. Credit cards accepted. Telephone/fax 670-0027.

Along the beach in Playa Hermosa is a complex with a small supermarket, a nice gift shop, a water-sports shop, and the Bar y Restaurante Aqua Sport, a restaurant with rustic decor and good food—seafood and Italian specialties, telephone 670-0450.

If you continue straight instead of taking the Playa Hermosa cutoff mentioned earlier, you arrive at two other popular beach destinations: Playa del Coco and Ocotal. A daily bus from San José and several from Liberia go to Playa del Coco each day.

Coming into Playa del Coco are two hotels: Hotel Resort La Flor de Itabo and Rancho Armadillo.

Signs will tell you where to turn left for Rancho Armadillo, a retreat in the mountains with a view of the coastline stretching in the distance. Actually, the hotel is only a bit more than a mile (2 km) from the beach , and a shuttle is provided. Owner Jim Procter offers six rooms with private baths (hot water), $45 for a double; a suite with a kitchenette, $40; and a house with a full kitchen, $80. The house is a beauty, with wooden pegs in the floors and dovetail joints in windows. The ocean-view restaurant, Wahoo Sports Bar and Grill, attracts locals as well as visitors, with a menu not to be found elsewhere in these parts: Cajun shrimp or blackened chicken, a Texas hamburger, chile without beans, foot-long subs, and more. A TV is hooked up to a satellite dish, especially for sports viewing. Jim is pleased to set up horseback riding, hiking, fishing, diving, and windsurfing, as well as a trip to pre-Columbian sites at Culebra Bay. VISA and MasterCard accepted. Telephone 670-0108, telephone/fax 223-3535; fax 670-0441, in the U.S. (305) 484-4255.

Hotel Resort La Flor de Itabo is less than a mile from downtown and the beach (1.3 km). It has eight air-conditioned rooms in the main hotel building, with phone, satellite TV, and private baths with hot water; single $50, double $55. Four apartments (for up to four people) have kitchenettes, air conditioning, and baths with tubs and hot water; $80. Ten bungalow rooms have ceiling fans and hot-water baths, $38. All rates include taxes, credit cards accepted. The restaurant, with views to the tropical gardens, specializes in seafood and Italian dishes, and there is a pool and a large bar and a casino. La Flor de Itabo runs its own tours: boating on the Tempisque River, horseback to Rincón de la Vieja, a barbecue at Zapotal Beach, visit to Lomas Barbudal reserve, and overnight to Arenal. Sportfishing is also a specialty. English, French, Italian, and German also spoken. Telephone 670-0011 or 670-0292; fax 670-0003.

In the town of Playa del Coco, which is popular with tico tourists, are a number of lodging possibilities. Here are three:

New to downtown is Hotel Coco Verde, a 33-room, two-story hotel that was not yet finished when I visited. There are broad open terraces above the street, with a pool, poolside bar, restaurant, and gift shop. Rooms are air-conditioned and have private baths with central hot water—room service available. Double $35, VISA and MasterCard accepted. English and Italian also spoken. Telephone/fax 670-0494.

Hotel Villa Flores is an eight-room bed and breakfast with ceiling fans and private baths and shower-head hot water. Single $25, double $35; $45 for two persons in the suite, which is air conditioned. Just 1½ blocks from the beach, the hotel is set in an ample garden, with an open dining and lounge area downstairs, where the coffee is always on. The restaurant specializes in pastas, and a full breakfast is served. Villa Flores has boat and surfing tours and a day trip to a beach in the Gulf of Papagayo. Telephone/fax 670-0269.

Hotel Luna Tica has 15 rustic rooms on the beach, clean but basic, and 16 in a two-story wooden addition across the road from the beach. Rates range from $13 for a single to $17 for a double, taxes included. A few have air conditioning, the rest fans—no hot water. VISA accepted. A large open-air restaurant is next to the beachfront cabins. where you can get a full breakfast for less than $2.50. Telephone 670-0279, fax 670-0127.

Many small sodas and restaurants are on the street into town and near the central park. Try the Papagayo across from the park for good dining.

Just 2 miles (3 km) from Playa del Coco is Ocotal Beach, small and beautiful. The tide pools are fascinating here. At the north end of the beach, caves shoot the water of the incoming tide back out with tremendous force. Big Guanacaste iguanas are almost always moving about at the edge of the sandy beach.

Hotel Ocotal has a spectacular view of coastline and sea from its rooms and restaurant on the cliff above the beach. Sunset from here is an occasion. Each of the 28 rooms and three suites on the cliffside opens onto a terrace with an unforgettable sea view. Make time to enjoy it from your terrace, the pretty tropical swimming pool area at the end of the path, or from the Jacuzzi. In addition, 18 rooms and three suites are along the beach below, and six duplex bungalows on the hillside contain 12 huge rooms with a large dressing area and bathroom. A pool is located by each of these areas, as well. Each of the tastefully furnished accommodations has air conditioning and ceiling fan, telephone, satellite TV, small refrigerator, coffeemaker, furnishings with bamboo accents, double or king beds with pretty comforters, and private bath with central hot water. Standard rooms are $80 for a single, $90 for a double; suites are $170, and bungalow rooms are $105. Rates are a bit more for Easter and Christmas seasons and less from mid-August to mid-December.

The restaurant in the main building serves a breakfast buffet and lunch and dinner either inside or on the covered terrace—again, the views invite lingering. Notice the great timbers in the remarkable roof structure of the dining room. Meal plans are available for $49, open menu, including tips and taxes. The Father Rooster Bar on the beach, open for lunch or dinner, has a "barefoot atmosphere" for informal dining and drinks. A shuttle for the beach, restaurant, and rooms is available with a phone call.

Hotel Ocotal offers an exercise room, car rental, and a lighted tennis court. Its tour desk arranges trips to see turtles, parks, and a volcano. Other activities include sportfishing, horseback riding, mountain biking, surfing, and boat cruises along isolated beaches and coastal islands. Scuba diving is a specialty here. A complete dive shop rents equipment, including cameras for underwater photography, and offers diving instruction. A two-tank boat dive is $55, a night dive $40. A $500 dive package, one of several available, includes five days and four nights, double occupancy, two days of boat diving, tanks, weights, guide, breakfast, and round-trip transportation from San José. Telephone 670-0321 or 222-4259; fax 670-0083 or 222-8483.

Hotel Villa Casa Blanca is a charming ten-room inn at Ocotal. Owners Janey and James Seip will probably join you for breakfast in the tropical

Ocotal Beach from Hotel Ocotal (Ree Strange Sheck)

garden setting in a rancho beside a small swimming pool. Both the company and the breakfast are delightful—besides the typical gallo pinto, guests find Belgian waffles, fruit, breads, and some of the best pancakes around. Splashes of color abound in the unique rooms: comforters, drapes, stool or chair cushions, shower curtains, artwork, and plants. The second-floor honeymoon suite, in blues and whites, has a canopy bed, a breakfast corner, high wood ceilings, comfortable couch, a view of the sea, and a bathroom with a raised tub on a tile platform, $80.

Staying in any of the rooms is like being in the guest room of an elegant home. Each has a private bath with central hot water, air conditioning ($5 extra) and ceiling fans. Single rooms are $40, doubles $50, including breakfast. A suite with a fully equipped kitchen living area and bedroom is $90. No smoking here. VISA and MasterCard accepted though there is a surcharge.

Though lunch and dinner are not served here, three restaurants are within walking distance. Tours to Arenal, the Tempisque River, Palo Verde, Santa Rosa, and turtle-nesting sites are arranged. Horses or kayaks can be rented for $10 per hour. The small gift shop has a nice selection of clothing and handcrafts, and a refrigerator in the reception area is stocked with cold beer and soft drinks. The Spanish-style villa, practically hidden in a tropical garden, is a short walk from the beach. The Seips also handle rental of three neighboring houses, some with pools and Jacuzzis, one with five bedrooms and four baths. Telephone/fax 670-0448.

Vista Ocotal has air-conditioned rooms, master studios, and villas, 26 in all. The master studios have two double beds, a microwave and refrigerator, and a bathroom with a Jacuzzi bathtub and bidet, $79 for two. Two-story villas have fully furnished kitchens, living rooms, and bedrooms, $90. Standard rooms are $50, single or double, including breakfast. There is a restaurant/bar, swimming pool, and barbecue area. Tours are arranged, including area excursions, diving, and horseback riding. Credit cards accepted. Telephone 293-4330 or 670-0429; fax 293-4371 or 670-0436; in the U.S. (800) 251-1962.

Another option for diving is Bill Beard's Diving Safaris, located at Ocotal on the road to the beach. Two-tank dive trips include a no-frills option for $40 (minimum four persons) or a deluxe trip (no minimums) for $60. Night dives are $45, and long-range dive trips are $80 to Catalina Island and $110 to Bat Island. Snorkeling trips are $26. Stop by the diving center, which hums with activity, or call to check on a variety of diving certification courses. Bill has been diving off of Costa Rica's shores for more than 20 years. His company also handles diving operations for several hotels at Playa Hermosa, Papagayo, and Ocotal. Telephone/fax 670-0012; in the U.S., telephone (407) 724-5474, fax (407) 768-1443.

For the next cluster of accommodations along the beach, continue south on Highway 21 to Filadelfia, Belén, and Huacas—a junction where you can go north, south, or west to beach areas. Let's go north first. Signs to hotels at Conchal, Flamingo, and Pan de Azúcar (Sugar Beach) will guide you.

The long curve of white sand beach at Conchal is beautiful. At press time, the luxurious Hotel Melia Conchal is under construction there. It may be open by your arrival. Telephone 654-4123 or 257-5505; fax 654-4181; e-mail mconchal@solracsa.co.cr.

The Hotel Aurola Playa Flamingo has 125 rooms, suites, and apartments in two complexes, one on the beach and one with a view of the bay. The hotel has three pools, restaurants, bars, parking, a boutique, casino, disco, gym, sauna, tour agency, boat charters, and diving (with instructor). Large rooms are nicely furnished, with air conditioning and fans, satellite TV, minibar, and baths with tubs, showers, and hair dryers. Single or double starts at $75 in the bay-view rooms, $110-$120 in the beach-side rooms, with suites starting at $150 and the apartment for six persons at $300. Credit cards accepted. The hotel offers transportation from San José on Monday, Wednesday, Friday, and Sunday for $30 one-way. Telephone 233-7233 or 654-4010; fax 222-0090 or 255-1036; in the U.S. (800) 2AUROLA.

Also on Flamingo Beach is Villas Flamingo. The 24 two-bedroom, three-bath villas sleep up to six people. Downstairs are the living room, dining area, bath, and kitchen with a full stove—no hot plates here. The master bedroom upstairs has its own balcony. Lots of glass on the front—views of the landscaped grounds, pool, and beach beyond. Villas Flamingo has no restaurant, but there are a number nearby, and there is daily maid service. The rate is $125 for one or two people, $135 for three, taxes included. Weekly and monthly rates are available. Telephone/fax 654-4215. There are daily public buses from San José to Flamingo.

Farther up the road is beautiful Pan de Azúcar beach and Hotel Sugar Beach. The tranquillity always makes me want to linger—the curve of the small bay, the rocky headlands, the forest. There is a sense of intimacy with nature here. An uncrowded, white sand beach beckons; the hotel's large open-air restaurant invites leisurely dining. Chefs prepare nightly specials— no fixed eating hours here, so guests can choose when to eat from 7:00 a.m. to 9:30 p.m. Each of 22 rooms in duplexes fronting the beach have windows on three sides, high ceilings, Spanish-tile floors, either hardwood or wicker furniture in the sitting area, a small refrigerator, air conditioning and ceiling fans, and private bath with central hot water (some tubs). Doubles from $90 to $125 depending on size. Four refurbished original rooms are $80 for two. A honeymoon suite is $150. An apartment suite with bedroom (king-size bed), living room with sofa sleepers, and kitchenette is $200. A beach house with three bedrooms, two baths, and equipped kitchen is $1,800 per week. Credit cards are accepted.

Hotel Sugar Beach has boat excursions to other secluded beaches, surfing trips to Witches Rock, and sightseeing trips. There are sea kayaks, canoes, surfboards, snorkeling equipment, boogie boards, etc. The hotel arranges fishing, scuba diving, turtle tours, horseback riding, estuary tours, and car rentals. There is a swimming pool. You are sure to hear monkeys and see iguanas, and the surrounding forest makes for good birding. No other hotels are on Pan de Azúcar beach. Sugar Beach offers a $20 round-trip pickup service from Tamarindo, which is accessible by bus and air. Telephone 654-4242, fax 654-4239; in the U.S. and Canada (800) 458-4735.

If you go west from Huacas instead of north, you come to Playa Grande and Las Baulas National Park, which protects an important nesting site of the big leatherback turtle. Hotel Las Tortugas is a few steps from the beach where the leatherbacks nest from October to March, and turtles can be seen year-round. Owners Louis Wilson and Marianela Pastor have worked to protect this important wildlife area and educate guests about turtle-watching. Because turtles are sensitive to light, none of the 11 rooms or suites has views to the south where the nesting beach is.

Each of the rooms is different, though all have private baths (some with hot water) and air conditioning or fans. Rooms are $85, larger suites with king-size beds and living areas are $125, including taxes. Credit cards are not accepted. There is a restaurant, small turtle-shaped pool, and Jacuzzi. Las Tortugas offers deep-sea fishing and estuary excursions by canoe or boat and also arranges horseback riding. Louis suggests that the express bus from San José to Santa Cruz is a good option if you do not have a car and do not want to fly. A taxi from the stand at the station to Playa Grande costs about $24; total time from San José is 4½ hours. Telephone/fax 680-0765. Rental houses are available.

Villa Baula is also at Playa Grande. Twenty rooms and five bungalows are in thatched wooden structures. All have private baths with central hot water and ceiling fans. There is a restaurant/bar and two swimming pools. Double rooms are $80. Bungalows, which have two bedrooms, a living area, and minibar, are $120. Credit cards are accepted. The hotel offers estuary trips, horseback riding, bicycling, and turtle tours in season. Staff will arrange kayaking, snorkeling, and surfing. Telephone 257-7676, fax 257-1098, telephone/fax 680-0869.

Before you get to the beach, you will pass Cabinas Playa Grande. Standard rooms are $21 for up to three persons; those with kitchenettes are $24 for two, up to $53 for six persons, taxes included. Rooms are basic but clean, with fans and private baths. The restaurant serves typical Costa Rican food. Staff will pick you up from the bus in Huacas or Matapalo. Telephone 237-2552, fax 260-3991.

The road southwest from Huacas goes through Villarreal to Tamarindo, a growing town that borders Las Baulas National Park (see Chapter 12), an area important for turtles, birds, crocodiles, and mangroves.

SANSA and Travelair make the 40-minute flight from San José to Tamarindo daily. The daily express bus takes about five hours. Here are some lodging possibilities.

On a hill above town is Hotel El Jardín del Edén, a complex of five Mediterranean-style villas, two swimming pools (one with a swim-up bar under a thatched roof), restaurants, and Jacuzzi. The beach is five minutes away. Each of the 18 rooms has an ocean view, air conditioning and ceiling fans, refrigerator, mini-bar, pretty bamboo furniture, and private bath with central hot water. Most have a terrace or balcony. The least-expensive single is $80; larger rooms are $105 for a single and $120 for a double. An ample buffet breakfast is included. There are two apartments with a full kitchen, dining room, and large terrace, $140 for two. Credit cards are accepted. The owners are Italian and French, a heritage reflected in the restaurant menu— fine dining. Herbs are grown on the property. Staff members will help arrange tours, and the hotel offers fishing packages. Telephone/fax 220-2096, 653-0111.

Hotel Tamarindo Diría is on the beach. A large garden area stretches from the terraces to the sand. To diminish impact on nesting turtles, the hotel has special lights in the garden and does not illuminate the beach. The 70 rooms in the three-story hotel are tastefully furnished and have both air condition-ing and ceiling fans as well as a mini-bar, telephone, and cable TV. Private baths even have hair dryers. There is a large swimming pool, tennis, a gift shop, restaurants, and car rental. Standard singles are $97, doubles $112, including a buffet breakfast. Credit cards are accepted. A hotel microbus charges $70 from San José. Telephone 289-8616 or 680-0080; fax 255-2981 or 680-0442.

Six thatched octagonal bungalows with a million-dollar view of the turquoise waters of Tamarindo Bay welcome guests to Bella Vista Village Resort. Under the high conical roof of each is an equipped kitchen, living area (with futon fold-out bed), and a sleeping loft with single and double beds. Full of light, with an airy feeling, each has a ceiling fan and a private bath with shower-head hot water. Spaced at varying levels around a pretty pool, the bungalows look like a tiny, planned village, with the bright white of their walls brilliant against rock wall terracing and the green of the gardens. It is a short walk down a gentle slope to town and the beach. Single $80, double $90, $15 per person extra. VISA accepted. Hosts Gabe and Judy promise personalized service in arranging nature trips, horseback riding, scuba, snorkeling, boating and canoeing, parasailing, or sportfishing—even making dinner reservations. Telephone/fax 653-0036.

Hotel Pasatiempo is downtown, about 2 blocks from the beach. Ten rooms in thatched bungalows are scattered in landscaped gardens, each with its own private terrace. Baths have central hot water, and some have bidets. Reading lamps and good lighting on the mirrors are nice features. Cooling is with ceiling fans or air conditioning. There is a pool near the restaurant and bar area, and owner Ron will help you set up guided tours, horseback riding, snorkeling, or scuba diving. Bicycles are available. Pasatiempo now has a cappuccino bar. Rooms are $59 for two people. Credit cards are accepted. Telephone/fax 653-0036.

Hotel El Milagro is across the road from the beach. You can hear the sound of the waves as you go to sleep. The 32 rooms have high wooden ceil-ings, tile floors, and central hot water in private baths. Wooden, louvered double doors open onto private porches to create a nice indoor-outdoor liv-ing space. English, German, and Dutch also are spoken. Be sure to talk with some of the young people waiting tables in the dining room. They are study-ing ecotourism and are enthusiastic about their work. The dining room is open to the pool and gardens. Staff members are helpful. Turtle-watching tours, estuary trips, horseback riding, and surfing are available. A room for two with a fan is $50 for a single, $60 for a double; buffet breakfast included. Air conditioning is $5 more. VISA and American Express are accepted. Telephone/fax 653-0096.

Cabinas Zullymar is at the center of town, with the restaurant on the beach and the hotel across the street. Note the pretty carved doors on each of the 27 rooms, which are simply furnished and clean; all have private baths. The hotel offers parking and car rental, and arranges tours of the estuary, surfing, and snorkeling. The rate for one or two people in rooms with fans is $24; with fans and refrigerators, it is $30; with air conditioning, refrigerators, and central hot water in the baths, it is $47. Credit cards are not accepted. Manager Edwin Martinez is a happy, helpful man. Telephone 226-4732; telephone/fax 653-0140; fax 286-0191.

As you drive over the back roads of the Nicoya Peninsula, you will see local residents looking for a ride; bus service is thin to nonexistent in some parts. You can meet some interesting people who just need a lift to the next town or crossroads. We once picked up a one-armed man waving a big saw; he turned out to be a deaf-mute, but he let us know where he wanted out. A few area hotels offer car rental, which allows you to get to the area initially by bus or air and then explore on your own. Road signs are far too sparse for strangers, though hotel signs help some. Four-wheel-drive is advisable on some of the unpaved roads in the rainy season.

The Junquillal area is another popular beach destination on the Nicoya Peninsula. Four express buses a day go from San José to Santa Cruz, where you can get a bus or taxi connection. There is also bus service from Liberia. If you are driving, you can get to Santa Cruz on paved roads either from Liberia or by crossing over to the peninsula via the Tempisque ferry. Santa Cruz is a picturesque town (population 16,611) with streets of paving stones.

The nearby town of Guaitil is worth a visit for Chorotega Indian-style pottery. Someone at the community gift shop can probably tell you who is making pots that day so you can see the process. Pots are also sold in front of potters' houses, and the shop will pack pieces so they are safe for travel. The outdoor ovens are used not only to fire pottery but also to bake bread or cook a pig.

From Santa Cruz, get to the Junquillal area on the road passing through Ventisiete de Abril to Paraíso. (I wonder how many towns named "Paradise" there are in Costa Rica.) Hotel Iguanazul—(watch for the signs)—is a friendly place on Playa Blanca, 19 miles (30 km) west of Santa Cruz. The 24 rooms have a Southwestern U.S. flavor with white plaster walls, red brick floors, and exposed beams on the high ceilings. Each has a private bath with central hot water, TV, ceiling fan, and potted plants. Each is decorated with folk-art rugs and wall hangings. A single with fan is $48, a double $60; with air, $60 and $75. Credit cards are accepted. The hotel sits on a bluff above the beach with nothing else around. The overall impression is one of sky and sea. The hub of activity is the dining room/bar/pool area, which has a grand view of the Pacific. The setting sun is spectacular. In addition to horseback riding, surfing, snorkeling, fishing, ping pong, billiards, volleyball, and the swimming pool, guests in high season may be treated to a typical night with marimba. Hotel Iguanazul is just one hour from the Ostional wildlife refuge, and beach walks from the hotel may bring you face to face with coatis, armadillos, iguanas, or monkeys. Ask about possibilities for hotel transportation from Santa Cruz or San José. Telephone 680-0783, telephone/fax 232-1423.

Playa Junquillal is also south of Santa Cruz, just beyond Paraíso. The long, uncrowded, dark-sand beach invites long walks. A few turtles find their way here to lay eggs. Two hotels attractive for nature travelers are Villa Serena and Hotel Antumalal.

Villa Serena is nestled among the palms. Once, as I ate a delicious lunch on the upstairs terrace looking out over the Pacific, a bird of the oriole family fed its young in a nest that seemed to hang by a thread from the tip of a palm branch. It is one of those terraces where you could probably sit happily for two or three years. The ten rooms are in the main two-story building and bungalows around the pool. Each has a fan and a large private bath with central hot water and a dressing area; $65 for two. Credit cards are accepted. A candlelight dinner with classical music and the sound of the ocean in the background brings each day to a restful close. The German owner has added a honeymoon suite—a round tower-like room—where even the bathroom has a view to the sea. There is even an ice machine, rare in small hotels in Costa Rica.

Guests at Villa Serena can stargaze at night—the telescope stands ready—and are welcome to use the library. Table games are available in comfortable lounges near the dining terrace. There is a tennis court and horse rental. Staff members can arrange turtle- and dolphin-watching, deep-sea fishing, and transportation from the airport at Tamarindo or from Santa Cruz. Telephone/fax 680-0573.

Hotel Antumalal is a piece farther down the road. It is beautifully situated in lush tropical gardens. The open-air restaurant and some rooms are on the gentle slope that descends to the sea. The rest of the 23 rooms are in bungalows tucked in gardens going down to the pool next to the beach. The high-ceilinged rooms are large, with red brick floors and rough-plastered white walls. Windows on two sides provide good ventilation, and there are ceiling fans. Each room has a porch with a hammock and table and chairs for dozing, reading, or watching the birds among the flowering plants. Private baths with central hot water also have bidets. Singles are $75, doubles $85. Nine suites with two king-size beds, small refrigerator, and living area are $100. Credit cards are accepted.

Guests can hike around a rocky headland at low tide to walk along the beach to an estuary for good bird-watching, or take a road through dry forest. I was delighted to spot a colorful member of the trogon family. Tide pools along the mostly unpeopled beaches invite exploration. You will hear howler monkeys, some of whom spend most of the day in trees near the dining area and upper rooms. I photographed a troop, including several babies, after breakfast; they were still dozing at lunchtime. The hotel offers excursions to Palo Verde, Caño Negro, Ostional, and Playa Grande, and has a tennis court and horse rental. From November to May, diving is offered. Meals in the open-air dining room have an international flair. Good food. Telephone/fax 680-0506.

I drove during the rainy season through the coastal hills from Junquillal all the way south to Playa Carrillo. Some of the stretches are gutbusters, and there are rivers to ford, but the landscape is interesting. Four-wheel drive is recommended; count on many 25-mph (40-kph) stretches. Places along this road may be reached more easily from Nicoya and Mansión or by flying to Sámara or Nosara. A word of rainy season caution on this coastal route: there are two large, as-yet-unbridged rivers, one between Junquillal and Ostional and the other between Ostional and Nosara. Ask at your hotel and in villages along the way whether they are passable.

Near Nosara is Ostional Wildlife Refuge (see Chapter 12). Along with Nancite Beach in Santa Rosa, it is among the world's important nesting sites for olive ridley turtles. During the day, there is good bird-watching along the estuary. If you are there on an evening when the turtle *arribadas* begin, you may see horses with sacks of turtle eggs slung over them, tied up at the local cantina. These eggs were taken legally in a managed harvest by the turtle cooperative that patrols the beaches against poachers.

South along the coast from Ostional is Nosara (population 3,430). Travelair and SANSA land there; a daily express bus from San José and a bus from Nicoya offer other options.

Hotel Playas de Nosara is one of those gracious beach hotels in harmony with its natural surroundings. Though many rooms offer a view of the sea, it is hard to spot the hotel among the trees from the beach just below. Expansive vistas of sky, sea, and shoreline from the open-air dining room would surely bring a bit of balance to even the most restless mind. Chefs

A place to dream—Hotel Nosara (Ree Strange Sheck)

from the San Francisco Culinary Academy serve Asian and Mexican specialties as well as fresh fish with a California flair.

Rock outcroppings on the beach create wonderful pools at low tide for exploration, swimming and snorkeling. The hotel arranges turtle nesting tours, river trips for birding, horse rentals, and a day trip to a nearby ranch, led by local guides. There are trails on the property. English, French, German, Greek, and Italian also are spoken by owner John Fraser.

The 20 rooms are in several buildings set among flowered gardens. Each is large, with brick floors, a ceiling fan, louvered doors to the balcony, decorative wall hangings, table and chairs, and private bath with central hot water. With a sea view, rooms are $100; without the view, singles are $75 and doubles $85. Credit cards are not accepted. From a spacious observation area above the dining room, one has a panoramic vista of the coastline, the pretty swimming pool below (finally finished!), and forest and gardens. Telephone/fax 680-0495.

Estancia Nosara, on a shady street a short walk from the beach, has eight rooms around a kidney-shaped pool. Rooms with air conditioning are $52 for a single, $62 for a double; with fans, $45 and $52. Each sleeps up to four people and has a kitchenette, dining nook, and private bath with showerhead hot water. Rooms have high wooden ceilings and Spanish tile floors. There is a pool and tennis court; horses are available, and there is a tour to

Ostional and a crocodile/bird tour on the Nosara River. There is a rancho bar and large open-air dining room. Telephone/fax 680-0378.

Rancho Suizo Lodge is just down the road. Ten rooms are in thatched bungalows, each with its own porch. Rooms are bright, with high ceilings, fans, and private baths with shower-head hot water. Singles are $30, doubles $40. Three new bungalows with large rooms, ceiling fans, and hot-water baths are $50. Credit cards are not accepted. The Swiss owners, René and Ruth, are gracious hosts and can help you out in English, French, Italian, and German as well as Spanish. The restaurant, open to the public, includes dishes from their homeland; flags of the Swiss cantons hang in the pleasant, thatch-roofed dining room. Tours go to Ostional for turtle-watching and to Nosara for bird-watching. Other options include hiking, snorkeling, horse-back riding, photo treks, and fishing. Ask about camping. A whirlpool in the garden and the Pirate Bar near the Playa Pelada beach are gathering places for guests. Though lodging is not on the beach, it is only steps away, close enough to hear the sound of the surf. Telephone 233-1888, fax 257-0404, telephone/fax 284-9669.

Nosara Retreat offers an adventure-wellness vacation in a pristine setting. Amba Camp and Don Stapleton are directors of this renewal center nestled among the hills and trees of Playa Guiones, offering hatha yoga classes, breathing and mediation classes, nutritional counseling, massage, reflexology, aromatherapy mineral bath, and Yogassage in elegant surroundings. The yoga pavilion has a floor of honey-colored pochote, archways, and copper pyramid roof, with views of the mountains, sea, and forest. Guests can choose an aquatic yoga class in the fresh-water swimming pool. Daily walks, water sports, mountain biking, and horseback riding are available. Standard rooms in the striking Mediterranean-style retreat center are $215 per person; deluxe corner suites with private balcony and spacious private baths are $235 per person; in a beach cabin, $185. The rates include lodging, delicious vegetarian meals served in a pleasant dining area with cushioned bamboo furniture and glass-topped tables, a yoga class, and hikes. Minimum stay of two nights. Packages are available. In the U.S. contact Wildland Adventures, (800) 345-4453; in Costa Rica contact Costa Rica Expeditions, telephone 223-0333, fax 257-1665.

Parrots and parakeets are among the many species of birds that help travelers forget the rough and sometimes dusty routes from many of these beach areas to another. Howler monkeys rest in tree branches hanging over the roads.

Between Nosara and Sámara is Bahía Garza. Thatched bungalows and a towering thatched restaurant lend an exotic, romantic flavor to the Villaggio La Guaria Morada Hotel. Located between the coastal hills and the sea, with forest along the beach stretching to Punta Guiones, the hotel arranges tours to the Ostional refuge, horseback riding, and sport fishing. It also can arrange transportation from the Nosara airport, and the San José–Nosara bus passes in front. Sounds of a group of howler monkeys, which the manager says are almost domesticated, drift to the bungalows at night and in the early morning. In this tranquil natural setting, the hotel's casino and discotheque seem out of place. A large swimming pool is next to the restaurant/bar. The 30 rooms are in well-ventilated bungalows with French doors that can open up one side of the room onto private terraces. Rooms have walls of rough white plaster, red-clay tile floors, bamboo ceilings, dressing room areas, louvered windows, large closets, fans, and private baths with shower-head hot water and bidets. The rate is $75 for a single or double, including continental breakfast. More units with kitchenettes may be available by your arrival. VISA and MasterCard are accepted. Telephone 680-0784 or 233-2476; fax 222-4073.

Sámara (population 2,631), along with Nosara and Tamarindo, offers travelers access by air as well as direct bus from San José. (See Practical Extras.) The 22 miles (35 km) from Nicoya to Sámara should be paved by the time you read this.

There are some modest-looking places in town, but Hotel Las Brisas del Pacífico is a quality hotel on the beach. Some of its 36 rooms are in bungalows close to the ocean; others offer fantastic views of the sea from an addition above the original complex. The pleasant, bright bungalows have louvered doors to the porches, baths with bidet and hot water, ceiling fans, and table and chairs. Suites are large, with balconies and air conditioning. If you can't get one with its own Jacuzzi, you can take advantage of the whirlpool beside the swimming pool and the open restaurant/bar (good food), surrounded by trees and tropical plants. The ocean is steps away through the hotel's gate to the beach. Las Brisas has parking and rents horses, boats, and equipment for windsurfing and water skiing. Inquire about tours. Rooms for up to two people are from $60 to $72; suites, $95. Credit cards are accepted. German and English also are spoken. Telephone/fax 680-0876, fax 233-9840.

Hotel Marbella is a two-story hotel with 14 rooms facing an inner courtyard with a small pool. The rooms are light, with ceiling fans and private baths with central hot water. A single is $30, a double $48. Six one-bedroom furnished apartments are $65, taxes included. A small restaurant upstairs serves breakfast, and there are nearby restaurants to choose from for other meals. The hotel arranges tours. English and German also are spoken. Telephone/fax 233-9980.

A few miles from town is Villas Playa Sámara, 56 classy villas on the beach. Motorized carts go through landscaped grounds from the reception area to the villas. Each red-tile-roofed villa has a fully equipped kitchen, ceiling fans, and tasteful furnishings in the living room, dining room, and bedrooms. Bamboo chairs with colorful cushions make the large terraces a comfortable outdoor living area. There is a large pool, children's pool, water slide, Jacuzzi, and restaurant. Some of the baths also have tubs. Villas Playa Samará offers snorkeling, surfing, waterskiing, sportfishing, scuba diving, bicycling, and horseback riding, and also arranges area tours. A one-bedroom villa for two is $125, a two-bedroom for four is $185, and a three-bedroom for six is $240. A master bedroom unit is $95. Breakfast is $7, lunch $14, and dinner $17. Credit cards are accepted. Packages are available. Hotel transportation from San José is $65 round trip. Telephone 256-8228, fax 221-7222. Access via Internet is http://www.greenarrow.com/travel/Samara.htm.

About 4 miles (6 km) south of Sámara is Playa Carrillo and the beautiful Guanamar Resort. There are 42 rooms in villas above the ocean and a mile-long (1.5 km) white-sand beach, with free shuttle from the resort to the beach. The pool, surrounded by a wooden deck, is at the edge of the bluff above the blue of the Pacific. Broad, shaded wooden walkways with white railings connect the areas of the resort. White wicker furniture with bright cushions stand out against the rich wooden floors and ceiling of the restaurant/bar, which is also open to the view of the sea and forest-covered hills. The restaurant is open to the public. Spacious, airy rooms are carpeted, with balconies or terraces, satellite TV, room service, air conditioning, fans, and fresh flowers on the table. Some baths have tubs as well as showers, all with central hot water. Rooms without a sea view are $110 for up to two people; with the view, they are $120. (Children under 12 are free.) Suites are $165, and some have balconies at treetop level for a close-up view of canopy wildlife. Monkeys have been known to drop by the reception area.

In high season, there is live entertainment at Guanamar, and there is also a casino. The resort, which has more than 1,000 acres (470 ha) of land, offers trail walks with local guides, horseback riding, mountain biking, kayaking, snorkeling, waterskiing, boat rental, and sportfishing (catch and release). Ask about special transportation possibilities by boat or air charter. The resort is part of Costa Sol International. Telephone 239-2000 or 239-4500; fax 239-2405; in the U.S. and Canada (800) 245-8420.

South of Carrillo is Hotel Punta Islita, which offers an extraordinary experience: unforgettable ocean views, secluded beaches, fine dining, rooms with a Santa Fe–style elegance; forest hikes, horseback rides, snorkeling, fishing, tennis, or hitting a few on the driving range. The beach and the sound of the howlers in the forest beckon. Setting off on mountain bikes seems appealing. Working out on the Cybex equipment in the small open-air gym—with what must be the most beautiful view in Costa Rica—is an option.

But frankly, tearing oneself away from the cool tranquillity of the hillside hotel is a struggle. An impressive, tall, thatched roof covers a huge, circular, open dining room made intimate with service, the right music, and decorator touches. Colonial-style wooden chests, dugout canoes, wooden barrels, and a wrought-iron candelabra (whose candles are lit only to celebrate the new year) are treasures that appeared in the movie *Christopher Columbus 1492, Conquest of Paradise.* Food is attractively served and good—a French chef presides over the kitchen. Harry's step-down bar on one side of the dining area is also a swim-up bar. The infinity pool that appears to flow off into the ocean below is connected to a sun-warmed Jacuzzi.

Twelve thatch and red-tile-roof bungalows contain 20 rooms and four suites. Rich earth tones predominate, along with marvelous blues. All have air conditioning and ceiling fans, hair dryers, bedframes of teak logs harvested from the property's plantation. They have cushioned bamboo chairs, mini-refrigerators chock full of drinks and snacks, and a private patio with hammock, table, and chairs—ocean views. Ivory Mexican-style round sinks with blue trim in the dressing area, separate from the bathroom, match the Mexican tile in the showers—central hot water.

Suites have a sun-heated Jacuzzi on the patio, a wet bar, a sunken living area, and attractive cane ceilings. Sets of two villas share an open-thatched kitchen and living area and a small outdoor Jacuzzi. Bungalow rooms are $110 single, or $132 double; suites $175 for up to two persons, breakfast included. Each two-villa/rancho complex is $300. A three-bedroom, 2½-bath villa with kitchen is also $300, for up to six people.

Guests can rent four-wheel-drive Kawasaki mules to drive around the property, to Norman's charming bar down the road to watch the sunset, to the tiny town of Islita, or on some of the roads of the almost 75-acre (30-ha) property, 70 percent of which is forested. In season, join a turtle-nesting tour to adjacent Camaronal Wildlife Refuge. Boat tours go to Carrillo and Sámara, and sportfishing is offered. The beach is a ten-minute walk away.

If you're lucky, René will guide you on a walk or horseback ride to the forest and beaches. You may fish with with local folks, hunt oysters or, at low tide, pass through a tunnel in the rocks of Punta Islita to discover yet another secluded beach. René can tell you about the animals and medicinal plants, and offer fascinating tidbits about the pioneers who settled this place.

The hotel is remote, not so much by distance as by lack of all-weather roads. Most travelers arrive here by air (Travelair or charter—50 minutes from San José), though when the river is down and the road dries up in dry season, the adventurous can come by four-wheel-drive car from Carrillo; the drive takes about half an hour. Check with the hotel for current road information. Roundabout road routes are also available through Coyote and San Pedro. Credit cards accepted. Telephone 231-6122 or 296-3817; fax 231-0715.

Nicoya (population 22,585) is a pretty town with a picturesque colonial church. Though most tourists just pass through on their way to somewhere else, it can be a pleasant destination, giving a flavor of small-town life on the Nicoya Peninsula.

Hotel Curime at the edge of town has 26 rooms in units scattered among landscaped gardens. It is a tranquil place with a resident parrot (uncaged) who hangs out near the large swimming pool alongside the open-air restaurant. Half of the larger rooms have air conditioning (a single is $28, a double $47), and the smaller ones have fans (singles are $16, doubles $28, taxes included). Both have refrigerators, a living room, and TV. Private baths have central hot water. The staff is extremely helpful. Zelmira called her dad to help me change a flat tire one Sunday morning, and he discovered I was driving around with a broken spring! That was not the end of helpful people in Nicoya—I was back on the road within a few hours. Call the Curime at 685-5238, fax 685-5530.

Southeast of Nicoya is Mansión, and just about 5 blocks (500 m) north of the Mansión junction on the main highway is a delightful little restaurant called Los Girasoles, owned by Marcial Flores. He loves to have a satisfied customer and says, "We cook with the heart, not in the kitchen." For us, he put together a dish of grilled chicken, shrimp, and beef that would have been fit for a fine city restaurant. We ate it in the thatched rancho in a large flowered garden as we watched parakeets in the trees. Los Girasoles is open for lunch and dinner. Tell Marcial hello for me.

From Mansión, you can head northwest for the ferry across the Tempisque River or a visit to Barra Honda National Park. At the entrance is a community ecotourism project—Barrio Cubillo—with a restaurant called Las Delicias and three clean, simple rooms with private baths but no hot water. They cost $11 per person. Credit cards are not accepted. Electricity may arrive at the park by the time you get there, but if not, there are candles. Fourteen camping areas with latrines and water are spaced in a forest frequented by howler monkeys. The cost is about $3 per person. You can also see deer and tepezcuintle projects. Guides lead three-hour trips to the caves in Barra Honda for $47 for up to seven people (with a minimum of two), and half-day hikes for about $19 for up to seven people. There is a small grocery. A handcrafts area has ceramics and carved gourds for sale. Call

685-5580 for reservations for rooms or tours. (Good luck—it's a public phone and often busy. Keep trying.)

The road to Puerto Humo and the Rancho Humo Hotel is also off of the highway between Mansión and the Tempisque ferry. The hotel, located on a bluff across the Tempisque River from Palo Verde National Park, offers a marvelous opportunity for travelers to enjoy the rich birdlife that lives in or migrates to this habitat. With the sun still low in the eastern sky and parrots moving noisily from tree to tree below, an iguana and I once watched rays of light travel over the green of Palo Verde to shimmer on the waters of the Tempisque. Guests do not have to go outside and sit with an iguana for this early morning treat, however; it can be savored from one of the 24 attractive rooms. Each room is air conditioned and has a terrace, a queen-size bed, and a private hot-water bath with a tub: $78 for up to two persons. Large picture windows in the rancho-style restaurant give almost a 360-degree view. Meals are served buffet style: breakfast $6.50, lunch or dinner $10. A meal plan is available.

Down the hill is a charming, rustic counterpart to the more luxurious hotel—Albergue Zapandi, built to resemble an Indian village. Eight rooms in four bamboo and thatch buildings around a central plaza share baths in separate buildings (four showers, four toilets). Each room has a ceiling fan: single $25, double $36. Good, ample food is in a serve-yourself screened, thatched rancho. Breakfast is $5, lunch or dinner $7. Don't be surprised to see howler monkeys in trees around the clearing.

Rancho Humo and Zapandí are connected by forest trails with Puerto Lapas, the dock for water trips (lapa is used for macaw, and you may see scarlet macaws here). The hotel offers boat trips to Pájaros Island and to the Palo Verde park ($62) or guests can mountain bike in the park ($87). A day trip to San Vicente to learn how local Indians make pre-Columbian pottery is $57, and a Barra Honda National Park tour, with a descent into the caverns, is $100. Guests can hike or horseback through the forests and floodplains on the ranch. Birds such as the roseate spoonbill, anhinga, jabiru, northern jacana, storks, and egrets are among the 279 species of birds identified in the area; 148 species of trees are known to exist here. Travelers can get to the hotel overland via the Tempisque ferry (turning at Quebrada Honda for Puerto Humo) or from Nicoya heading via Corralillo to Puerto Humo), or by boat from the ferry or from Palo Verde—check with the hotel about prices. The ranch has an airstrip for charter flights. Credit cards accepted. Telephone 255-2463, fax 255-3573.

The road east of Mansión soon heads south for Playa Naranjo. When the pavement stops, it is slow going—plenty of time to take in the countryside and a character or two. One rainy afternoon, I noticed an old, bearded man on the bank along the road, half-hidden as he squatted in the tall grass. As the car approached, he rose slightly, carefully aimed his machete, and fired. Hilarious. In the rear-view mirror, I watched as he resumed his station, presumably waiting for the next passerby.

When you get close to Lepanto, notice the salt beds. Then it is Playa Naranjo and the dock where the car ferry from Puntarenas comes in. This is where some travelers begin their journeys on the Nicoya Peninsula. Descriptions of this southern part of the peninsula are in the earlier Puntarenas–Montezuma Route.

10

What to See and Do: Southern Costa Rica

The Talamancas, the highest mountains in the country, are in the region we are looking at here, along with beautiful mid- and southern-Pacific beaches; plantations of pineapple, African palm, and bananas; virgin forest; and some lands that knew only indigenous peoples and a trickle of pioneers until the Inter-American Highway to Panama pushed back the frontier in the 1950s.

Road travel into the region from San José is via three routes: along the Inter-American Highway through the highlands; the old Spanish road through Orotina and then south along the coast; or the Inter-American to Puntarenas, then turning south for Puerto Caldera and Orotina. Scheduled flights get you to towns such as Quepos, Golfito, and Puerto Jiménez. See Practical Extras for schedules. Some of the largest and some of the smallest national parks are here, along with biological reserves, wildlife refuges, and some private nature reserves. This chapter has sections on the highland route, the Osa Peninsula, and the coastal route.

The Highland Route

An early start is recommended for a trip on the Inter-American Highway south from San José. Fog or rain become likely at higher elevations as the hours pass. If you are driving, have your money ready for the tollbooth (60 colones, at this writing). Some lanes are for exact change only. After you pass through the colonial capital of Cartago and turn at the sign for San Isidro de El General, the road begins to climb out of the Central Valley. Fields of agave plants called *cabuya* (hemp) grow on hillsides. Then small farms with dairy cows dominate the landscape.

If you have not had breakfast, several restaurants along this road offer the

▲ The morpho butterfly makes any day special (Ree Strange Sheck)

▼ Solitude at sunset, Nosara (Ree Strange Sheck)

▲ Orchids at Excazú oxcart parade (Ree Strange Sheck)

▲ Gran Hotel Costa Rica, downtown San José (Ree Strange Sheck)

▼ Perfect sunset at Rainbow Adventures, north of Golfito (Ree Strange Sheck)

Colorful ponciana tree (*malinche*) against seasonally dry landscape at Ocotal
Beach (Ree Strange Sheck)

▲ Decked out for Independence Day (Ree Strange Sheck) ▲ Hanging orchid (Ree Strange Sheck)

▼ The rhinoceros beetle, a show stopper (Ree Strange Sheck)

Day's end at a local watering hole near Punta Islita—ask for Norman's place
(Ree Strange Sheck)

Steam rises from hot waters at Tabacón, near La Fortuna (Ree Strange Sheck)

▲ Bring binoculars—you'll be sorry if you don't (Ree Strange Sheck)

▼ Infinity pool at Hotel Punta Islita (Ree Strange Sheck)

▲ Author, a tall person, next to
tree buttresses at Hacienda Barú
(Jack Ewing)

▲ Heliconia
(Ree Strange Sheck)

▼ Hotel Villa Casa Blanca at Ocotal (Ree Strange Sheck)

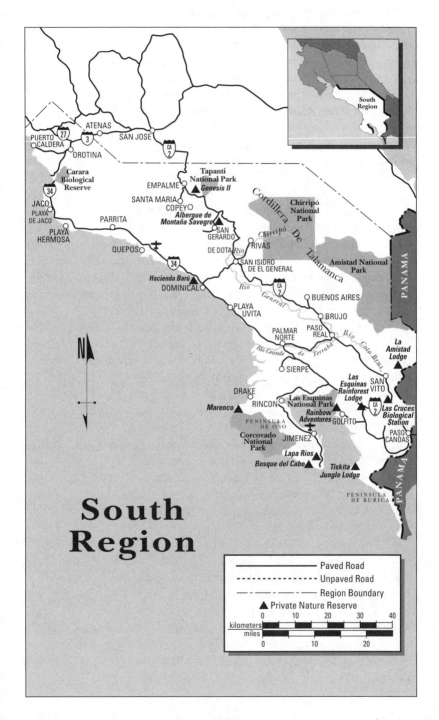

South
Region

Paved Road
Unpaved Road
Region Boundary
▲ Private Nature Reserve

kilometers
miles

typical gallo pinto and coffee or agua dulce. Or you can order a *papusa, gallos* (tortillas filled with practically anything—usually meat, potatoes, or arracache), or cheese or bean empanadas. All are good. At kilometer 60 and kilometer 77, you'll find Chesperitos. Las Georginas on the other side of Cerro de la Muerte (kilometer 95) has good food, buffet style.

On the left near kilometer 58 on the Inter-American Highway is the little yellow church of Cañon. For a taste of the Talamanca cloud forest and a stay at the private nature reserve called Genesis II, take the unpaved road beside the church for about 2.5 miles (4 km). Genesis II is as intriguing as its name; read about it in Chapter 13.

Albergue de Montaña Tapantí, named for nearby Tapantí National Park, is at kilometer 62, just before La Trinidad. The albergue has six apartments, some for up to four people, and four double rooms. A single or double costs $53, including breakfast. Each has heaters (the elevation is close to 10,000 feet, or 3,048 meters) and a private bath with hot water; furnishings are comfortable. There is a conference room, cozy lounge with a fireplace, library, table games, and restaurant—great trout dishes. Tours to go trout fishing or seek out the quetzal can be arranged. Telephone/fax 232-0436.

For a taste of real Costa Rican rural hospitality, stop by Finca Los Lagos Madre Selva on the left near kilometer 64 and meet the Solano Serrano family. You can sit by the trout ponds or enjoy the rushing mountain stream from covered picnic areas on their farm for an admission fee of less than $1 per person. Join one of the brothers for a three-hour guided walk in the forested mountains, with a good chance of seeing quetzals from October to March—many other birds year-round; cost, $6 each. The words will be in Spanish, but these young men know the mountains well and will help you discover the beauty. Open 6:00 a.m. to 6:00 p.m. daily. Telephone 224-6388.

At about kilometer 70, watch for signs to Albergue Mirador de Quetzales, a rustic retreat where you will receive a warm welcome from the Serrano Obando family: the parents and their eight children. The small lodge has seven rooms with bunks of rough-hewn wood—total capacity 29. Two shared baths, very clean, have shower-head hot water. Good smells emanate from the kitchen, with much of what is served from the farm itself—fresh milk, cheese, blackberries (*mora*), rainbow trout, and homemade bread. The charge is $25 per person, including lodging, breakfast and dinner, and a guided walk. No credit cards. Eight trails wind through the farm's 106 acres (43 ha). Son Jorge says quetzals are seen here year around, along with about 100 other species of birds so far identified. Day visitors are also welcome to the guided walks, $6 per person. Rubber boots are available. Contact Albergue Mirador de Quetzales by calling 454-4746 or 534-441; your

Striking *páramo* landscape of Cerro de la Muerte (Ree Strange Sheck)

message will be radioed to the Serranos. The lodge is 700 meters after the turnoff from the Inter-American Highway.

Near kilometer 73, watch for the small refuge that sheltered early travelers and settlers who made the difficult journey over Cerro de la Muerto by foot or by horseback. The two-room adobe has been partially restored. You can walk into the small room where travelers stopped to rest and escape from the cold; you can see where the fire was made for cooking. A plaque commemorates the pioneers of the southern zone at this Casa Refugio de Ojo de Agua, and an exhibit reports that the route was built in 1869, serving settlers until the highway was built in 1945.

Cerro de la Muerte got its name, Mountain of Death, because of the danger in crossing it due to storms and frigid nighttime temperatures. This is the northernmost true páramo in the hemisphere, and its plants are associated with Andean climes. At this top-of-the-world vantage point, when conditions are right, it is possible to see both coasts. The highest point of the cerro is near kilometer 89.

The turnoff for San Gerardo de Dota is at kilometer 80, famous among natural history travelers for its cloud forests and the resplendent quetzal who lives there. The road down into the valley is narrow, with a few hairpin curves and unforgettable vistas. Three lodging possibilities to consider in the San Gerardo area are, in their order along the road, Trogon Lodge, Cabinas de

BANANAS

Costa Rica is the world's second-largest exporter of bananas, after Ecuador. More than 91,000 acres of land (37,000 ha) are devoted to bananas in Costa Rica.

Bananas originally were brought to the New World from Asia in the fifteenth century. Both bananas and the United Fruit Company got their start in Costa Rica in the 1880s. United Fruit was formed by Minor Keith, the builder of the railroad from Limón to San José, and his associates. Under the name of Chiquita Brands, it continues as a major foreign company in the banana business in Costa Rica, along with Standard Fruit and Bandeco (owned by Del Monte).

Each trunk in a banana plant produces one bunch, then it dies. But a continuous supply of new trunks emerges from the plant's base. It generally takes about nine months from the start of a trunk to the cutting of the fruit, three months from flowering to harvesting of a bunch. On a plantation, there may be 2,000 plants per 2.5 acres (1 ha).

Blue plastic bags are put on a bunch at about two weeks. The bags concentrate heat so that the fruit gets fatter and longer more quickly, and they are also impregnated with insecticide and fungicide.

At harvest time, a cutter in the field removes the still-green stalk of bananas from the trunk and places it on the shoulder of another worker, who carries it to a cable. When 25 bunches are on the cable, a runner pulls the "train" to the packing plant. The plastic is removed, and workers cut "hands" of bananas from the bunch, tossing them into water, where they stay at least eight minutes to let latex drain from the cut stem. The fruit that survives the selection process is washed again, stacked on trays, and sprayed with fungicide. Each banana gets a label, is loaded into a box lined with plastic, and put aboard a container. Government inspectors check at the boxing stage—once the container's doors are closed, they are not opened until they reach their destination. Containers are trucked to the port for shipment.

Costa Rica's bananas go mainly to the United States, but also to Germany, Belgium, Italy, and the Netherlands.

The banana industry has come under attack from people concerned about the cutting of forests for plantations and about the eco-impact of pesticides and the plastic bags, which can end up in rivers and oceans. Several banana companies are working toward a green seal of approval under an ECO O.K. program tied to environmental improvement by industry.

Quetzal, and Albergue de Montaña Savegre. I enjoy walking along the road in this valley for the scenery, the birds, the friendly people, and the peace.

Trogon Lodge has mountain air, a rushing river, forest, flowers, cabins, and trout ponds, creating a living landscape painting. Nights can be chilly at 7,000 feet (2,134 m), so each room has an electric heater and the dining room has a cast-iron wood stove that radiates warmth. The ten rooms with private baths and hot water in the showers are in six cabins on the slopes above the beautiful Savegre River. Striped comforters, reading lamps, built-in closet and luggage space, and glass windows with louvered shutters make for comfort in this highland retreat. A single is $40; a double, $55. Meals are served family style (breakfast $7, lunch or dinner $9). While eating you can watch five species of hummingbirds feed outside the windows. Kitchen staff told us what time quetzals would be feeding in a tree near the dining room, and they were.

A walk on the trails may give you a glimpse of the acorn woodpecker, Baird's and elegant trogons, black guan, emerald toucanet, or flame-colored tanager. A two-hour guided walk is $24 for guests or day visitors, $5 unguided. Horseback riding is $25 per person. Fishing is allowed in the eight trout ponds. Tour packages are available from San José: one day $72, two days and one night $166, and three days and two nights $237, including transportation, lodging, meals, and guided walks. Credit cards accepted. Trogon Lodge belongs to Grupo Mawamba, telephone 223-7490 or 223-2421; fax 255-4039 (no telephone at the lodge). The office in San José is 3½ blocks north of Paseo Colón on Calle 24.

Cabinas del Quetzal is a small family operation with two cabins for guests, $27 per person including meals. One is a log cabin, which has a living room with a fireplace and two rooms with beds for six persons; the other has a wood-burning stove in the living room and four rooms that sleep eight. Each has a bath with shower-head hot water. Rodolfo Chacón, his wife, and three children are your hosts. Family members can lead you on trails to a waterfall and mirador and to see quetzals. The river is behind the cabins, so its sounds will lull you to sleep. Telephone 771-2376.

Six miles (10 km) from the turnoff is Albergue de Montaña Savegre, known to many as Cabinas Chacón. It was the first of these lodges and is a delightful private nature reserve owned by Efraín Chacón and his family. See Chapter 13 for a description.

Continuing south on the Inter-American offers one of the most spectacular drives in the country. In 28 miles (45 km), the road drops from its highest point at 10,938 feet (3,334 m) to 2,303 feet (702 m) at San Isidro de El General. You pass from páramo vegetation to a forest with red bromeliads shining in the sun and then to tree ferns, vines, and sombrilla del pobre—

walls of greenery on both sides of the road. As the vista of the General Valley opens up, you may catch a whiff of heliotrope from plants growing along the road.

Just below the statue of Christ above the highway on the right (about kilometer 127) is a *trapiche* (sugar mill cum restaurant) on the left. The mill is in operation Wednesday and Thursday, 8:00 a.m. to 2:00 p.m., when you can see oxen turning the press to extract liquid from the sugarcane. The restaurant is open daily from 6:00 a.m. to 10:00 p.m. Roadside stands sometimes offer wooden *bateas* for sale. You can occasionally still see a woman washing clothes on one in the countryside, but these small versions make beautiful trays or centerpieces loaded with fruit or flowers.

San Isidro de El General (population 41,116) is the commercial center of this rich agricultural area. It can easily be a hub for travelers as they visit Chirripó, Cerro de la Muerte, the Wilson Botanical Garden at San Vito, hot springs at Canaan de Rivas, the Savegre Caverns, or beaches at Dominical. Buses run frequently between San José and San Isidro, a distance of 85 miles (137 km).

San Isidro is a pleasant place to wander around in for the flavor of a small Costa Rican town. I stumbled onto a double wedding in the church on the plaza one evening. Shortly after, a dog ambled in through the open door, made its way down the aisle, sniffing and looking, and then ambled out again. Nobody got upset or even paid any attention. Since church doors often stand open in this country, it is not uncommon to see a bird flying above the altar or to hear chirping from the ceiling in the quiet of the day.

This valley will be familiar to those who have read books by one of its most famous residents, naturalist and ornithologist Alexander F. Skutch. (See Practical Extras, Recommended Reading.) His farm in Quizarrá was purchased by the Tropical Science Center (TSC) in 1993 with a commitment to maintain it as a bird sanctuary and protect its flora and fauna. Dr. and Mrs. Skutch live on the farm and he continues his bird research. Santuario Los Cusingos is open to visitors with a reservation through TSC. The fee is $8 per person. Contact TSC at Apartado 8-3870-1000, San José; telephone 253-3267 or 225-2649; fax 253-4963. Some area hotels arrange visits.

Several hotels in downtown San Isidro are available. One is Hotel Iguazú, in front of Banco Nacional, only 1 block from the bus stop. Above Superlido, the hotel has 21 clean modest rooms, 16 with private baths and shower-head hot water. Rooms with shared baths start at $9, while rooms with private baths range from $12 for a single to $20 for a double. Credit cards accepted. Telephone 771-2571.

Two others just minutes from San Isidro offer some of the area's spectacular views and the sounds of nature: Talari Mountain Lodge on the way to Chirripó National Park and Hotel del Sur, 2.5 miles (4 km) heading south on the Inter-American Highway.

On clear days at Hotel del Sur, you can sit by the large pool and gaze at the impressive Talamanca Mountains above the trees. The 47 rooms are on two floors around a pretty garden with a fountain, and ten cabins for up to five people are farther back on the property. Each of the 20 deluxe rooms has two queen-sized beds, TV, reading lamps, desk, lounge chairs, and a stocked minibar. A beautiful wood door, white tile floors, and pretty watercolors say welcome. Modern baths have solar hot water. Eight have both air conditioning and ceiling fans; the rest, fans only. Two are accessible to the handicapped. Single $47, double $56. Carpeted standard rooms, plainer, have ceiling fans, table and chairs, and combinations of double and single beds, all with private baths and hot water. Single $29, double $36.

Cabins, which can sleep five, have refrigerators, shower-head hot water, and ceiling fans, $77. In addition to pools for adults and children, there are tennis and volleyball courts and bicycles for rent. Tropical plants abound on the ample grounds. A new open-air snack bar next to the pool attracts tourists and locals alike for a Friday night dance, but the music stops at midnight to allow a few hours for tranquil sleeping. All rates include an ample buffet breakfast.

The hotel has a minibus to take guests to Dominical, to the farm of Alexander Skutch, or other local destinations. It is available for airport pickup. Bilingual naturalist guides can also be arranged. Credit cards accepted. Telephone 771-3033, 234-8871; fax 771-0527.

To get to Talari Mountain Lodge, about 5 miles (8 km) east of San Isidro, turn left at the first road after the Jilguero River heading south out of town— the same road that goes to Chirripó. Each of the cabins is named for one of the area's birds, with a painting of the bird decorating the white outside walls. More than 125 species of birds have been identified so far on Talari's 20 acres (8 ha). The eight rooms are light and comfortable. Private baths have big towels and shower-head hot water. Half of the rooms have a small refrigerator and a terrace. Rooms range from $27 to $34 for singles and $37 to $46 for doubles, including breakfast. The swimming pool has an area for children. Hosts Pilar and Jan—they describe themselves as a tica-Dutch blend— are gracious and attentive.

The reception area has a nice lounge area with reading material, and the pleasant restaurant serves good food, some grown at Talari: corn, beans, yuca, and a variety of fruits including star fruit and *chirimoya* (anona). Do not miss the guava ice cream. On Friday evenings, enjoy music with dinner— Jan plays their Russian piano. The restaurant is open to the public for dinner

Thursday to Saturday from 6:00 to 9:00 p.m. and Sunday and holidays from noon to 7:00 p.m.

There are a number of trails on the property—to the General River, through interesting secondary forest, and to an area being reforested with native species. Jan and Pilar also offer tours to Chirripó including all equipment, guides, and bearers. A four-day, five-night package, including two nights at Talari, is $182 each for four to eight people; a three-day, two-night trip is $155 per person for one to three persons. A three-day, two-night horseback trip through forest to a waterfall is $160 for one person, dropping to $95 each for two to four persons. Telephone for Talari is 771-0341. Taxi from San Isidro is less than $4, or the lodge will pick you up with advance notice.

Just minutes from Talari is the town of Rivas, where the pavement ends; the Chirripó National Park is less than 6 miles (9 km) from there. (See Chapter 12 for park information.) You can do the trip to Chirripó on your own, of course, but tour companies also make arrangements. One is Camino Travel, which runs a three-day trip. The first day gets you from San José to base camp in a park refuge at 11,155 feet (3,400 m), requiring an eight- or nine-hour hike of 10 miles (16 km). Day two is the trek to the peak, San Juan Lagoon, and Los Crestones. The return to San Gerardo de Rivas on the last day takes only four hours, which gives you an idea of the terrain. The cost is $357 for transportation, meals, guide, cook, and park fees, and a $5 donation to the park. You need your own backpack and sleeping bag. Minimum is three people. Telephone 225-0263 or 234-2530; fax 225-6143.

Just 22 miles (35 km) west from San Isidro via a paved road are Dominical and lovely Pacific beaches. This route allows the traveler to make a loop that joins up with the southern coastal route discussed later in this chapter, a way to get to the middle Pacific without returning to San José. Many choose the highland road to get to Dominical, combining a mountain experience with the coast. See the following Coastal Route section for a description of the Dominical-Uvita area.

For those continuing south from San Isidro, the Inter-American Highway goes through farm and ranch country and then into mile after mile of pineapples. In less than an hour, you can be in the Buenos Aires area, where there is a Pindeco pineapple processing plant. The chamber of commerce in San Isidro can give you information on tours of the plant. Try fresh pineapples at a roadside stand.

Past El Brujo there is a guard checkpoint where you may be stopped and a pleasant, buffet-style restaurant), a few miles on the right, is a lovely waterfall on the Rio Catarata that Indians in the area believe has a special quality. Healers use the water in medicinal preparations. Just before the Inter-

American Highway crosses the Río Grande de Térraba is the junction to Paso Real. This is the road that will take you to San Vito and two special private nature reserves: the renown Wilson Botanical Garden at Las Cruces Biological Station, operated by the Organization for Tropical Studies, and La Amistad Lodge, which is near Las Mellizas and the Panamanian border and is within the Amistad Biosphere Reserve. (See Chapter 13 for descriptions of these two reserves.)

The paved road to San Vito passes through beautiful country, where travelers can come across cowboys and cows going down the road along with the usual menagerie of bicycles, dogs, chickens, and pedestrians. The Talamanca Mountains in La Amistad Park, an international biosphere reserve, rise up to the east. A four-wheel-drive vehicle is recommended to reach park headquarters at Las Tablas.

Italian immigrants helped settle the area around San Vito, arriving in the early 1950s to clear and farm the land. In this town of 12,725 people, you will find several Italian restaurants (try Lilliana or Mamma Mia) and hear the language spoken on the streets. (There are gas stations.)

Hotel El Ceibo has 40 modest rooms, all with private baths and hot water. Newer rooms have individual terraces. The single rate is $14, double $22. MasterCard and VISA are accepted. There is a large, pleasant dining room/bar and ample parking. Telephone/fax 773-3025.

If you are heading northeast from San Vito toward Las Mellizas and La Amistad Lodge, you will see some of the large coffee plantations that produce the fine coffee of this area. The paved road goes to gravel after Sabalito, passing through several small villages.

Heading south from San Vito, watch for the sign for Cántaros, a small farm where Gail Hewson has created a library for local young people, a gift shop, a park, a small reforestation project, and lodging for visitors. Entrance fee to the park is a bit more than 50 cents. The natural lake brings aquatic birds, including the striking purple gallinule. Camping underneath a large rancho is $5, which includes access to electricity, shower, toilet, and beautiful views. Inside the colorful farmhouse is a gift shop chock-full of the unusual—Boruca Indian masks, primitive wood carvings, books, carved gourds, embroidered and silk-screened T-shirts, ceramics, jewelry, and more. A small suite offers a living area and bedroom, with a shared bath and use of a kitchen area. Cántaros is open from 8:00 a.m. to 4:00 p.m., closed Monday. Telephone 773-3760.

Just about 2 miles (3 km) past Cántaros is the Wilson Botanical Garden, where visitors can see a remarkable collection of plants from around the world (see Chapter 13). The garden is open for day visits as well as overnight lodging. The road continues on through the mountains and then drops spectacularly to the lowlands, Ciudad Neily, and the Inter-American Highway, where one can go south to Panama or head back north for Golfito or San Isidro.

For those who continue on the Inter-American rather than taking the Paso Real cutoff to San Vito, the road winds along the Térraba River. At the Indian village of Rey Curré, pull off for a visit to the local craft cooperative across from the school. If it is closed, go to the house next to the school. Children and adults carve plants, animals, and indigenous designs on gourds. It is much more fun to buy the gourds here than in San José. At the cooperative, each gourd has the name of the person who made it and the price he or she wants for it—very inexpensive. Sometimes there are woven purses for sale. If you buy at the house by the school, where the chickens have more bravado than feathers, check to be sure there are no ants living in the gourds. You do not want to be cooped up in a car when the creatures decide to come out—the voice of experience.

Palmar Sur, where both SANSA and Travelair flights land daily, is often the route for travelers heading to the Sierpe River or Drake Bay. These destinations are described in the Osa Peninsula section. A fantastic opportunity for nature travelers is to the west, off the Inter-American at kilometer 37: in Chapter 13, read about Esquinas Rainforest Lodge, next to Piedras Blancas National Park.

About 40 miles (65 km) south of Palmar on the Inter-American is the turnoff for Golfito, some 14 miles (22 km) away. From San José, by air, the trip takes about an hour; by bus, almost eight hours. Golfito (population 13,928) is a port town on the Golfo Dulce and was a busy center for banana exportation when the Bananera Company, a subsidiary of United Brands, was operating in the area from 1938 to 1985. African palms have replaced bananas on much of the land, though bananas are being planted again now. The biggest news in Golfito in the last few years, however, has been the "duty-free" shopping complex known as the *depósito* which opened in 1990. People come from around the country to shop there, especially on weekends. The town itself is a narrow strip of about 4 miles (6 km) between the water and the mountains. If you fly in, you may wonder as you approach where there is enough level land for a runway.

Driving in, one of the first hotels encountered is Las Gaviotas. A pleasant open-air restaurant—with fresh flowers on the tables—is near the reception area and gift shop; another is beside attractive swimming pools for children and adults next to the Golfo Dulce, looking across to the Osa Peninsula. Each of the 18 rooms and three bungalows has private baths with hot water, and they open onto pretty gardens that reach to the shore. Rooms, a bit dark because they open onto covered individual porches, are brightened by quilted bedspreads. Each contains a desk and chair. Bungalows have two bedrooms and a living room/kitchen area with a hot plate and refrigerator. Rates for a single or double range from $33 to $41, depending on whether cooling is by air conditioning or fans. Bungalows with kitchenette and TV go to $82, taxes included. Credit cards are accepted. Near the shore are the remains of a minesweeper used in World War II, which now often serve as a picturesque roost for land and sea birds. Telephone 775-0062, fax 775-0544.

At the opposite end of Golfito, near the duty-free facilities, are three other lodging possibilities. Hotel Sierra, between the airport where the daily flights from San José land and the depósito, has 72 tastefully furnished rooms, each with a private bath with hot water and both air conditioning and ceiling fan. Furnishings include two double beds with bright bed coverings, a pretty wood dressing table and big mirror, remote-control TV, telephone, and a table and chairs. Floors are a pretty, cooling green tile. In the landscaped courtyard between the two wings of rooms are swimming pools for children and adults, the latter with a wet bar. There is a restaurant/bar, lounge, and conference room, plus secured parking. Singles are $39, doubles $47. Credit cards are accepted.

The hotel offers guided half-day hiking tours for $25 in the Golfito Wildlife Refuge next door, a $65 day-tour to Zancudo Beach or Playa Punta Encanto, half-day horseback tours, and a day trip to Wilson Botanical Garden, which costs $65. Fishing is offered. Ask about tours to Corcovado.

Las Gaviotas Hotel at Golfito (Ree Strange Sheck)

In San José, telephone 257-7676, fax 233-9715; in Golfito, telephone 775-0666, fax 775-0087.

Hotel Golfo Azul is in a residential area, the American Zone of United Fruit days, with well-kept wooden houses. The hotel's 24 simply furnished rooms, of varying sizes, have nice private baths with hot water and either air conditioning or fans. Rates range from $24 with fan to $39 with air conditioning. There is a restaurant and secured parking. Credit cards are accepted. Telephone 775-0871, fax 775-1849.

Also north of downtown right along the gulf is Samoa del Sur with its huge, distinctive, thatched-roof restaurant/bar. New to the complex are 12 rooms and one suite behind the restaurant. Each large, airy room has two double beds, desk, ceiling fan, and a pretty tiled bath with hot water. Doubles are $43, credit cards accepted. By the time you arrive, a shell museum should be open, and there is a book-exchange library and small game room. The restaurant is open to the public from 7:00 a.m. to midnight, closed only on Christmas and New Year's Day. Telephone 775-0233, fax 775-0573.

Getting around in Golfito is no problem. Taxis constantly run the major street from one end of town to the other, picking up passengers for about $1, and the public bus is even cheaper. Across from the downtown dock is Restaurante Luis Brenes where you can get typical, inexpensive food—Luis speaks English and seems to have answers to most questions about how to get where. Open 6:30 a.m. to 9:00 p.m. Monday through Saturday and until 2:00 p.m. on Sunday.

Forty-five minutes by boat north of Golfito is lodging at secluded, captivating Rainbow Adventures, a private reserve with a mix of sea and forest. South of Golfito is the Pavones Bay area, which draws surfers and nature travelers alike—surfers for the big waves and nature travelers for Tiskita Jungle Lodge, a biological reserve and experimental station where exotic tropical fruits are grown. (See Chapter 13 for descriptions of Rainbow Adventures and Tiskita.) A private botanical garden, Casa Orquídeas, is on Playa San Josecito, north of Golfito. Access is by boat only; ask about a trip at your hotel or at the local dock.

The Golfito Wildlife Refuge, which practically surrounds the town on its landward side, Piedras Blancas National Park, and Corcovado National Park across the gulf are good options for nature travelers. (See Chapter 12.) For those who want to cross the Golfo Dulce to Corcovado, Puerto Jiménez, and other destinations on the Osa Peninsula, the daily launch leaves Golfito at 11:30 a.m. The $3 trip takes less than 90 minutes. Passengers are often treated to views of dolphins who keep company with the boat for a ways. Boats between Golfito and Puerto Jiménez can be chartered.

Osa Peninsula

The Osa Peninsula has Corcovado National Park, private nature reserves, lodging from rustic to a certain tropical elegance, rivers and coastline, and some spectacular wildlife. Access is by air, boat, bus, or car.

Let's start with Puerto Jiménez (population 6,819), just across the Golfo Dulce from Golfito. In addition to the launch between the two towns, both Travelair and SANSA have flights into Puerto Jiménez (see Practical Extras). Here is where you find an office for Corcovado National Park and the Osa Conservation Area to help you with visits to Corcovado. Also look for an information office and gift shop run by La Palma Feminine Association.

Lodging in this small town is modest. Hotel Manglares has ten rooms and a restaurant; six of the rooms are next to the street and restaurant, and four are behind in a pleasant garden. A thatched rancho with hammocks offers a place for guests to enjoy the tropical flowers and the birds. Watch for the resident crocodile and scarlet macaw. Each room has a private bath—but no hot water—and fans. Singles are $25, doubles $30, taxes included. VISA and MasterCard accepted. The hotel offers a boat trip in the gulf, horseback riding, and tours to Corcovado. A hiking venture to the Río Tigre includes gold-panning. Phone 735-5002, fax 735-5121. Other clean, small establishments with lower rates are Cabinas Marcelina and Cabinas Puerto Jiménez.

Heading south of town toward the tip of the peninsula are two private nature reserves well worth a visit. See Chapter 13 for descriptions of charming Bosque del Cabo and architecturally distinctive Lapa Rios.

Corcovado Lodge Tent Camp, owned by Costa Rica Expeditions, is further along this road near Carate at the southern edge of Corcovado park. Twenty tents on wooden platforms have two single beds, and guests share two common bath houses. Electricity from a small generator is mainly for the screened-in, thatched dining room and the bath houses, so this is flashlight country after dark. Single $58, double $97, including all three meals. A thatched hammock house and bar complete this jungle complex, with forest behind and a palm-fringed beach in front. Neighbors include magnificent scarlet macaws.

A self-guided loop trail is free to guests; other hiking tours range from easy to hard, some in Corcovado park. A sunset horseback ride is $30. Enjoy life in the canopy from a platform in a 200-foot (61-m) *ajo* tree. See two species of monkeys and a feast of feathered friends: honeycreepers, toucans, aracaris, tanagers. Half-day is $69, and arrangements can be made to spend the night on the platform. Packages for two persons run from overnight without guided walks ($371, double occupancy) to a three-day, two-night with a guide for $853 (including a platform trip and half-day guided trip in Corcovado park). These include air charter, transfers, lodging, and meals. Telephone 257-0766 or 222-0333; fax 257-1665; Internet crexped@ sol.racsa.co.cr, or World Wide Web http://www.cool.co.cr/crexped.html. A taxi from Puerto Jiménez can take you to Carate, and the walk to the lodge along the beach is about 30 minutes.

An unpaved road goes from Puerto Jiménez to Rincón to join the Inter-American, opening up the eastern and southern parts of the Osa to road travelers. Access to the western shores of the peninsula can be by air, by boat from other Pacific ports, or by road for 7 miles (11 km) from Palmar (where SANSA and Travelair land) to Sierpe and then by boat on the Sierpe River to Drake Bay and points south.

The trip on the Sierpe River can be fascinating, with an opportunity to see kingfishers, tiger-herons, crocodiles, turtles, parrots, monkeys, blue herons, muscovy ducks, perhaps even a roseate spoonbill. But how much you actually do see may depend on the speed at which you travel. Some boat captains seem to view the river pretty much as a highway, a means of getting from one place to another as fast as possible. Others, like Mike Stiles, owner of the Río Sierpe Lodge, slow down for wildlife viewing and explore some of the estuaries, enjoying the trip as much as his guests. A hard rain in the mountains had brought an avalanche of water hyacinths downriver on my return trip with him, transforming the water into a floating garden—beautiful but tricky for navigation. The mouth of the Sierpe can be treacherous at times—be sure to go with a seasoned boatman.

The Río Sierpe Lodge is 15 miles (24 km) from Palmar by boat. At that point, the river is more than a half-mile (1 km) wide and 50 feet (15 m) deep. Along the opposite shore are some of the tallest mangroves in the world. The lodge, on a narrow piece of land between the river and the mountains, consists of 11 rooms with private bath, some in the main house and others a few steps away. All have private baths with passive-solar hot water. Rooms are plain but comfortable, with thoughtful touches such as mirrors in both the bathroom and bedroom. Electricity is from a generator, and battery-powered reading lamps function after the generator goes off at night. Windows are screened, and there is a wall fan. Rubber boots and snorkeling equipment are free for guests. Food is plentiful and tasty, with lots of fruits, vegetables, and seafood—Mike serves a mean spaghetti. Rates of $65 per person, double occupancy, include lodging, meals, soft drinks, transportation between Palmar and the lodge, and taxes. Guests can be picked up at Quepos, Dominical, or Playa Piñuela at added cost.

Tours with local naturalist guides include Corcovado or Caño Island for $55, an overnight hiking trek for $65, an overnight horseback trip for $125;

a half-day excursion to Violin Island for $25, or a Laguna Sierpe boat trip for $50. Hiking trails near the lodge are free. Ask about packages. Mike also offers scuba-diving and fishing trips, and there are archaeological ruins to visit and beaches where you can swim, snorkel, or marvel at huge sand dollars and other sea shells.

The lodge has a reference library, including bird books to help you identify the myriad you will see. Some 175 species are spotted regularly, including the mangrove hummingbird, which Mike says often comes at breakfast, and the Baird's trogon. Telephone 284-5595 or 220-2121; fax 786-6291.

The Sierpe River is also the gateway for many travelers headed for Drake Bay, named for Sir Francis Drake, who sailed these waters more than 400 years ago. Though the area is remote, accessible by charter flights or boat, a growing number of nature tourism sites exist between the Sierpe and Corcovado National Park. Three are a short hike from the village of Drake Bay. Remember that boat landings on beaches will be wet, so come prepared with suitable shoes and clothes.

Aguila de Osa Inn is an upscale, 14-room complex of rooms, open-air restaurant, and dock. On a bluff overlooking the bay, the rooms have hardwood floors, screened windows, ceiling fans, carved doors, and private tiled baths with hot water. Some bathrooms have sunken tubs, and a two-bedroom suite with a conical roof has windows on three sides. Singles are $105; doubles $90, suites for two $225, including meals. Transportation from Palmar to Sierpe is $30 for up to four by taxi, and from Sierpe to the Aguila de Osa, it is $30 each by boat. A horseback tour is $55, a jungle hike in Corcovado $65, diving at Caño Island $110, archeological hike at Caño $65. Telephone 296-2190, telephone/fax 232-7722.

Just across the Agujitas River is the Drake Bay Wilderness Camp, a relaxing, laid-back kind of place where one soon settles into tropical time, pausing to delight in the antics of two squirrel monkeys who spend a lot of time in the fruit-laden gardens (they even play with a domestic cat), making a date with a spectacular sunset, lounging in hammocks. One of the prettiest natural tide pools I have been in beckons at low tide.

Part of the wilderness camp is on the point between the river and the Pacific; the rest faces the ocean, backed by forest. Nineteen rooms with private baths, most with solar hot water, are in seven buildings scattered on the property. Newer units have tile floors and tile baths. All simply furnished with ceiling fans, brightly flowered sheets, luggage racks, even washcloths. Four 10-by-10-foot oceanfront furnished tents (with electricity) offer an alternative, with occupants sharing a two-shower, two-toilet communal bath. Rates are $66 per person, double occupancy, in the rooms, $44 in tents, meals included. Same-day laundry service is available.

A four-day, three-night package that includes lodging, meals, day trips to Corcovado and Caño Island, bilingual guide, and airplane and boat transportation from San José is $520 each for doubles. Pickup and drop-off at Quepos, Dominical, and San José can be arranged. Credit cards are accepted, at an additional charge. Good food is served family-style in a separate dining room. Complimentary bocas at 5:00 p.m. in the thatched, open-air lounge bring most guests together to talk over the day's adventures.

A horseback tour along beach and through forest is $35, and the Corcovado or Caño tour ranges from $35 to $50, depending on the number of people. I treasure the memorable morning I had on the $35 Río Claro tour. Walking on beach and forest trails with Fernando, a knowledgeable naturalist guide, was a treat. We saw 12 scarlet macaws feeding in distant trees, a white hawk (which Fernando explained follows white-faced monkeys, waiting for the chance to take a young monkey—and then we saw the monkeys). We watched a spectacular blowhole and a "walking beach" alive with hermit crabs. River otters were playing in the Río Claro.

Guests swim up the beautiful river, outfitted with life vests and fins, and float back down with the gentle current. Tall trees are on both banks; kingfishers fly by. It is special. You can snorkel in a lagoon if you like, or visit a waterfall. I recommend it. An all-day trip by horseback to a butterfly farm is $40, and you can take kayak lessons or sign up for kayak tours.

The owners and hosts at Drake Bay Wilderness Camp, Herbert and Marleny (Marleny's family homesteaded this land), will help you work out the details of your visit. Ask about scuba diving at Caño Island, either for the day or as part of a package. Fishing is also available. It is now possible to arrive by seaplane. Telephone/fax 771-2436 at the camp itself, or telephone 284-4107.

Do not miss the hanging bridge over the Agujitas River between Drake Bay Wilderness Camp and the Aguila de Osa Inn. It is on the traditional path that villagers and travelers have walked for years connecting the town of Drake Bay with areas farther down the Osa Peninsula. Continuing toward the south on this path from the wilderness camp is delightful La Paloma Lodge, owned by Mike and Sue Kalmbach. The hilltop retreat has spectacular views of the Pacific and landscaped gardens that provide a rich setting for the tropical birds that abound in this area. Fiery-billed aracaris were feasting regularly on *almendro* trees when I was there. Their calls mixed with those of chestnut-mandibled toucans, parrots, and macaws in appropriate jungle melodies, blending nicely with distant sounds of the sea.

The centerpiece of the complex is a large, thatched-roofed structure that contains the dining room, bar, lounge area, a small library with reference books and magazines, and a marvelous veranda along the ocean side with

Hanging bridge over the Agujitas River (Ree Strange Sheck)

lots of chairs for sunset-watching at complimentary boca time before dinner. Food is served family-style, and it is excellent. Homemade bread is on the table at every meal, and nighttime brings rich desserts. Do not be surprised if Mike sits down with you at dinner. Sue is generally the one who helps with arrangements by phone or fax. A swimming pool has been added near the clubhouse, with a dramatic ocean view.

There are five rooms and five thatched, two-story ranchos to house guests. The comfortable, spacious rooms open onto a big veranda with hammocks. The ranchos have private porches, with beds and bath downstairs, and a marvelous, spacious bedroom upstairs open between the waist-high walls and the overhang of the tall thatched roof. The views are of forest and sea. Both rooms and ranchos have private tiled baths (solar hot water), ceiling fans, and orthopedic mattresses. Electricity is a combination of solar and generator power. Rates per person for double occupancy, with meals, are $70 for the rooms, $90 for the ranchos. A three-night package is $540 for the rooms, $610 for ranchos, including round-trip air and boat transportation from San José, meals, and guided tours to Corcovado and Caño Island, park fees, and taxes. Four- and five-night packages are available.

Accompany the lodge's experienced naturalist guide, and you may see and learn about toucans, manakins, scarlet macaws, parrots, monkeys, sloths, herons, and iguanas. For pure pleasure, go on a gentle canoe or kayak trip on the Agujitas River, taking a dip in the cool water—a contrast to the warmer water of the bay—and enjoy bird-watching. You can go with the guide or alone. The beach is a short walk down the trail.

La Paloma Lodge offers guided day trips to the Río Claro for $50 and to Corcovado or Caño Island for $65. Ask about sport fishing and diving rates. Telephone/fax 239-0954.

A bit farther along the trail is Cocalito Lodge. Rustic rooms in the main lodge and cabins with decorative bamboo house up to 25 people. Each unit has a private bath with hot water. A small hydroelectric project plus solar power provide electricity, but there are no electric outlets in rooms. The restaurant serves organic produce along with seafood and pastas—by candlelight in the evening. There is traditional music and dance after dinner. Rooms are $50 per person, cabins $65 per person (quadruple occupancy), meals included. Cocalito Lodge, on the beach, offers guided tours to Caño, Corcovado, or the Río Claro for $50 each, a waterfall hike for $15, and an overnight trip to Los Planes for $100. There is also fishing and scuba diving ($90 for two dives). Ask about packages. Telephone/fax 786-6150.

Corcovado Adventures Tent Camp is also on the beach. Each tent, on a base that also provides a private porch, is furnished with a single and a double bed, night stand, and battery-powered lamp. The dining room and kitchen are powered by solar panels. In the communal bath houses are five toilets and five showers. The cost is $60 per person for lodging and meals. Corcovado Adventures offers a full-day trip to Caño or Corcovado with a local guide for $60 and horseback riding to the park or snorkeling in park waters for $55. Ask about sea kayaking, fishing, and transportation from Quepos or San José. Telephone 223-2770, fax 257-4201.

The trail farther south continues to wind through forest and along the beach to Marenco, a marvelous private nature reserve described in Chapter 13.

Coastal Route

You can take the Inter-American west from San José and either turn off a ways past the international airport to Atenas or continue on toward Puntarenas, turning south for Puerto Caldera, Orotina, and Jacó. The route to Puntarenas is covered in Chapter 9 (Northwest Costa Rica).

Part of the route through Atenas to Orotina was the old Spanish trail from San José to the Pacific. Founded in the sixteenth century, Atenas (population 6,036), is a pretty town in an area known for the quality of its fruits. Ticos travel to Atenas and Garita on weekends just to buy them. As you travel along the mountain road to Orotina, you pass through picturesque villages, farms, coffee fields, and patches of forest. Notice the "living fences." A branch cut off a tree of certain species is stuck in the ground, and it grows there. Besides serving as fence posts, the trees are windbreaks, and some of them offer fodder for cattle. *Madero negro* and *poró* (showy red flowers) are two of the species used. Sometimes the indio desnudo is chosen. Photosynthesis can take place through the bark of this species.

Other trees with bright blossoms on this route are the *llama del bosque,* "flame of the forest" (with red flowers), and *cortesa amarilla* (with yellow flowers).

While you are in Costa Rica, you may hear talk of a dry canal, referring to a land route from coast to coast that Costa Rica can offer as an economical alternative to the Panama Canal. There are road possibilities here and farther north through Guanacaste. As a matter of fact, the one here is functioning already with containers trucked between Puerto Caldera on the Pacific and Moín, near Limón on the Caribbean. The missing highway segment that will streamline the route is between Ciudad Colón and Orotina, a route farther south than this one. El Cafetal Inn is a delightful bed and breakfast just a few minute north of Atenas. See Chapter 7 (Central Costa Rica) for a description of the ten-room country house.

Descending toward Orotina on the historic route, notice the almost perpendicular hillsides cleared for pastures. The terrace-like appearance is created by the horizontal trails of grazing cows.

At San Mateo, just before Orotina, is Rancho Oropendola—helpful signs to guide you. The five separate cabins ($45) are spaced around a pretty tropical garden. Two are suites ($55, $65) with a living area and large screened in porch. Ceiling fans keep the comfortable rooms cool—one has air conditioning. Beds with orthopedic mattresses are double, queen-, or king-size. Private baths have shower-head hot water, with washcloths and fluffy towels. A river flows at the back of the property. Owner/manager Ted Woodford prides himself on his swimming pool pod; the water is cleaned with the same system used in space shuttles—no chlorine needed. Tours can be arranged to the gold mine at nearby Desmonte, where you can either enjoy the waterfall, pools, and rocks or enter the mine itself. Rancho Oropendola is only 20 minutes from Carara Biological Reserve and near Iguana Park. Telephone/fax 428-8600.

At Orotina (population 8,287) you can take a side trip to visit Iguana Park, about 6 miles (10 km) away, Rather than taking the road to Jacó, bear left and take a right turn toward Coopebarro. (Be forewarned about the one-lane suspension bridge—you are on the right road.) In the portion of the 1,000-acre (400-ha) park open to visitors, you can learn about the project to save the endangered green iguana through captive breeding and release. A visitor center offers educational materials and a video as well as a gift shop

Iguana Park near Orotina (Ree Strange Sheck)

with posters, T-shirts, and items made locally from iguana leather. In a garden enclosure at the center, you can see iguanas of various sizes or take a guided walk on one of forest trails and see them in the wild. The restaurant features what else but iguana meat.

Dagmar Werner, president of the Iguana Verde Foundation, began the iguana breeding in Costa Rican in 1988. The green iguana management program, which has released 100,000 iguanas to date, aims not only to recuperate iguana populations but also to conserve and restore tropical forest and train local communities in sustainable use of forest and wildlife. The foundation also carries out research on captive breeding of scarlet macaws and has a training program for monitoring of resident and migratory birds and their habitats. Iguana Park is open 8:00 a.m. to 4:00 p.m. daily, $10 per person. For more information write to Fundación Pro Iguana Verde, Apartado 692-1007, San José. Telephone 240-6712, fax 235-2007.

For another view of Iguana Park, you can join The Canopy Tour, climbing into the upper layer of the forest, moving from tree to tree and platform to platform via cables, $85. The day tour from San José, Puntarenas, or Jacó includes transportation, lunch, and guides. Among birds you might see are trogons, toucans, tanagers, tityras, motmots, and scarlet macaws. Make reservations with The Canopy Tour, telephone 255-2463, fax 255-3573.

Past Orotina is a turnoff northwest to Puntarenas and the Caldera dock, where cruise ships stop regularly. Between Puerto Caldera and the junction to Orotina are Dundee Ranch Hotel and Hacienda Doña Marta Lodge, both of which offer nature tourism on a working ranch; guests have a chance to explore this tropical dry forest-moist forest transition zone and to work alongside ranch hands. Watch for signs near Cascajal off the Caldera route; the back road from Orotina to either can be bad in rainy season.

Dundee Ranch Hotel has a large reception/lounge/dining room building, a sparkling swimming pool, 23 rooms, and a small conference/bird observation structure across a shallow lagoon connected to the rest of the complex by a wooden walkway. Colorful northern jacanas, egrets, and black-bellied whistling ducks were enjoying the water when I was there. The hotel has a list of some 100 birds compiled sporadically over a four-month period at the ranch, and another for the nearby estuaries, giving each its scientific, English, and Spanish names. You may see the crested caracara, hummingbirds, trogons, kingfishers, hawks, and cuckoos. Other animals include monkeys, crocodiles, coatis, and anteaters.

The comfortable rooms are bright, with red clay tile floors, colorful bedspreads, big closets, table and chairs, air conditioning and ceiling fans, TV, and modern baths with hot water. The rate is $76 for one or two people, including continental breakfast. Credit cards accepted.

Optional tours include horseback riding in the Valley of the Monkeys ($28) or Rainbow Safari by Cricket (a tractor-tram) within the farm ($28). An estuary and mangrove boat trip can be arranged, $56. Your visit may coincide with an Elderhostel group taking a class in pottery-making, with the traditional mud oven in use. Transportation from San José is $15 per person. Dundee belongs to Alvaro and María Batalla, who also have Hotel Chalet Tirol in the Central Valley. Phone 267-7371, 428-8776; fax 267-7050, 428-8096.

Hacienda Doña Marta, just down the road from the Dundee, belongs to another branch of the Batalla family. Part of the fun of doing this book is discovering a totally unexpected delight to share: Hacienda Doña Marta made my day. It is open, however, only from December through April. The *hacienda* (house) has been restored to include a small dining room and lounge area for guests. Details of decoration in each of the six rooms create the impression that one is visiting a fine home and has been put up in a family bedroom. My favorite is the "hat room" with a wonderful collection of hats hanging on a long wall rack. Trophies for horseback riding, old family photographs, and fine antiques make each room distinctive and personal. The headboard of one bed is made of decorative metal gates with a landscape painted on the wall behind. Original art is in the private bathrooms—

which have hot water. There are high bamboo ceilings, ceiling fans, and screened windows. Doubles are $60. Breakfast is $5, lunch $10, dinner $14, plus tax.

Guests can swim in the pool, ride with cowboys, go horseback riding ($20), take trails in the forest, or visit rivers. The farm has cattle for milk and meat production (stables and corral near the main house), a *pochote* reforestation project, and mango groves. Phone 234-0853, 428-8126; fax 234-0958.

Just ten minutes from these two lodges is the Tarcoles River and Carara Biological Reserve. Bring binoculars for a stop near the bridge over the river. Crocodiles bask in the mud along its banks; birds enjoy the waters. You might see a wood stork, blue heron, or American egret. Near sundown, watch for scarlet macaws flying overhead. Restaurant Los Cocodrilos is beside the bridge.

Because of one-day nature tours from San José, Carara has become a popular natural history destination. Seeing it with a guide is recommended. One disappointed young woman told me she had gotten off the public bus at the entrance to Carara and walked on the trail without seeing anything spectacular. I think she had expected the birds and animals to come out and greet her. Guides know animal territories, which trees are in fruit, and what to look for. They can point out orchids that a visitor might not even spot. (See Chapter 12 for information on Carara and Chapter 14 for some tour possibilities.) Area lodges and hotels also offer Carara tours.

In the little town of Tarcoles, about 1 mile (2 km) from Carara is Cabinas Carara, quite basic but clean accommodations. Rooms have fans, no hot water. Singles are $13, doubles $21; cabin for six is $32. There is a small restaurant and pool. Visits to Carara can be arranged. VISA and MasterCard accepted. Telephone 224-0096.

Jungle Crocodile Safari also operates out of Tarcoles with an office at Cabinas y Restaurante La Guaria. The two-hour boat tour takes you for a close-up look at this endangered species as well as the many species of birds found here. Cost is $30 per person, children under 12 not allowed. Call for departure times: 661-0455.

Farther down Tarcoles' main street is Tarcol Lodge, geared to birders and naturalists. At high tide, the five-bedroom, two-bath lodge at the mouth of the Tarcoles River is almost surrounded by water. At low tide, guests may see as many as 2,000 birds on the sand flats. The rooms in the 30-year-old, two-story house are simply furnished. The food is good. The rate is $99 per person, including round-trip transportation from San José, meals, taxes, and lodging. There is a three-day minimum stay if Tarcol Lodge provides transportation. With your binoculars, in the evening you might be able to see thirty to forty pairs of scarlet macaws in a tree across the river.

Possible tours include Carara, horseback riding on the beach, turtle watching at Playa Hermosa, or an estuary trip. Some tours are included in your stay, depending on its length. The owners of Tarcol Lodge, the Erbs, also have the private nature reserve Rancho Naturalista, near Turrialba. Reservations necessary. Telephone/fax 267-7138; in the U.S. (800) 593-3305.

Hotel Villa Lapas is a next-door neighbor to Carara, on a former cattle ranch whose pastures have been returning to forest for eight years now. The 47-room modern hotel is built in the forest along the Tarcolitos River; the sound of its waters lull one to sleep at night. A flock of scarlet macaws may squawk in a nearby tree as you eat in the pretty open-air dining room, and a toucan will probably drop by. One birder spotted more than 75 species of birds in 30 minutes.

Large rooms with high ceilings are in nicely spaced units facing the river. Nice touches include a desk with storage drawers, a large mirror, an ample closet (in the bathroom), and one of the best hot showers in the country—the water flow is perfect. Most rooms have ceiling fans; some have air conditioning. There is a small conference center, a gift shop, library area, table games, TV and video room, and facilities for badminton and ping-pong as well as a swimming pool. A single or double is $75. Credit cards accepted.

Service and food are good in the dining room; the freshly made tortillas are excellent—go for them instead of bread at least once. Try the banana flan. The restaurant is open to the public from 7:00 a.m. to 10:00 p.m. A guided walk in the Villa Lapa forest lasts two hours on well-maintained trails, while a six-hour trek takes you to a nearby spectacular three-tiered waterfall. Tours to Carara, only five minutes away, and to Manuel Antonio are available. Call about day visits. Telephone/fax 293-4104 or 293-4265.

Just 1.5 miles (2.5 km) south of Villa Lapas is Steve N' Lisa's Restaurant, where you have one of those tantalizing beach views right from the outdoor terrace. Open from 6:00 a.m. to 10:00 p.m. daily, it has a varied menu, from chilidogs and BLTs to shrimp and lobster, and good prices. No credit cards. Telephone 222-5113.

From Carara, the road drops down to the coastal lowlands, with tantalizing views of the Pacific. Architectural variations are more common in this region, the most striking being the sharply pitched, thatched roofs on huts and open-air ranchos.

Next is Punta Leona Hotel and Club, set amid 740 acres (300 ha) of forest and beach. From the entrance on the highway, a 2.5-mile (4-km) drive passes through exquisite forest. Some of Punta Leona's forest is now a government-recognized private wildlife refuge. This is scarlet macaw country, and Punta Leona is the site of an effort to increase numbers of these beautiful birds in the wild by placement of artificial nests. Chicks born here will be out of reach to nest-robbers who sell macaws on the black market.

Lodging options abound, from rooms, chalets, and bungalows to condos in buildings set among the trees—a total of 180 rooms. The pretty Selvamar sector offers a single room for $72; double, $82. Chalets run from $58 to $125, and the newest development, Leona Mar Condominium Hotel, has furnished kitchens, cable TV, air-conditioning, and king-size or twin beds, plus washer and dryer in every unit, starting at $120 for up to four people. The Punta Leona complex has three pools (one in the forest), miles of nature trails, three restaurants, tennis and basketball courts, game room, small store, pharmacy, and gift shop. Equipment rental for water sports is available, as is horseback riding. An on-site tour company arranges visits to Carara and other sites as well as sunset cruises. A shuttle takes people from lodging areas to the white-sand beaches on either side of the rocky outcrop known as Punta Leona. A day visit to Punta Leona is $10 per person. Credit cards accepted. Telephone 231-3131 or 661-2414; fax 232-0791 or 661-1414.

Visitors can also climb into the canopy of Punta Leona's forest with The Canopy Tour company, moving among platforms in tall trees on horizontal cables. The one-day tour from San José, Jacó, or Puntarenas is $85 a person, including transportation, guide, and lunch. The canopy experience is about three hours, including the walk on a trail to the site, and the day includes a chance to spend time on the beach. Telephone The Canopy Tour at 255-2463 or 223-5595; fax 255-3573.

Just a bit more than a mile (3 km) south of the Punta Leona entrance on the main highway and 56 miles from San José (100 km) is Villa Caletas. More than 1,000 feet (350 m) above the sea, the hotel has a commanding view of the coastline from the Nicoya Peninsula to Jacó. Tones of French colonial and Victorian architecture lend distinction. The main building has two restaurants, a bar, conference rooms, elegant hallways and conversation areas, and eight guest rooms with queen or twin beds.

Twenty villas are tucked among tropical gardens down the slope, each with a bedroom, living room with sofa bed, and private terrace. Art and antiques decorate rooms and villas, almost all with sea views. No telephones or TVs here to pull you away from the natural serenity; ceiling fans and sea breezes quietly cool. Indian artifacts and jewelry are in the boutique near the reception area, along with glass-encased insect exhibits and Chinese vases.

The swimming pool seems to float on the edge of forever. A small Greek-style amphitheater, which hangs on the side of the cliff—not for those with a fear of heights—is the site of concerts and even weddings.

Sunsets are spectacular from here, and guests can watch scarlet macaws fly by in late afternoons. The property includes 250 acres of forest (100 ha). Do not be surprised to see wildlife, especially birds and small mammals. Free transportation is provided to the beach below, and trips are arranged to Manuel Antonio, Carara, Herradura Beach, and Jacó, as well as to Tortuga Island. Water sports and bicycle riding are also available. Rooms are $115 for a single or double; villas start at $136. A breakfast buffet is $9 and lunch or dinner (a la carte) is $20. Credit cards accepted. Telephone 257-3653, fax 222-2059.

Jacó, on the beach, is popular with Costa Ricans. Tour companies often take tourists there, too. There are hotels, cabins, restaurants, a disco, car rental, and rental of surfing and other water-sports equipment. Swimmers and surfers should read the tips on water safety (Chapter 5); riptides are not uncommon. ICT can give you information on lodging possibilities in town, where there always seems to be a lot of activity for a place with only 2,827 people. Here are three hotels away from downtown that, for me, offer a sense of place:

Hotel Club del Mar is tucked away on a peaceful cove at the south end of Jacó Beach. Light, nicely furnished rooms nestle among the trees and tropical gardens, with the Pacific only a few steps away. The view of the surf and headland is fantastic. The 18 rooms offer a cool, soft respite from the coastal sun—all have ceiling fans, some have air conditioning. A lovely sea-green floor tile adds a peaceful air. Carved wooden lintels, floor-to-ceiling louvered doors, rattan furniture with deep cushions, and balconies or porches are among the attractive features of superior rooms. Economy and standard rooms have equipped kitchenettes and colorful cushioned furniture. Doubles are $65 for economy rooms, $77 for standard, and $90 for superior rooms. Credit cards are accepted but discouraged. There is a sparkling swimming pool and a library.

Philip and Marily Edwardes, owners and hosts, along with son Simon, help guests with custom trips. The hotel offers turtle walks during egg-laying season (August 15 to October 15), a horseback trip into the forested mountains with a member of the Madrigal family, and a picnic at a hidden waterfall. As a local agent for Fantasy Tours, Club del Mar offers guests tours to volcanoes and parks, boat trips, and rafting. They speak English and French. If you cannot stay at Club del Mar, stop by for a gourmet meal at its Las Sandalias restaurant. Telephone/fax 643-3194.

Near kilometer 59 is a big gasoline station open 24 hours a day. A bit further is Terraza del Pacífico, a 43-room hotel just 3 miles (5 km) south of Jacó,

Club del Mar on Jacó Beach (Ree Strange Sheck)

where Playa Hermosa begins. Rooms in the two-story hotel open onto porches or balconies facing the swimming pool and garden, looking toward the ocean. Hand-painted birds and butterflies decorate the curtains. The air-conditioned rooms have cable TV, telephone, and private bath with hot water and tub. Rooms are $66 for up to two persons. A package including breakfast and taxes is $85 for singles and $98 for doubles. Ask about packages that include other meals. Credit cards are accepted.

Cars and horses can be rented, and tours are arranged to area attractions. Italian specialty dishes in the restaurant reflect owner Eugenio Scorsone's heritage, but since he also has restaurants in New York, he promises a U.S.-style hamburger and can do club sandwiches and BLTs. Try the papaya milk shake. Telephone 643-3222, 643-3444; fax 643-3424.

Leaving the Jacó area and continuing south along the *costanera* highway, you pass through large cattle ranches. Roadside signs advertise other lodging on Playa Hermosa, which is a favorite with surfers and also is a sea-turtle nesting site. The next group of small hotels is on the long expanse of Esterillos beach, which has several entrances from the highway. Two small beach hotels with an intimate flavor, where you will be understood in English, Spanish, or French, are off of the Esterillos Este turnoff: Auberge du Pélican and Fleur de Lys. Neither accepts credit cards at the moment.

Mariette Daignault and Pierre Perron are your hosts at Auberge du Pélican. In front of a palm-fringed beach, the ten-room inn (two rooms accessible to the handicapped), has a pool with lots of comfortable lounging chairs, barbecue grill, ranchos and hammocks on the beach, and a screened-in dining room. The restaurant serves full breakfasts, buffet lunches of cold cuts and salads, and dinner with at least two choices—perhaps between seafood and steak. Vegetarian is always possible.

The six upstairs rooms, with shared baths, open off of an ample corridor that channels a breeze from the sea by day and from the mountains by night. Each room has its own flavor, with decorator touches, and all have fans and reading lamps. The two shared baths are large with hot-water showers and royal blue fixtures; the women's bathroom has a bidet. Two downstairs rooms have private baths, and the two rooms adapted for the handicapped, shared bath, are by the pool. A boat is available for fishing or to get out among the dolphins. Double with shared bath is $30; with private bath, $40. Telephone/fax 382-1623 or fax 779-9108.

Cabinas Fleur de Lys has ten rooms in cabins set among tropical gardens, each with a private bath and hot-water shower. Large, bright rooms with high, pitched, wooden ceilings have wardrobes, fans, and colorful sheets. The open-air dining room looks out on the garden and the beach beyond. Thatched ranchos shelter hammocks and lounge furniture. Marcelle Coté and family are your hosts. Rooms with one double bed are $40; a double and a single, $45; and two doubles, $50, including taxes. Telephone 779-9117, fax 779-9108.

Another entrance to the beach will lead you to Hotel Bejuco and Hotel Delfin—watch for signs. Bejuco is a tent camp. Each of the 15 tents is divided into sleeping and living areas and have electric lights. Restrooms and showers are in units for men and women. Cost is $10 per person including breakfast. If you bring your own tent, cost is less than $4 for the site and use of facilities. The small restaurant is rustic, picnic table style with dirt floor.

Two-story Hotel Delfin has 15 rooms; each opens from the land side and has a balcony or terrace looking out to the ocean on the other side. The large rooms have either fans or air conditioning, TV, private baths with hot water (big towels), and a table with chairs. A beautiful curved stairway goes up from the large, circular ground-floor dining area/bar, which is two stories high with arched openings to the sea view. The restaurant serves local and international dishes. A rancho under the palms near the pool offers a nice lounge area and a nearby beach has lots of shells to enjoy. Single $60, double $75. Credit cards accepted but a surcharge is added. Reservations via telephone/fax 289-8845. Telephone at the hotel is 779-9246.

Continuing south, waving fields of rice for a nearby processing plant draw birds. Near Parrita, groves of African palm appear. In 1945, the Bananera Company started the first commercial palm plantation in the area, replacing banana plantations that had been badly affected by Panama disease. By 1965, African palm plantations reached as far south as Golfito. Oil extracted from the plant is used not only for fat, margarine, and cooking oil but also in soaps and perfumes. Be alert for one-lane bridges, a long one just out of Parrita. Pay attention to the yield signs.

On Palo Seco beach, just south of Parrita, are Beso del Viento and Hotel La Isla. Beso del Viento is a small inn 3 miles (5 km) from Parrita. Huguette and Jean are your hosts. One room has a private bath ($50 including breakfast), six rooms share two baths ($40 single, $45 double), and two furnished apartments have private baths ($80). Credit cards accepted. Baths have shower-head hot water. A grassy garden with hibiscus is shaded by palm trees, and the pool has a distinctive lavender edge. Rich colors, in fact, accent the inn inside and out.

The restaurant is presided over by a French chef in high season. Beso del Viento (kiss of the wind) offers an estuary tour through mangroves for birdwatching. French, English, and Spanish spoken. Guests can be picked up in Parrita, or take a taxi for about $3. Reservations via fax: 779-9108; in Canada, telephone (514) 383-7559, fax (514) 383-0971.

Hotel La Isla, 5 miles (8 km) from Parrita, is on a narrow peninsula between the river and the sea. Its 16 rooms and 16 apartments are in buildings surrounded by a garden with lots of fruit trees that attract birds, fruits such as guava, papaya, grapefruit, limes, and oranges, as well as coconut palms that provide plenty of *pipas* for those who want to try this natural drink. The large rooms have two double beds, air conditioning and fans, TV (local channels), and private baths with central hot water. Singles are $60 and doubles $70, including breakfast. Fully furnished apartments have a living room and two bedrooms, capacity up to six persons, with fans, kitchenette, and large private bathrooms with hot water. Apartments are $50 for one, $60 for two persons, and $80 for six.

Guests may use rowboats and motorboats for estuary trips and horses for beach rides at no extra charge. One-day tours are offered to Manuel Antonio park and to Carara, and a guided natural history tour goes to a nearby forest that is a biological corridor. An agricultural tour can be arranged. La Isla has a pool for adults and one for children, a Jacuzzi, and an outdoor barbecue area. The restaurant/bar is open to the garden. Breakfasts are $5, lunch and dinner $10, box lunches $7. Telephone 255-3158, 222-6561; fax 233-5384; in the U.S. and Canada (800) 391-3961.

Just 6 miles (10 km) on the left past Parrita is the entrance to the Rainmaker Mountain Project and the opportunity to experience a canopy walkway that is more than 800 feet long (250 m), moving through six trees above waterfalls and a river. The hanging bridges (perhaps you have read of a similar walkway at Iquitos in the Amazon) are 155 to 235 feet (47 to 72 m) above the ground; platforms on each tree allow visitors to observe the diversity of flora and fauna in this important biological corridor of the Fila Chonta. Rainmaker encompasses almost 5,000 acres (2,000 ha), of which a small portion is being developed for nature tourism. Afraid of heights? Rainmaker still has lots to offer. In addition to the canopy walkway, there is a river walk graced by four waterfalls, a medicinal plant trail and garden (labeled plants), a three-hour hike in the forest to a spectacular waterfall, and a four-hour strenuous hike to El Mirador, a lookout point.

Camping is possible at El Mirador, equipment provided. The admission fee of $39 entitles visitors to try all trails with a bilingual naturalist guide, in groups no larger than 12 people. First tour of the canopy walkway is at 9:00 a.m., the last at 1:00 p.m. From the highway, Rainmaker Mountain Project is 4 miles (6.4 km) down the road through an African palm plantation—signs indicate the route. Telephone/fax 779-9080.

The town of Quepos, 110 miles (177 km) from San José, is the gateway for visits to Manuel Antonio National Park. Express buses from San José make the trip in about 3½ hours, and Travelair and SANSA have 20-minute flights. If you come by bus, you can get off at Quepos and make reservations for your return trip before continuing to Manuel Antonio. There are also buses to Quepos from San Isidro de El General and Puntarenas. (See Practical Extras for plane and bus schedules.) Car rental is available in Quepos and Manuel Antonio.

Quepos (population 13,254) was named for the Quepo Indians who once roamed these parts. Artifacts turn up in surrounding pastures and fields. Mogote Island, a sheer-sided land with a crown of thick vegetation visible from Cathedral Point in Manuel Antonio National Park, was Quepo ceremonial ground. Today Quepos is the center of an agricultural area where cattle are raised and rice, beans, sorghum, papayas, and mangoes are grown.

The Buena Nota gift shop on the road to Manuel Antonio, between the Arboleda and Karahé hotels, serves as an informal information center for the area. The original downtown shop has closed. The large, beautiful new building has clothing and beachwear designed by Anita; pottery, jewelry, handcrafted wooden items, books, maps newspapers, and lots more.

Anita answers questions with amazing patience. She and husband Donald, who have lived here almost 22 years, have worked hard on beach safety and on environmental issues in the area. Donald, who built the new store, talks about the history and the archaeology of the area on Tuesday and Thursday at 5:00 p.m. when he is in town—no charge. La Buena Nota is open from 8:00 a.m. to 7:00 p.m. daily. Telephone/fax is 777-1002.

Donald and Anita also have two attractive, fully furnished houses for rent past the Mariposa Hotel—with gorgeous views of Cathedral Point, the beach, and forest. The one-bedroom is $400 per week and the two-bedroom, with a front deck where one could sit for a few years, is $600. Call La Buena Nota for reservations.

Quepos is a bustling town with lots of small shops that serve area residents as well as the growing number of tourists. One of the small restaurants I like on the street facing the beach is El Gran Escape (The Great Escape), open from 7:00 a.m. to 10:00 p.m. but closed Tuesday. The menu includes Mexican food (fajitas, tacos), seafood, sandwiches (burgers, club sandwiches), black bean soup, and lots more—VISA accepted.

Just down the street is Restaurante Isabel, closed Wednesday, which has pastas as well as typical dishes and seafood. Do not miss Café Milagro, on the same street, open 6:30 a.m. to 9:00 p.m. in high season, fewer hours in low season. Coffee is roasted on site daily, and you can buy it here or have it mailed to you. You can get pastries along with your iced coffee, espresso, or cappuccino—brownies to die for. The small gift area also has pottery made in Costa Rica. VISA accepted.

On Calle 5 near the church is La Botánica, where you can buy local organically grown spices raised on the farm of María Ester Bekins and

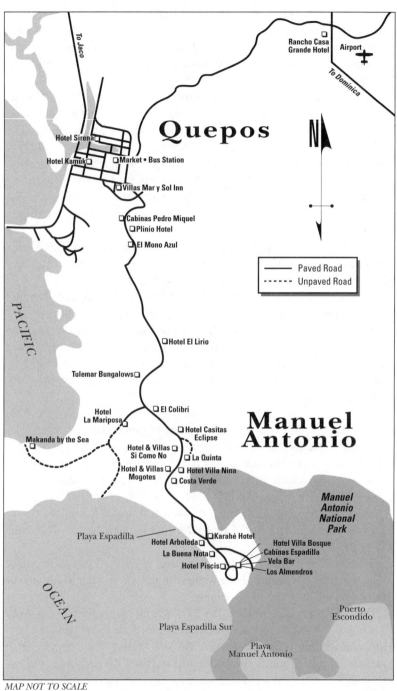

Quepos

Manuel
Antonio

PACIFIC

OCEAN

To Jaco

Rancho Casa
Grande Hotel

Airport

To Dominica

N

Hotel Sirena

Market • Bus Station

Hotel Kamuk

Villas Mar y Sol Inn

Cabinas Pedro Miquel

Plinio Hotel

El Mono Azul

Paved Road

Unpaved Road

Hotel El Lirio

Tulemar Bungalows

El Colibrí

Hotel
La Mariposa

Hotel Casitas
Eclipse

Makanda by the Sea

Hotel & Villas
Si Como No

La Quinta

Hotel & Villas
Mogotes

Hotel Villa Nina

Costa Verde

Manuel
Antonio
National
Park

Playa Espadilla

Hotel Arboleda

Karahé Hotel

Hotel Villa Bosque

La Buena Nota

Cabinas Espadilla

Hotel Piscis

Vela Bar

Los Almendros

Puerto
Escondido

Playa Espadilla Sur

Playa
Manuel Antonio

family. She also has medicinal herbs and does consultations. The spices, marketed under the Especias Ceilán label, make good gifts. The attractive store is open from 8:00 a.m. to 4:00 p.m. Monday through Friday, half-day on Saturday. María Ester will probably offer you a refreshing glass of mint tea. Telephone 777-1223.

Three other favorite restaurants of mine are along the road to Manuel Antonio. Hotel Plinio's restaurant has a nice atmosphere and excellent food from appetizers to desserts, specializing in Italian/German cuisine. The Barba Roja has been the place to eat in Manuel Antonio for years—shrimp, lobster, steak. It has a quiet atmosphere with a nice view and good service. Closed Monday. Karolas, closed Wednesday, has full breakfasts (including banana pancakes or huevos rancheros), light lunches, and dinner menus that can include anything from enchiladas and chicken cacciatore to fish dishes. Try the macadamia pie for dessert.

Two of the several tour operators operating in the area are Lynch Tourist Service in downtown Quepos and Iguana Travel in a shopping center near Hotel y Villas Si Como No on the road to Manuel Antonio.

Lynch Tourist Service can fix you up with a whole range of eco-adventure tours, including bird-watching, rafting, and horseback tours. The four-hour Manuel Antonio park tour is $45. Guides carry spotting scopes for close-up looks at wildlife. A horseback ride to a waterfall is $65. Lynch offers a water taxi to Drake Bay, crossing in three hours; one way is $60, round trip $99. Lynch is a SANSA and Travelair ticket agent. Telephone 777-0161, 777-1170; fax 777-1571.

Iguana Travels offers white-water rafting or kayaking on the Savegre ($70) or Naranjo ($55) Rivers as well as a number of kayaking or boat tours with a naturalist bent and hiking or horseback forest ventures (from $40 up). A guided tour of Manuel Antonio park is $45. Several packages are available, including photo safaris from one to three days with a professional photography guide. Telephone/fax 777-1262, 777-0574.

Eqqus Stables, also on the road to Manuel Antonio, has guided horseback tours. Its beautiful stables make it a kind of horse heaven. Telephone 777-0001.

Quepos offers lodging options with a range of prices. If you would rather be in town than stay in one of many hotels on the way to Manuel Antonio or nearer the park, here are some options.

The three-story Kamuk Hotel has 28 rooms that range from $71 to $112 for a double, breakfast and taxes included. Price depends on the size of the room and whether it has a balcony. VISA and MasterCard accepted. Each tastefully furnished room is air-conditioned and has TV, a telephone, and private bath with hot water. A third-floor restaurant/bar offers sunset views and a coffee shop on the ground floor is good for people-watching. Telephone 777-0379, fax 777-0258.

The two-story Hotel Sirena has 14 double rooms with air conditioning, private bath, and central hot water. The pleasant rooms are simply furnished and open onto a courtyard with the pool and bar/restaurant. A single is $40, a double $50, breakfast and taxes included. Credit cards are accepted. The conservation-minded owners have put together interesting tours.

On the $60 Savegre River horseback venture, travelers may see crocodiles, white-face monkeys, and some of 150 species of birds as well as habitats that include mangrove, primary forest, beach, and river. A look at local agriculture—cattle, rice, and African palm—is included. Two-night, three-day packages can include horseback riding, park tour, bilingual guide, lodging, and breakfasts for $158; or horseback riding and a tour in a yacht equipped for fishing and diving for $224. Telephone 777-0528, fax 777-0171.

You might also try Villas Mar y Sol Inn, about a block east of the bus stop and central market. The eight rooms are air conditioned and have private baths with central hot water. Single $25, double $30. Telephone 777-0307, fax 777-0562.

About 4 miles (6 km) northeast of Quepos on the road to the airport and Dominical is Hotel Rancho Casa Grande, 14 rooms and ten one- and two-bedroom bungalows, swimming pool, tennis courts, whirlpool, and a restaurant that is open to the public. Rancho Casa Grande has its own walking paths through a humid tropical forest frequented by squirrel monkeys (*monos titi*), some 70 species of birds, and 38 of butterflies. The large, pleasant rooms have ceiling fans and air conditioning, two queen-size beds, cable TV, telephones, hair dryers, coffeemakers, and a small refrigerator. The bungalows also have living rooms, dinettes, and kitchenettes with microwaves.

Rancho Casa Grande has a tour agency. Guests can go horseback riding, rent cars, take a guided nature walk in the private reserve, visit Playa de Rey or Manuel Antonio. Babysitting is arranged. Rooms are $95 for a double; the one-bedroom bungalow is $110, the two-bedroom $125. Credit cards accepted. Telephone 777-0330, 777-1646; fax 777-1575.

Manuel Antonio is less than 5 miles (7 km) south of Quepos. A proliferation of small sodas in recent years has created a kind of shantytown near the park entrance and raised questions about pollution, but Manuel Antonio park itself continues to be a small jewel. It protects beautiful beaches as well as the flora and fauna of the tropical forest. Visitors must wade across an estuary to reach the entrance, an adventurous introduction to the special experience ahead. A bus between Quepos and Manuel Antonio passes about every hour in front of the hotels sprinkled along the road.

The following hotels along the road between Quepos and Manuel Antonio are listed according to rates (see map for locations). Remember that many of them have considerably reduced rates during the "winter" months of May to November. Taxes are not included in price except where specified.

Something about Hotel La Mariposa seems to suspend time, so that the most important thing is simply being, and being there. Maybe it is because the view of forest, sea, and white-sand beach curving out to Cathedral Point touches the eternal within. Ten villas, refined in their simplicity and tasteful decor, are woven into the greenery of the hillside: Spanish clay tile red roofs, white walls, bright colors in art and fabrics, bathrooms that incorporate tropical gardens (hot water, of course). Big windows, ceiling fans, balconies that open off comfortable living rooms.

The restaurant in the main building serves international cuisine (it is open to the public, but a reservation is necessary from December to April). No credit cards accepted; no children under 15. Rates include breakfast and dinner. Villas are $160 for a single, $240 for a double. The penthouse is $140 for a single and $220 for a double. Shuttles to the airport and beach are provided. Telephone 777-0355, 777-0456; fax 777-0050. U.S. telephone (800) 223-6510; Canada (800) 268-0424.

From the top of the hill, the octagon-shaped roofs of Tulemar Bungalows seem to hover among the trees like visiting spacecraft. Each of the 14 bungalows is spaced for maximum privacy and dynamite views of the blue Pacific. Half of the eight walls in each of the spacious bungalows are full-length glass, with sliding screened windows. High wooden ceiling beams radiate out from a bubble skylight. Peaches and blues are in full-size sofas in the large living area, comforters on the two double beds, and upholstered wooden chairs at the low breakfast bar. Kitchens equipped for four have microwaves, cooktop stoves, and refrigerators. Each has air conditioning and ceiling fans, TV and VCR, telephone, hair drier, bathrooms with maroon fixtures and large showers—a washcloth and big towel place.

A steep paved road leads down through forest to a secluded beach, where I watched squirrel monkeys jump from tree to tree. Kayaks are available for Tulemar Bungalow guests free of charge, and there are nature trails and some small waterfalls on the 42-acre (17-ha) property. A snack bar is by the infinity-type pool that seems to stop in midair. Bungalows are $180 for up to four persons. Credit cards accepted. Telephone 777-0580, 777-132; fax 777-1579.

Makanda by the Sea is as elegant as its name. Located about halfway between Quepos and Manuel Antonio down the road that passes the Hotel Mariposa, it is surrounded by tall forest. Squirrel monkeys like it here, and sloths come to call. The secluded beach is down a short trail through the trees. Each of the seven studios and villas has an ocean view. Colorful purples and greens contrast with slate-gray tile. Louvered doors open up rooms to the natural world. Cushiony sofas, king- or queen-size beds gracefully draped with mosquito netting, kitchenettes or full kitchens, ceiling fans (one with air conditioning), reading lamps, split-level rooms, hot-water showers, balconies or terraces, hammocks and lounge chairs, individual Japanese gardens—these are some of the features. The large "infinity" pool and Jacuzzi are in a forested setting. The peace is palpable. Studios are $125, villas $170. Credit cards not accepted. No children under 16. Telephone 777-0442, fax 777-1032.

Hotel & Villas Si Como No is not just a place to spend the night—it is an experience. From the swimming pool with a waterslide and a Jacuzzi fed by a waterfall to a laser theater/conference center and nature trails through the forested property, Si Como No reveals the thoughtful planning of owner Jim Damalas. Energy-efficient air conditioners (remote-controlled), a water management system that processes gray waters for landscaping and turns hotel sewage into fertilizer, and insulated roofs and windows to conserve energy are features not likely to be found elsewhere in Costa Rica.

Each of the 29 apartments, villas, and suites has an unobstructed view of forest, sea, and sunsets. Villas and suites are split-level with balconies, while apartments have terraces. Built-in sofas have brightly colored cushions—purples, reds, and oranges; beds are king or queen size, and every pillow has a reading light focused directly at it. Accents of cane adorn cabinets and furniture. The large atrium lobby incorporates tall trees where they took root long before Si Como No was born as a dream. A snack bar by the pool is the scene of breakfast and light lunches, while the dining room for dinner should be open by the time you arrive. Two-room, two bath villas are $185, suites are $120, and apartments $85, all double occupancy and including breakfast. Children under 12 are free. Credit cards accepted. Telephone for Si Como No is 777-1250, fax 777-1093 or 777-1893. In the U.S. and Canada (800) 237-8201. E-mail sicomono@sol.racsa.co.cr.

Dazzling white walls of Mediterranean-style villas stand out against the green of the forest at Hotel Casitas Eclipse. Light and white furnishings inside contrast against the dark tile floors and rugs in the 25 suites and rooms. White columns and drapes separate the living area from the bedroom in first-floor suites, which also have a kitchenette and a large white-tiled bath with blue accents, including rich blue towels and washcloths. Second-floor rooms with wood ceilings are large and also comfortably furnished, with a private balcony. Both have ceiling fans and air conditioning. Each has a private entrance. Three pretty blue pools are surrounded by nice clay tile lounge areas. A chef from St. Tropez presides over the restaurant.

The tropical gardens include fruit trees, which attract wildlife—the property is backed by Manuel Antonio Park. Rooms are $91 for up to two; suites, $109. Credit cards accepted. English, French, Italian, and German also spoken. Telephone/fax 777-0408, 777-1738.

Hotel Arboleda has 32 rooms plus two family units with kitchenettes, living area, two bedrooms, and private bath, built on a hillside going down to the beach. There are two restaurants, a pool, gift shop, and kayak rental at $10 per hour, or $40 for a guided tour to Manuel Antonio. The hotel also has a half-day tour to Isla de Damas. Beds are large and long for king-size guests, sheets are bright. Some rooms are in a two-story building, others in bungalows. Private baths have shower-head hot water. Air-conditioned rooms are $95 for one or two people; rooms with fans are $85. Credit cards are accepted. Airport pickup is available.

Ask about the rustic cabins at the mouth of the Naranjo River. The Barahonas, owners of the Arboleda, make them available to people doing research or who are interested in helping protect the turtles that nest there. The cabins have no electricity or hot water. Telephone 777-1056, telephone/fax 777-0092.

Hotel y Villas Mogotes has eight rooms; four one- and two-bedroom villas, some with ocean views and kitchenettes; and four suites with kitchenettes and ocean views. The bright, modern baths have hot water. Bamboo accents are found in the furniture and lampshades, and rooms have ceiling fans. Breakfast is served in a thatched dining area near the Jacuzzi and swimming pool. Double rooms are $60 to $70, depending on the view; villas are $100; suites, $90. Credit cards are accepted. A guided tour is available to the park and to Isla de Damas, with lunch on a floating restaurant. Telephone 777-1043, fax 777-0582. This was the summer home of singer Jim Croce.

The Karahé Hotel has nine small villas, eight rooms tucked away in gardens up a hillside, and 16 air-conditioned junior suites in a two-story addition near the beach. The newer oceanfront suites, light with large windows and pretty quilted bedspreads, open onto balconies or terraces that overlook an attractive pool and whirlpool, and the sea beyond. The separate riverstone villas involve some climbing on paths through pretty gardens. Each has a private porch, kitchenette with a refrigerator but no stove, louvered windows with screens, and a large nicely furnished room. Villas for two people are $70, upper rooms $80, and beachfront rooms $100, breakfast included. Credit cards are accepted. Telephone 777-0170, 777-0152; fax 777-1075.

Costa Verde has a special feeling about it. It has wide tiled balconies with classy leather rocking chairs, terraces, gardens, big sliding wood-framed glass doors, tití monkeys moving through the trees, and a panoramic view of forest, sea, and Cathedral Point. The openness of the 46 rooms built on hillsides above Manuel Antonio connects them with the forest just outside the door. All have kitchenettes, ceiling fans, and private baths with hot water. Sixteen have a Jacuzzi and air conditioning. Superior rooms have a king and double bed; standard rooms have double and twin beds. One restaurant serves lighter fare, while the original restaurant has a full menu—good food attractively presented. At 4:00 p.m., it is "Monkey Hour" here. Relax with your camera and a drink while you wait for the squirrel monkeys to drop by. Bring your camera and binoculars to breakfast for that matter—a sloth rested in an eye-level treetop not 10 feet from the open-air dining room the last time I was there.

Tours include a guided walk in the park, horseback tour, rafting, and an estuary boat trip. Costa Verde rents kayaks by the hour and also offers guided kayak tours and a mangrove tour. Single or double superior rooms are $90, standard rooms are $65. Credit cards are accepted, but there is a fee. Telephone 777-0584, 777-0187; fax 777-0560. The Costa Verde in Manuel Antonio is affiliated with the Costa Verde Inn in Escazú, just outside San José.

Hotel El Lirio has nine rooms, some with a Southwestern U.S. flavor: rough-plastered white walls, tile floors, and a splash of color from the bedspreads. Rooms are large, with queen-size beds, ceiling fans and private baths with hot water. Four are in the two-story house next to the road; five are across a pretty garden where orchids bloom. A garden breakfast gazebo restaurant is next to the swimming pool. Rooms are $65, taxes included. Credit cards are accepted. Telephone/fax 777-0403.

Plinio Hotel attracts people from all over the world. It is the kind of friendly place where you hear, "If you are ever in Sweden, look me up." The restaurant is a favorite with locals and visitors alike—cooking with a European flair. A wide variety of sleeping accommodations is available. There is the Jungle House with a king-size bed plus a queen-size in a loft, living area, kitchen facilities, a deck and a bath with a tub, for $75. Or there are three-story family suites with a rooftop sun deck, a big living room, a balcony overlooking the swimming pool, beds, and sofa beds for $120 for four. There are two-story ocean-view studio suites for $75 and rooms from $50 to $60, double occupancy. All the units have hot water and ceiling fans or air conditioning. Those red, red bathroom fixtures are from Germany, the tiles from Italy. Plinio also has 3 miles of nature trails through its forested mountain slope, one that leads to a 60-foot (18-m) wooden outlook tower that lets you see canopy level and above—on clear days to Talamanca, Dominical, and the Nicoya Peninsula. Isolde and Roger are wonderful hosts. They invite you to come enjoy the canopy from the tower whether you stay here or not. Afterwards, you might want to drop by the restaurant and order a natural *piña* (pineapple) drink or a banana daiquiri. Credit cards are accepted, but there is a surcharge. Telephone 777-0055, fax 777-0558.

La Quinta consists of five pleasant, peaceful cabins above Manuel Antonio, all with a balcony or porch and an ocean view, and private baths with shower-head hot water; all but one have cooking facilities. There is a pretty pool in a landscaped garden, and an outdoor terrace where breakfast is served. English, French, and Hungarian also are spoken here. Cabins are $65 for two persons with kitchenettes, $50 without. Credit cards are not accepted. Telephone/fax 777-0434.

The ten bungalows at El Colibí have the forest of Manuel Antonio Park as a neighbor. They are pleasing and private. Louvered doors open onto terraces with a table and chairs for eating out and lounge chairs or a hammock just for relaxing and enjoying the landscaped gardens of tropical flowers and trees, pools, and fountains. Pleasant paths lead through the gardens to the swimming pool near reception. Each room has cooking facilities, private bath (shower-head hot water), a ceiling fan, barbecue grill, and high wooden ceilings; some have king-size beds. A single is $50; double, $60. VISA is accepted. El Colibrí does not accept children under 8. Telephone/fax 777-0432.

Hotel Villa Nina is a charming pink multistory building with eight rooms tucked away here and there, each with its own decorator touches. Three are air-conditioned with queen beds, a refrigerator, and private balcony ($63). Three have ceiling fans, standard beds, and views of the sea from balconies ($52), and two, closest to the road, have ceiling fans, standard beds and a semiprivate balcony ($43). A breakfast of fruits, cereal, and toast is included in the rates. All have private baths with central hot water and coffeemakers. A rooftop sun deck is next to a thatched, open-air bar; tropical foliage surrounds the pool. Owned and operated by a Costa Rican family, the hotel is friendly and comfortable. There's even an icemaking machine. Credit cards accepted. Telephone 777-1628, 777-1554; fax 777-1497.

Cabinas Pedro Miguel is also a family affair, where the hosts say people enter as strangers and leave as friends. Each of the 14 rustic rooms is different, some with hot water, all clean and simply furnished, surrounded by forest. There is a small pool and an open-air restaurant with an unusual twist. At dinnertime, salads and meats are set out, and guests cook their own meat over a long grill. The restaurant is open to the public, so drop by about 6:00 p.m. if you want to join in the fun. Doubles range from $26 to $45 (with hot water), and there is a cabin, with kitchen, for $70 for up to five persons. Telephone/fax 777-0035.

El Mono Azul de Manuel Antonio is an eight-room hotel with a natural food restaurant open to the public. Some rooms have air conditioning, each has a private bath with hot water. There is a sparkling pool (candlelight dinners beside it), and nightly movies—the first to arrive gets to choose the film. The restaurant features salads, pizza, hamburgers, fish, pastas, and pastries—all baking is done on the premises. Double $35 to $45, breakfast included. VISA accepted. Telephone 777-1548; telephone/fax 777-1954.

The following hotels are near the end of the Manuel Antonio Road, close to the park entrance:

Hotel Villa Bosque has 16 rooms in a two-story modern building; each opens onto a terrace or balcony that runs the length of the structure. Most have air conditioning, others ceiling fans, all with private baths with hot water, and carved wooden doors with palm motifs. A bamboo-framed mirror, soft green floor tile that suggests the sea, and lots of potted plants are nice features. A room is $90 for up to two people in air-conditioned rooms, $80 with fans, taxes included. Credit cards are accepted. The attractive open-air restaurant is in a separate building. A bilingual local guide leads four-hour tours to the park for $25. Telephone 777-0463 or 777-1152, fax 777-0401.

Los Almendros has 21 rooms; 12 units have hot water in the bathrooms and are air-conditioned; others have ceiling fans. Porches and balconies with lots of chairs look out on a palm-studded garden that includes a pool and Jacuzzi. A spacious open-air restaurant is across the garden—its music flows to the rooms. The older rooms are $50 for up to three people, the newer ones $60, taxes included. Credit cards are not accepted. Telephone/fax 777-0225.

Cabinas Espadilla has a pleasant two-story annex across the street from the original rooms. Some have kitchenettes. Sixteen of the 32 rooms are air-conditioned and have shower-head hot water in private baths. Rates for one or two people are $35 for the rooms with fans, $55 for air conditioning; VISA is accepted. Telephone/fax 777-0416.

Hotel Vela Bar adjoins the protected forest of Manuel Antonio. There are ten rooms with balconies or terraces that are furnished with hammocks and open onto a pretty tropical garden. (I once found an exquisite hummingbird nest on the branch of a tree by the path.) Rooms have fans. Singles range from $20 to $57, doubles from $25 to $48, taxes included. Credit cards are accepted. A one-bedroom casita for up to three people is $63, and a one-bedroom apartment for two is $45, with fan, refrigerator, and hot water. A local bilingual guide leads a morning park tour for $35. Telephone 777-0413, fax 777-1071.

Hotel Piscis has 18 rooms, some with private baths. The older rooms are a bit dark and open onto a long shaded porch, but they are immaculate, and there are fresh flowers on the table. The newer cabins are brighter. All the units have fans. The restaurant is in a separate building. A double is $35 with a private bath; the shared baths are $25, taxes included. Credit cards are not accepted. Telephone 777-0046.

From Quepos, it is about 28 miles (45 km) farther along the coast to Dominical, where the road to San Isidro de El General comes in, offering an alternative route back to San José, described in the earlier Highland Route section. Or you can choose that option to continue south on the Inter-American.

If you do drive from Quepos to Dominical, allow about 90 minutes even though distance is short. The road is unpaved and there are several one-lane bridges, so going is slow. Birding is usually good along the road as well, so do not be in a rush. See Practical Extras for bus schedules between Quepos and Dominical.

This road is part of the famous Costanera Sur, envisioned since 1963 as an all-weather road offering an alternative to the part of the Inter-American Highway south of San José that passes over Cerro de la Muerte. The costanera allows you to go all the way to Ciudad Cortés and connect with the Inter-American at Palmar Norte. At this writing the road is still unpaved from south from Quepos, but major rivers south of Dominical now have bridges. Asphalt was in the original plan—you can see the progress for yourself when you arrive.

Near Dominical are approximately 30 miles (50 km) of sandy beaches with names like Matapalo, Barú, Playa Hermosa, and Uvita. Ballena National Marine Park and Caño Island Biological Reserve are easily reached from here. The town of Dominical is still very small (fewer than 200 people), and everybody knows everybody else. There are a growing number of restaurants and places to stay.

San Clemente Bar and Grill has Mexican food. There is also a pizza place and typical Costa Rican food restaurants. Hotel restaurants add to the culinary picture. Stop by the small Plaza Pacífica shopping center for souvenirs and groceries.

Dominical is earning a name for itself in Costa Rica as a community concerned with protecting the environment. A number of the hotels are on forested property and cater to natural history travelers.

Radio communication is the order of the day here because of the lack of phones. You will notice that several lodging possibilities have the same phone/fax number for reservations, which is the number for Selva Mar, a tour company that works mainly in the Dominical-Uvita area. Calls come in to an office in San Isidro de El General, and then bookings and information are radioed to the appropriate business. It works. Selva Mar has an impressive booklet of possible ecotourism activities along with lodging possibilities. Telephone 771-4582, fax 771-1903. Another office is at Hacienda Barú, minutes north of Dominical as you come in from Quepos.

Hacienda Barú is a private nature reserve, part of which is now recognized by the government as a private wildlife refuge. It covers a variety of habitats, from beach to coastal range primary rain forest, offering overnight facilities, both in tent camps in the forest and in six cabañas ($50 for a double) near the beach. Jack and Diane Ewing and Steve Stroud are marvelous hosts. Whether you stay at Barú or not, you can sign up for its walking or horseback tours in the tropical forest or climb up for a look at the forest canopy, $45 for tree climbing or $35 for a canopy platform experience 100 feet (30 m) up. See Chapter 13 for details.

In Dominical proper is Hotel Río Lindo, an attractive ten-room, two-story hotel with rooms priced at $40 (with fans) and $45 (with air conditioning) for up to three persons. Rooms are airy, with bamboo furniture, screened windows, and private baths with central hot water (some with huge showers). A pool and Jacuzzi have been added in the gardens. The Maui Restaurant next door belongs to the hotel. Telephone 771-2009, fax 771-1716. VISA and MasterCard accepted.

Ann and Richard Dale are the charming owners of Albergue Willdale. Set among the trees alongside the Barú River, the albergue has seven very clean and simply furnished rooms—cement floors painted red, bright sheets, some lovely purple heartwood, fans, and private baths with shower-head hot water. The cost is $30 for one person plus $5 for each additional person. There are bikes, an inflatable paddle boat, and kayaks. A floating dock on the river is great for bird-watching. A stem of bananas is always out for guests. Therapeutic massages are available.

The Dales also have a two-bedroom mountain villa, Cabeza de Mono, for those who seek solitude in beautiful surroundings. A spectacular view stretches from Punta Catedral in Manuel Antonio to Isla de Caño and Corcovado. The two-bedroom villa has a swimming pool and comes furnished with food for two meals per day; $125 a day or $900 per week, taxes included. VISA and MasterCard are accepted only if absolutely necessary. Telephone 787-0023 or through Selva Mar, telephone 771-4582, fax 771-1903.

Hotel Posada del Sol is a small, new inn downtown with four rooms, private bath with shower-head hot water, and ceiling fans. Single $20, double $25. An upstairs furnished apartment is $40 for up to four persons. Very clean. Fax 771-3080.

Hotel Villas Río Mar is just east of town along the Barú River, a complex of 40 thatched bungalows, restaurant, poolside bar, Jacuzzi, tennis court, mini-gym, and conference center set in lush tropical gardens against a backdrop of 16 acres (6.5 ha) of forest. Bungalows are a delight, with bedrooms opening via double louvered doors an outdoor living area with a wet bar, small refrigerator, breakfast bar and stools, bamboo coffee table and comfy

Villas Río Mar at Dominical (Ree Strange Sheck)

cushioned bamboo armchairs. Sheer tied-back drapes and the thatched over-hang of the roof lend an intimate privacy to the open-air living space. Bedrooms have king or twin beds and bathrooms feature lighted mirrors, hair dryers, and showers with sliding glass doors. Ceiling fans cool bedroom and terrace. Doubles $75. Credit cards accepted. The restaurant is open to the public from 7:00 a.m. to 11:00 p.m.

Río Mar has mountain bikes and a stable and offers guided walks or horseback rides in the forest, diving, snorkeling, shuttles to the beach, and park tours. Telephone 283-5013, 787-0052; fax 787-0054; telephone/fax 224-2053.

South of Dominical along the costanera are a number of destinations for nature travelers. Two are on the same road off of the main route. Four-wheel-drive is recommended, especially in rainy season. Watch for signs on to left to Bella Vista Lodge and Escaleras Inn about 2 miles (3.5 km) south of Dominical.

Bella Vista Lodge above Punta Dominical lives up to its name—there is a gorgeous view of forest and sea. Woody and Lenny Dyer have turned the old farmhouse made out of hand-cut hardwood into a rustic, delightful place to get away from it all. A wide veranda surrounds the heart of the house. The four small bedrooms are off a central hallway that is open to catch the breeze. There are two shared baths with solar hot water. A single is $25, double $40.

There are no power lines here, so it is battery power at night. A full break-fast is $3.50, lunch is $4, and dinner is $7. Do not anticipate a strict rice and beans diet—some gourmet dishes come along with the candlelight on the porch. A number of horseback tours are available for overnight guests and day visitors. An all-day rain forest-waterfall tour to double-tiered Nauyaca is $40, beach rides $30, and a beach and Pozo Azul waterfall tour $35. There also are walking trails in the forest. Transportation from Dominical can be arranged. Woody also oversees rental of a house near the lodge for up to ten people, at about $45 for two plus $5 for each extra person. Telephone 771-4582, fax 771-1903 (Selva Mar).

Just ½ mile (1 km) farther down the road is Escaleras Inn, an upscale retreat 1,200 feet (374 m) above the sea. Three pretty rooms in the main house, one (adapted for the handicapped) by the sky-high pool, and a more secluded cabin enjoy a view of the coastline all the way to the Osa Peninsula. Michael Holm and Denise Richards are attentive hosts. This is a shoes-off place to protect the beautiful purple heart floors, which also tends to make one feel right at home. Shades of blue abound from Guatemalan textiles in curtains and a gorgeous patchwork bedcover to pottery and stems of the wine glasses. Private bathrooms have pressurized hot water.

The main room downstairs, which serves as a library, bar, and gourmet restaurant, opens onto a wide terrace. The restaurant serves a full breakfast, a light lunch (different every day), and a three-course dinner featuring Thai and Italian specialties. It is open to the public for dinner with a reservation ($12.50 to $17 per person). Colorful artwork and tropical plants are featured throughout. Guest rooms have high ceilings, louvered glass windows, and queen-size beds with orthopedic mattresses. Single $80, double $85, breakfast and taxes included. No smoking is allowed inside the buildings and no children under 12 are permitted. Activities at Escaleras include surfing and boogie boarding, bird-watching, hiking, and whale-watching, while a canopy climb, horseback rides, and a visit to a botanical garden can be arranged. Telephone/fax 771-5247.

Back on the costanera and up a turnoff to the left is Pacific Edge, four large, private, hillside cabins that combine indoor and outdoor living. Each has a kitchenette, big bathrooms with solar hot water, the sleeping area, and a living area that is half in and half out on a beautiful balcony. Hosts George and Susan were yacht captains for years, and their experience is reflected both in the cabins and in the cuisine. Electricity is from solar panels. Single $35, double $40, with $5 a day extra for use of the kitchenette. Ask about rates for long-term rental. Because of its location and architecture, Pacific Edge is not suited for small children. Telephone 771-4582, fax 771-1903 (Selva Mar).

A piece further down the costanera to the right is the turnoff to Cabinas Punta Dominical, situated high on the point at Punta Dominical with the sea on both sides. If you drive straight from Dominical, it is only about ten minutes. Four spacious cabins of tropical hardwood, nestled discretely among the trees, have tremendous views of the ocean. Rooms have louvered floor-length shutters on three sides, polished wood floors, ceiling fans, screened windows, and private baths with hot water. Each has a porch with a hammock. It is a peaceful, private place. Single $35, double $50, taxes included. The thatched, open-air restaurant, open to the public, has excellent food, and it is worth a trip just to sit here and drink in the panorama of sea and coastline, with Ballena National Marine Park at center-stage. Telephone 787-0016, fax 787-0017.

Cabañas Escondidas is less than 6 miles (9 km) south of Dominical. Each of the nine very private cabañas is unique: Rancho Bamboo has Japanese-style sliding screen doors; Rancho Ambrosia is next to cacao trees; Treehouse appears to be in the branches of the trees and remains without electric lights—nothing to dim the starlight. Electricity, however, has arrived for other cabañas, so baths now have shower-head hot water. El Sueño, Amapola, and Tesoro (with river rock decorating the shower) are near the beach, and Panorama is a hexagon. Cabañas are $35 to $55 for a double, plus $10 for each additional person; weekly and monthly rates. VISA and MasterCard accepted. Food is Thai, Chinese, and vegetarian gourmet, served in a thatched restaurant with a spectacular view of forest and ocean. Scrumptious desserts may include pineapple upside-down cake or specialties made with organic chocolate. Breakfast is $3.50, lunch $5, dinner $10 (by reservation only).

Owners Gailon and Patricia have created beautiful gardens of native plants and trees around cabañas and dining room, but 80 acres (32 ha) remain in natural forest. A four-hour five-waterfall guided walk is $20, and other walking tours range from $10 to $25. There are mountain bikes and horses and a path leads to a secluded beach with tide pools for safe swimming.

Escondidas is a gentle, laid-back place, where you can take a Tai Chi Chuan class, do a Chi Kung or Sunset Jungle meditation, or have a therapeutic massage ($55). Kathy, who has been at Escondidas for several years, says work-study programs are available from December to April, where people help out and learn either Tai Chi Chuan, Chi Kung, massage, or vegetarian cooking. Write to Cabañas Escondidas, in care of Selva Mar, AAA Express Mail, 1641 NW 79th Avenue, Miami, FL 33126. For reservations, telephone 771-4582, fax 771-1903 (Selva Mar).

Las Casitas de Puertocito has seven thatched split-level bungalows with a single bed, living area with bamboo furniture, and bath with central hot water on the first level. The upper level has a queen-size bed, and both have ceiling fans. The outside porch has lounge furniture. If guests stay longer than one week, cooking equipment is provided. The casitas are $49 for two persons, with breakfast. VISA and MasterCard accepted. English, Italian, German, French, and Dutch also spoken. The restaurant specializes in Italian food. Jungle hikes around the finca, swimming on three unspoiled beaches, and horseback rides (some multiday) are options. The property has three rivers with waterfalls. Telephone 771-4582, fax 771-1903 (Selva Mar).

Oro Verde Private Biological Reserve above Uvita, managed by the Duarte family, offers day visits as well as overnight stays in rustic cabins with private bath. A visit involves a horseback ride and a hike in. It is a cultural as well as an ecological tour, with a chance to experience something of life on the Duarte farm. You may see an anteater, howler monkey, or tepescuintle. You will see birds, butterflies, and waterfalls. Day tours are $35, cabins about $10 per person and another $10 a day for meals. Telephone 771-4582, fax 771-1903 (Selva Mar).

Rancho La Merced is near Punta Uvita, adjacent to Ballena Marine National Park. The working cattle ranch has 988 acres (400 ha) set aside as a private wildlife refuge containing primary and secondary forest, mangroves, and habitat on both the Morete River and along the beach. Lodging is available in a house on the farm that has two bedrooms, private bath, no hot water (but owner Walter Odio explains that it is not cold either), living room, and equipped kitchen. A generator gives electricity for three hours at night. Double is $35, with $10 for each additional person. Meals can be provided.

Tours are available, such as playing cowboy for a day; a five-hour hike and horseback tour including the river, mangrove, beach, and forest ($35); a six-hour horseback trip to Hermosa Beach, Ballena park, and waterfalls ($55); and two- to four-hour hiking tours in the refuge. The Profelis Center, which works on reintroduction of cat species into protected areas, is open to visitors for $10, free to Rancho La Merced guests. The visit includes audiovisual information, observation of the felines, and a talk with the biologists carrying out the research. Reservations for Rancho La Merced or the tours is through Selva Mar, telephone 771-4582, fax 771-1903.

Cabinas Ballena has three cabins along a river and six fronting a beach with Ballena Island in the foreground. Lighting is mostly by candlelight or lantern. Lodging is rustic-comfortable and each cabin is different. One has a bedroom on either side of an open living-kitchen area, the house raised off the ground. One is two-story with bedrooms above and a balcony looking out to the sea. Another has solar panels. Rates are from $25 to $60. Horses are $20 a day, and Caño Island is only a 45-minute boat ride away. Typical Costa Rican fare can be arranged at a small restaurant. Telephone 771-4582, fax 771-1903 (Selva Mar).

11

What to See and Do: Costa Rica's Caribbean Coast

The Atlantic Coast is shorter than the Pacific and has a more extensive coastal plain. The area offers long, uncluttered beaches, high forested mountains, coconut palms, plantations of cacao and bananas, national parks and wildlife refuges, sleepy villages, and a commercial port.

Route to Limón

The newer highway through Guapiles and Braulio Carrillo National Park cuts travel time to 2½ hours by road from San José to Limón. Even when you have left the park, though, keep your eyes peeled for sloths in the trees. If you are driving, be careful of heavy fog and landslides, especially through the park, and also of speeding drivers. (Note safety recommendations for the park in Chapter 12.) See the North Central section (Chapter 8) for a description of other destinations on this route. I arbitrarily fixed the boundary between these two sections just past the turnoff to Horquetas, a road that ties the north central part of the country to the Caribbean. The older highway from San José through Cartago and Turrialba, described in the Central section (Chapter 7), requires about four hours of travel time. The two highways join at Siquirres for the final lap into Limón.

Just a note here about travel on this route from San José to Limón through Braulio Carrillo Park. If a landslide closes the road on your return to San José, officials where cars are stopped usually can tell you how long it may be before Braulio Carrillo is clear. You can wait or consider two alternate routes: one is through Puerto Viejo de Sarapaquí, which will take at

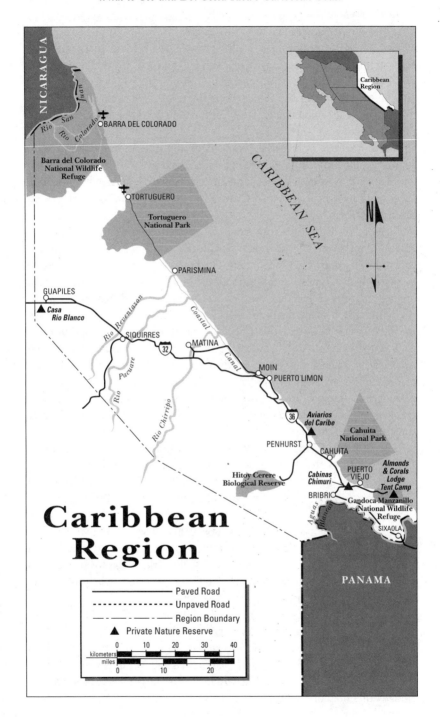

NICARAGUA

Rio San Juan

Rio Colorado

BARRA DEL COLORADO

Barra del Colorado
National Wildlife
Refuge

CARIBBEAN SEA

TORTUGUERO

Tortuguero
National Park

N

PARISMINA

GUAPILES

▲ *Casa
Rio Blanco*

Rio Reventazon

Coastal

SIQUIRRES

32

MATINA

Canal

MOIN

Rio Pacuare

PUERTO LIMON

Rio Chirripo

36

*Aviarios
del Caribe* ▲

Cahuita
National Park

PENHURST

CAHUITA

Hitoy Cerere
Biological Reserve

*Cabinas
Chimuri*

PUERTO
VIEJO

*Almonds
& Corals
Lodge
Tent Camp*

BRIBRI ▲

Aguas Blancas

Gandoca-Manzanillo
National Wildlife
Refuge

SIXAOLA

Caribbean
Region

PANAMA

Caribbean
Region

———————— Paved Road

------------ Unpaved Road

—·—·—·— Region Boundary

▲ Private Nature Reserve

kilometers 0   10   20   30   40

miles 0   10   20

least 3½ hours, or you can go back to Siquirres and return through Turrialba, at least 2½ hours. Both routes involve narrow, mountainous roads with potholes. If it is getting toward night, my advice to you is to seek lodging at some of the places mentioned below and wait until morning.

The large pipelines you notice along the road carry petroleum products from the port at Limón to a RECOPE refinery near Cartago. From Siquirres pipelines follow the Turrialba route.

Many travelers from earlier years made the journey from San José to Limón via the famous Jungle Train, discontinued in 1991. Even though the national railway system gave up the ghost in 1995, ending any remaining freight and passenger service in Costa Rica, the imprint of the steel rails on this area is deep.

Signs point to towns whose names tie them to the railroad: Linea B, 28 Millas. Many short lines provided transportation in this area, some with rail cars pulled by burros until the 1950s. The main line took from 1871 to 1890 to build, with Chinese and West Indians brought in as workers. To help finance the project, bananas were grown for export (and to feed the workers), and that brought in more blacks from British colonies, many from Jamaica. That is how the United Fruit Company got its start in Costa Rica.

Though only about 3 percent of the country's residents are African American, the percentage in the province of Limón is about one-third. Their cultural influence adds to the flavor of the Caribbean zone and, because many speak English, broadens communications for monolingual English-speaking tourists. It is, however, a Creole English whose expressions may surprise and delight you.

The Indian influence in the Caribbean is more heavily felt as you go farther south to the Talamanca coast—land of the Bribrí and Cabecar Indians. There are three Indian reserves: KéköLdi, Talamanca-Bribrí, and Talamanca-Cabecar. The rich mix of Indian and black cultures in the area is unique in Costa Rica.

For the nature traveler, the Caribbean area has much to offer. Just 36 miles (58 km) from San José, or about 10 miles (17 km) after the ranger station on the eastern edge of Braulio Carrillo park, is Casa Río Blanco, a small private nature reserve, well-managed by a dedicated, delightful couple, Thea and Ron. See Chapter 13 for a description.

Stop by La Ponderosa restaurant, a local landmark, if you are hungry or need a break. It is a steak house and *chicharronera* (*chicharrones* in Costa Rica have no resemblance to the pork skins sold in the United States). Open from 6:30 a.m. to 11:00 p.m. daily, credit cards accepted. Yes, it is named for the TV program—a photo of Ben Cartwright and his boys hangs above the bar, along with a map of the Old West namesake.

Continuing on past Guapiles y Guácimo, watch for the Agricultural School of the Humid Tropical Region (EARTH) on the left. The college has a four-year program for students from Latin America, focused on balancing agricultural production and resource conservation in the humid tropics. Research at the school's banana plantations, whose earnings help provide scholarships for students, is aimed at developing an environmentally safer fruit. You can visit the plant where banana waste is recycled into paper and buy products made from it in the gift shop on campus. Other tours encompass a banana plantation or packing plant and nontraditional plant crops such as *pejibaye*, yuca, pepper, plantain, and *ñampi* (a tuber).

A star attraction is EARTH's 865-acre (350-ha) forest reserve, mostly regenerating secondary forest, where you may be able to see the great green macaw, monkeys, toucans, poisonous frogs, a fer-de-lance snake, or the morpho butterfly. Ninety-five species of timber trees have been identified so far. Cost of the three-hour student-guided forest tour is $5 per person. Call 255-2000, extension 4601 or 4603, to make arrangements—mornings are recommended for the walk.

EARTH offers short courses for small farmers and other groups. When the 32 rooms in the training center are not in use, travelers may stay overnight there: double $40, single, $25. Airy rooms have ceiling fans and private baths with hot water. Guests can eat in the dining hall. Call 255-2000, extension 5001 to inquire about space.

A stone's throw farther on the other side of the highway, just before the town of Pocora, is Hotel Río Palmas, a place I like. A delightful nature trail behind the hotel winds through riparian habitat, mostly between two rivers, the Palmas and Dos Novillas. I recommend walking it early in the morning when the light just begins to play on the waters. Kingfishers, herons, toucans, and poison dart frogs (red with blue limbs) will reward you. Cement walkways allow you to cross over and walk through the water at several points. Just before the first long cement walkway along the water's edge, notice the woody vine that tied itself in a knot.

You are likely to see an armadillo on the hotel grounds, along with colorful basilisks. Owner Erick Berlin, also in the tropical plant business, has more than 500 varieties of tropical flowers on the property, some of which you can see next to the hotel. A palmito plantation provides fresh heart of palm for the restaurant. Many plants in the garden are labeled; there are loads of heliconias. Rooms with private baths and very hot water are around a flowered courtyard, with a small swimming pool and thatched rancho at one end. Original watercolors provide accents, along with quilted bedspreads in hues of rose, turquoise, and green. The 32 rooms have high pitched ceilings, and are cooled by ceiling fans. Each room also has television (local channels).

Río Palmas Hotel between Braulio Carrillo and Limón (Ree Strange Sheck)

Single $39, double $44; standards (no hot water) $29 and $34. Credit cards accepted.

Hotel Río Palmas will arrange your tour at EARTH and offers a two-hour tour of its own trail plus a visit to a large tropical ornamental plant farm, which exports 30 varieties around the world. Other tour options are a macadamia farm, a medicinal plant farm, a three-hour horseback ride, or, for the truly fit, a six-hour trek to the Pocora waterfalls. Tortuguero tours can easily be arranged from here. Public buses to Limón and points south pass in front of the hotel. Telephone 760-0305, fax 760-0296.

Whether you stay overnight at the hotel or not, the Río Palmas restaurant, open 6:00 a.m. to 10:30 p.m., offers good eats. It is a good place to try natural fruit drinks such as cas, mango, or guanabana, and if you have not yet tried fried yuca, you can do it here. Tired of gallo pinto? Breakfast can be pancakes or an omelette. Try your hand at cracking macadamia nuts found in the typical cart at the rear of the restaurant.

Continuing on toward Limón, the highway crosses two mighty rivers of white-water rafting fame: the Reventazón just before Siquirres and the Pacuare after. Remember Siquirres is where the older road from San José through Turrialba comes in, offering an alternate loop for your return.

Notice changes in architecture as you drop into the Caribbean lowlands—houses raised off the ground or two-story houses with main living quarters above for added ventilation. You'll see lots of bananas and plantains;

near the Río Cuba, watch for a mixed plantation of coconut palms and *cacao* trees on the right. Cacao, whose seeds give us chocolate, was once the country's top cash crop. Its seeds were still used as currency in the 1700s.

If you are driving, you may want to fill up at one of the several large gas stations along the highway—they are harder to find going south after Limón.

Limón, or more correctly Puerto Limón (population 55,866), is capital of the province of Limón and the principal port on the Caribbean coast. Christopher Columbus dropped anchor offshore near La Uvita Island, in front of Limón, on September 18, 1502. Though he stayed about 20 days, he apparently never set foot on the mainland. At that time, present-day Limón was called Cariay by the Indians who inhabited the area.

Around October 12, the day traditionally commemorating Columbus and his discovery and which ticos celebrate as Día de las Culturas (to recognize contributions of all cultures), Limón throws a party that draws about 200,000 people. It may not be Río, but this carnival is five days of music, parades, dancing, bullfights (the bull is never killed in this nation of peace), and local arts and crafts.

During the rest of the year, Limón is a center of commerce (with deep-water docking facilities at nearby Moín) for fishing, shipping, agriculture, and tourism. If sloths have so far eluded you, go to Vargas Park near the seawall, where several live. If you cannot spot the well-camouflaged mammals, a passerby will usually help. If you go to the Municipal Market, stop by one of the food stands to try rice and beans, or a fried cake, or *agua de sapo*, literally "toad water" but actually a kind of cold agua dulce with lemon.

In Limón and south, you still see a few signs of the April 22, 1991, earthquake that walloped the region, though reconstruction of buildings and damaged roads and bridges has whittled away at the physical evidence. The quake, which registered 7.4 on the Richter scale, raised the Atlantic coast about 5 feet (1.5 m) at Limón, diminishing to about a foot (30 cm) farther south at Gandoca near Panama. So you will note some changes along the beaches. A positive note is that scientists predict no major earthquake here for about another 100 years.

Surfers find the breaks at Playa Bonita and Playa Portete, north of downtown, and at Uvita Island, with December-January and June the best months, along with hurricane season.

My pick of hotels in and near Limón includes the following, some on the water, some with forest, and one downtown.

Hotel Jardín Tropical Azul, north of Limón on the road to Portete and Moín, is on a hillside across the road from the sea. White buildings with red roofs are scattered among gardens and trees. A pool for adults and one for children are near the thatched La Rumba bar. The Bastón del Emperador restaurant has an international menu and also offers Caribbean specialties such as rice and beans and *rondón* (smoked fish).

All 32 rooms are air-conditioned with color TV and have private baths with hot water. Sixteen rooms have pretty forest-green bathroom fixtures, tile floors, dark green comforters on double and single beds, and private porches: single $46, double $52. Sixteen family units have carpeted bedrooms and attractive living rooms with glass-topped mimbre tables, cushioned sofas, glass-topped dinettes with chairs, and small refrigerators: $87 for up to three persons. Credit cards accepted.

Trails are being developed in the forest belonging to the hotel, both for walks and horseback riding. Tours are through a local tour company. The hotel will arrange transportation from San José or Limón. Telephone 798-1244, 798-1237; fax 798-1259.

At Hotel Maribú Caribe, a single is $68, a double $78. Fifty-two air-conditioned rooms are located in 14 upscale thatched bungalows, some with ocean views. The hotel has a restaurant specializing in international food, a snack bar, swimming pools, a gift shop, and parking. Credit cards are accepted. It offers tours to watch turtle-nesting during the season plus one-day tours to Tortuguero for $65 and visits to Cahuita National Park for snorkeling at $75 and diving at $85. If you do not have time to go all the way to Tortuguero, you can take a three-hour tour on the canals for $35. The hotel is situated on a hill, with grassy grounds going down to the Caribbean. Hotel transportation from San José to Limón is $40. Telephone 758-4543, 758-4010; fax 758-3541, 234-0193.

At Hotel Matama near Playa Bonita, a room for one or two people is $76. The open-air restaurant/bar and rooms in scattered bungalows are nestled among the trees. Some of the bathrooms have small tropical gardens growing under their skylights. The 16 rooms are nicely furnished; cushioned wicker chairs add color. There is also a pool, air conditioning, car rental, and parking. Credit cards are accepted. There is a short botanical trail and a walk to an orchid garden on the property, and horseback rides can be arranged. Day trips to Tortuguero are $65. Every Thursday, live music by local groups brings the sounds of salsa, reggae, and calypso, while Saturday brings a disco for dancing. The restaurant is open to the public from 6:30 a.m. to 11:00 p.m. Telephone 758-1123, 758-4200; fax 758-4499.

Across the road from the Matama is Apartotel Corobicí, with its open-air restaurant and a patio area next to the ocean and a dynamite view of Playa Bonita next door. Resident owner María de McGuinness says a pool may be in by the time you arrive. Rooms in the two-story hotel with wide verandas are small, clean, and simply furnished, with private baths and hot water. Six of the 21 rooms are air-conditioned: single $28, double $50. Rooms with

CACAO

Cacao trees were cultivated in Costa Rica before the Spaniards arrived. The plant, whose seeds provide us with cocoa, chocolate, and cocoa butter, is native to tropical America. The name it was given in Latin, Theobroma, *means "food of the gods."*

Spanish explorers found cacao fields at Matina in 1540. During colonial times, it was the most important cash crop until coffee was introduced, and cacao beans were even used as money up to the late 1700s. Climatic conditions continue to make the Atlantic lowlands the major region for cacao plantations; you will see them on the road south from Limón to Puerto Viejo and between Braulio Carrillo park and Limón.

Cacao is a short tree, about 26 feet (8 m) in height. It has some interesting biological peculiarities. Leaves are both green (mature ones) and red (young ones). They go from a horizontal to a vertical position depending on the amount of sunlight—the more intense the sun, the more they droop. The fruits or pods (called mazorcas*) grow directly from the trunk or branches, hanging*

like ornaments. As the pods ripen, they change from green to yellow or red. As many as 60 seeds—the commercial cocoa beans—can be in the oval-shaped fruit. The one opened for me had 43, all covered in a slippery, soft pulp that is quite tasty.

Harvest is year-round, but it peaks in April and May and from October to December. Mature pods are hand-picked and cut open. The seeds are fermented for a few days and then dried, either in the sun or mechanically. They are then shipped to factories—there are three large ones in Costa Rica—for processing. If you take a side road off the main highway in the Penhurst area, you will see platforms with cacao spread out to dry.

Costa Rica was once Central America's leader in cacao export, but disease damaged many trees in 1978. Gradually, production has increased since then. CATIE, the agricultural research center at Turrialba, has worked with disease-resistant strains and distributes hybrids.

Most of the cacao crop exported from Costa Rica goes to the United States, France, and Germany.

ceiling fans are $21 for a single, $38 for a double. Six apartments, which can sleep up to five people in two rooms, have cooking facilities and refrigerators: $53. Credit cards accepted. Telephone 257-4674 or 758-2930; fax 255-3702.

At 39-room Hotel Acón downtown, a single is $20, a double $26. The hotel has a restaurant, private baths with hot water, air conditioning, TV, and a discotheque and arranges trips to Tortuguero. Telephone 758-1010, fax 758-2924.

Express buses for Limón depart hourly during the day from San José at Avenida 3, Calles 19/21, near the national park. You may want to purchase your ticket a day in advance to ensure a seat.

Northern Caribbean

Tortuguero and Barra del Colorado National Parks on the northern Caribbean coast are popular destinations for nature travelers. SANSA and Travelair offer air options. (See Practical Extras for schedules.) The most convenient way to get to either from San José is by taking a prearranged one-day or multiday tour that includes transportation by bus and boat or airplane, hotel, and meals. Some offer guided exploration of the waterways off the main canal. Hotels and travel-related businesses from Limón south also arrange tours to Tortuguero. You can do the trip yourself, too, arranging boat transportation from Moín outside Limón, finding your own lodging, and hiring a boat and local guide once you arrive at Parismina, Tortuguero, or Barra del Colorado.

The canals that run parallel to the sea were built in the 1970s, connecting existing rivers and lagoons to provide an 80-mile (129-km) inland waterway from Moín, just north of Limón, to Barra del Colorado. Roads have yet to link some of this area with the rest of the country, so this lifeline of canals and rivers is the highway for canoes loaded with bananas and coconuts, logs that are floated south, and barges carrying supplies north. Families travel in tiny dugouts. Sometimes the narrow canals open into wide lagoons; signs give distances and directions. A trip on these waters is fascinating, and one notes a courtesy in traffic lacking in San José. Large boats propelled by motors generally slow down when small craft appear, to avoid swamping them. Once, when the tour boat I was on died between Tortuguero and Barra del Colorado, the first boat by took all of us on, luggage and all.

Fishing draws visitors to this area as well, especially for snook and tarpon. Lodges at Barra del Parismina, Barra del Colorado, and Tortuguero offer fishing.

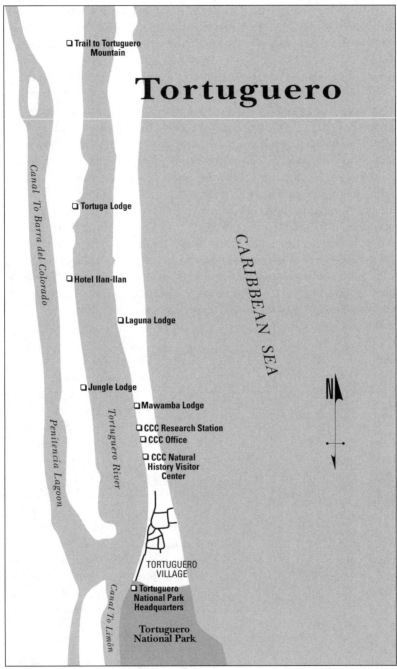

Trail to Tortuguero Mountain

Tortuguero

Canal To Barra del Colorado

CARIBBEAN SEA

Tortuga Lodge

Hotel Ilan-Ilan

Laguna Lodge

Jungle Lodge

Mawamba Lodge

CCC Research Station

CCC Office

CCC Natural History Visitor Center

Penitencia Lagoon

Tortuguero River

N

TORTUGUERO VILLAGE

Tortuguero National Park Headquarters

Canal To Limón

Tortuguero National Park

MAP NOT TO SCALE

Isolated for so long—the first public telephone was installed in 1972—Tortuguero yet feels like an out-of-the-way place despite the thousands of tourists who arrive every year. Many of these visitors never get to the village, but I hope you do. The Tortuguero experience is turtles and forest and rivers, but it is also a special brand of people who live on this edge of land and sea.

The village of Tortuguero is small—about 450 people who work mainly in farming (rice, coconuts, fruits, and vegetables) and tourism. Stop by the Joshua B. Powers Information Kiosk to learn about the area's history, from settlement by peoples related to the Maya to its fame by the 1700s among merchants and seamen for the thousands of turtles nesting here to the impact of the Atlantic railroad and the canals. There is information on green turtles and the parks. The kiosk is also where you can sign up for the night-time turtle walks led by local guides from July 1 to October 15. The office is open from 4:00 to 6:00 p.m., and the cost is $5 per person and 100 colones that go to the local development association. Remember to wear dark clothes for the walk, stay quiet. Cameras are no longer permitted. Please respect your guide's instructions—the rules have reason behind them. The most intense nesting period for green turtles is June to September, March to May for leatherbacks. Loggerheads and hawksbills also come ashore here.

Several sodas and gift shops are tucked away on the few paths that meander through the village. The Travelair office is at Paraíso Tropical, a gift shop with artisan offerings and clothing as well as basics for travelers. Open from 8:00 a.m. to 7:00 p.m. Owner Jessie makes some of the things. She still has a first edition of my book on her shelves—I signed it, hoping somebody buys it someday. The Jungle Shop and Tienda de Artesanía also offer gifts.

A five-minute walk north of the village is the Caribbean Conservation Corporation's (CCC) H. Clay Frick Natural History Visitor Center—a must. Beautiful, colorful, informative exhibits focus on ecological relationships, highlighting turtles and the area's other diverse wildlife as well as work of the CCC. Founded in 1959 to support the work of the late Dr. Archie Carr, CCC is the oldest sea turtle conservation organization in the world. It strives to preserve sea turtles and other marine and coastal life through research, training, education, and protection of natural areas. You can purchase some of Dr. Carr's books, T-shirts, and information packets on turtles and other gift items. An 18-minute video in English or Spanish describes Tortuguero's unique relationship with sea turtles. A biologist is always on hand to answer questions. Open from 10:00 a.m. to noon and 2:00 to 6:00 p.m. Admission is $2 for adults, children up to 12 free. Credit cards accepted.

If you are interested in volunteering for either the CCC turtle-tagging program or neotropical bird study on both resident and migratory species, contact the U.S. office for schedules and costs (room, board, and transportation)—one-week minimum stay. Call (800) 678-7853, or write to P.O. Box 2866, Gainesville, FL 32602. In Costa Rica, the CCC address is Apartado 246-2050, San Pedro; telephone/fax 224-9215 or 710-0547.

Small cabins as well as larger lodges are on both sides of the Tortuguero River (see map). Three on the other side of the river from the village and the turtle beaches are Tortuga Lodge, Jungle Lodge, and Hotel Ilan-Ilan, all of which run their own tours to Tortuguero from San José. Tours from San José generally include a brief stop in Braulio Carrillo and at one of the banana plantations. Tour prices listed are for double occupancy.

Operated by Costa Rica Expeditions, Tortuga Lodge has 24 rooms opening onto shady verandas with the typical Costa Rican tall-backed leather rocking chairs that invite you to sit and watch life on the river in front or bird life in a garden loaded with palms, heliconias, and colorful crotons. Deluxe rooms, large and airy, have screened windows on three sides, simple furnishings, ceiling fans, and private baths with hot water—a shower you could have a small party in. Standard rooms are small and darker. Meals are served family style—good food and lots of it. Cover yourself with repellent and venture into the forest behind the lodge on a short loop trail (boots available for $1 per day). Optional activities include a night boat tour ($28), Cerro Tortuguero tour, boat rental, and turtle walks ($15). Whether you go on the turtle walk or not, do not miss the excellent natural-history slide presentation about Tortuguero, the turtles and other wildlife, and the park—free of charge. Canal/river trips with a local guide are included in some packages. The one I took with Wallace as the guide was magical—a flock of collared aracaris, my first look at the beautiful chestnut-colored woodpecker, a days-old howler clinging to his mother, bare-throated tiger herons, crocodiles, three-toed sloths, kingfishers, crocodiles, and Jesus Christ lizards. Wallace can also tell you about trees and plants.

Guests can fly both ways or opt to do one way via the canals. Two-day one-night trips start at $333 per person, double occupancy, including transportation (one-way by air), lodging, meals, and taxes. The three-day two-night trip is from $396. For lodging alone, standard single $69, double $81; deluxe single $98, double $118, all plus tax. Credit cards accepted. Reserve for Tortuga Lodge through Costa Rica Expeditions: telephone 257-0766 or 222-0333; fax 257-1665. E-mail crexped@sol.racsa.co.cr; World Wide Web http://www.cool.co.cr/crexped.html. Offices of Costa Rica Expeditions in San José are at Avenida 3, Calles Central/2.

The Jungle Lodge, operated by Cotur, S.A., has 48 comfortable rooms in buildings scattered between the forest and the Tortuguero River, many connected by covered walkways. Peach-colored quilted bedspreads and peach

The Jungle Lodge at Tortuguero (Ree Strange Sheck)

and turquoise drapes contrast with polished dark hardwood floors. A full-length mirror adds a nice touch. Cooling is by ceiling fan. Private bathrooms are large, all with hot water. Happy hour is offered nightly in a thatched bar, and tasty buffet-style meals are served in the separate dining room. A short loop trail in back of the hotel will take you to the Penitencia Lagoon and into a forest corridor. Remember repellent.

A two-hour trip in a canoe or motorboat through canals is $15, as is the bird-watchers' special, from 5:30 to 7:30 a.m.—a real delight. The naturalist guide told us how the howler monkey makes his remarkable sound. He told us about mating habits of the northern jacana—the male cares for the nest and the young—and about the buttress roots of the gavilán and other large trees. Seeing the ringed kingfisher in early morning light is a thrill. A night tour is $18. Packages include transportation (by canals—extra to fly one or both ways), food, lodging, and taxes. The day trip is $115. A two-day, one-night trip, at $176 per person, double occupancy, includes the night turtle tour during the season and a morning canal tour. The three-day, two-night tour, $239 per person, includes a tour to Tortuguero National Park and a hike to Tortuguero Hill. A hotel boat will take you across the river to the village so you can visit the CCC and shop, or go to the beach. A butterfly farm is in progress that will allow guests to see the stages of butterfly development. Tours run daily. Credit cards accepted. Telephone 233-0133 or 257-4142;

fax 233-0778. Cotur offices in San José are at on Calle 36, Paseo Colón/ Avenida 3, just around the corner from Toyota.

Hotel Ilan-Ilan, operated by Agencia Mitur, S.A., offers 24 rooms in two cement buildings. Rooms are large with private baths, set in what the company calls at 20-acre (8-ha) botanical garden. Staff tells about the Italian biologist who would not believe that the "walking palm" really walks, so he took measurements and returned to see for himself—it did. The record for an individual bird count while staying at Ilan-Ilan is 300 birds in 72 hours. Every guest has the opportunity to plant a tree. The boat for the canal trip, carries 44 persons and leaves from a new dock in Hamburgo.

Three miles (5 km) of trails offer a good half-day excursion. One kilometer is cement, fully wheelchair accessible, and the hotel has one room suitable for the handicapped. Tours depart daily. The two-day, one-night tour is $160 per person; the three-day, two-night tour is $215 per person, transportation, meals, lodging, and taxes included. Ask about an optional Puerto Viejo de Sarapiquí-Tortuguero route. Make reservations through Mitur: telephone 255-2031 or 255-2262; fax 255-1946; Internet mitour @sol.racsa.co.cr. The Agencia Mitur office is on Paseo Colón, Calles 20/22, just west of the Children's Hospital.

On the east side of the river, Mawamba Lodge is walking distance north of the village of Tortuguero and the CCC natural history center. Forty comfortable rooms have ceiling fans and private baths with hot water. There is a pool and a conference room for daily natural history programs as well as a 7-acre (3-ha) private reserve with trails. Food is served family style, and there is an honor bar.

Night tours are $17 per person, and the turtle walk from July through September is $10. A one-day tour to Mawamba is $72. The two-day, one-night tour from San José is $201, single or double, including ground transport from San José, meals, lodging, taxes, guide, and regular tours. A three-day, two-night tour is $252. Credit cards accepted. Options also include air transport one or both ways or coming through Puerto Viejo de Sarapiquí—inquire about costs. Telephone 223-2421, 222-5463; fax 255-4039. Mawamba offices in San José is 3½ blocks north of Paseo Colón on Calle 24.

Laguna Lodge has 20 rooms with ceiling fans and private baths (no hot water), also on the ocean side of the river. The standard two-day, one-night tour is $187, a three-day, two-night tour is $259. Credit cards accepted. Options with different rates include one way by air as well as one way through Sarapiquí. Telephone 225-3740, fax 283-8031.

North of Tortuguero is Barra del Colorado Wildlife Refuge and a number of lodges that offer natural history tours along with their primary focus on sportfishing. Two of them are Rio Colorado Lodge and Silver King Lodge.

Río Colorado Lodge pioneered the boat tour to the Caribbean coming from Puerto Viejo de Sarapiquí, following the Sarapiquí River to the San Juan and then on the Colorado River. Passengers go by bus to Puerto Viejo, where they board the Colorado Queen for Barra del Colorado. The return trip is through Tortuguero, with a stop at the park, and on through the canals, to be picked up by bus, traveling through Braulio Carrillo National Park to San José. The two-day, one-night trip is $196. Built right on the water, the lodge has 19 rooms with private baths, some with air conditioning. Cost per day for those not on a tour is $90 per person, including lodging, meals, and happy hour. Telephone 232-4063 or 232-8610; fax 231-5987; in the U.S. and Canada (800) 243-9777, fax (813) 933-3280. The office of Río Colorado Lodge in San José is in the lobby of Hotel Corobicí, which is north of Paseo Colón near La Sabana park.

Silver King Lodge has large rooms with tongue-and-groove floors and walls, bamboo ceilings, queen-size beds, orthopedic mattresses, and private baths with hot water—coffeemakers in each room. Laundry service is complimentary and there is a ten-person Jacuzzi. Aluminum canoes and fiberglass kayaks are available for estuary trips into the rainforest at Barra del Colorado, navigable only by these small craft. Private paths also lead into the jungle. Guided tours are available into the wildlife refuge as well as to Tortuguero and to see turtle nesting (July through September) or crocodiles at night. A two-day, three-night option is $528 each for double occupancy, including round-trip airfare from San José, lodging, food, soft drinks, and two boat tours of Barra del Colorado and Tortuguero canals. A two-day, one-night package is $353 per person, double occupancy, including round-trip airfare, lodging, food, soft drinks, and a tour through the Barra del Colorado refuge. Ask about a package that includes a guided canoe trip, lodging, meals, and drinks, $175 per person, double occupancy. Telephone 381-0849, fax 381-1403; in the U.S. (800) 847-3474, fax (813) 943-8783.

Southern Caribbean

South from Limón you can travel by road all the way to Panama. The direct bus from San José to Sixaola at the border will take you by Cahuita National Park and to the Indian village of Bribrí. It does not go all the way in to Puerto Viejo. There is a direct San José–Puerto Viejo bus, however, and there are buses from Limón to Cahuita and Puerto Viejo. (This is Puerto Viejo de

Limón.) See Practical Extras for bus schedules. Several tour companies now offer nature-oriented tours to the southern Caribbean region, and lodges and hotels in the area arrange visits to the parks and reserves.

With the Caribbean on the left and forest remnants and farms on the right, there is much to take in. Some fields contain coconut palms, banana plants, and cacao trees together.

About 20 miles (30 km) south of Limón, just before the Estrella River, is a delightful destination for nature travelers: Aviarios del Caribe. Luís and Judy Arroyo own and operate this refuge (see Chapter 13). It is open for overnight or day visits—terrific birding.

At Penhurst, a road west goes through miles of cacao plantations. Platforms are covered with seeds spread out to dry. You may see guanábana fruit covered with the same blue plastic bags impregnated with insecticide that you have noticed over bunches of bananas. The size of the guanábanas is astounding. Follow this dirt road through big banana plantations to the Hitoy-Cerere Biological Reserve. Little visited, it holds treasures for those who reach its forests.

Back on the main road, a few miles farther is the town of Cahuita and Cahuita National Park. A pedestrian entrance to the park is downtown; another is further south at Puerto Vargas.

Cahuita, 27 miles (44 km) south of Limón by paved road, has only about 3,682 people. Though hotels and lodges are still small, tourism is increasingly big business here.

The thriving tour company Cahuita Tours and Rentals (telephone 755-0232 or 755-0273; telephone/fax 755-0052) is a full-service operation where you can send a fax; exchange money; buy newspapers, handcrafts, or postage stamps; make reservations; and find a public telephone. Owners Antonio Mora and Rudolfo Henriquez offer general information about the area. Snorkeling equipment is available, as well as bikes and scuba gear. For $20, you can spend four hours in a glass-bottomed boat viewing the marvels of the coral reefs offshore. Other tours include a morning guided nature walk ($18), a visit to the Bribrí Indian reserve ($25), and visits to Manzanillo and the Gandoca-Manzanillo refuge and to Tortuguero National Park. A tour to Hitoy-Cerere Biological Reserve with a bilingual local guide is about $35 per person, with a minimum of three people. Open from 7:00 a.m. to noon and 1:30 to 7:00 p.m. daily. Credit cards accepted.

Here are some of Cahuita's hotels, starting with those off the first entrance to town, almost 2 miles (3 km) before the main entrance. Watch for hotel signs.

The Magellan Inn, tucked away on a street back from the beach, has six delightful rooms. Original oil paintings adorn the white walls. There are big closets, a long desk, and beautiful woods in carpeted rooms. Each room has French doors that open onto a terrace facing the pool and a tropical garden colored by bright bougainvillea and hibiscus flowers as well as avocado, guava, orange, and lime trees. Baths have king-size towels, washcloths, and hot, hot water. There are ceiling fans not only in the rooms but also on the individual terraces, which have cushioned bamboo furniture. Owners are Elizabeth Newton and Jean Paul Fevillatre.

The dining room and bar is also open to the garden. Classical music sets the tone for breakfast, quiet jazz for a candlelight dinner. Daughter Terry and husband Etervé, in charge of the restaurant, serve dinners with a French Creole–Polynesian flavor. Dessert of the day may be puffed pastry with vanilla ice cream and chocolate sauce or banana flambé. Lunches feature salads and sandwiches on baguettes, and anytime you can ask for regular milk shakes or milk shakes with a zing—for example, After Eight, with chocolate and creme de menthe. The restaurant, closed Wednesday, is open from 6:00 to 9:00 a.m., noon to 3:00 p.m., and 8:00 to 10:00 p.m.

Toucans, parrots, parakeets, and hummingbirds like the place, and sloths are not uncommon here. A garden path by the pool leads down to a coral hole that was once under the sea. Guests may choose an exclusive morning canoe trip with an Indian guide on a river where even a manatee has been spotted—but no promises. Perhaps you can be content seeing monkeys, birds, orchids, and crocodiles. The cost is $26 per person. Guided horseback rides and beach and Tortuguero tours can be arranged. Rooms at the Magellan Inn are $55, single or double, including continental breakfast. Credit cards accepted. English, Spanish, French, and Italian spoken. Telephone/fax 755-0035.

Chalet y Cabinas Hibiscus is by the sea. Three bungalows; two two-story, two-bedroom houses; and a one-bedroom house are scattered on palm-studded grounds. Private baths with hot water feature showers lined with smooth river stones. Lace curtains cover the windows, and mosquito nets are draped over the beds, though the owners, the Grafs, say they are more for show than necessity. The houses have balconies, sitting rooms, and completely furnished kitchens. The two-bedroom houses are $100 each; the one-bedroom, $50. Bungalows are from $40 to $55. Credit cards are not accepted. English and German also are spoken. The Hibiscus has no restaurant, but several are nearby. Telephone 755-0015, fax 755-0021.

The Hotel Jaguar has 45 rooms across the road from the beach on the north end of town, close enough to go to sleep to the sound of the surf. The building design incorporates cross-ventilation and thermo-siphoning, resulting in passively cooled rooms that have queen-size beds with orthopedic mattresses and private baths with hot water. Louvered shutters cover screened windows. Just outside the front door are lounge chairs on long porches facing the beach. A variety of fruit trees draw birds to the hotel grounds. Watch for the flash of the scarlet-rumped tanager and listen to the parrots. Superior rooms are $46 and have hot water; standards without hot water are $39. VISA and MasterCard are accepted.

Paul and Melba Vigneault own the hotel and are creators of a menu fit for a gourmet, true elegance by the sea, with such delicacies as avocado omelets for breakfast and French-Caribbean cooking that uses fresh herbs and spices in ten sauces served with fish, beef, or chicken. The sea bass with heart of palm sauce is memorable, or try the chicken with cashew fruit sauce. If you cannot stay at the Jaguar, stop by for a meal. The restaurant is open for breakfast beginning at 7:30 a.m., and dinner is served from 7:00 to 9:00 p.m. Lunches are light—salads and sandwiches.

Nature trails on the 18 acres (7 ha) offer hotel guests the possibility of seeing a crocodile, armadillo, sloth, kinkajou, agouti, or colorful frogs. Trips can be arranged to Tortuguero for $55 ($75 for overnight), to the Bribrí reserve for $25 per person, and across to Panama for $30. A rental shop has boogie boards, beach mats, fins, and snorkeling equipment as well as books and souvenir items. Telephone 226-3775 or 755-0238; fax 226-4693. Transportation from Cahuita is available if you come by bus. Taxi to Cahuita from Limón is about $25.

Next door is charming Bungalow Malú. Four rooms in river stone and wood bungalows are nestled among colorful tropical vegetation in expansive gardens across the road from the beach. Bathrooms have river stone floors and showers with shower-head hot water. Decorator touches abound. Wood washed ashore after storms has been polished and used as door handles and light fixtures—natural sculptures. Rooms have a built-in desk, reading lamps, and a small refrigerator, some have queen-size beds. The closet and headboards are made of wood and bamboo. Stone paths lead to a pavilion where owner Alessandra Bucci will offer breakfast, light lunches, and a fixed menu for dinner. There is a *pila* and lines, so guests may do their own laundry if they wish. Rooms are $30 for two, with $3 more per extra person—two can sleep up to three persons; two, up to four. Credit cards not accepted. No telephone yet, so you will have to take your chances for space.

El Atlántida has 30 rooms, each with its own porch separated by a cane division from adjoining porches and fringed with a thatched-roof overhang. Rooms have fans, reading lamps, cane furniture, wooden shutters over screened windows, and private baths with shower-head hot water. The single rate is $53, the double $65, full breakfast and taxes included. Credit cards are accepted. There is an open-air restaurant, pool, parking, gift shop, and a tour desk in the reception area—don't miss the antique crank cash register.

El Encanto Bed and Breakfast at Cahuita (Ree Strange Sheck)

Managers Luc Généreus and Francine Darveau have added to the gardens, ablaze with color. A small bridge over a fish pond connects the pool and the snack bar. Playa Negra is in front. Atlántida offers eight tours, including a four-hour jungle walk, a snorkeling tour, or a visit to Bribrí ($20 per person), bird-watching at Aviarios del Caribe ($30), a tropical farm tour or visit to an orchid farm ($10), and an iguana farm tour ($15). Horseback riding to a waterfall is $35. Telephone/fax 755-0213.

El Encanto, 300 meters from downtown on the road to Playa Negra, has three roomy bungalows, each furnished with a queen-size bed and trundle bed, ceiling fan, reading lamps, table and chairs. Royal blue towels, wash-cloths, and bath mat offset the light sea color of the tiled bath, which comes with hot water. Each bungalow has a walk-in closet. Owners Michael and Karen Russell offer a full breakfast of fruit, toast or muffins and eggs, or pan-cakes or waffles. The dining room/lounge area is open to the large garden through arches on three sides. Tours with local guides, certified by the Talamanca Association for Ecotourism and Conservation, take guests for forest walks, horseback riding, and on reef tours. A single is $40 with break-fast, $37 without; a double is $45 with breakfast, $40 without. Credit cards accepted. Telephone/fax 755-0113.

Cabinas Vaz in downtown Cahuita has 14 older, basic rooms. All have fans and some have shower-head hot water in the private baths. Single $14, double $16, tax included. In a new addition in back, big air-conditioned rooms have an equipped kitchenette, double and single bed, private baths with hot water, and striking glass and carved-wood doors—$80 per room for up to three persons. VISA and MasterCard accepted.

The Vaz restaurant is a good place to watch people while you eat. Prices are reasonable, and you can get typical dishes as well as spaghetti, octopus, lobster, and shrimp. Try *patacones* (fried green plantains). Owner Charles Wilford Vaz, who has lived here for 32 years, will personally prepare breadfruit for you—the right way—if you make arrangements the day before. Telephone for Cabinas Vaz is 755-0218, fax 755-0283.

Practically next door to the entrance to Cahuita National Park is Kelly Creek—with four large, high-ceilinged rooms; lots of louvered wooden shutters, and hardwood floors. The glass-doored shower has shower-head hot water. A covered veranda goes around the rectangular structure. Double $55, no credit cards. Grilled dishes and Spanish food (paella and gazpacho available) highlight the menu in the attractive restaurant, which is open to the public. Perhaps you will spot the caiman who lives in the creek in front of the restaurant. No phone.

You will find music in downtown Cahuita—just walk down the street until you find the kind you like. You will also find a community at work on taking care of the natural resources in and out of the park and security of residents and visitors alike. The Cahuita Development Association, aided by the Tourism Chamber and other local organizations, is spearheading a grassroots effort to protect the park near the downtown entrance. Under an agreement with national parks, the community administers the downtown entrance. On Friday and Saturday, join local people in beach cleanup and trail maintenance. The cabin at the entrance, staffed by local residents, has been rebuilt and holds photos documenting the progress so far. Javier Mullings, head of the association, urges visitors to help. Donations can be monetary, but assistance is also needed in cleanup or training, or you can give binoculars to be used for security.

Continuing on the highway a little more than a mile (2 km) past Cahuita, you will pass the entrance to the Puerto Vargas sector of Cahuita National Park, administered by the park service (see Chapter 12).

The turnoff to Puerto Viejo is near Hone Creek (some maps and signs say Home Creek), about 3 miles (5 km) from the village of Puerto Viejo de Limón. The main highway continues on to Bribrí and Sixaola. There is a direct bus from San José to Puerto Viejo as well as buses from Limón.

Not long after taking the turnoff and where pavement turns to gravel, watch on the right for a sign about the Iguana Farm in the KéköLdi Reserve, open daily from 8:00 a.m. to 4:00 p.m., admission about $1 (road is just past

Cabinas Pingüino). The entrance is about 200 meters down that road. When I was there, the sign was practically hidden, so go slowly and watch on the left. If no one is in the small thatched artisan building, continue to the right up the hill—the iguanas are behind the private house there and someone will show you around. Juana was my guide. KéköLdi people are raising green iguanas, an endangered species. Iguanas traditionally are important to these people for their meat and skins; even their fat is used for medicinal purposes. At the small shop, you will find carved gourds, baskets, drums, and other items made by children and adults. Hikes into the reserve can also be arranged here, led by certified local guides. A tour of the green iguana project and/or walks in the Indian reserve can also be arranged in Puerto Viejo at the ATEC office (see below).

As you near Puerto Viejo, a sign to Cabinas Chimuri, a privately owned nature reserve, is on the right. See Chapter 13 for a description of this unique destination. At Pulpería Violeta, as the main road bends to the right into town, the road left goes to Beach Cottages and Cabinas Black Sand, both thatch-and-bamboo experiences, and to La Perla Negra, a new hotel between ocean and forest.

Beach Cottages is owned and managed by Mauricio Salazar, a Bribrí Indian, and his Austrian-born wife, Colocha. Two bungalows are for rent by the week ($150 for two persons) or the month ($250). Each has a private bath with shower-head hot water, a porch facing the beach across the road, equipped kitchen (small refrigerator and hot plate), and a bedroom upstairs. Furnishings are pleasingly simple. You may have met Mauricio and Colocha at Cabinas Chimuri, which they also own. Mauricio continues to guide there. Telephone/fax 798-1844.

Cabinas Black Sands is next door, also on the road parallel to the beach. This rustic retreat, owned by Diane Applebaum, is on grounds sprinkled with banana, papaya, other fruit trees, pineapple, and palms. Three rooms and a kitchen are in the cabin. There is an outhouse with a flush toilet, and the outdoor shower is open enough to let you watch the birds while you bathe. The cost is $12 for one person, $20 for two. Telephone/fax 758-3844.

Continuing down the road along the beach, you will find a gem, La Perla Negra Hotel. Set against the backdrop of the forest, the two-story hotel is made of beautiful tropical woods. Twenty-four tasteful rooms have either a view of the open sea ($66) or the forest ($61). Some rooms have a sleeping loft, all have nicely designed bathroom areas with a separate room for the toilet and a large dressing area, shower-head hot water, ceiling fans, screened windows, and reading lights. Owners Marlena and Julian Grae designed and supervised the building—he is an architect—and nice touches abound. Double doors open onto balconies or terraces. The restaurant has an international menu, and a swimming pool may be in place by the time you come. La Perla Negra offers bird-watching, boating, and nature walks with local guides. VISA and MasterCard accepted. English and Polish also spoken. Telephone/fax 381-4047.

Back on the main road into town is El Pizote Lodge,. which has its own nature trails where you are almost guaranteed to see small colorful frogs. Lodging is in eight rooms in a U-shaped wooden building with shared baths ($34 single, $50 double) or in six bungalows with private baths ($83 single or double). None has hot water, but the baths are otherwise modern with the delightful feature of high windows so you can watch birds in the tall trees while you shower. There are bright bedspreads, screened windows, cane ceilings, and ceiling fans. A two-bedroom casita has a king-size bed and two doubles—$110 for up to three persons. VISA and MasterCard accepted. Kayaks, snorkeling equipment, and bicycles are available for rent, and El Pizote Lodge offers jungle hikes, tubing, and bird-watching tours. Telephone/fax 229-1428, telephone at lodge 798-1938.

The village of Puerto Viejo de Limón is to the Caribbean what Montezuma is to the Pacific side. Laid back, it has its own beat—a slow and sultry beat. A mecca for surfers, it is also home to ATEC, the Talamanca Association for Ecotourism and Conservation that works from Cahuita south to Gandoca. ATEC promotes ecologically sound tourism and small-scale, locally owned businesses along with cultural interchange and ethnic pride among indigenous and African-Caribbean people of Talamanca.

The ATEC office is on the first main north-south street off the main road. Stop by to find out about tours and guides: for example, four different walks in the KéköLdi Indian Reserve, culture and nature walks to Cahuita and Punta Uva, coral reef snorkeling or fishing, rain-forest hikes and horseback rides, birding tours, and nightwalks. Most tours range from $15 to $30 per person. Buy a copy of *Coastal Talamanca* there to learn more about the culture and ecology of the area. The office is a hub of activity, having one of the few telephones around. (You will notice that many of the hotels use the same numbers—the two public phones. Promised lines may be in before the next edition of this book.) Current bus schedules are posted. Open weekdays from 7:00 a.m. to noon and 1:00 to 9:00 p.m., Saturday 8:00 a.m. to noon and 1:30 to 9:00 p.m., and Sunday 8:00 a.m. to noon and 4:00 to 8:00 p.m. Telephone/fax 798-4244. Write to ATEC, Puerto Viejo de Talamanca, Limón, Costa Rica, but allow four to six weeks for a response.

For downtown lodging, try Cabinas Casa Verde. Surrounded by pretty gardens in a residential neighborhood, the 12-room hotel encompasses several small buildings, including a separate bathhouse. Singles in rooms with shared baths range from $10 to $15; doubles, $15 to $25. The four rooms with private baths are $25 for up to two persons. Baths have shower-head hot water. All rooms have fans. English and German also spoken. No telephone.

Hotel Maritza just off the main road downtown has 14 simple rooms with private bath and shower-head hot water ($19 for two) and ten with shared baths ($14 for two). All have fans. VISA and MasterCard accepted. Telephone/fax 798-1844.

Pura Vida has ten rooms at the edge of town near the soccer field. Clean and comfortable with basic furnishings, rooms with shared baths are $15 single and $19 double. A room with private bath is $25 for two. All baths have hot water. Breakfast is served. No telephone.

A number of restaurants offer a variety of foods. Stanfords is a landmark in the old two-story building by the ocean at the southern edge of town. You can still get delicious patacones there and other good food, though the disco downstairs can be loud. The Garden Restaurant has good food, and for pizza or Italian dishes, try El Coral. The Juice Joint, open 6:00 a.m. to 5:00 p.m. Tuesday through Sunday, serves sandwiches (BLT if you have missed it), Mexican food, waffles and pancakes, hot and cold espresso drinks, and slushies and smoothies. Desserts are scrumptious.

Another local tour option is to the Botanical Gardens just north of El Pizote Lodge. It's a working tropical farm where black pepper and tropical fruits are grown commercially. You can learn about chocolate production and enjoy the flowering plants, poison dart and harlequin frogs, toucans, and other birds. Open Friday through Monday, 10:00 a.m. to 4:00 p.m., entrance fee less than $3, $8 with a guide.

Not far out of the village going south is Hotel Casa Blanca, a family-run operation with four clean rooms: two doubles are $25 each and two triples are $30. No hot water. Breakfast is served, and soft drinks are always available. No credit cards. Spanish and English also spoken. Send a fax to Martina Gehlen at 798-4244 or 798-1844.

La Isla Inn, also past the edge of town going south, has three rooms upstairs that open on to a large balcony facing the ocean. Built-in benches along the railing make it comfortable for bird- and butterfly-watching, sea watching, and people-watching. The downstairs room is next to an open-air restaurant and lounge area where breakfast and snacks are served. I hope you make time for interesting conversations with owners José Luis and Petra. Furnishings are simple, but everything is neat as a pin. There are built-in tables and closets, ceiling fans, and private baths with shower-head hot water—large, fluffy towels and washcloths. The inn has a four-hour nature walk in the forest, along the river, and by farms, $20 including a bag lunch. Do not miss Petra's banana milk shakes. Three rooms are $40 each for up to two persons; a larger upstairs room is $50 for two, $10 per person extra. No credit cards. English and German also spoken. Fax 798-4244 (the ATEC office).

La Costa del Papito is small and charming. Three tropical-wood cabins have wraparound verandas with bamboo rails. Each is large, with wood and bamboo tables, ceiling fans, pitched ceilings, shuttered windows, and two double beds. Big, open bathrooms have royal blue tile and fixtures, and shower-head hot water. Pretty gardens to the road contain heliconias, palms, bananas, papayas, guanábana, plantains, and passion fruit; the ocean is beyond. Owner Eddie Ryan arranges bicycle and horse rentals. Cabins are $50 for two, $5 for each additional person. Breakfast is available if ordered the night before, about $3.50. No credit cards. Fax to 798-4244 or 798-1844 (those public phones again).

On Playa Cocles you will see a red-tile-roofed complex called Villas del Caribe, 12 two-story villas for up to six people each; doubles are $79, plus $10 for each additional person. Credit cards are accepted. The sitting room and fully equipped kitchenette downstairs open onto a private terrace with lounge chairs and an outdoor shower for rinsing off when coming in from the beach. Upstairs balconies have hammocks. Bedrooms are large, with hardwood floors, ceiling fans, desk, and occasional tables and chairs. Bathrooms have plants in the shower area under a skylight; there is central hot water. The view is through scattered coconut palms and gardens that go right to the Caribbean. Enjoy the fragrance from the heliotrope hedge.

Villas del Caribe rents horses for about $6 an hour, and guests can ride on roads in a 125-acre (50-ha) forest. There is a motorboat with an English-speaking guide for trips along the coast, and you can rent surfboards, boogie boards, bicycles, and snorkeling equipment. Nearby is an old-fashioned *trapiche*, so you may have a chance to see sugar extracted from cane with oxen power. Telephone 233-2200, fax 221-2801. By the way, there is a *pulpería*, or small grocery, near the entrance.

As you make your way south, you will probably glimpse the brilliant flash of scarlet-rumped tanagers as they fly across the road.

Hotel y Restaurante Yaré on Cocles Beach probably has the most colorful decor on the coast. Rich Caribbean red and green, purple and green, gold and turquoise, orange and chartreuse gladden exterior walls. Inside, colorful bedspreads and matching curtains continue the festive mood. High-ceilinged rooms have private baths with hot water, and fans. Some have kitchenettes. Raised, covered walkways join lodging areas with the thatch-roofed restaurant and pool. The restaurant is open to the public, 7:30 a.m. to 9:00 p.m. Tours are offered to botanical gardens, the KéköLdi Indian Reserve, and Gandoca-Manzanillo Wildlife Refuge, while a local guide offers a three-hour nature walk. Single rooms are $40, doubles $50;

Clear waters and unspoiled beaches near Manzanillo (Ree Strange Sheck)

those with kitchenettes are from $50 to $75. Credit cards accepted. Telephone/fax 284-5921.

Less than 3 miles (5 km) south of Puerto Viejo is Hotel Punta Cocles, an inviting place from which to explore the nearby parks and reserves or just sit and watch the toucans and parrots fly by. The complex of 60 rooms, restaurants, and good-sized pool is surrounded by tall trees, with several well-maintained nature trails through a 35-acre (14-ha) forest reserve. Watch for small, brightly colored frogs, but do not touch them. Those bright colors usually warn of strong toxins. Guests can make one- to two-hour self-guided forays into the lush forest. A checklist of birds found in the area list 326 species in 55 families.

Trails from the hotel lead across the road to golden sand beaches, with the seaside Blue Crab Bar where drinks and snacks are sold. Other hotel amenities include a Jacuzzi and ice machines. Rooms are in bungalows connected to the restaurant and pool area by covered walkways. Each has its own terrace, private bath with central hot water, and both fans and air conditioning. Five bungalows have furnished kitchens. Rooms are $70 for up to four; bungalows with kitchens, for up to six people, are $90.

A tour desk is in the lobby. The hotel also rents binoculars—a nice feature—as well as bicycles, rain ponchos, boogie boards, and snorkeling equipment. Hotel Punta Cocles will pick up guests who take the direct bus to Puerto Viejo. The Limón to Manzanillo bus passes in front. Telephone 234-8055, fax 234-8033; or in the U.S. (800) 325-6927.

Three lodging experiences await at the next beach down—Playa Chiquita. First along the road is Miraflores Lodge, a bed and breakfast nestled in an exuberant tropical garden. Owner Pamela Carpenter Navarro not only attends personally to her guests but raises flowers for export. Guests live among 200 varieties of heliconia, ginger varieties (including the flamboyant torch ginger), Calatheas, Costus plants, and Musas (of the banana family), most of which are planted under pruned cacao trees. She has bromeliads, orchids, and a medicinal plant garden. The plantings produce flowers, fruit, nectar, and seeds for animals and birds.

Each of the ten rooms in the house is different. Decor throughout reflects Pamela's years of living and traveling in Central America and her commitment to simplicity. Two upstairs rooms share a living area and bath, $45 per room. Downstairs suites, with accents in bamboo and cane, have private baths (shower-head hot water in all baths), $50 per room. Downstairs rooms are $40 and dorm rooms with bunkbeds are $10 each, including breakfast. Total capacity is 45 people. The rancho restaurant, constructed by Bribris, has the typical split chonta-palm floor—stop by to see it and have a cooling fruit drink.

Tours include an early morning bird walk to see toucans, the iguana farm, the Indian reserve, a visit with a basketmaker, and a dugout ride to Panama. She also coordinates with ATEC for tours, and takes people to Bocas del Toro in Panama. No credit cards. Telephone/fax 233-2822.

New on the scene is Shawandha, created by Maho Diaz and Nicolas Buffile. Each of the 12 bungalows is unique, with its own theme and furniture designed by Maho. Spacious rooms open onto private terraces, each with a small sofa, table, and hammock. The bathrooms are enchanting —sinks with designs in small mosaic tiles, showers down spiral steps—no two alike. Shower-head hot water. There are three double-bed rooms, five rooms with queen-size beds, and four with extra long king-size beds. A gift shop features neo-primitive jewelry. The open-air restaurant and bar, with carved stone motifs reminiscent of Mexico, is striking with its towering rancho-style roof. Sofa, lamps, chairs, and tables offer a place to relax with a drink. A French chef presides over the restaurant, open to the public for dinner from 6:30 to 10:00 p.m.. Bungalows are $80 for two, including a breakfast buffet, with $15 per person extra. Credit cards accepted. Trails lead to the beach and into the forest on the hills behind. French, English, Spanish, and Portuguese also spoken. Telephone 284-9360, fax 240-3558.

Just across the road is the reception area for Playa Chiquita Lodge, which definitely has a jungle feeling to it. On the beach side of the road, wooden buildings seem to rise out of the abundant plant life. A thatched rancho serves as the dining room and central gathering place. Rooms have forest views even out of the bathrooms (no hot water), screened windows, ceiling fans, and rocking chairs on the porches for bird-watching and relaxing to the sound of howler monkeys. A walkway leads to the beach. Single $25, double $40. Owner Wolf Bissinger has built new two-story units on the forest side of the road, near Shawandha, that feature large rooms with balconies or terraces, some with spacious showers and striking blue fixtures in the bathroom, shower-head hot water. One unit has two bedrooms and two baths with a full kitchen, $110 a day for eight people, with weekly and monthly rates. VISA accepted. Guests can rent bicycles, snorkeling equipment, and boogie boards. Tours go to Gandoca, Punta Mono, and Cahuita. Telephone 233-6613, fax 223-7479.

The road goes past Punta Uva, which many claim is the prettiest beach on the Caribbean. You are already in the Gandoca-Manzanillo Wildlife Refuge, which has mixed private and government ownership. Though the road peters out after Manzanillo, there are walking trails that continue in and out through forest and beach. Standing on a rocky point near Punta Manzanillo, you can see all the way along the coast to Puerto Vargas and Cahuita National Park. Spectacular scenery. Hiking tours and boat trips to the Gandoca Lagoon are available through local hotels and agencies. Stop by Maxi's Restaurant and Bar in Manzanillo.

Not long before you get to Manzanillo is Almonds and Corals Lodge Tent Camp, which offers an unforgettable experience for nature travelers. See Chapter 13 for a description.

12

National Parks, Biological Reserves, and Wildlife Refuges

Today more than 16 percent of Costa Rica's land is in parks, refuges, and biological reserves; almost another 16 percent is legally set aside as forest reserves, protected zones, and Indian reserves.

Natural history travelers today follow in the footsteps of naturalists and explorers who have been drawn to the biological diversity of this small country since the mid-1800s. Five percent of all the plant and animal species known on the planet exist here, in a space that takes up only three ten-thousandths of the Earth's surface. The protected areas are showplaces for the wealth of species found in Costa Rica. The National Biodiversity Institute, which is at work on an inventory of all plant and animal species in the country, so far has these numbers: mammals, 209 species; birds, 850; reptiles, 220; amphibians, 163; freshwater fish, 130; and arthropods (insects, spiders, and crabs with segmented bodies and jointed limbs), 366,000. Among the 13,021 species of plants discovered are 1,500 trees and more than 1,400 orchids.

Today both public and private organizations recognize the importance of coordinating their efforts to preserve biodiversity, not only within Costa Rica but perhaps also in links reaching from Mexico to Colombia. Biological corridors that connect protected sectors help create areas large enough for survival of tapirs, cats, and birds that migrate altitudinally, such as the quetzal, and help ensure survival of the biodiversity that is jeopardized in isolated units—the philosophy of "the whole is greater than the sum of its parts."

Since the park service was set up in the 1960s, emphasis been on preserving areas before they are destroyed. Though money is still needed to

FOR INFORMATION

Telephone Hotline: 192
From Monday to Friday, call 192 for information on national parks, biological reserves, and wild-life refuges once you are in Costa Rica. From 7:30 a.m. to 5:00 p.m., English- and Spanish-speaking staff give information on services in each area, how to get there (complete with bus and ferry schedules), weather, entrance fees, and hours each area is open. Remember that some protected areas are closed for one or two days a week. You cannot make reservations via this number, but staff can give you the appropriate number to call. Information can also be sent by fax.

Conservation Area Numbers
Reservations are now made directly with the appropriate conservation area. Following is a list of conservation areas and their components with telephone and fax numbers.
Amistad Pacífico: *Telephone 771-3155, fax 771-4836*
  La Amistad, Chirripó, Tapantí
Amistad Atlántico: *Telephone/ fax 758-3996*
  Cahuita, Gandoca-Manzanillo, Hitoy-Cerere

Arenal *Telephone 695-5908 or 222-4161; fax 695-5482 or 221-0249*
  Alberto Manuel Brenes, Arenal Volcano, Caño Negro, Tenorio Volcano
Cordillera Volcánica Central: *Telephone 256-2611 or 256-2717; fax 256-2986*
  Braulio Carrillo, Guayabo, Irazú Volcano, Juan Castro Blanco, Poás Volcano
Guanacaste: *Telephone/fax 695-5598*
  Guanacaste, Junquillal, Rincón de la Vieja, Santa Rosa Isla del Coco
Osa: *Telephone 735-5036, fax 735-5276*
  Ballena, Caño Island, Corcovado, Golfito, Piedras Blancas
Pacífico Central: *Telephone/fax 428-9792*
  Carara, Manuel Antonio
Tempisque: *Telephone 671-1062, telephone/fax 671-1290*
  Barra Honda, Curú, Las Baulas, Lomas Barbudal, Ostional, Palo Verde
Tortuguero Plains: *Telephone 710-2929 or 710-2989; fax 710-7673*
  Barra del Colorado, Tortuguero

purchase the approximately 12 percent of the park land still privately held, more attention now can be directed toward better protection of those areas and amenities for visitors, which up to now have been quite limited.

No monorail systems transport people through this fantastic kingdom of plants and animals; only a few parks offer roads; waterways wind through a handful, but maintained trails exist in a growing number. Overnight lodging is available at camping areas in a few of the protected areas and, when space permits, in park or refuge stations. Visitors can also stay in research stations in places such as Guanacaste, Santa Rosa, Corcovado, and Palo Verde if there is an empty bed.

Housing, from humble to fine, may be available nearby. For day visits on your own, take food and drink; generally, there are no restaurants or souvenir shops selling candy bars.

The men and women who work in the parks are delightful to know and will help you get oriented. However, the staff is usually shorthanded, so do not expect a personal guided tour. Printed brochures with maps have been made for most parks. You should get one with your admission fee. Some refuges have printed guides.

Even parks where you will see the most people, like Poás or Manuel Antonio, may not be crowded on weekdays except at Easter or Christmas. Your group may meet no one else on a trail through pristine country. Your chances of seeing the wildlife, of course, depend on you. Proceed quietly, be patient, and be alert. For safety's sake and to minimize impact, stay on the trails.

Admission fee for any national park or biological refuge is $6, while national wildlife refuges maintain a fee of about $1. No advance purchase is necessary, and tickets may be purchased at the park, reserve, or refuge entrance. Camping fees are about $2 per person per night.

The information center for the National Parks Service in San José is at Calle 25, Avenidas 8/10 for the time being. Plans are to open a larger center at another location. It may be open by your arrival.

Contact individual parks, biological reserves, and wildlife refuges about overnight space or reservations through the appropriate conservation area (see "For Information" box). The conservation areas were created to facilitate the regional protection of ecosystems and cultural resources. Each has an office to coordinate conservation efforts within its area and to work with communities in the buffer zones around the protected areas.

In contrast with national parks, which by law should belong to the government, wildlife refuges can also include areas either partly or completely in the hands of private owners. The state can authorize farming, homes, recreational activities, businesses, research, and industries in those areas.

VOLUNTEERS IN PARKS, RESERVES, REFUGES

If you are open for a different kind of vacation—a working vacation—are 18 years of age or older, and speak at least basic Spanish, the National Parks Service may have a deal for you. As a volunteer in the parks, you can work alongside rangers or in the San José office. The minimum time to volunteer is 45 days.

Depending on your skills and interests, you could be a lifeguard at park beaches during the high tourist season, work on an archaeological dig, help fight forest fires, protect nesting sea turtles, cook, or maintain trails. Extra hands and minds are always needed in environmental education and assisting visitors.

The work can be hard, the hours long, and living conditions rustic. You pay for your food (about $7 a day) and transportation. You wash your own clothes in a pila. Some stations have no electricity, with the only outside contact by radio phone.

Bring your own sheets. Both men and women are welcome, and there is no upper age limit.

What does a volunteer get out of all this? A rare opportunity to experience Costa Rica's parks in a way no tour or day visit can offer, to learn, and to contribute to conservation efforts in a real way. Parks are understaffed and for the most part work within severe budget constraints.

If you are interested, write to ASVO, Servicio de Parques Nacion-ales, Apartado 11384-1000, San José. State when you are coming—writing in Spanish may speed up your answer. You will receive information and an application. Allow at least three months for the exchange of letters to arrange your stint. Telephone/fax 222-5085. The office is at Avenida 21, Calles 25/27. Open weekdays 9:00 a.m. to noon and 1:00 p.m. to 4:00 p.m.

The region of the country where each park, reserve, or refuge is located is noted in parenthesis in the descriptions of each that follow. You can read about accommodations and the surrounding area in Chapters 6 through 11, or look up nearby private reserves that offer accommodations in Chapter 13. Look for specifics in Chapter 14 on companies specializing in nature tours.

The brief descriptions here tell you how easy or difficult it is to get to the site, what visitor facilities are available, and highlight some of the magic you will encounter. I mention those with at least some facilities for visitors.

Parks and Biological Reserves

La Amistad Costa Rica-Panama International Park (South)

La Amistad means "friendship," and the international park was created with an understanding that a counterpart park would be established across the border in Panama.

La Amistad is a gigantic national park, 479,199 acres (193,929 ha), big enough to sustain a healthy population of animals that require large areas for hunting and reproduction, such as the tapir, jaguar, puma, and harpy eagle. Probably the largest population of resplendent quetzals in the country resides in this refuge of rainforest, cloud forest, and páramo, along with at least 400 other bird species. Epiphytes abound in the tall cloud forests, where you can see oak, elm, magnolia, and sweet cedar. More than 130 varieties of orchids have been found in the southwest corner of the park alone. There are 263 species of amphibians and reptiles. Spread across the rugged Talamanca Mountain Range, the highest in Costa Rica, the park protects not only endangered plants and animals but important watersheds as well. It is within the Amistad Biosphere Reserve.

Elevation ranges from about 328 to 11,644 feet (100 to 3,549 m); temperatures vary accordingly, with upper altitudes rainy and sometimes cold.

Though much of the fantasy land of geology and wildlife has yet to be explored, some trails do exist, and it is possible to get into La Amistad more easily now because of some lodges and private nature reserves (Chapter 13) that have opened near its borders.

The park administration office is at Las Tablas, about 25 miles (40 km) northwest of San Vito de Coto Brus. If driving, ask about the condition of the road to La Amistad. The highway is good to San Vito, which is about five hours from San José near Panama.

Arenal Volcano National Park (North Central)

Called one of the most active volcanoes in the world, beautiful Arenal Volcano dominates the landscape of this park and of the region. It erupted in 1968 after having been considered by most as extinct, though some fumarole activity had been noted as early as 1937. Some 5,358-feet high (1,633 m), the volcano has three craters, one of which is currently active. Its eruptions send clouds of ash into the sky and throw fiery materials into the air. Lava flows, visible with binoculars in daytime, are spectacular at night.

Though Arenal Volcano is the most popular attraction, the park also includes habitat along part of Lake Arenal's shores and protects part of some important watershed for Lake Arenal, whose waters feed the largest hydroelectric project in the country.

Arenal Volcano, blowing and going since 1968 (Ree Strange Sheck)

Temperatures here are between 55°F (12.6°C) and 64°F (17.5°C), and average annual rainfall is from 138 to 197 inches (3,500 to 5,000 mm). Though it only became a national park in 1994, it had previously been in a protected zone.

Entrance to the park station and a viewing area within the park is 10 miles (16 km) west of La Fortuna. Rangers there advise you that it is best not to go farther than the mirador, or lookout. There is a self-guided trail, Las Coladas, that goes to a 1992 lava bed—allow 90 minutes. Los Tucanes trail goes across the lava flow and into forest, about three hours. There are five species of toucans here—hence the name. Howler and white-face monkeys also live here.

The park is open from 7:00 a.m. to 10:00 p.m., since many visitors come for nighttime viewing. There is a restroom, but no camping facilities. Remember to observe warning signs—this volcano has killed.

Ballena National Marine Park (South)

Created in 1990, the Ballena park was established to protect marine resources. It encompasses 13,282 acres (5,375 ha) of ocean and 272 acres (110 ha) of land. The coast is about 6 miles long (10 km) between Punta Uvita and Punta Piñuela along the Pacific south of Dominical, an area rich in well-preserved mangroves.

Ballena Island and the smaller rocky protrusions called Las Tres Hermanas are nesting sites for frigate birds, pelicans, and boobies. The park gets its name from the humpbacked whales that visit from December to March. Dolphins are common here.

It is the first marine park in Costa Rica to involve a fishing community. There is a guard station, but the park is not developed for tourism. Visitors can, however, snorkel around the coral reefs, dive in the protected area or visit by boat. Visits can be arranged from Dominical and Uvita.

Las Baulas National Marine Park

Fortunately the mangroves and big leatherback turtles (*baulas*) that this area was set up to protect do not care what the place is called. It began life as a government-protected area under the name of Tamarindo Wildlife Refuge, but in 1991 the area was enlarged and decreed to be Las Baulas de Guanacaste National Marine Park to give it a higher status of protection under the law. The legislative assembly did not approve the decree: the issue was complicated by the fact that the expanded area includes expensive private lands difficult for the government to purchase. National parks are theoretically government owned, while wildlife refuges can be mixed ownership. So the area was again a wildlife refuge. But guess what? It has once again been declared a national park. This is why you will hear it referred to as both Las Baulas and Tamarindo.

Whatever its eventual name, it encompasses beaches that attract one of the largest populations of leatherback turtles in the world. The peak nesting months in the refuge are October through January, when as many as 200 females may come ashore per night. Smaller but noticeable numbers continue to arrive until March, but there are actually turtles there year-round. Each nest contains from 70 to 100 eggs, and the babies hatch in about 70 days. Warmer temperatures in the nest produce females; cooler temperatures, males.

The baula is the largest sea turtle living today. The female can be 6 feet (1.8 m) long and weigh more than 1,300 pounds (590 kg). The species has a tough skin or hide instead of a true shell—hence the name in English.

The major dangers to survival for these sea creatures are not only loss of habitat, egg-poaching, and accidentally being caught by fishermen but also plastic pollution. Plastic resembles jellyfish in the water and may be ingested by the turtles, who love the jellyfish that most sea animals steer clear of: the Portuguese man-of-war. Olive ridley turtles also sometimes come ashore to lay their eggs, though not in the massive arribadas experienced at Nancite in Santa Rosa park or at Ostional Wildlife Refuge.

To see the protected mangrove, you can take a boat. All five species that live in Costa Rica thrive here: black, white, buttonwood, tea, and the red, with its stilt or prop roots. You may be surprised to see what can decorate the woody plants: orchids, bromeliads, termite nests.

Las Baulas is a good bird-watching area. Lowlands attract the wood stork, white ibis, jacana, roseate spoonbill, and American egret—at least 174 species of birds have been identified. There are estuaries where the American crocodile can be found, and there is a fragment of tropical dry forest. A large pochote tree at Langosta is 9 feet (2.8 m) in diameter. Crabs abound: ghost crabs, hermit crabs, and mouthless crabs, those garish creatures with black bodies, orange legs, and purple pincers.

Access to the park is easiest at the town of Tamarindo and at Playa Grande. Lodging exists at each (see Chapter 9), and several hotels and tourist businesses in the region operate tours. Boats can be rented for trips in the estuaries. There is daily bus and air service between San José and Tamarindo. (See Practical Extras.) The bus trip takes 5½ or six hours, depending on the route.

Barra Honda National Park (Northwest)

The main attraction at Barra Honda is a network of caves through a peak that once was a coral reef beneath the sea. Located just west of where the Tempisque River flows into the Gulf of Nicoya, Barra Honda still holds many secrets. Of the 42 caves discovered, only 19 have been explored. The human remains and pre-Columbian artifacts discovered have yet to yield their stories. But the exploration has revealed several large caverns adorned with stalactites, stalagmites, pearls, soda straws, columns, popcorn, and other intriguing formations. Nature's underground artistry is most profuse in the Terciopelo (fer-de-lance) Cave, so named because early speleologists found a snake of this species smashed on its floor. Terciopelo contains the Organ, a columnar formation that resounds with different tones when gently tapped. This is the only cave open to the public. The deepest cave, Santa Ana, is almost 790 feet (240 m) beneath the surface.

The shafts into these caves are mostly vertical, and there are no elevators to carry you down or caverns lit with colored lights. Descending into the caves is not for the fainthearted or infirm: straight down a metal ladder almost 90 feet (27 m) and back up the same way. Arrangements should be made at least four days beforehand by calling 685-5580. A local community association, Barrio Cubillo, conducts the tours. A guide and caving equipment costs about $47 for up to seven people. The maximum time in the cave is 45 minutes, though the tour is three hours. Besides offering tours, the association maintains the trails and helps with park protection.

For noncavers, the 5,673-acre (2,296-ha) park offers trails that lead to a view point overlooking the Gulf of Nicoya and Chira Island, a tall evergreen forest, and waterfalls over natural travertine dams. The summit of Barra Honda Peak at 1,312 feet (400 m), pocked with large and small holes and decorated with sculptured rock, hints of the artistry in the caves below. Los Laureles Trail, about 3.5 miles (5.5 km) long, is open to the public. The first 40 minutes are uphill, but then it levels off. Bring water (it is hot), and keep to the trail. Two tourists became lost and died here in 1992. Half-day guided tours are $19 for up to seven persons. Trail visits are limited to five hours.

Below-ground wildlife includes bats, insects, blind salamanders, fish, and snails, while above-ground visitors might see the white-faced monkey, Amazonian skunk, long-nosed armadillo, white-nosed coati, coyote, and orange-fronted parakeet. The vegetation of the tropical dry forest, moist province transition zone, is mostly deciduous.

The average annual rainfall ranges from 59 to 79 inches (1,500 to 2,000 mm), and the average temperature is 81°F (27°C). The highest elevation is 1,886 feet (575 m).

The Cubillo community organization has clean cabins and campsites in the forest next to the park entrance. (See Chapter 9 for details.) Monkeys move through the trees around the small campsites. This project is an example of park neighbors helping with and benefiting from a protected area.

To get to the park from San José, turn off the Inter-American Highway about 6 miles (10 km) before Cañas and take the Tempisque ferry. Go through Quebrada Honda and Tres Esquinas to Barra Honda. Two streams you need to cross can rise rapidly with rains, so inquire in the village of Barra Honda if in doubt. The road deteriorates past the town. From Liberia, take Highway 21 south and turn north just before the town of Mansión to get to the park. There is a bus from Nicoya, 9 miles (14 kilometers) away, to Santa Ana, a little more than a mile (2 km) from the entrance.

Barra Honda is open from 7:00 a.m. to 4:00 p.m. daily, but visits to the caves are allowed only from 8:00 a.m. to 1:00 p.m.

Braulio Carrillo National Park (Central Valley)

Braulio Carrillo is a symphony in green. Waterfalls, deep canyons, and raging rivers lend their tones. The exciting part is that the concert begins only 20 minutes from San José—and on a paved road.

While roads through virgin forest usually spell ecological disaster, this particular road spurred creation of a national park that now encompasses 113,525 acres (45,943 ha) of majestic beauty. Braulio Carrillo was born out of the conflict between the need for a new highway to the Atlantic and the determination to preserve the largely primary forest it would pass through. The park was established in 1978, and the road through this rugged, largely

Barva sector of Braulio Carrillo with gigantic *sombrilla del pobre* leaves
(Ree Strange Sheck)

untouched land opened in 1987. Most of the traffic between San José and
Limón now passes on a ribbon laid down through this awesome landscape.
Be alert for landslides.

The park offers many levels of enjoyment; just driving through it is a
thrill. View points provide safe places to pull off. A trail I took led from highway to primeval beauty, complete with waterfall and morpho butterflies that
fluttered up and down above the sparkling stream. A *tepezcuintle*, the wonderful Spanish name for the paca, jumped from a cave hidden by vegetation
into the pool where we had just been swimming and disappeared behind the
waterfall. It is a timeless, hushed place—one of nature's gifts.

As for established trails, there is one of about a half-mile (1 km) from the
main ranger station at Zurquí, 30 minutes from San José on the highway to
the Caribbean. Two trails take off from the station close to the Limón end of
the highway: Botarrama (which takes about two hours) and the longer La
Botella. Camping is permitted.

Just 19 miles (30 km) from San José through Heredia and Sacramento is
an entrance at Barva, one of two volcanoes in the park. It is about 2.5 miles
(4 km) from Sacramento to the ranger station on one terrible road, at least
in rainy season—four-wheel-drive only. The trail from the ranger station to
Laguna Volcán Barva, 1.8 miles (3 km) of breathtaking beauty, climbs gently in spots and is almost level in others. Remember the air is a bit thin here,

with an elevation of around 9,500 feet (2,900 m). The view from the mirador above the crater lake is worth the climb, sparkling in sunshine and magically shrouded in mists. I suggest you linger a bit on the chance of seeing the magnificent hummingbird feeding in nearby flowers. From the first lake, it is about 1.5 miles (2.5 km) to Copey, a shallow lake that becomes isolated ponds in dry season. The third lake, Danta, is the largest and least accessible. Quetzals are seen more here between January and March when they are nesting, though some stay year-round—125 bird species have been identified here. Mammals are not as commonly seen in this lofty sector of the park, though tracks of jaguar and tapir are found.

Camping is allowed at the Barva station and bunks in a small refuge can be rented when not in use by parks. Bathrooms and a covered picnic area are at the entrance.

Special permission is required for a multiday trek from Barva Volcano through a protected zone added in 1986 to join Braulio Carrillo with land protected by the Organization of Tropical Studies' La Selva Biological Station, all the way to Puerto Viejo de Sarapiquí. The journey goes from 9,514 feet (2,900 m) to 112 feet (34 m). This is the only place in the country where an altitudinal variation of this magnitude is protected, which is extremely important for species that migrate, including some of the 515 bird species identified so far.

If you are going through Braulio Carrillo on the highway to Limón, try to reach the park early to reduce the chance of fog narrowing your views. Dropping into the lowlands, you may see a sloth in a tree alongside the road. Watch the *guarumo* (cecropia) trees in particular. Other animals that live in the park include three species of monkey—also frequently spotted at lower elevations—kinkajou, deer, and ocelot. In all, there are 135 species of mammals here. The bare-necked umbrellabird knows these forests, as do eagles, trogons, hawks, curassows, and guans. Bromeliads and orchids adorn the trees. This is a good place to see the poor man's umbrella (*sombrilla del pobre*), a plant whose leaves grow up to 7 feet (2 m) across. People caught out in the rain in the countryside have used them for protection. If you are caught driving in the rain, which averages 177 inches (4,500 mm) a year, enjoy the waterfalls that pour down the roadside and keep your eyes open for landslides.

Because of the topography and range of elevation within the park, temperatures can be 59°F (15°C) at Zurquí, 37°F (3°C) at Barva, or 86°F (30°C) in the Atlantic lowlands, where rainfall can be 315 inches (8,000 mm) a year.

Primary access to Braulio Carrillo is at the stations at either end of the highway through the park (Zurquí and Quebrada González), and at the

LIFE IN A CECROPIA TREE

Discovery of relationships between trees, other plants, insects, and animals opens a window on understanding the intricacies of life in the tropical world. One such symbiotic relationship has evolved between the cecropia tree, called guarumo *in Spanish, and Azteca ants.*

The cecropia tree, a member of the mulberry family, grows throughout the country at elevations up to approximately 6,500 feet (2,000 m). It is called a pioneer species because it is among the first to come back on cleared land or to grow when forest is opened up by the fall of a big tree. It grows rapidly and requires a lot of light. You will notice it along road cuts. Look for a tree with a ringed trunk that resembles bamboo; leaves are large and lobed, resembling hands.

Because it is a relatively short-lived tree, maybe 20 years, the cecropia has not developed chemical protection such as toxic leaves, which longer-lived trees tend to have. However, its hollow stems are home to some species of aggressive Azteca ants, which tend to live in large colonies and swarm out over the tree

at the slightest disturbance, attacking unsuspecting caterpillars, other ants, and even a lightly placed hand on the tree. Aztecas do not seem to bite birds, who eat the fruits and scatter the tree's seeds, but they zero in on epiphytes and vines—chewing off any vine that starts up the trunk. In return, the tree provides glycogen-rich food at the base of each leaf stalk for the ants to feed on and hollow stems for them to live in.

But the ant patrols are not effective against all predators. Sloths are among the animals that like cecropia leaves and fruit. You are more apt to spot them in a cecropia tree than others they feed on because of the openness of its growth. Apparently their heavy fur gives sloths some protection. Howler monkeys also eat in cecropia trees.

Countless symbiotic relationships exist in the natural world. Some we know about; others remain to be discovered. Even in this tree-ant relationship, all the answers are not in on why the tree has developed lodging and food to attract these ants or the degree of protection the ants actually give.

Barva Volcano station. Nature travel companies and lodges and hotels offer day visits to the park.

Remember to stay on trails and to check in at the ranger station before setting out. Vegetation is extremely dense in this rugged region. Experienced hikers have gotten lost; as one Costa Rican put it, the forest has eaten several small planes and a few people. Unfortunately, theft has become a threat in the park. Do not leave items in a car parked along the road and do not park in isolated areas.

Cabo Blanco Strict Nature Reserve (Northwest)

Cabo Blanco Strict Nature Reserve is important historically as well as biologically. It was set aside as a protected area in 1963 before Costa Rica had a park service, largely through the efforts of Olof Wessberg and Karen Mogensen, who had come to live on the Nicoya Peninsula in 1955. Because of their love of nature and concern about rapid destruction of the forest on the tip of the peninsula—plus personal commitment and a good measure of persistence with funding sources and bureaucracy—this forest and sanctuary for seabirds exists today. You will see a memorial plaque honoring Olof at the reserve entrance. Doña Karen died in 1994.

The reserve is a treasure. Visitors often see howler monkeys and an admirable assortment of birds and butterflies before even leaving the picnic area next to the ranger station at the entrance. The reserve claims 119 tree species and possibly the largest pochote tree in any park. It is 115 feet high (35 m) and almost 10 feet (3 m) in diameter. Predominant species are gumbo-limbo, lemonwood, frangipani, dogwood, trumpet tree, and cedar.

Though the land portion of the park is only 2,896 acres (1,172 ha), wildlife is plentiful: deer, white-faced and howler monkeys, agoutis, pacas, margays, ocelots, coyotes, coatis, tamanduas, and raccoons. Birds are abundant, too—one birder counted 74 species in four hours. Land species include manakins, woodpeckers, trogons, crested caracaras, parakeets, and chachalacas. The reserve also protects 4,423 acres (1,790 ha) of marine habitat.

Cabo Blanco (White Cape) got its name from the small island a short distance off the point, though there is dispute about whether the name comes from deposits of bird guano or a white cliff or the light-colored soil. Pelicans, frigate birds, and brown boobies hang out there. The area is rich in marine life: octopus, starfish, sea cucumber, lobster, giant conch, and fish such as snapper and snook.

Look in at the small museum before setting off on one of the well-maintained trails. A 90-minute trek through low mountains, steep in places, leads to Cabo Blanco Beach, a sandy spot on a mostly rocky shoreline. Though visitation has increased, you may still have the beach practically to yourself for a bit except for colored crabs and seabirds. The famous English pirate Captain John Cook died off these shores in 1684 and was buried here, site unknown.

To protect this small, fragile place, no camping is allowed, and the number of visitors is being monitored. Plans call for guided walks. Remember that this is a small reserve, a place that could be loved to death. Safeguards are aimed at preventing that. Park hours are 8:00 a.m. to 4:00 p.m., closed Monday and Tuesday. Telephone/fax 671-1290.

Montezuma, 7 miles (11 km) away, offers hotels, restaurants, and tour possibilities; some small lodges are closer to Cabo Blanco. The road from Montezuma piddles down to one lane just before the Cabo Blanco reserve. It can be a muddy track in the rainy season, and since you must also ford a river en route, a four-wheel-drive vehicle is recommended for those months. There is no bus between Montezuma and Cabo Blanco, but taxis are available, along with bike and horse rentals. (See Chapter 9 for area facilities.)

Cahuita National Park (Caribbean)

Take white sands, coconut palms, a coral reef, the wreck of an eighteenth-century slave ship just offshore, and clear Caribbean waters; add to these at least 123 species of fish, an abundance of bird life, and an assortment of other animals from monkeys to caimans. The winning combination is known as Cahuita National Park, 27 miles (44 km) southeast of Limón. One entrance is in the town of Cahuita, and another is at Puerto Vargas, a few miles farther down the main road toward Puerto Viejo.

At present, a community group is administering an information center at the town entrance to the park, maintaining trails, and organizing beach cleanup. Visitors are invited to lend a hand.

The 1,483-acre (600-ha) reef encircles Cahuita Point, forming a rich undersea garden of 35 species of varicolored coral some 1,640 feet (500 m) from shore. Brightly colored fish such as rock beauty, blue parrotfish, and angelfish swim among the formations. There also are sea urchins, barracudas, moray eels, sharks, lobsters, sea cucumbers, and green turtles, which feed on the expanse of turtle grass.

But there is trouble in paradise. Increased erosion from deforestation in the Talamanca Mountains has brought silt carried by the Río Estrella that is affecting the reef, a vivid reminder of the distance trouble can travel from a mismanaged forest.

Snorkeling and scuba diving are allowed. Tours in glass-bottomed boats are available from the town of Cahuita. Though the Puerto Vargas area was closed after the 1991 earthquake, camping and hiking are once again possible there. A 4-mile (7-km) nature trail lets visitors experience the exuberance of tropical moist forest vegetation. The abundance of land and sea birds makes it a bird-watcher's delight. Troops of up to 25 howler monkeys roam the area, and coatis and raccoons are abundant. You might also encounter a three-toed anteater, an otter, a four-toed armadillo, or a three-

Beaches and forest beckon at Cahuita National Park (Ree Strange Sheck)

toed sloth. The park encompasses 2,639 acres (1,068 ha) of land and about 55,350 acres (22,400 ha) of sea.

The colors of the sea on a sunny day run from almost transparent near the white sand to bright green, turquoise, and aquamarine. At some points, you can wade quite a distance from shore without getting wet above your knees. Some areas have strong currents where swimming is not safe. In general, the first 400 meters after the park entrance are dangerous, and there is another very dangerous area at the Puerto Vargas entrance. Pay attention to the warning sign.

The park receives a little less than 118 inches (3,000 mm) of rain a year, and the distinction between the wet and dry seasons is not as clear as in the Central Valley. Visibility around the reef, however, is better from December to April.

Tour companies, lodges, and hotels offer day trips. You can hire a local guide trained by the nonprofit Talamanca Association for Ecotourism and Conservation (see Chapter 11). Lodging is available along the route from Limón through Cahuita to Puerto Viejo and farther south.

Caño Island Biological Reserve (South)
Located 12 miles (20 km) west of the Osa Peninsula in southern Costa Rica, Caño Island is of interest largely as an archaeological site and for its marine life. About 494 acres (200 ha) rising to 361 feet (110 m) above the Pacific,

the land contains tall evergreen forest, a prehistoric cemetery, and mysterious round stones sculpted by the Indians who once walked here. Unfortunately, many graves were plundered before the island came under the protection of Corcovado National Park. The most abundant pottery dates from A.D. 220 to 1550.

The crystalline waters are a snorkeler's delight. Five coral reefs, containing 15 species of stony coral, create a marine wonderland that almost made me forget my fear of being so far from shore in deep waters. Lobster and giant conch live here, as do eels, octopuses, sea urchins, brittle star, and countless fish—jacks, grunts, and triggerfish. Manta rays, sailfish, sea turtles, humpback whales, and dolphins have been seen near the island. Snorkeling and diving are limited to the sea in front of the ranger station. In all, the reserve protects 6,672 acres (2,700 ha) of marine habitat.

Wildlife on the island is scarce, consisting mainly of pacas, opossums, boa constrictors, a few species of bees, moths, butterflies, beetles, frogs, bats, rats, lizards, and ants. Among the birds are ospreys, brown noddies, brown boobies, terns, and egrets.

The forest is largely made up of locusts, wild figs, rubber trees, wild cacaos, and milk trees, which exude a white latex that can be drunk as milk.

Rangers are stationed on the island, and a trail climbs through the forest to points of archaeological interest. High cliffs rise from the coastline, with only a few small, sandy beaches that largely disappear at high tide.

Most visitors to Caño Island arrive as part of a tour. Private nature reserves in the area offer optional day trips to the island, as do several coastal hotels. (See Chapters 10 and 13.) Check with the Osa Conservation Area in advance to arrange an independent trip.

Carara Biological Reserve (South)

You can spot the Carara Biological Reserve before you see any sign as you come from San José through Orotina toward the Pacific coast. Its green forest stands tall against the eroded hillsides—land whose soil, once the trees were cut, tired out quickly when turned into fields for crops or pastures for cattle. In a transition zone between the dry north Pacific and the more humid south, Carara has an average rainfall as high as 126 inches (3,200 mm) in the interior and as low as 79 inches (2,000 mm) near the coast. A large lagoon and rivers and streams supply life-giving moisture.

The reserve has archaeological importance, with Indian sites dating from 300 B.C. to A.D. 1500. Artifacts include gold objects, pottery, and large rectangular stones. These sites are not accessible to visitors.

Most of the 11,614-acre (4,700-ha) reserve is in primary forest, with regal giants that spread their branches in a tall canopy. Some plants live up in the trees and send their roots to the ground; vines wind up trunks toward the light. Epiphytes, ferns, and palms soften the setting.

Because of the lush vegetation and relative ease in seeing the abundant wildlife, Carara Biological Reserve can be an excellent choice for a traveler's first experience in a tropical forest—especially when accompanied by a naturalist guide. I had crossed the Tarcoles River there a dozen times and never knew crocodiles bask along its banks until the guide pointed them out. Naturalist guides know where the wildlife is, which trees have fruit to attract animals, and when the orchids are blooming.

Let me share with you what we saw in about three hours: a fiery-billed aracari, blue-gray tanager, spectacled owl, boat-billed heron, crested guan, anhinga, brown jay, white-tailed kite, wood stork, blue heron, orange-bellied trogon, roseate spoonbill, yellow-headed caracara, chestnut-mandibled toucan, dotted-winged antwren, blue-crowned motmot, great kiskadee, scarlet macaws, crocodiles, white-faced monkeys, iguanas, squirrels, leaf-cutting ants, and lizards. We did not see the snakes that live there, or the morpho butterfly, sloth, coati, agouti, peccary, porcupine, anteater, coyote, or howler or spider monkey. Perhaps you will.

You certainly can see flocks of scarlet macaws if you time your visit right. From near the bridge over the Tarcoles, you can see them between 5:00 and 6:30 a.m. and again between 4:00 and 5:30 p.m. Dozens of red, blue, and gold scarlet macaws fly between the reserve and nighttime resting places in mangroves along the ocean—a spectacular sight. Some 300 macaws live here now.

Visitors should go first to the Quebrada Bonita ranger station to pay the admission fee and arrange for a walk on one of the trails. The Las Aráceas Trail leaves from there, with a maximum walking time of one hour. The Laguna Meándrica Trail starts between the Tarcoles River and Quebrada Bonita. If you are traveling alone, check with the rangers about joining up with a guided group. A maximum of sixty people at a time is allowed on each trail. Carara is open from 7:00 a.m. to 5:00 p.m. No camping is allowed, but there is a picnic area, latrines, and water.

The dry season is from December to April. The terrain is hilly, and though the maximum altitude is only about 2,087 feet (636 m), you may find yourself huffing and sweating. Average temperatures are from 77° to 82°F (25° to 27.5°C). Take it easy.

Parataxonomists working with the National Biodiversity Institute collect insects at Carara. I saw cases of insects so tiny they can barely be seen, as well as flashy butterflies and bizarre-looking beetles. This multiyear project aims to identify all the species in this biologically diverse country.

Carara is always in need of volunteers, especially bilingual persons

(English and Spanish) who are willing to work with visitors, giving out information and staffing the casita at the entrance to the Meándrica Trail. Contact the ASVO office (see Volunteers box in this chapter).

Carara is 56 miles (90 km) from San José along the old Spanish highway. No camping is allowed. It is an easy day trip from the capital or a stopping place on the way to Jacó or Quepos. A number of hotels and lodges all the way from Puntarenas to Quepos arrange tours to Carara. (See Chapter 10. Chapter 14 lists some tour companies that offer trips.)

Chirripó National Park (South)

Geologists, botanists, mountain climbers, biologists, adventure seekers, and just plain nature-lovers make their way to Chirripó National Park, 94 miles (151 km) south of San José near San Isidro de El General. The park contains the highest peak in the country, Chirripó Peak at 12,529 feet (3,819 m), glacial lakes, rivers, and habitats ranging from mixed forests, fern groves, and swamps to oak forests and páramo.

On a clear day, visitors can see both oceans from the peak. There are cloudy and clear days throughout the year, but the driest time is February and March. Annual rainfall is between 138 and 197 inches (3,500 and 5,000 mm). Some long-time visitors say that they cannot resist trips in the rainier times, when the exuberance of the vegetation defies description.

At whatever time of year, take warm clothes. Though maximums in the 80s are possible, count on cold at night in the upper elevations. There can be strong winds. Extremes between day and night can vary by 43°F (24°C); the lowest temperature recorded is 16°F (-9°C). You may wake up to a frosty world, finding ice on lakes and stream banks.

Marked trails traverse the 123,921-acre (50,150-ha) park. Refuges offer bunks with foam mattresses, a wood-burning cook stove, and a dining table. This building is being enlarged and baths moved inside. Bring a warm sleeping bag and be sure to carry enough liquids. While the ascent to the summit appears daunting, it is not so difficult if taken slowly and carefully. Allow at least ten hours to get to the top. If you are going to the Crestones Base, you must leave the San Gerardo ranger station no later than noon. Tent camping is generally not allowed, nor are open fires—you will see signs of a huge forest fire that raged here in 1992.

Endangered species protected at Chirripó include the margay, puma, ocelot, jaguar, tapir, and quetzal. Birds and animals are more abundant in the forest zones, though there are hummingbirds even in the high páramo. Plants seem to cover every inch of trees in the cloud forest: orchids, bromeliads, mosses, and ferns. On the way to the summit, you pass through seven distinct forest types. The higher you climb, the more stunted the vegetation.

Names like Savanna and the Lions, Valley of the Rabbits, and Moraine Valley hint of what early explorers found when they scaled these heights (the lions were actually pumas). Discovery awaits today's visitor to Chirripó National Park, a place where you can look down on rainbows.

The entrance to the park is 9 miles (15 km) northeast of San Isidro at San Gerardo de Rivas, where there is a ranger station. Buses run from San Isidro to San Gerardo. The hardy inhabitants of San Gerardo have been known to actually run up the mountain and are often sought out as guides. If you are going independently, call the conservation area for information about guides or pack horses and to reserve space in a shelter. Space is limited, so reserve as early as possible. The San Gerardo de Rivas station is open from 5:00 a.m. to 5:00 p.m.

Cocos Island or Isla de Coco National Park (South)

A small green island in the Pacific more than 370 miles (500 km) off Costa Rica, Cocos was an early haven for explorers, privateers, pirates, and whalers because of its abundant fresh water and its coconuts; *coco* is Spanish for coconut. Today, it attracts treasure hunters, divers, scientists, and natural history travelers.

More than 500 expeditions have uncovered only a few tantalizing pieces of three treasure caches believed to lie hidden on Cocos Island. Some believe that stories of these treasures fired the imagination of Robert Louis Stevenson for his *Treasure Island.*

Scientists and tourists come in search of other riches: Many endemic species—those that occur nowhere else—have evolved on this isolated piece of land. Its wild beauty encompasses spectacular inland waterfalls and others that plunge into the sea, dense vegetation, and underwater caves and coral gardens. Seventy of the 235 plant species identified so far are endemic, two species of lizards, 64 of the island's 362 species of insects, and four of the 85 bird species. There is an endemic palm named for Franklin D. Roosevelt, who visited the island four times. Cocos is an important nesting site for seagulls, noddies, and boobies. Another nesting bird is called the *Espíritu Santo,* or Holy Spirit. A small white bird, it often hovers in the air, unafraid, a few feet above a visitor's head. Its more prosaic name in English is white tern. Eleven species of shark move through the island's waters, including huge whale sharks, hammerheads, and white tips, among 200 species of fish.

A fragile environment maintains this living laboratory for the study of evolutionary processes. Species introduced by people, such as pigs, deer, rats, coffee, and papaya, endanger the delicate ecological balance. Fishing and increased tourism also are having an impact on this special place, as is its extreme popularity with divers. Historically, the island's isolation minimized human impact; its inclusion in the park system is aimed at protecting it in a shrinking world. An international commission has been set up to work for conservation of this resource, with Jean-Michel Cousteau a member.

The rugged coastline of high cliffs makes access possible at only two bays, Chatham and Wafer. Inscriptions dating to the 1600s on the rocky coast at Chatham provide evidence that sailors sought safe harbor here. Though the island is only 4.7 by 2 miles (7.5 by 3.3 km), its rugged terrain and dense vegetation call for caution. In 1989, a tourist became separated from her group and has never been found.

A park station on Cocos Island has radio contact with the mainland. Permission is necessary for a visit. Most travelers come as part of an organized tour. There are no overnight facilities for visitors.

Rainfall averages up to 276 inches (7,000 mm) a year. The highest point on the island is Iglesias Peak at 2,080 feet (634 m), and upper elevations are covered by cloud forest; epiphytes abound. Of volcanic origin, the island contains rocks that are 2 million years old. It is the only outcrop of the Cocos Ridge, a chain of volcanoes reaching from Costa Rica almost to the Galápagos Islands. The park contains 5,930 acres (2,400 ha) of land and 240,268 acres (97,235 ha) of coastal waters.

Corcovado National Park (South)

Corcovado, on the Osa Peninsula in southwest Costa Rica, is a remote park. It is big—134,766 acres (54,539 ha) of land plus 5,930 acres (2,400 ha) of marine habitat.

The administrator of the park told me he had once counted 150 scarlet macaws flying in two groups near the Madrigal River. I sat at the Sirena station one morning and watched two of these large members of the parrot family preen their brilliant red, yellow, and blue plumage, eat, and gracefully glide from treetop to treetop.

Herds of white-lipped peccaries have sometimes treed visitors along the trails. Five hundred species of trees, one-fourth of all those found in Costa Rica, live here, including probably the tallest in the country, a *ceiba* or kapok tree that soars to 230 feet (70 m). Eight habitat types exist: montane forest, cloud forest, alluvial plains forest, swamp, palm forest, mangrove, and rocky and sandy vegetation.

You are likely to encounter scientific researchers studying everything from how jacamars know not to eat toxic butterflies, to the life habits of the squirrel monkey to why some South America species are found here but not in Panama or on the Atlantic side of Costa Rica. Researchers often work out of the Sirena station, which is where overnight tourists generally lodge on a space-available basis. If you are on trails in the park, you may not see anyone else. Six trails from Sirena offer 1- to 2-mile (2.5- to 3.5-km) forays into the forest.

The beach along the Pacific adds a marine component to the park. Sperm whales have been sighted offshore, and marine turtles nest on its beaches. There is a live coral reef at Salsipuedes. Among endangered species protected at Corcovado are five species of cat (including the jaguar), giant anteaters, sloths; and the harpy eagle, the largest bird of prey in the world (last seen in 1977). Identified so far are 367 species of birds, 500 species of trees, 104 species of mammals, and 117 species of amphibians and reptiles. Visitors sometimes actually see the elusive tapir. On one of my trips, a fellow traveler spotted one at the Río Claro.

Though its remoteness and heavy vegetation protected the area now encompassed by the park, Corcovado does have some interesting human history. Local lore holds that Cubans trained along its beaches before the Bay of Pigs landing and that Sandinistas sought its isolation for training for a brief period before President Anastasio Somoza of Nicaragua was overthrown in 1979. Miners invaded its confines to pan for gold in the 1980s but were evicted in 1986. Small farms and forestry operations had made inroads in the virgin forest before the park was established in 1975.

Much of the terrain is hilly, rising from sea level to 1,932 feet (782 m). December through March are the driest months; rainfall is 197 inches (5,000 mm) a year in the mountains. The average temperature is 77°F (25°C).

You can get information about Corcovado at the Osa Conservation Area office in Puerto Jiménez. If you plan to stay overnight, you will need written permission, obtained at either the Osa office or the ranger station where you enter. Permits are based on the availability of space in the park refuges or in designated areas next to the refuges. Reservations for overnight camping are not accepted more than a month in advance. Bring mosquito netting.

Public trails in the park go between several ranger stations, basically between Sirena and La Leona, Los Patos, and San Pedrillo (from December to April only). They range from 4 to 12.5 miles long (6 to 20 km). Shorter trails fan out from the ranger stations at Sirena, Los Patos, La Leona, and El Tigre. A $1 booklet of information and maps is available at the Osa office.

Puerto Jiménez is accessible by air, land (turn off the Inter-American Highway toward Rincón), and sea (across the Golfo Dulce from Golfito).

From Puerto Jiménez, the closest ranger station is Los Patos, which involves getting a ride to La Palma and then about a two-hour trek by foot.

Several private nature reserves and lodges in the area offer day tours of the Corcovado, visiting sites along the Pacific side of the park. (See Chapters 10 and 13.)

Guanacaste National Park (Northwest)

Established in 1989, Guanacaste encompasses dry tropical forest and rain forest and stretches from lowlands along the northern Inter-American Highway to the mountains of the Guanacaste Range. It contains 80,337 acres (32,512 ha), and is a crucial piece in the puzzle of ecological interdependence being fitted together in northwestern Costa Rica.

Preservation and restoration of one of the last remaining tropical dry forests, protected in adjoining Santa Rosa National Park, was an impetus for forming Guanacaste National Park. Tropical dry forests once stretched along the Pacific from central Mexico to Panama, but most have fallen prey to agricultural and residential use. Studies at Santa Rosa on the forest's seasonal patterns, distinct life forms, and interactions between plants and animals helped determine the size and habitats necessary to sustain healthy populations of species. Seasonal migration of some of the animal life from Santa Rosa to rainforests in mountains to the east meant protecting those forests as well. Animals are crucial to the life cycle of the forest as seed dispersers. Even the place of insects in the food chain cannot be overlooked.

The idea began as preservation and grew to regeneration, allowing the original dry forest to reinvade large areas cleared for agriculture and pasture, a long-term project its initiators will not see completed in their lifetimes. But they and natural history visitors can measure the progress of this innovative experiment with each season. Environmental education programs for visitors, who range from local schoolchildren to foreign travelers, communicate what is being learned.

Guanacaste is big enough to maintain the needed habitats for plants and animals that have historically lived in the area and to open up places for intensive use by visitors and researchers. The good news for nature lovers is that biological stations in the park offer accommodations for tourists as well as researchers on a space-available basis. Lodging is $19 per person.

Cacao Biological Station sits in cloud forest at 3,609 feet (1,100 m). Cacao Volcano, at 5,443 feet (1,659 m), looms above. Sleeping quarters are in one of the station's three wooden buildings: four rooms for eight

Squirrel monkey (Ree Strange Sheck)

people each, blankets provided. A panorama of forest and distant coastline unfolds from the long covered porch. The station is rustic: no electricity, cold-water showers. The other small buildings house a kitchen and a laboratory or meeting space. Virgin forest behind the buildings holds tapirs, cats, bellbirds, orchids, and bromeliads. Howler monkeys announced the day when I was there. Hiking back out in the afternoon, we saw howler, spider, and white-faced monkeys within a hundred yards of each other. There is a trail to the Maritza Biological Station, about three hours away by foot, and one to the top of Cacao. Getting to Cacao is a trip—you can go only so far on the bad roads and then it is foot or horseback. The trail is not well marked, so a local guide is recommended.

Maritza is also accessible by a road that is best covered in four-wheel-drive vehicles. I can attest to that personally, having slid the entire 11 miles (18 km) after a serious downpour. Maritza lies on the skirts of Orosí Volcano in a windier, cooler area. A more modern facility, the station can house 32 tourists and researchers, with shared baths. Meals can be arranged if requested in advance. Research on aquatic insects has been going on here for several years.

In forests around the rivers, wildlife is abundant: toucans, bellbirds, peccaries, sun bitterns, monkeys. Jaguars have been known to kill cattle in the area. I arrived too late to see a band of 15 peccaries that had appeared on the trail near the laboratory that morning. Coatis frequently visit the station. Less than two hours from Maritza by foot is Llano de los Indios, an open pasture with petroglyphs carved in volcanic stone. The more than 80 pieces of rock art are both abstract and representational.

In the Atlantic watershed, Pitilla Biological Station can hold 32 people, shared cold-water baths. Both the facilities and the road leading to it are rustic; there is no electricity, and four-wheel-drive is necessary. (Enter via Santa Cecilia.) Views from Pitilla include the Lake of Nicaragua, Orosí Volcano, and the rain forest around it.

A research station is now on the Murciélagos Islands—the Institute of Biological Investigations San José, on San José Island. Scientists are studying the abundant marine flora and fauna as well as that found on the land. Inquire about the possibility of visits and camping.

The fee for camping is less than $2 a day. Telephone or fax the Guanacaste Conservation Area for reservations. The nearest lodging outside the park is at Liberia or some of the private nature reserves in the area. (See Chapters 9 and 13.) Access is via the Inter-American Highway north of Liberia. Several buses a day run from San José to Liberia, a trip of about four hours; the bus from San José to La Cruz passes by. However, you will not see much from the highway. Trails for visitors are limited to those connected with the biological research stations.

Guayabo National Monument (Central Valley)

Guayabo is the blue morpho butterfly, the yellow flash of a Montezuma oropendola flying through the tall trees, flowing water, patches of profuse pink impatiens, and ancient carved stones. It is the quiet of centuries-old ruins hidden in the rain forest.

The only archaeological park in the country, Guayabo protects the remains of a city that flourished and disappeared before the Spaniards arrived. People may have occupied the area as early as 1000 B.C.; at its peak Guayabo is estimated to have had 300 to 500 residents, though perhaps as many as 10,000 lived in surrounding villages, supplying labor and revenue to this religious and political center. There was little new building after A.D. 800, and the site was abandoned by 1400.

Visitors today see cobbled roads (*calzadas*), stone-lined tanks to store water, open and covered aqueducts that carried water through the site (many still in use), and mounds (*montículos*) with stone-covered bases. Information signs at the park depict conical houses believed to have been built on the mounds out of wood and palm leaves. Trails lead past covered and open tombs, plundered before the park was established. Stylized forms of a jaguar and caiman decorate a striking monolith. Sixty-three petroglyphs picture birds and animals as well as art whose meaning has yet to be deciphered.

A conservation and excavation project begun in August 1989 may shed light on some of the mysteries of people and place. The project increases the excavated area to half of the almost-50-acre (20-ha) site. Among items found in the area are golden bells, carved stone tables, roasted corn kernels, beautiful pottery, a copper and gold frog, and a sacrificial stone. Some of the works of art are exhibited at the National Museum in San José. In 1991, four fragments of Nicoya pottery were discovered that were precisely dated, A.D. 1359. According to park administrator and archaeologist Rodolfo Tenorio, the find indicates a contact between Guayabo and Nicoya at that time that perhaps went beyond commercial interchange. One hypothesis is that the contact was at a diplomatic/political level.

In addition to the archaeological site, Guayabo protects the only remaining primary forest in the province of Cartago, accounting for 22 percent of the park's 538 acres (218 ha). More than 80 varieties of orchids and other epiphytes adorn the trees; toucans are present, as are chachalacas, woodpeckers, and brown jays (ticos call them *piapias* and say they are the scouts of the forest, their warning cries signaling that an intruder is near). Notice

MONKEY BUSINESS

Four species of monkeys live in Costa Rica: the white-faced capuchin (called cara blanca *in Spanish), the howler (*congo*), spider (*mono colorado or araña*), and the squirrel (*tití or ardilla*). The Spanish word for monkey is* mono. *Howlers, the most abundant, are fruit and leaf eaters, as are the acrobatic spider monkeys, while the capuchins and squirrel monkeys eat everything from fruits to insects to lizards.*

The small squirrel monkey, or tití, is found only in the southern Pacific lowlands. At Manuel Antonio National Park, Grace Wong of the wildlife management program of the National University of Heredia has studied the titís in the area, which are a subspecies endemic to Costa Rica. Another subspecies farther south is endemic to Costa Rica and Panama, though few remain in Panama.

Grace has identified 14 troops totaling about 681 individuals, with six of the troops, varying from 15 to 65 individuals, ranging mainly inside the park.

From May to October, when fruit is abundant, the titís have more time to rest and play, but by November, they spend most of the day looking for food. Up at 5:00 a.m., they retire for the night about 6:00 p.m.

The young are born from the end of February to the end of March, one birth per pregnancy. Females have young every two years. Babies are carried for their first three months, with other adults taking turns helping the mother.

When food is scarce, there is some competition between capuchins and titís. Grace says that when they clash, the smaller tití leaves; she has seen a capuchin grab a tití and throw it to the ground. When food is plentiful, they eat together. In Manuel Antonio, natural enemies of the tití are mainly boa constrictors and tyras, minklike animals.

Though human activity does not seem to drive titís away, Grace is concerned. The increase in tourists and tourism infrastructure has reduced the habitat of monkeys and other animals living outside the park, in some cases destroying corridors that forest monkeys move through and isolating troops. Another impact of tourism is that monkeys near a trail or road where people stop to observe them spend more energy on guard and less time foraging.

Tropical Storm Gert in 1993 also influenced habitat in the park. About 60 percent of the canopy, or upper layer of the forest, was affected, reducing sites where the monkeys look for insects and fruits. Though short-term effects of this natural destruction are negative, Grace says that in the long-term, it can be beneficial because of the mosaic of different types of forest that will regenerate.

the abundance of long, hanging nests built by oropendolas. Mammals include sloths, coatis, rabbits, squirrels, and armadillos.

With advance notice, local guides can accompany visitors on Sendero de los Montículos, the interpretive trail that leads through the archaeological site to a mirador with a fantastic view of the ruins below, the valley where Turrialba lies, and mountain peaks. Guayabo is open from 8:00 a.m. to 3:30 p.m. daily. A new trail lets visitors watch excavation of a road that ran from Guayabo to an outlying area. Visitors can walk alone on the Los Cantarillos nature trail, which makes either a short loop or a longer one down to the Lajitas River. It can be muddy in the wet season. Rainfall averages 138 inches (3,500 mm), and the average temperature is 68°F (20°C). The highest point in the park is 3,609 feet (1,100 m).

Do not miss the visitor center across the road from the park entrance. The nearby camping area has been revamped to provide ten camping sites scattered among the trees and one group-camping area. There are bathrooms and potable water.

The nearest lodging outside the park is a ten-minute walk away in the town of Guayabo; hotels in Turrialba 11 miles (19 km) away can be reached in 30 minutes by paved road. Tour companies, lodges, and hotels offer guided trips to the park (see Chapter 7). Bus service from San José to Turrialba is frequent and takes less than two hours to cover the 40 miles (65 km). There also is bus service from Turrialba to Guayabo. Taxi fare between the two runs about $12 one way.

Guayabo, Negritos, and Los Pájaros Biological Reserves (Northwest)

These four small islands in the Gulf of Nicoya are havens for large populations of resident and migratory birds, mainly seabirds. No visitor facilities exist; in fact, along with protection of the birds, another reason for making them biological reserves was to avoid their "development" for tourism or other purposes—to keep at least some of the gulf islands in a natural state.

Guayabo welcomes peregrine falcons in the winter and holds the largest of the country's four nesting colonies of brown pelicans. Located 5 miles (8 km) southwest of Puntarenas near San Lucas Island, Guayabo is also home to brown boobies, frigate birds, laughing gulls, lizards, and crabs. It has cliffs, a small beach, and sparse vegetation.

Two islands make up the Negritos, separated by a narrow channel that harbors whirlpools. Brown pelicans, frigate birds, boobies, and gulls live here, too, along with parrots, doves, raccoons, and iguanas. Artifacts indicate that Indians have been to the islands, either to live or bury their dead. Coral reefs make access difficult, but the waters support dolphins, giant conch, and oysters. Forests of palm, cedar, gumbo-limbo, and frangipani survive. The Negritos are almost 11 miles (17 km) south of Puntarenas near the Nicoya Peninsula. The Guayabo and Negritos reserves cover 355 acres (144 ha).

Isla de los Pájaros means "island of the birds." Less than 550 yards (500 m) from the coast, 8 miles (13 km) north of Puntarenas, it has some low-growing forest and fresh water. Again, seabirds, mainly pelicans, are the predominant species. It is the smallest of the four islands at 10 acres (4 ha).

There are no facilities at these reserves and camping is prohibited; however, you can enjoy the bird life through your binoculars as you pass by on one of the popular day cruises of the Gulf of Nicoya.

Hitoy-Cerere Biological Reserve (Caribbean)

Off the beaten path, Hitoy-Cerere is not a stopping-off point on the way to somewhere else but a destination in itself. Your map may not even show a road in, but there is one, passable even in the wettest months. The reserve is 37 miles (60 km) southwest of Limón, 90 minutes from Cahuita.

Parts of this rugged portion of the Talamanca Mountains have yet to be explored. We do know some of the animals that live on its 22,622 forested acres (9,155 ha): tapirs, jaguars, peccaries, pacas, porcupines, weasels, white-faced and howler monkeys, agoutis, anteaters, armadillos, kinkajous, sloths, squirrels, otters, and deer. Among the 276 bird species identified are the blue-headed parrot, keel-billed toucan, squirrel cuckoo, spectacled owl, green kingfisher, and slaty-tailed trogon. Frogs, toads, insects, and snakes have not been counted. Perhaps you will spot one of the remarkable Jesus Christ lizards, so named because they can walk on water. Their secret is quick movement and large hind feet with flaps of skin along each toe that allow them to skip over the surface of streams and ponds.

The forest canopy hovers at about 100 feet (30 m), but some species protrude through the top, reaching more than 160 feet (50 m). Buttresses from the trunks of these giants widen their base of support. Some trees begin as high as 7 feet (2 m) above the ground and have a horizontal reach of almost 50 feet (15 m). There are black palms with spiny stilt roots, tree ferns, orchids, and bromeliads. Mosses and lichens cushion trunks and branches.

Trails in this perpendicular place are difficult and not well marked. One researcher found it easier to stick to the rivers, though moss-covered rocks make streambeds slippery. (The reserve is surrounded by legally protected Indian lands.)

Water flows through the reserve. "Hitoy" in Bribrí refers to moss- and algae-covered rocks in the river of that name, "Cerere" to another river's clear waters. Pools surrounded by exuberant vegetation invite a solitary dip, while waterfalls almost 100 feet (30 m) high inspire awe. Bring rain gear—

there is no defined dry season. Yearly amounts average 138 inches (3,500 mm). Humidity is high year-round; temperatures average 77°F (25°C). Elevation goes from about 328 to 3,363 feet (100 to 1,025 m).

To stay overnight, check with La Amistad-Atlántico Conservation area. A small biological station constructed with funds from Holland may be completed by your arrival. Day trips can be made from lodging in Limón, Cahuita, Puerto Viejo, or spots in between.

Irazú Volcano National Park (Central Valley)

Irazú Volcano has a history of showing off. Its awesome power is evident long before one reaches its impressive craters. Near Cartago, notice the devastation from the most recent major eruptions, from 1963 to 1965. Whole areas were buried in mud, floods were significant, and volcanic rock still peppers the countryside. But as you travel along the paved road to the park, give the volcano credit for the rich soils that now produce cabbages, potatoes, onions, and grasslands for dairy cows.

The highest peak in the Central Volcanic Range, Irazú reaches 11,260 feet (3,432 m). It has been known to send ash as far away as the Nicoya Peninsula; steam clouds have billowed 1,640 feet (500 m) high, and debris has shot up 984 feet (300 m). The rumbling giant tossed boulders weighing several tons from its innards in 1963 and send tremors to rattle buildings miles away.

Today, with Irazú in a sometimes-restless resting phase, visitors can ride right to the top of a lunar landscape that muffles its fiery nature. But thin streams of steam or gas and occasional tremors remind us that it is not dead; it only sleeps. People can walk along the rim of the main crater, peering down into a bright green lake almost 1,000 feet (300 m) below. Volcanic grays and blacks are highlighted by swatches of reds and oranges in the steep sides. The diameter is 3,445 feet (1,050 m). There are four other well-defined craters: Diego de la Haya, Playa Hermosa, La Laguna, and Piroclústico.

Tenacious plants dot the largely empty areas around the craters, some bravely sporting bright flowers. On slopes, where the green of secondary growth gives testimony to nature's powers of recovery, old, barren branches rise like ghostly fingers above the new forest.

Animal life is scarce at the park as a result of both human activity and the eruptions. Where cougar and jaguar once thrived, today you may see rabbits, coyotes, armadillos, or even a tiger. Hummingbirds are numerous, and you might also spot a volcano junco, mountain robin, ruddy woodcreeper, or ant-eating woodpecker.

For clearest views and a chance to see both oceans, go early. I have a memory of Irazú at sunset, however, that I would not trade. Buffeted by a

Mushroom artistry (Ree Strange Sheck)

cold wind, I stood on a narrow path between two craters and watched as the setting sun lit swirling clouds of mist with rich tones of orange and gold.

Whatever time of day you visit, take a jacket and something for rain, just in case. The average temperature is 45°F (7.3°C), with a lowest recorded temperature of 26°F (-3°C). When it is cold, it is very, very cold. Frost is possible from December through February. The annual rainfall is 85 inches (2,158 mm) in the 5,706-acre (2,309-ha) park.

Irazú park is the birthplace of several rivers that eventually flow into some of the country's major water-ways: Chirripó, Reventazón, Sarapiquí, and Río Grande de Tárcoles. The Indians who lived on the mountain's slopes named it Iztarú, which means "mountain of trembling and thunder."

Irazú Volcano Park, open from 7:00 a.m. to 5:00 p.m., is a two-hour drive from San José. Take the main highway to Cartago, then watch for signs telling where to turn. The park is 19 miles (31 km) from Cartago. Up on the mountain, there is a pleasant view point with picnic facilities where you can safely pull off the road and drink in the expansive view of the valley below and peaks beyond. Most San José tour companies offer trips to Irazú, some in conjunction with a visit to the Lankester Gardens, Cartago, or the Orosi Valley. Perhaps by your arrival a new visitor center will be in place.

Lomas Barbudal Biological Reserve (Northwest)

My impression of Lomas Barbudal was birds— everywhere, so many to peer at through binoculars that we could hardly make progress driving along the dirt road. The species list is up to 180; the sheer quantity is overwhelming. Three species particularly important—because they are disappearing in other areas—are the king vulture, great curassow, and yellow-naped parrot. The man on the street will tell you that yellow-naped parrots are the best talkers in the parrot family. Trapping is no doubt a factor in their disappearance, along with loss of habitat. Curassows make for good eating.

Enthralled with the birds, we had little time for the bees, one of the reserve's claims to fame. About 250 species are thought to live here, some found nowhere else in the country. About 60 species of moths and butterflies and wasps are also abundant. Congo and white-faced monkeys move about the reserve, as do coatis, peccaries, white-tailed deer, armadillos, and raccoons.

Four species of endangered trees survive here, only three of which are familiar to most people: mahogany, Panama redwood, and rosewood. Deciduous forests make up 70 percent of the 5,631-acre (2,279-ha) reserve. One of the species that flowers profusely in the dry season, when its branches are bare of leaves, is the yellow cortez, *cortesa amarilla*. With a profusion of yellow blossoms, the trees resemble giant bouquets. Flowers in a single tree last only about four days, but it may bloom two or three times during the dry season. A curious tree is the cannonball. You will know it when you see it. The fruit looks like big balls hanging on strings down the trunk and on lower branches.

Water sources are plentiful in this region, which is classified as tropical dry forest. Rainfall averages 59 to 79 inches (1,500 to 2,000 mm). Rivers such as the beautiful Cabuya flow year-round; its natural, sandy-bottomed pools are ideal for a swim under the big trees along its banks, where monkeys and birds escape the afternoon heat. Students from Bagaces High School constructed a trail that begins between the information center and the river pools—delightful. There are more than 20 natural springs in the reserve.

Lomas Barbudal, which means "bearded hills" in Spanish, is three hours from San José on the Inter-American Highway toward Nicaragua, or 30 minutes south of Liberia. Turn west 6.8 miles (11 km) north of Bagaces and continue about 4 miles (6 km) to the visitor center, which is operated in conjunction with Friends of Lomas Barbudal. Inside the reserve are picnic areas, trails, a lookout, and a place to swim in the river. Lodging is available in Liberia or at nearby privately owned nature reserves. For more information, stop by or call the Tempisque Conservation Area office in Bagaces.

Manuel Antonio National Park (South)

This park is special. White-faced monkeys leap from tree to tree along the beach in dazzling displays of aerial skill. Shier squirrel monkeys, an endemic subspecies found only in this area, peek from behind leaves along trails. Slow-moving sloths turn a lazy look at visitors from their high vantage points. I had my first close-up look at a coati and an agouti in the wild on the forest trail in Manuel Antonio. Large iguanas rustle through leaves on the forest floor or sun themselves on logs along the beach.

The warm waters of the Pacific are home to a variety of marine life; snorkelers, divers, and even watchers at the tide pools see brightly colored fish. Do not miss the tiny bright blue ones in pools among the rocks at the western end of Manuel Antonio Beach. Whales pass by, and dolphins swim offshore. There are ten species of sponge, 17 of algae, 78 of fish, 19 of coral, and 24 of crustaceans.

Researchers have identified 184 species of birds and 109 species of mammals, more than half of which are bats rarely seen by visitors. Among marine birds are brown pelicans, magnificent frigate birds, and brown boobies. Land birds include parrots, Baird's trogons, green kingfishers, gray-headed chachalacas, and golden-masked tanagers.

The fun begins at the entrance to the park, reached by wading across an estuary that can be waist-high on a short adult at high tide or barely cover the feet at low. There is no bridge, so wear shoes and clothes that can get wet. Carry whatever you want to eat or drink.

Once inside the park, you can choose a wide trail through the tall forest or walk along South Espadilla Beach. Toward the far end of the beach, you can enter the forest and cross over to gentler Manuel Antonio Beach or take the path to Cathedral Point, which separates the two beaches. From Cathedral Point, you can see Mogote Island—one of 12 included in the park—rising up sharply from the sea, its high cliffs crowned with vegetation. Both Mogote and Cathedral Point were sites of prehistoric Indian activities.

These two white-sand beaches are lined with lush vegetation almost to the high-water line. The clear waters are warm. Espadilla is steeper with bigger waves. Puerto Escondido, rockier, not as kind to the feet, lies farther down a trail through the low mountains. Its beach disappears at high tide. Check with rangers before you start out. Guided walks on the trail to Puerto Escondido and a lookout point are limited to groups of no more than 15, with a total of 45 people allowed on the trail at a time.

Allow time for a leisurely walk along the short Perezoso Trail, named for the sloths you may see there. No more than 30 people at a time may be on this trail.

At Manuel Antonio Beach, face the sea and look at the far right end near the rocks for a prehistoric turtle trap built by the Quepo Indians. Most easily visible at lowest tides after a full moon, the trap is a semicircular rock barrier that forms a pool at the beach's edge. Low and high tides vary about 11 feet (3.4 m) here. Female turtles would come in on high tide over the rock wall, but some would be caught in the pools when they tried to return to the sea as the tide went out and the water level dropped below the barrier. Both green and olive ridley turtles lay eggs here, though not in mass nestings.

A visitor center for exhibits and audiovisual presentations is in the works. Certified local guides, trained by park personnel, are available.

The park, which covers 1,687 acres (683 ha) of land, does have a dry season from December to March, but rains are possible even then, and clear days, especially mornings, in the rainier months permit hours of quiet enjoyment on the beach. The annual rainfall is 150 inches (3,800 mm); the rainiest months are August, September, and October. The average temperature is 81°F (27°C). The park also protects 135,905 acres (55,000 ha) of marine habitat.

In addition to primary and secondary forest and beaches, there are marshes, a mangrove swamp, lagoons, and woodland. Warning signs point out the manzanillo tree along the beach; its leaves, bark, and applelike fruit secrete a white latex that stings the skin and is toxic.

The park is open from 7:00 a.m. to 5:00 p.m., closed on Monday. It is crowded at Easter, Christmas, and during the two-week school vacation in July. Even though it is one of the most-visited parks, it is sometimes possible on a midweek visit to have the beach practically to yourself. No more than 600 people are admitted at a time during the week, 800 on weekends. The park has its own telephone (777-0644) and fax (777-0654).

To protect both vegetation and animals in this small park, camping is no longer allowed. Please do not feed the monkeys. Some are becoming aggressive because of this practice. Accommodations are available in the adjacent town of Manuel Antonio and along the road to Quepos, less than 5 miles (7 km) away.

Daily express buses travel between San José and Manuel Antonio. The trip takes about 3½ hours. There are daily scheduled flights from San José to Quepos. (See Practical Extras at the end of the book.) A local bus runs frequently between Quepos and Manuel Antonio.

Palo Verde National Park (Northwest)

Palo Verde National Park, which includes what was formerly known as the Dr. Rafael Lucas Rodríguez Wildlife Refuge, covers 41,523 acres (16,804 ha). Lying along the east bank of the Tempisque River above where it empties into the Gulf of Nicoya, the area encompasses lakes, swamps, grasslands, savanna woodlands, and forest—probably 15 habitats in all. It is one of the most important sanctuaries for migrating waterfowl in Central America. Along with the thousands of migratory birds that arrive every year, there are many resident species. Up to 279 species of birds have been counted, but it is believed that as many as 300 are here because other species have been seen nearby.

Herons, ibis, ducks, storks, and jacanas are among those that descend on the lowlands to feed and mate. The rare, endangered jabiru stork nests here, most commonly seen from November to January. The largest stork in the world, the jabiru has a white body, gray neck and head, and a rose-red necklace. The only scarlet macaws left in the tropical dry forest of the Pacific live in this area.

In the rainy season, flooding of the plains is widespread. In the dry months of November through April, some waterholes disappear, and those that remain attract both birds and other wildlife, allowing the patient visitor a good chance to see them. An observation tower open to visitors is near a marsh.

Approach the mango trees near the Organization for Tropical Studies

(OTS) station quietly for a chance to see some of the many mammals that make their home in the region. Peccaries, iguanas, deer, monkeys, and coatis feed on the fruits. The white-tailed deer who watched us while we watched him did not seem the least bit frightened. The park is home to 177 species of mammals.

A good trail system takes visitors into the forest past flowing springs that attract wildlife, past a natural cactus garden, to a superb lookout over the Tempisque floodplain, through a marsh (a printed guide recommends this as the best place to see a tropical rattlesnake or boa constrictor), through second-growth forest that is reclaiming pastureland, and to virgin tropical dry forest.

Friendly park staff greet visitors at the entrance stations. On one visit, the ranger on duty rushed from the forest to urge me to come with him quickly—he had just come across a snake eating a frog and wanted me to see it. You can go to the Catalina sector of the park (about 9 miles or 14 km by car) or continue to the OTS station and Puerto Chamorro (about 7.5 miles or 12 km) on the banks of the Tempisque, where you will surely see huge iguanas foraging. Signs point to the Sendero Pizote (Coati Trail), Sendero Venado (Deer Trail), a 2.5-km loop, and others.

Isla de los Pájaros in the Tempisque River is an important nesting site for some spectacular birds. The small island seems covered with birds. On river trips past it, you can see the lovely color of the roseate spoonbills as they nest and fly overhead. There are wood storks, glossy ibis, anhingas, and great egrets. Many boas inhabit the island, feeding on bird eggs and nestlings. The river has a 13-foot (4-m) rise and fall with the tide. Sometimes it flows backward. Crocodiles and caimans can often be seen along the banks.

At the park, you may see cattle grazing; it is part of a management plan to keep the marshes open. Nearby farmers lose more of their crops than they like to birds, who do not recognize boundaries, so now automatic cannons help keep them from the fields. A fire-prevention program has resulted in a 95-percent reduction in forest fires since 1991.

The elevation ranges from 33 to 689 feet (10 to 210 m) above sea level. The annual rainfall is 90 inches (2,295 mm), and the average temperature is 81°F (27°C).

In the dry season, most trees lose their leaves to conserve water, but many wear bright flowers. The palo verde tree which gave the park its name, has pretty yellow flowers that adorn its green, thorn-clad branches. Temperatures can reach 105°F (41°C) at midday, but nights and early mornings are cool. While it is windy in the dry season and insects are scarce, the rainy season brings humidity, little breeze, and mosquitoes and gnats.

Camping is allowed in the park. If the rustic Palo Verde Biological Station belonging to OTS is not filled with researchers, tourists can stay there. The cost is $53 with meals. Make reservations at OTS. Telephone 240-6696, fax 240-6783.

The main land route is by the Inter-American Highway to Bagaces, between Liberia and Cañas. Turn west at the sign just across from the Tempisque Conservation Area office. The pavement ends, but the road is passable year-round. Just follow the signs. Keep your binoculars and cameras handy, because birds are everywhere. The 17-mile (28-km) trip from Bagaces can take a while, depending on how often you have a binocular stop. You can get from San José to Bagaces on one of the frequent buses that go on to Liberia. From Bagaces, you will need to hire a taxi.

The second route is to turn off the Inter-American and take the Tempisque ferry; once across the river, head for Puerto Humo. There you can hire a boat to take you along the meandering Tempisque to a dock at the park. It is a little more than a mile (2 km) by foot to the park headquarters. Tour companies and hotels offer both land and water trips to Palo Verde. Boat trips on the Tempisque to Isla de los Pájaros are attractive for natural history travelers—some tours include shore time at Puerto Chamorro for lunch and hiking. For information, contact the Tempisque Conservation Area. Attention birders: the park is open at 6:00 a.m.

Poás Volcano National Park (Central Valley)

At Poás Volcano, you can stand at the edge of a multicolored crater almost a mile (1.5 km) in diameter, look down 984 feet (300 m), and watch geyser-like eruptions that leave no doubt this mountain still has something to say.

Its message was so clear in 1989 that the park was temporarily closed. The intensity of eruptions, the gases, and the ash made visits inadvisable. Forests and agriculture, especially coffee grown on the slopes below, suffered from acid rain. Some nearby residents were evacuated. Today the park is open from 7:00 a.m. to 4:00 p.m. No camping is allowed. You will see evidence of the acid rain.

Volcanologists cringe when they hear Poás called the largest geyser in the world, but the fact that it is not takes nothing away from the beauty and power of this 8,884-foot (2,708-m) giant. There are actually five craters on the mountain, but two get the most attention from visitors: the newer active crater responsible for the recent lava, rocks, ash, and steam, and an extinct one that now cradles Botos Lake, a 20-minute easy climb through dwarf forest from the active crater.

From the view point constructed along the edge of the active crater, you have a spectacular view of the greenish hot-water lake. The earlier you go, the better chance you have of an unimpeded look. Clouds that drift in as the day

POETRY ON THE ESCALONIA TRAIL
POÁS VOLCANO

I am light and shadow
Shining sun
Cold kiss of clouds
Fertile home of ancient trees
Of flowers just born
And of the red-green hummingbird
All pass their days
In my arms
Free
I am the cloud forest

progresses can completely obscure the bottom. While waiting for a column of mud and water to shoot into the air, notice the fumaroles, and look for small measuring devices scattered around the crater. Costa Rica has a fine Volcanological and Seismological Observatory at the National University in Heredia; its staff keeps a close watch at Poás and other sites around the country. Depending on the wind direction, you may get a good whiff of sulfur.

The park, with 13,838 acres (5,600 ha), has more to offer, though, than volcanic craters. Trails lead through shrubs, dwarf forest, and cloud forest covered with epiphytes. Because of volcanic activity, hunting, and deforestation outside the park, few mammals remain. Coyotes, rabbits, frogs, and toads are common, and at least 79 bird species are at home here. A park ranger told me he has seen resplendent quetzals fly over the road between the park entrance and administration building in early morning. Hummingbirds are easy to see. If you take some of the less-traveled trails, you might spot an emerald toucanet, brown robin, black guan, or masked woodpecker.

The trail to Botos Lake, named for the Botos Indians who lived on the north slope when the Spaniards arrived, begins near the view point. At this altitude, take your time, enjoy the tangled vegetation, and try to figure out the birds you are hearing but may not be able to spot.

My favorite is the Escalonia Trail, which begins at the picnic area. Trees soar overhead, bromeliads are everywhere, and trail markers full of poetry do justice to the forest's magnificence. They are only in Spanish; I have translated one of them for you (see box).

The visitor center houses exhibits, a nature shop, restrooms, and an auditorium. The visitor center restaurant, which is and has been operated by Café Britt serves good food.

Bring a jacket and rain gear. Rainfall is 106 inches (2,700 mm), and though temperatures average between 48°F and 55°F (9°C to 13°C), a minimum of 21°F (6°C) has been recorded. On a bright, sunny day, it can be 70°F (21°C).

Poás lies about 90 minutes from San José through Alajuela and San Pedro de Poás. The drive is spectacular, through coffee farms, nurseries where ornamental plants are grown for export (under those huge expanses of black shade cloths), strawberry fields, and dairy farms. If you are going by tour, check to see if it gets to Poás by 9:30 a.m. at the latest and how much time it allows there. Some give you 30 minutes, barely enough time to peer into the crater. Other nature tour companies offer more time or a naturalist guide to take you on a day trip to the area.

Public bus is not the easiest way to get to Poás. The only direct bus is on Sunday, and it is crowded. Daily buses go from Alajuela to San Pedro de Poás, and you can hire a taxi there. If several people are going, you can hire a taxi from San José and split the cost.

Rincón de la Vieja National Park (Northwest)
From the porch of the century-old ranch house that now houses park rangers, an exhibit room, and an administrative office at Rincón de la Vieja park, I watched a doe and fawn at the edge of the clearing. They walked without fear. On the way up the mountain, a morpho butterfly had fluttered across the road; four species of this brilliant butterfly live in the park. Tapirs roam here, as do howler, capuchin, and spider monkeys. The armadillo is so abundant it could practically be the symbol of the park. Peccaries are common, and there is evidence that jaguar and puma stalk this 34,801-acre (14,084-ha) preserve.

The white-fronted Amazon parrot and spectacled owl are among 257 species of birds. Doves are everywhere; you have a good chance of seeing the curassow at lower elevations. The park ascends from 1,968 to 6,545 feet (600 to 1,995 m). There are kites, toucans and toucanets, redstarts, and motmots. A small cicada with the voice of a frog lives under the ground, its imitation fooling even the experts.

The park, in the Guanacaste Mountain Range, is the source of 32 rivers. As much as 197 inches (5,000 mm) of rain falls at higher elevations, practically year-round. The park's forests are important not only in preventing rivers that flow to the lowlands from disappearing in the dry season but also in keeping them from flooding in rainy months. The area's importance as a water source is one reason the park was established.

Two volcanoes crown this mountain mass: Rincón de la Vieja, which is active, and Santa María, which is dormant. In fact, Rincón de la Vieja has two craters; the dormant one has a crystal clear cold-water lake, while the lake in the other crater steams. Rincón erupted again in 1995, spewing ash and sending hot mud to area rivers. The best time to climb to the craters is in the driest months, February through April, but of course climbing is subject to volcanic activity.

Visitors have access to the scenic beauty and geologic attractions of the park through two entrances, both on bad roads. The ranch house, or *casona*, entrance on the slopes of Santa María is 16 miles (25 km) from the center of Liberia. This is called the Santa María sector. (Jeep taxi from Liberia is about $35 one way.) The Enchanted Forest Trail begins here. A walk through that fairyland of tall trees, delicate orchids (the national flower, the *guaria morada* orchid, thrives in the park), ferns, and mosses touches a primeval chord within. A small waterfall makes it picture perfect.

A shorter Sendero Colibrí (Hummingbird Trail) or a walk to a mirador with a view of Liberia and Miravalles Volcano are other possibilities. Less than 2 miles (3 km) away are sulfur waters that many say are medicinal. A 5.6-mile (8-km), three-hour trek takes you to Las Pailas, a magic land of bubbling mud pots, pools of hot water, and steam and gas vents at the other entrance to the park.

The second entrance is reached by turning off the Inter-American Highway about 3 miles (5 km) north of Liberia and continuing 12 miles (19 km) through the village of Curubundé to the park. This is called the Las Pailas sector. After checking in at the ranger station, visitors can hike on forest trails to Las Pailas. The walk starts out by crossing a river—no bridge—which was about knee-deep when I waded across one August.

Various trail possibilities exist from this entrance also, including the climb to the craters and to waterfalls. Camping is permitted in designated areas. Bring rubber boots for hiking. The average temperature is 59°F to 79°F (15°C to 26°C)—it can get cold at night.

Contact the Guanacaste Conservation Area for information. If you drive from Liberia to the casona, you may have to wait for the river at the edge of Liberia to go down after a hard rain before you can get across—there is no bridge. The park is open from 7:30 a.m. to 4:30 p.m.

Hotels, lodges, and tour companies offer visits to Rincón de la Vieja. There are some small lodges and private reserves near park entrances. (See Chapters 9 and 13.)

History-filled La Casona at Santa Rosa National Park
(Ree Strange Scheck)

Santa Rosa National Park (Northwest)

In times past, Indians have walked this land, and hunters, woodcutters, cowboys, and soldiers, too. Footprints today belong mainly to researchers, park rangers, and nature lovers. What had been virgin tropical dry forest, cleared pastures, and a battlefield now is Santa Rosa National Park, a piece of property where history is still being written.

The historical significance of Santa Rosa was the primary reason it was protected by the government, first as a national monument and then as a national park. Soon, however, the ecological importance of its flora and fauna and of the habitats that exist in this dry Pacific region was recognized.

It is the ecological battle that is making history now, an effort not only to protect but also to restore some of these habitats. Research at Santa Rosa is shedding light on plant and animal interrelationships and how forests regenerate themselves—discoveries that make a difference here and around the world.

A young park ranger told me that most Costa Ricans who visit Santa Rosa National Park come initially because of its history, but they leave excited about the intricacies of nature. She carries the park's environmental education program to nearby village schools, and walks with the children when they come on tour.

The historical drawing card is the site of the Battle of Santa Rosa on

March 20, 1856, which pitted a well-trained and well-armed invading army against a ragtag band of Costa Rican peasants who had become soldiers overnight. The patriots won, routing the forces of adventurer William Walker in 14 minutes. The battle took place around La Casona, the house at Hacienda Santa Rosa. Visitors today can walk through the big house and see the historical displays, stand on the wide wooden veranda and look toward the 300-year-old stone corrals, or step into the kitchen and see where cheese was hung over the wood stove to preserve it.

A stately *guanacaste*, the national tree of Costa Rica, stands nearby. Its wood is good for construction, and its ear-shaped fruit, which gives the tree its English name of ear fruit, has been used to wash clothes and is food for horses, cows, and small forest mammals.

Climb the short view-point trail behind La Casona or take the short, well-marked nature trail. Keep your eyes open: I was within spitting distance of a handsome 5-foot (1.5-m) boa constrictor before I could discern it draped over a tree root by the path. Its natural camouflage is remarkable. The trail is called Indio Desnudo for the gumbo-limbo tree, identifiable by its reddish-brown bark, which inspired the popular name—*indio desnudo* means "naked Indian." Since the reddish skin has a tendency to peel, ticos sometimes irreverently refer to it as the "tourist tree." Some of the trees are labeled, and the well-maintained trail is a delight. Look for Indian petroglyphs along the trail.

Two of Santa Rosa's beaches are famous as sea turtle nesting sites: Naranjo, about 8 miles (12 km) from park headquarters, and Nancite, 11 miles (17 km) away. Though three species come ashore to lay eggs, it is the hundreds of thousands of Pacific or olive ridley turtles on small Nancite Beach that get the most attention. From July to December, mass nestings, called *arribadas*, occur periodically, while single turtles come ashore every night in this peak season. The other two species are green and leatherback turtles. Nancite is in a study area, so permission to visit is required.

The park does have a pronounced dry season from November to May. Rainfall for most of its 91,719-acre (37,118-ha) land surface is about 63 inches (1,600 mm). Average temperature is 79°F (26°C). The park also protects some 193,000 acres (78,000 ha) of marine habitat.

Entrance to this part of Santa Rosa, which also includes the park headquarters, is 22 miles (36 km) north of Liberia via the Inter-American Highway, paved all the way to La Casona. At the entrance booth, you can buy a map of the park, and the ranger can help you decide what you can see in the time you have.

Entrance to the Murciélago section of Santa Rosa is farther north on the Inter-American, turning off to Cuajiniquil at the rural guard station. If you do not see a sign for Murciélago when you get to the village, ask for directions. The road is unpaved, and a couple of rivers must be forded to reach the ranger station. I did it in the rainy season in a standard pickup, but I would have worried less in four-wheel-drive; there is lots of mud. Better to attempt it in dry season.

Stop along the narrow road and take a close look at the acacia tree for a lesson in plant and animal relationships. The tree provides food for acacia ants, and the ants protect it from animal predators and foreign vegetation. They even keep a circle cleared around the tree. Find the small hole near the base of one of its thorns and watch what happens when the tree is disturbed. Do not get your fingers in the way of the ants rushing out: Their stings are painful. If you unwittingly brush against an acacia branch along a trail, you will find out for yourself.

Murciélago ("bat" in English) belonged to Anastasio Somoza when he was president of Nicaragua. Talk to the delightful cook at the ranger station there; she can share stories from those days. She can also tell you about the coyotes and monkeys that come into the yard. You can travel on to the coast at Playa Blanca (11 miles, 17 km) or Santa Elena Bay or walk on the trail to the Pozo del General, which has water year-round, and is important for animals in the dry season.

Santa Rosa National Park has capuchin, howler, and spider monkeys, deer, armadillos, coatis, raccoons, and even some cats—115 species of mammals in all, about half of them bats. Studies have identified more than 3,000 species of moths and butterflies among more than 30,000 of insects. Magpie jays and parrots make lots of noise, while some of the 253 species of birds get attention with their coloring: Look for orange-fronted parakeets, elegant trogons, and crested caracaras.

Santa Rosa park includes Bolaños Island. Located up the coast from mainland Santa Rosa west of the town of La Cruz, Bolaños is in a small bay whose waters lap on both the Costa Rican and Nicaraguan shorelines. Rising 266 feet (81 m) out of the Pacific, this rocky mound protects seabirds. Magnificent frigate birds and American oystercatchers nest here, and this is one of four nesting sites in the country for brown pelicans.

Winds seem to be an important factor in determining where frigate birds build a nest: They need help landing and becoming airborne because of their small bodies, short feet, and long wings and tails. The wind on Bolaños during the dry season—nesting time—is consistent and strong. There are as many as 1,000 of these birds, called *tijeretas* (tea-hay-RAY-tahs) in Spanish because of their scissorlike tails. During mating season, the male blows out a bright red throat pouch to attract a female, who lays a single egg.

No facilities for visitors exist at the bird sanctuary, but watching through binoculars at a tactful distance is not against the rules. The island is less than 3 miles (5 km) from Puerto Soley.

Camping is possible near the administrative center at Santa Rosa, at Playa Naranjo, and at Estero Real as well as at Pozo del General in the Murciélago sector. Beds are sometimes available at the Tropical Dry Forest Research Center in Santa Rosa's administrative area, though priority goes to researchers and students, $19 per person in shared rooms, shared baths. Soft drinks and snacks are available at the cafeteria, meals only with advance notice. Contact the Guanacaste Conservation Area for information or to make reservations.

Area hotels and some private nature reserves offer day trips to Santa Rosa. Several nature tour companies have trips to the park, and it is easy to find on your own if you are driving. Buses to Peñas Blancas or La Cruz will let you off at the park entrance, though you will have a 4-mile (7-km) walk to the headquarters. Or you can hire a taxi from Liberia for a day trip to the park. Santa Rosa is 4½ hours from San José. The information booth at the entrance is open from 7:30 a.m. to 4:30 p.m.

Tapantí National Park (Central Valley)

"Dripping forest" is not a scientific term, but for me, it describes the Tapantí National Park in the Talamanca Mountain Range. Inside the forest, raining or not, the air is moist, plants seem wet, the earth smells fresh. The sound of running water can be pervasive: 150 rivers and rivulets run here, important sources for hydroelectric projects. Reports give an average rainfall of about 256 inches (6,500 mm), though it has on occasion totaled 315 inches (8,000 mm). Even in the drier months of January through April, wise travelers bring rain gear. The average temperature is 68°F (20°C).

A number of trails near the entrance lead through the extravagance of rainforest vegetation. Tree crowns form a leaky umbrella under which grow delicate ferns (including 18 species of tree ferns), orchids, bromeliads, lianas that tempt one to take a swing, mosses, and multi-colored lichens. Along the road and on forest slopes grows a plant with immense leaves and a tall reddish flower that Costa Ricans call "poor man's umbrella." I have seen its leaves used in the countryside by people caught in the rain.

Tapantí is a favorite with bird-watchers. Among the more than 260 species identified here are the ones everybody wants to see: quetzals, exotic hummingbirds, toucans, parakeets, parrots, great tinamous, and squirrel cuckoos. Endangered mammals live here, too: jaguar, ocelot, tapir. Animals you are more likely to see are squirrels, monkeys, raccoons, opossums, coyotes, agoutis, and red brocket deer: 45 species of mammals. There are porcupines, silky anteaters, otters, and lots of toads. Butterflies are everywhere. Your day may be blessed by the appearance of a blue morpho.

An exhibit room at the entrance is a good starting place to orient yourself and talk with a friendly ranger. A map and booklets on forest fauna published by the wildlife service (in Spanish) can be purchased here. About ½ mile (1 km) from the ranger station is the Oropendola Trail, which has covered picnic shelters, popular swimming spots in the frigid river water, and a place designated for fishing. Hike another 2½ miles (4 km) to a vista point marked by a sign with a large eye. Climb the short trail for a splendid view of a waterfall in the densely forested mountains across the river. In all, the refuge covers 12,634 acres (5,113 ha). There are covered shelters at a picnic area. Contact La Amistad-Atlántico Conservation Area about the possibility of staying in research facilities.

The gravel road is excellent because the Costa Rican Electric Institute (ICE) has a dam about 9 miles (15 km) from the entrance. You can continue along it for views of magnificent virgin mountain forest. The Río Grande de Orosí which flows here produces hydroelectric energy and helps supply San José with water.

Tour companies offer day trips to Tapantí. If you go by the Orosí–Río Macho bus from Cartago, you still end up more than 5 miles (9 km) from the refuge entrance, though you can hire a taxi to go the rest of the way. You may want to consider a taxi from Cartago or Paraíso, where they are more plentiful. If you are driving, take the highway to Cartago, and continue to Paraíso and Orosí, taking the bumpy road for Purisil. Watch for the Tapantí sign. The park is open from 7:00 a.m. to 5:00 p.m.

Tortuguero National Park (Caribbean)

With very little imagination, you can see yourself as Hepburn or Bogart on the *African Queen* as you wind your way through the rivers and canals to Tortuguero National Park on the northern Caribbean coast. Flora, fauna, and the condition of the boat may differ, but the feeling is there—you and the water, vegetation, and wildlife in an intimate and solitary encounter.

If you travel to Tortuguero by boat from Limón, the contrast of settled lands along the water with these protected lands vividly portrays the difference a park can make. From the air, the park is a mass of greens from the coastal plain to the Sierpe Hills, broken only by narrow ribbons of water.

However you get there, to explore Tortuguero is to discover a crocodile along the bank, a small turtle sunning on a trunk in the water, a monkey or sloth asleep in a tree, vultures peering down from a lofty perch. Perhaps a river otter will slip into the water as the boat approaches. Water and land birds keep your binoculars busy: At least 405 species live here. Watch for green macaws, herons, egrets, parrots, kingfishers, oropendolas (notice their large, hanging nests), tanagers, toucans, and bananaquits.

Tortuguero is tall forest and palm groves, lianas trailing into the water, and floating gardens of water hyacinths. The endangered West Indian manatee feeds on these and other aquatic plants. This large sea cow can be 13 feet (4 m) long and weigh about 1,300 pounds (600 kg).

Tortuguero is also beaches, important nesting sites for the sea turtles (*tortugas*) that gave the place its name. Green, leatherback, hawksbill, and occasionally loggerhead turtles return to these beaches every year to lay eggs. Some come in massive arribadas, others singly. Though you could see a turtle any night, there are peak times. The best time to see hawksbills is from July to October, leatherbacks from February to July with a peak in April and May, and green turtles from early July into October, peaking in August. Rangers from other parks are brought in to help patrol the beaches during the busiest months to prevent eggs from being stolen. Researchers at the nearby Caribbean Conservation Corporation have been tagging nesting turtles since 1955. The female green turtle comes ashore to lay eggs an average of two or three times during her season there, staying not far offshore in between. It may be up to four years before she returns to Tortuguero.

There are many crustaceans (prawns feed under the water hyacinths), eels, 52 species of freshwater fish (including the gar, considered a living fossil because species of that genus lived 90 million years ago), and sharks.

Self-guided nature trails take off from ranger stations on the water at either end of the park. On foot in this tropical wet forest, perhaps you can spot the small, brightly colored frogs that live here. Some of the mammals include peccaries, raccoons, kinkajous, ocelots, pacas, cougars, and skunks. The park protects more than 15 endangered mammal species, including the tapir, jaguar, giant anteater, and three species of monkeys. Rain gear and rubber boots come in handy.

Rainfall averages about 197 inches (5,000 mm), but it can go up to 236 inches (6,000 mm) in parts. Elevation reaches from sea level to 1,020 feet (311 m) in the Sierpe Hills. It is hot and humid, with an average temperature of 79°F (26°C). The park covers 46,818 acres (18,947 ha) on land and also protects 129,147 acres (52,265 ha) of marine habitat.

Camping is allowed in the park. The nearest lodging is in the villages of Tortuguero at the northern end or Parismina at the southern end. It is possible to visit Tortuguero park in a day trip, but being there overnight allows for an after-dark boat ride to see nighttime animal life on the river, a chance to see the turtles, or simply more time to savor the flavor. You can also make your own arrangements for boat and hotel, but you save yourself that hassle by going with a tour company leaving from either San José or a site on the

Caribbean. Tour companies offer boat or plane trips or a combination of the two (see Chapter 11). Some lodges in the north central area offer boat trips to Tortuguero via the San Juan River.

Canals sometimes get low, and boats have to proceed slowly. I have heard tales of passengers getting out to push; I have seen the captain do it. If you do not take a tour, you can hire a small boat or sometimes get a ride on a cargo boat. There is daily air service (see Practical Extras).

Wildlife Refuges

Barra del Colorado National Wildlife Refuge (Caribbean)

The Barra del Colorado refuge is as far north as one can go on Costa Rica's Caribbean coast. On the other side of its northern border along the San Juan River is Nicaragua. Access within the park is by its waterways. Virtually no land trails exist. Part of the western region has yet to be explored.

Travelers get to Barra del Colorado by air or by boat. Boats come through Tortuguero park or the Sarapiquí–San Juan–Colorado River route. There is plenty to see from the network of rivers, channels, and lakes in the reserve. Among the endangered species are the West Indian manatee, tapir, cougar, jaguar, ocelot, and jaguarundi. Species you are more likely to see are caimans and crocodiles, white-faced and howler monkeys, red brocket deer, and sloths. Birds include the great green macaw, great curassow, herons of various kinds, the red-lored Amazon parrot, great tinamou, cormorant, and keel-billed toucan.

A very wet rain forest, the area averages from 158 inches (4,000 mm) of rain on the western edge to 221 inches (5,600 mm) at the town of Barra del Colorado. However, my two-day visit in one of the rainiest months was sunny and beautiful. Go prepared for rain, but take your sunscreen.

You will see swamp forests, swamp palm forests, and mixed forests growing above the swamps in this 242,158-acre (98,000-ha) refuge. *Caña brava,* a wild cane, grows mainly along the rivers. Its stiff, solid stems are used to make decorative ceilings and prop up banana plants. Another forest species with commercial value is *cativo,* which is used in plywood. If you come via the canals, you may see lumber being floated down to Moín; supposedly, it is all being cut outside the park lands.

A variety of fish live in the lakes, rivers, and estuaries, among them snook, tarpon, mackerel, snapper, gar, and guapote (a tropical rainbow bass). The area draws many sportfishers.

Lodging is available inside the reserve at private lodges near the town of Barra del Colorado. Tour companies offer one-day or multi-day trips to the reserve. You can easily combine a trip to Tortuguero and Barra del Colorado,

THE RESPLENDENT QUETZAL

The name is exotic. The bird is exotic. A member of the trogon family, the resplendent quetzal was a symbol of freedom and independence to some indigenous Central American peoples. It thrives in Costa Rica. Travelers are more likely to see it here than in Guatemala, where the quetzal is the national bird, because of the protected forests at the elevations where they live: 5,000 to 10,000 feet (1,524 to 3,048 m) in the Central and Talamanca ranges, above 4,000 feet (1,219 m) in the Tilarían Cordillera.

Though Monteverde Cloud Forest Preserve is the more famous site for seeing this fantastic iridescent bird with its blue-green head, neck, and body and its crimson belly, Braulio Carrillo, Poás, and Chirripó National Parks are also home to the quetzal as well as other forests in the Talamanca Mountains. Some birders say the easiest place to see it is near San Gerardo de Dota off the Inter-American Highway before Cerro de la Muerte. Dr. Alexander F. Skutch, who wrote a classic descriptive account of the natural history of the quetzal, lives near San Isidro de El General. He says that in the 1970s, he often saw quetzals at 7,000 to 8,000 feet on the road from San José to San Isidro.

The birds are endangered because of the destruction of their habitat. Though they eat many kinds of fruits and other things such as insects and lizards, they depend heavily on fruit from the laurel family, a relative of the avocado. At Monteverde, quetzals move seasonally, apparently following the fruiting patterns of the different species and migrating from Monteverde to unprotected land. As reserves such as Monteverde become isolated by deforested land, the survival of migrating species is endangered.

Not only do quetzals depend on laurels, but laurel trees also depend on the quetzals to distribute their seeds. Swallowing the fruit whole, the bird coughs up the seed after digesting the nutritious part.

The breeding period is from March to June, peaking in April and May. This is the easiest time to see quetzals because they come down lower in the trees to nest, making do with a hole already hollowed out by a woodpecker or excavating space in rotting limbs or dead tree trunks. The female generally lays two blue eggs, which hatch about 18 days later. As soon as the first babies fly away, she lays eggs again. Both male and female take part in building the nest, incubating the eggs, and feeding the young. The end of the male's longer tail streamers can sometimes be seen protruding from the hole when it is his turn on the nest. The main predators of the eggs and chicks at Monteverde are short-tailed weasels and perhaps snakes.

either with a tour or by hiring a boat to take you from one to the other. Scheduled airlines fly from San José to Barra del Colorado in 30 minutes; the canal trip to Barra from Moín takes six hours. Boat tours also arrive from Puerto Viejo de Sarapiquí via the San Juan River—a marvelous trip.

Caño Negro National Wildlife Refuge (North Central)

The centerpiece of this 24,633-acre (9,969-ha) refuge for resident and migrant birds is Caño Negro Lake, which covers some 2,225 acres (900 ha) with up to 10 feet (3 m) of water in the rainy season. As the dry season progresses, it diminishes to a few pools, streams, and an arm of the river that feeds it. I have only visited the refuge in wet times, but in the drier months from January to April, the lake turns to pasture, and birds and animals come to the shrinking waterholes to drink.

The largest colony of neotropic olivaceous cormorants in the country are found here, and it is a good place to see the roseate spoonbill, wood stork, species of ducks you never imagined existed, snowy egrets, five species of kingfisher, and green-backed herons. Seventeen of the huge jabiru storks are sometimes here.

During a few magical hours on a boat, I saw some of these birds plus jacanas, two groups of spider monkeys, three of howlers, a red-lored parrot, a black-bellied whistling duck, anhingas with their wings spread to dry, caimans, iguanas, great egret, and, for the thrill of the day, a common potoo looking for all the world like a part of the branch on which it was perched. How the boatman spotted it is a mystery.

A number of endangered mammal and reptile species live at Caño Negro: tapir, jaguar, ocelot, cougar, and crocodile. Other animals include white-faced, howler, and spider monkeys; sloths, river otters, peccaries, white-tailed deer, silky anteaters, bats, and tayras. What is a tayra, you ask? It looks like a large mink, colored chocolate brown to black, with a long, furry tail. It lives in a den under the ground but searches for food both on the ground and in trees. Tayras probably include bird eggs and nestlings in their diets. In the dry season, visitors who wait patiently and discreetly in sight of the remaining waterholes can watch a variety of animals come to drink.

From January to April, less than 4 inches (100 mm) of rain falls. Since the year's total rainfall averages 138 inches (3,500 mm), you can see that the other months are damp. South and west of the lake, where the land rises from the plain abruptly to the Guanacaste Mountain Range, rainfall can reach 158 inches (4,000 mm) a year.

One aim of the wildlife refuge is to help improve the economic well-being of those who live in and around it. Under an agreement with the local development association, the wildlife department allows grazing of cattle on the dry lake bed in summer. Cattlemen pay less than a dollar a head for grazing rights, with 80 percent of the income going to community projects and the rest to conservation. A tree nursery established with area families provides trees to reforest parts of the refuge and the basin of the Río Frío, with some sold for profit. Fresh-water turtles are being raised—30 percent are released and the rest sold. Families are allowed to fish in the lagoons when they are drying up, and the refuge assists in finding a market for the fish caught.

There are two main entrances to the Caño Negro refuge. The head-quarters is at the town of Caño Negro, accessible by road from Upala, San Rafael de Guatuso, and Los Chiles, near Nicaragua (the latter by very bad road). The other entrance is by boat from Los Chiles on the Río Frío. Many organized tours take the river route but do not go all the way to the headquarters. Hotels in the north-central section offer one-day tours. (See Chapter 8.)

A visit to the refuge could be combined with a trip to Arenal or Guananaste parks and private nature reserves, using the Upala route. There are buses from Upala to Caño Negro and from Ciudad Quesada to Los Chiles.

Camping at the refuge costs $2 per person. Limited overnight space in a house at the ranger station in Caño Negro is $7 per person. Call 460-4164 or the Arenal Conservation Area for overnight reservations. In the dry season, visitors can explore on foot or rent horses, but in the rainy months, boat rental at $4 per person is necessary—rowboats only, no motorboats. Ask about the availability of a local guide. The refuge is open from 8:00 a.m. to 4:00 p.m.

Curú National Wildlife Refuge (Northwest)

The Curú refuge has a deserted island kind of feeling, even though it is on the Nicoya Peninsula. Perhaps the reason is the coconut-strewn beach, or the mangrove swamp, or the jungled hills rising up at the end of the bay. Walking through the tall forest behind the palm-fringed beach, one senses the wild-ness of the place.

Boa constrictors are at home here, as are pacas, agoutis, ocelots, white-faced and howler monkeys, rattlesnakes, iguanas, white-tailed deer, herds of peccaries, mountain lions, and margays (a small, spotted cat with a long tail). Waters along the beach host giant conch, lobster, and oyster—there is good snorkeling. Hawksbill and olive ridley turtles come ashore to nest. The mag-nificent frigate bird soars overhead. Parrots squawk. Hummingbirds, tro-gons, hawks, swallows, egrets, motmots, tanagers, roseate spoonbills, and fish eagles are among the 223 species of birds. There are 78 species of mammals and 87 of reptiles.

Small islands jut up in the Pacific in front of Curú Beach, one of three sand beaches in the refuge. On the distant horizon is the mainland.

Creation of the Curú refuge was the doing of Federico and Julieta Schutt, who established Curú Hacienda in 1933 for commercial logging, reforestation, and agriculture. When squatters took over more than 980 acres (400 ha) of the farm in 1974, the Schutt family looked for ways to protect habitat and wildlife. Refuge status was secured in 1983 for 208 acres (84 ha) of fragile marine and beach habitat, leaving the surrounding Schutt farm with 2,698 acres (1,092 ha), two-thirds of which is forest and one-third pasture.

Visitors can explore ten trails with names like Mango, Killer, Laguna, and Río, rated from very easy to difficult. On some, the scientific names of plants are marked. The Finca de los Monos (monkey farm) trail has a printed guide, with lists of trees, birds, and mammals.

Besides running the farm, the family manages Curú as a living laboratory for students on directed projects. To walk with Doña Julieta or her children is to walk with the best guides around. Doña Julieta took me to the corral to see baby white-tailed deer. Captured by a nearby landowner on private property, they were brought in to be cared for until they can be relocated on protected land. Doña Julieta had predicted that white-faced monkeys would be at the corral at that time of day to get bananas, and they were. We climbed a ladder to the second floor of a barn to look at a makeshift museum of shells, bones, rocks, and other research projects. Near the forested mountain, she told of a leader of the Costa Rican conservation movement who got lost overnight in the dense jungle; he shall remain nameless.

Walking with daughter Adelina, I received an introduction to the forest, to the swamp, to the life she has in this wonderland, where boas can be found in bedrooms, and dinner can be for just family or for hungry hordes of researchers. Adelina has spearheaded environmental education programs, leading more than 750 students from 16 area schools on walks and giving talks. The naturalist guides who have been trained to lead trail walks are from Valle Azul, the town begun by the squatters of twenty years ago. The town is also opening a naturalist gift shop.

The whole family is elated by the recent birth of a spider monkey. This little fellow is special because his parents were captive animals, brought to Curú, and he was born in the wild. This is the second birth in the reintroduction program. Spider monkeys became extinct in the area in the sixties. This species has disappeared in many areas of Costa Rica because of hunting pressures and habitat loss. Other recovery efforts at Curú include an artificial reef for marine species, built of old tires, and the rearing of sea turtles in captivity for release into the Pacific in cooperation with the National University in Heredia.

Though the rustic cabins along the beach at Curú are primarily for researchers, space may be available for a overnight stay. Meals, served family-style, are ample and tasty. Lodging and meals cost $25 per day; day tours are $5. Doña Julieta requests a call in advance, even for a day visit: 661-2392 (this number is also a fax—evenings only).

The entrance to Curú is about 4 miles (7 km) south of Paquera off the main road to Cóbano. Buses to Cóbano and Montezuma pass by. The refuge is 1.5 miles (2.5 km) from the highway. Several area establishments offer day tours.

Gandoca-Manzanillo National Wildlife Refuge (Caribbean)

Gandoca-Manzanillo, which touches the border with Panama on the Caribbean, is a mixed-management reserve. That means its goal is not only to conserve the rich biological resources but also to work with the community in sustainable use of those resources to promote economic development. Tourism is one of the components in the development formula; a number of hotels and lodges exist on private land within the refuge.

Nature has spread a visual feast there. Go and enjoy. Take the road south from Limón past Cahuita and Puerto Viejo. Since the tourism institute and roads people are adding more signs, perhaps there will be one to tell you where the refuge starts. If not, know that you are already in the refuge when you get to Punta Cocles. Maybe an information center at Manzanillo will be open by the time you arrive; an office is already there.

Some call the beaches around Punta Uva the most beautiful on Costa Rica's Caribbean coast. They are often pictured on postcards. And gorgeous they are: white sand, graceful palms with jungle-looking vegetation beneath, just the right amount of logs and coconuts washed up on the shore. Coral reefs about 650 feet (200 m) out create a snorkeler's paradise: blue parrotfish, green angelfish, white shrimp, red sea urchins and long-spined black ones, anemones, sea cucumbers, lobsters, sponges. Turtle grass sometimes attracts Pacific green turtles that feed on it.

Explore the land portion of the refuge by foot from Manzanillo or take a boat to a more southern shore and then go by foot. It is about a four-hour hike to the Gandoca Lagoon, but even a short walk on a trail that meanders from forest to beach to forest will reward you with unexpected beauty. From the mirador, you can look down at tropical fish through dazzlingly clear water or view the whole coastline all the way north to Puerto Vargas.

Terrain in the refuge ranges from flat to rolling country with small, forest-covered hills. You might discover a freshwater marsh, the only

Stunning shoreline of Gandoca-Manzanillo refuge (Ree Strange Sheck)

natural banks of mangrove oysters in the country, or the place where tarpon fish larvae grow to adulthood. Endangered species protected there include the manatee, crocodile, and tapir. There are also pacas, caimans, opossums, five species of parrots, sloths, ocelots, margays, otters, bats, falcons, hawks, frigate birds, pelicans, chestnut-mandibled toucans, and collared aracaris.

As for weather, forget the Costa Rican rule of thumb for wet and dry seasons. Rain falls year-round, though the driest months are March, April, May, September, October, and November. Expect cooler temperatures with wind and rain in December and January. The temperature averages 82°F (28°C). The total area of the refuge is 23,348 acres (9,449 ha).

Check with the wildlife office about camping. Consider Limón, Cahuita, Puerto Viejo, or places along the road linking them for lodging. Buses and taxis will get you to Manzanillo. Several hotels, lodges, and tour agencies along the Caribbean coast offer tours to the refuge (see Chapters 11 and 13).

Golfito National Wildlife Refuge (South)

Virgin forest covers about half of the 5,683 acres (2,300 ha) of Golfito National Wildlife Refuge. Preservation of that forest is the reason the refuge was created, not only for the species of plants and animals that live there, some of them endangered, but also for the community of Golfito it surrounds. The tall evergreen forest on this rugged terrain safeguards water sources for today's population and future generations while it also reduces the danger of landslides that would affect the town.

Rainfall is heavy in this area of southwestern Costa Rica, almost 196 inches (4,976 mm) a year, and temperatures are warm, averaging 82°F (28°C). The combination creates a marvelous tropical wet forest where mosses, lichens, bromeliads, and 31 species of orchids make a greenhouse on the limbs of a single tree. Heliconia plants splash their exotic, showy flowers of red, orange, and yellow against the vibrant greens of the understory. Eleven of the thirty or so species of heliconia found in the country are here. Pollinated by hummingbirds, their berry fruits are food for many birds. Indigenous peoples used the bananalike leaves medicinally and for building, thatching and wrapping food.

Some tree species reach almost 165 feet (50 m) high. The purple heart tree grows at Golfito; you see its beautiful purple wood made into salad bowls and earrings in souvenir shops. There is manwood, whose wood can lie on the ground for more than thirty years without decomposing; ceiba; and bully tree, whose red leaves stand out against the canopy.

Among the 146 bird species identified so far are the endangered scarlet macaws, great tinamous, parrots, herons, pelicans, ibis, owls, parakeets, and trogons. All four species of monkeys found in Costa Rica (including the squirrel monkey, or tití) live in the Golfito refuge, as do cats such as jaguarundi and margay, anteaters, bats, pacas, and agoutis. A number of trails, short and long, crisscross the refuge. A visit to the other side of the airport may allow you to see monkeys who come to eat the exotic fruits planted here by the banana company. It will certainly allow you to see a variety of birds.

The driest months are January through March, but bring your rain gear even then. Check with the Osa Conservation Area about camping in the refuge. Since it is at the edge of the town of Golfito, lodging is nearby. Some Golfito hotels offer guided tours to the refuge. By bus from San José, the 213-mile trip (342-km) trip takes eight hours. There is daily airline service between San José and Golfito.

Junquillal National Wildlife Refuge

Formerly classified as a recreation area, Junquillal became a refuge in 1995. It protects a diversity of marine resources as well as wildlife on the shore. Leatherbacks and olive ridleys nest in this area, and some 59 species of birds have been identified, including the jabiru, wood stork, yellow-naped parrot, and brown pelican. Humpbacked whales are sometimes seen during dry season.

Visitors may picnic or camp at in the refuge—latrines and showers available. The recreation area is on the beach. Entrance fee is less than $3.

SEA TURTLES

Six of the world's eight species of sea turtles nest on Costa Rica's coasts. Though it is possible to see a turtle laying eggs on a beach almost any night of the year, there are times when turtles arrive in large numbers (arribadas) at particular sites.

The turtle species and their Spanish names are green (verde), leather-back baula or canal, hawksbill (carey), olive ridley (lora or carpintera), Pacific green (negra), and loggerhead (cabezona). The Pacific green, hawksbill, and leatherback are found on both coasts, while the ridleys are only on the Pacific. The loggerhead is mainly in the Caribbean. Hawks-bills, loggerheads, and leather-backs usually are solitary nesters; the greens come ashore to lay eggs in concentrated colonies; and the ridleys come singly, in small colonies, or in massive arribadas.

The most important nesting beaches are listed here.

Tortuguero: Green turtles nest from June to September; hawksbills are also easiest to see here at this time, though they nest year-round on both coasts. Leather-backs nest from March to May, as do loggerheads.

Playa Grande in Las Baulas National Marine Park: Peak nesting for leatherbacks, the largest sea turtles, is from October to March.

Ostional Wildlife Refuge: July to December are peak months for olive ridley turtles, though there are nesting turtles or hatchlings almost all year.

Santa Rosa Park: July to December brings arribadas of olive ridley turtles, especially on Nancite Beach. Leatherbacks and Pacific greens also nest at Nancite and Playa Naranjo.

Barra de Matina Beach, north of Limón: Leatherbacks come ashore from February to July, with peaks in April and May; green turtle nesting peaks from July to September; hawksbills also come ashore.

Green turtles are prized for their meat, especially in the Caribbean area. Hawksbills are hunted for their shells (source of tortoiseshell jewelry) along both coasts. While eating turtle meat is not a tradition on the Pacific, the eggs are prized as aphrodisiacs. Turtle protection and conservation programs in Costa Rica range from patrolling beaches and public education to egg hatcheries, controlled harvesting of eggs, and setting of legal catches of turtles to be sold for meat.

Practice proper turtle-watching etiquette. Stay still when a turtle comes onto the beach—movement may scare it back into the water. Light disturbs the turtles, so restrict use of flashlights; no flash cameras. Wear dark clothing. Wait until turtles are laying their eggs before drawing near. Be quiet!

Two estuaries are nearby for exploration. Contact the Guanacaste Conservation Area for more information. The entrance is off of the Inter-American Highway between Liberia and La Cruz, about 9.5 miles (15 km), most of which is unpaved.

Ostional National Wildlife Refuge (Northwest)

The night was very dark. A young man led us across the beach of the Ostional National Wildlife Refuge to the high-tide line, where a Pacific or olive ridley turtle was patiently digging a hole in the sand with her back flippers. She dug as far as the flippers would reach, flinging sand out behind her shell.

Practically as soon as the flying sand had settled, soft eggs began to drop into the hole—one, two or three at a time—plopping on top of each other until there were about a hundred. Once the egg-laying began, the guide could briefly use his flashlight without disturbing the creative process. We could hear the whishing of sand off to the left, another hole begun.

Within 25 minutes, the digging and laying were done, and the turtle began methodically pushing sand back in, using both front and back flippers. Then she pounded her body against the surface to pack it down and moved around in a circle, scattering sand, leaves, and beach debris over the spot to obliterate any evidence of her buried treasure. Within an hour of emerging from the sea, she was back in it.

Nesting turtles can be found on this beach practically any night of the year, though massive arrivals, called arribadas, peak from July to December, when as many as 120,000 ridleys nest over four- to eight-day periods. Arribadas are usually about two weeks apart, but they can stretch to a month apart.

Harvesting of turtle eggs for food (there is a popular but apparently false idea that they are aphrodisiacs) along with the killing of adults for their meat or the leather trade threaten these and other species of sea turtles around the world. The Ostional refuge, on the west coast of the Nicoya Peninsula, was set up to protect the nesting sites of the ridleys, leatherbacks, and occasional green turtles that also come ashore. In an innovative program, local residents, who once plundered the nests and now live mainly off subsistence agriculture, harvest some of the eggs from the first arrivals on the beach and then patrol it to prevent illegal egg-taking. About 30 percent of the eggs deposited during an arribada are lost anyway when turtles dig up eggs laid earlier, so everybody is happy with the arrangement. Visitors who come for the nesting should join a guide from the turtle cooperative at the rancho at the upper edge of the beach. An administrative station for the refuge is scheduled to be built.

Ridley eggs hatch in about 50 days, with many hatchlings picked off on their way to the water by vultures, crabs, or frigate birds, while others become food for predators in the water, including other turtles. Survival rates are low, making the protection of eggs all the more important. Ostional and Nancite in Santa Rosa Park are the major nesting sites for olive ridleys in Costa Rica.

The 790-acre (320-ha) land portion of the refuge also has a few patches of forest that contain howler monkeys, kinkajous, coatis, and basilisks. The estuary of the Ostional River offers good bird-watching—190 species have been identified. The marine portion of the refuge is 19,768 acres (8,000 ha).

You may notice a sign for a University of Costa Rica laboratory at Ostional. Under an agreement between the university and the refuge, scientists are conducting turtle research as well as carrying out education programs on the rational use of eggs.

Rainfall averages almost 67 inches (1,700 mm) a year; the temperature averages 82°F (28°C). Unpaved roads are slow going and rough. Your best bet is to rent a car or take a tour to Ostional. If you plan to come from Sámara or Nosara, inquire about the road—there are rivers to cross. (See Chapter 9 for lodging.)

Tamarindo National Wildlife Refuge (Northwest)
See Las Baulas National Marine Park.

13

Privately Owned Nature Reserves

P rivately owned nature reserves catering to natural history tourists are springing up around the country. These are more than just lodges or hotels. They encompass tracts of protected ecosystems that range from large areas of virgin forest to river habitats to ribbons of primary and secondary forests surrounded by pastures. These reserves offer not only a chance to spend the night where monkeys live and toucans fly but also to learn about the ecosystems on guided walks or horseback rides. Some have bilingual biologist guides, others use local people with varying commands of English who are naturalists by life experience. Accommodations range from bunk beds to comfortable lodges with hot water and fine dining. Some provide transportation; others help arrange it from San José or other locations.

Some people thrive on adventure: tromping along muddy trails through a jungle miles from nowhere is bliss. Others prefer to view plant and animal life from a shady veranda or to stroll along a quiet beach. The privately owned reserves run the gamut. There is something for everyone. This chapter tells you which offers what, with details on how to get there, costs, and some idea of what you may see. Reserves are listed in alphabetical order in each region.

If you call or fax from outside Costa Rica to make reservations, first dial the international area code (011) and then the country code (506); for example, 011-506-000-0000. Places that accept credit cards are noted; many do not. I no longer include mailing addresses because service can be very slow. I recommend using phone or fax. Some are now accessible by computer.

Central Valley

Rancho Naturalista

Fields of cane and coffee spread out below the mountain retreat of Rancho Naturalista, while Irazú and Turrialba volcanoes dominate the skyline to the northwest across a vast valley. Tropical forest is steps away from the lodge. Tranquillity is the key word.

Located 1.7 miles (2.8 km) southeast of Turrialba up a dirt road from the village of Tuis, the ranch belonging to the Erb family caters strictly to nature travelers. "Anybody else would probably be bored," said John Erb. Boredom does not seem likely, however.

Enthusiastic, knowledgeable guides lead visitors on the trails and farm roads to look for the birds, butterflies, and moths that abound. More than 345 species of birds have been seen within 2 miles of the lodge. All of the guides are biologists/ornithologists or expert birders. With their encouragement, even neophytes experience the thrill of spotting species after species— maybe even a rare bird. You may see a blue-crowned motmot; notice the telltale tick-tock motion that motmots make with their racket-tipped tails. You are likely to see toucans, manakins, trogons, tanagers, and a world of hummingbirds. Perhaps you will also spot a scarlet-thighed dacnis or a green honeycreeper.

If you have yet to see the gorgeous morpho butterfly, this could be your chance. Several of the six Central American species of this butterfly live near the lodge. The blue flash of one of these against the green of the forest is a treasure that glows forever in the mind's eye.

The Erbs don't claim to have all 12,000 species of moths found in Costa Rica, but they believe they have enough to keep you occupied. Just ask, and they will put up a sheet and plug in a lamp outside at night to attract them. The variety is awesome. Guided night walks are available.

A neighbor down the road has a trapiche, the old-style sugarcane press. Horses are available at no extra charge, and you may want to explore along roads in the 125-acre (50-ha) farm or outside the farm on neighboring roads or along the Tuis River.

If you stay a week, the Erbs offer you a complimentary all-day field trip to an area with a different elevation, so you may see different flora and fauna. Popular choices are the Tapantí National Park or Irazú Volcano. Tours can be arranged to volcanoes, beaches, or national parks at an additional cost, as well as white-water rafting on the nearby Reventazón River.

The two-story main house has six large, comfortable bedrooms, one a suite. Three of the bedrooms have private baths; the others, a shared bath. There is great birding from the upstairs balcony and the long porch off the downstairs living room. A one-bedroom and a two-bedroom cottage with private baths are nearby. All the baths have central hot water, some with tubs.

Meals are family-style, and the food is plentiful and delicious, ranging from filet mignon to Mexican food, with some Costa Rican cuisine as well. The Erbs are gracious hosts who have lived in Costa Rica for many years and are pleased to share their knowledge with you.

A minimum stay of three days is required if transportation is provided. The Erbs say most guests stay at least a week. Laundry service is part of the package, at no extra charge.

The lodge is at 2,953 feet (900 m) and is in the transition zone between premontane wet forest and premontane rain forest. Daytime temperatures are usually in the 70s (21°C–26°C), nights in the 60s (15°C–20°C). Afternoon rain is common, especially from May through November. Rubber boots are recommended. Four main trails on the ranch are well-maintained and not difficult. You will find shelters and benches along the way where you can sit and wait for nature to reveal its treasures. A cable car crosses above a waterfall on one trail.

A stay of a week or more can be split, for the same rates, between Rancho Naturalista and the Erbs' other location, Tarcol Lodge near the Pacific, not far from the Carara Biological Reserve. (See Chapter 10.)

Transportation: Transportation to and from San José is provided as part of the package, but you can arrange for pickup at the airport or elsewhere instead. There is a moderate transportation charge on optional tours.

Rates: $114 a day per person or $690 a week per person, double occupancy. The rates include meals, lodging, guided walks, horseback riding, tours in the Erbs' reserve and up the Río Tuis Valley to the Chiripó reserve, and for at least a three-night stay, transportation to and from San José.

Reservations: Telephone/fax 267-7138.

North Central

Arenal Observatory Lodge

At 4:30 in the morning, a thunderous explosion brought us from our beds to the door in one swift leap. Outside, the cone of Arenal Volcano, about 1.2 miles (2 km) away, was sharp against the dark blue of the night sky. Stars were brilliant. From the crater, red rocks and thin streams of lava began to make their way down the slopes.

Arenal Observatory Lodge has a front-row seat for viewing eruptions of one of the most active volcanoes in the world. Built in 1987 as a laboratory and base for scientists carrying out long-term geological and biological research, the facility is now a top destination for nature travelers.

The small group I was in had already jumped up twice during dinner to pay homage to the spectacle in a steady rain. Later, two of us sat patiently on the elevated, covered observatory platform trying to elicit a command performance, but Arenal seemed uninterested in our schedules. The real show began after everyone was in bed. In all, I jumped up for four explosions—and saluted two rumbles from underneath the covers.

That was in the old days before volcano-view rooms were added, rooms from which one theoretically could lie in bed and watch what some call "cosmic fireworks"—I for one cannot do it, however. Each explosion brings me to my feet—the power and the beauty somehow demand it.

Three of the ten observatory rooms have direct views of the volcano, all now refurbished with private baths and hot water. The newer Smithsonian block of nine rooms, across a long suspension bridge from observatory rooms and the dining room, is beautiful. Plate-glass windows bring the energy of the fiery colossus into each room. These larger rooms have Tiffany-style lamps, ceiling fans, and pretty comforters—some beds are king-size. A volcano-viewing room upstairs offers yet another perspective. The five-room original farmhouse a short distance from the lodge has two hot-water baths and a sitting area with a fireplace. Guests have a view of lake and volcano from the porch.

In the dining room, guests sample fruits from the area and such typical meals as *olla de carne* (a meat and vegetable soup) or *arroz con pollo* (chicken and rice), buffet style. Huge windows face the volcano, so diners will not miss an eruption.

After a 400-year dormancy, Arenal devastated more than 4 square miles (10 sq km) in the last three days of July 1968. It has been continuously active since then. The flow comes from a horseshoe-shaped crater—one of four—that is open to the northwest, west, and southwest. Fortunately, the observatory is to the south. Arenal is young as volcanoes go—about 4,000 years young—and relatively small—5,358 feet (1,633 m) high. It is in the Tilarán Mountain Range.

Scientists from the Smithsonian Institution stay at the observatory while monitoring the volcano, and Earthwatch groups have used it as a base.

When you are not watching eruptions, you can turn your eyes to the tranquillity of Lake Arenal, just down the hill, site of Costa Rica's largest hydroelectric project. Visitors may want to arrange optional tours for fishing in its waters or a three-hour boat tour.

Visitors to the observatory have access to almost 300 acres (120 ha) of primary and secondary forest on the property, a 432-acre (175-ha) reforestation project of pine, eucalyptus, and macadamia. Trails through lush forest lead to Cerro Chato, an extinct crater near Arenal and its

Volcano on the doorstep at Arenal Observatory Lodge (Ree Strange Sheck)

green-colored lagoon, or to a lovely waterfall. Trails as well as roads through
the farm offer excellent bird-watching as well as a chance to see the spectacular morpho butterflies. Walking is easy around the farm and along the roads,
but the trail to the crater is for the physically fit. It is steep. Incredibly beautiful forest lures one on step after step, however, even when it is bathed in
cloud or washed by rain. Once there, you can canoe on the lake. A guided
walk to Cerro Chato is $5.

The farm also offers a firsthand look at agricultural operations, where
you can watch macadamia nuts being harvested and husked. A horseback
tour is $7 per hour. Free to overnight guests are guided walks to the water-
fall and lava flow. There is a night lava tour, night tour to Tabacón hot
springs, and guests can choose day trips to Caño Negro National Wildlife
Refuge ($65) or to raft on the Sarapiquí River ($70). A mountain biking tour
is $60.

Elevation at the observatory is 2,428 feet (740 m), and annual rainfall is
197 inches (5,000 mm). The drier months are from December through May,
but rain can occur anytime, so bring your gear.

Transportation: If you are driving, you can go through either Varablanca
or Zarcero to La Fortuna, or head north from San Ramón to La Tigra and
La Fortuna. From the west, you can head around Lake Arenal from Tilarán.
The turnoff from the paved road is the same as for Arenal Volcano National

Park; just follow the signs on 5.6 miles (9 km) of gravel road. A bridge over the river makes access quite tame now. Packages from San José include transportation.

Rates: Observatory standard rooms are $45 single, $55 double; Smithsonian superior rooms are $65 single, $75 double; the Casona farmhouse is $35 single, $40 double. Breakfast buffet is $7, dinner $10, box lunches $6, plus tax. Rates including breakfast and dinner are available. A three-day, two-night tour is $345 (double occupancy), including round-trip transport from San José, lodging, most meals, guided waterfall and lava flow walks, and hike to Cerro Chato. As about other packages. Credit cards accepted.

Reservations: Telephone 255-3418, 221-0303; fax 255-4410; e-mail suntours@sol.racsa.co/cr. Arenal Observatory Lodge is owned by Sun Tours, which has offices at Avenida 4, Calle 36.

Chachagua Rain Forest Hotel

Peck, peck, peck. Peck, peck, peck. Where else can one wake up to such a good-morning greeting from two collared aracaris at the window? Chachagua Rain Forest Hotel, less than 8 miles (12 km) south of La Fortuna, offers an out-of-this-world experience.

In a ten-minute drive up a dirt road from the paved highway, one moves from the workaday world to a rain-forest hideaway that in some wondrous way helps put that other world in better perspective. Seventeen of the prettiest individual bungalows one could imagine in this setting offer creature comforts. The warm, natural color of broad wooden-plank walls and polished hardwood floors harmonizes with the soft rose and blue colors in comforters and matching drapes. A ceiling fan, big dresser and mirror, two queen beds, reading lamps, artwork, and flower arrangements of heliconia, anthurium, and varicolored tropical leaves complete the picture. Wood and glass doors open onto a generous terrace with benches and chairs. The piece de résistance, however, has to be the bathroom, as large as some hotel rooms. The bi-level room has two small garden areas, mirrored windows that afford privacy and the outdoors at the same time, and an open chest-high shower—central hot water, of course. Big bath towels and washcloths, too.

Wood and cement walkways lead from bungalows across a steam to reception, a natural swimming pool, outdoor rancho/bar, and the open-air dining room. It is a tablecloth place with excellent service by friendly staff. Meals are delicious—you may find owner Carlos Salazar in the kitchen adding his special touch, especially at breakfast. Some of the food served is grown here—pineapple, papaya, yucca, squash, and black beans, and the beef, poultry (an ocelot has been cutting into the chicken population, however), eggs, milk, and cheese are also produced on the ranch.

Dining was embellished one morning with a flight overhead of at least 60 red-lored parrots. An anteater appears more often than not at 8:00 a.m. The resident scarlet macaw, who hangs out at the dining room, may deign to speak to you.

Chachagua is an almost 250-acre (100-ha) ranch with glorious rain forest. The magic of the contiguous International Children's Rain Forest spills over into this rich reserve. Trails go to small waterfalls, along rivers, and through forest inhabited by sloths, white-faced and howler monkeys, keel-billed toucans, blue morpho butterflies, and poison-dart frogs. Have the guide show you the Blood of Christ plant and monkey ladders, and watch for the large, beautiful golden spider that lives here. Boots and walking sticks are provided.

The hotel can be a base for trips to nearby Arenal, to Tabacón hot springs, and to Caño Negro wildlife refuge. Packages include some of these tours. Half-day horseback tours are also available.

Groups who come to Chachagua are invited to give donations to the school in the nearby community for books, supplies, and building improvements. Individual travelers may do the same.

Transportation: From San José, proceed northwest on the Inter-American to the San Ramón turnoff; head north through La Tigra and San Isidro and start watching for hotel signs before the town of Chachagua. From La Fortuna, go south. Transportation is provided with fixed-departure packages.

Rates: Single or double occupancy in the bungalows is $80, $90 for a triple. A full typical breakfast is $6, and lunch or dinner are $10. A three-day package is $370 single, and $274 each for a double, including lodging, meals, visits to Sarchí and Tabacón, and a night visit to Arenal plus a guided walk at Chachagua and a natural history slide presentation. The four-day package includes a visit to Caño Negro, $616 for a single, $430 each for a double.

Reservations: Telephone 239-1049, 239-0328; fax 293-4206. Contact with the hotel is by radio.

Eco-Lodge, Lago Coter

You will learn about such things as flying sticks and why some tropical trees shed their bark (to keep epiphytes from getting a hold). You can see a huge mound built by busy little leaf-cutter ants and marvel at the free-form sculpture of a vine called monkey ladder.

On the 13 marked trails that wind through the Eco-Lodge property, bilingual, well-trained naturalist guides can help guests appreciate that tropical forests are more than monkeys jumping from branch to branch, than coatis darting across a trail, than the turquoise flash of a scarlet-thighed dacnis as it flies against the rich greens of the trees and plants. It is these things, but it is also the tiny flower almost hidden among fallen leaves, an insect disguised as a dried leaf, an animal track in the mud, the elegant tree fern, thousands of species of plants and animals intertwined in a web of life.

In the distance, Arenal Volcano rumbles. It seems to rise out of Lake Arenal from some vantage points on the property. Though it is not visible from the lodge, it is from a covered observatory and bungalows.

Eco-Lodge is a comfortable place from which to wander forest trails or go horseback riding, fishing, windsurfing, canoeing, or sailing either on Lake Arenal or Coter Lake. The lodge can be the base for trips to the volcano, to caverns at Venado 90 minutes away, to Ocotal beach, to Palo Verde or Caño Negro, or for rafting on the Corobicí. Rubber boots, flashlights, and rain ponchos are provided.

The main lodge building has the feel of a mountain lodge with its spacious living/recreation area, welcoming fire in the fireplace, conversation areas, TV and VCR with a supply of videos, billiard table, bar, and dining room. Ample, tasty meals are served buffet style. Interesting photographs, many of an earlier Costa Rica, adorn the walls of the lodge. One of the most intriguing is of a flying saucer near Arenal Volcano and mysterious, heart-shaped Coter Lake. The friendly staff can show you books commenting on the authenticity of the photo.

Twenty-two cozy, carpeted rooms in the lodge are of rock and wood, each with pretty comforters and a private, hot-water bath (some tubs). Twelve attractively furnished rooms have been added in six bungalows within a five-minute walk from the lodge. The rooms are larger than in the lodge, with high ceilings and a glass wall that faces the porch and the volcano, Arenal and Coter lakes, and the nighttime lights of Nuevo Arenal. Each room has a table and chairs both inside and on the porch. Baths are private with central hot water.

Guests are invited to record the animals see and where. More than 350 birds have been sighted. Leafing through the book, one finds monkeys, brocket deer, keel-billed toucans, the bare-necked umbrella bird, squirrel cuckoo, and coatis, among others. Guests are invited to a complimentary two-hour natural history presentation.

The dry season is not as pronounced here as in some other places in the country: rainfall amounts to about 152 inches a year (3,857 mm). The elevation varies, but the lodge is at about 2,329 feet (710 m). The forested slopes have characteristics of both rain forest and cloud forest.

Transportation: Eco-Lodge is 17 miles (28 km) from Tilarán above the northwest section of Lake Arenal near the kilometer 46 marker. Buses between Tilarán and Ciudad Quesada (San Carlos) pass by on the highway less than 2 miles (3 km) below. Transportation can be arranged from San José or Tilarán for a minimum of four people.

Rates: A single in the bungalows is $50, a double $66; rooms in the lodge are $41 for a single and $49 for a double. Breakfast is $5, and lunch and dinner are $10 each. Packages include lodging, meals, and some of the activities. For example, the two-night, three-day tour ($301 each double occupancy in the lodge or $321 in the bungalows) includes hiking, horseback riding, biking, one water sport, and an Arenal Volcano and hot springs tour. Credit cards are accepted.

Reservations: Telephone 257-5075, fax 257-7065.

La Laguna del Lagarto Lodge
Spider monkeys moved through tall treetops, sometimes with spectacular leaps. I would swear I saw one slide down a long liana. Sitting on a bench across a small pond from them, I watched as they hung from their tails to feed on fruits in the tall forest. Flock after flock of noisy parrots and parakeets flew in, stayed for a bit, and moved on. Jesus Christ lizards skittered across the water. On the short walk to the pond from the lodge, I had stopped to watch white-fronted parrots, a Montezuma oropendola, and squirrels eating pejibayes. This was all before breakfast.

La Laguna del Lagarto, 93 miles (150 km) north of San José, is a trip. It is a watery world—lagoons, rivers, swamps—but also a place of striking forest. Owner Vinzenz Schmack has almost 250 acres (100 ha), and a neighboring forest of 1,000 acres (400 ha) extends the habitat for such species as white-faced, howler, and spider monkeys, tepezcuintle, the great curassow, araçaris, chestnut-mandibled and keel-billed toucans, and great green macaws. Almost 200 bird species have been identified so far. With luck, Vinzenz says, one can see the scarlet macaw.

Ten miles (16 km) of marked trails open the forest for exploration. The tiny red frogs with blue legs, known as poison dart frogs, can be easily seen on the forest floor. The small green frogs with black spots are more elusive— I saw only one. A highlight of the hike was finding the track made by a tapir.

A different habitat can be explored by canoe in two swamp lagoons. Moving silently, with only the sound of the oar dipping into the water, brings one close to the spirit of the place. On my quiet trip, the green-backed heron made several appearances, kingfishers flashed by, and a lineated woodpecker perched on a lifeless trunk standing in the water. Vinzenz pointed to another trunk where small sleeping bats made a dark line down the tree. Orchids and bromeliads were everywhere.

A nighttime walk with a good flashlight can reveal the bright eyes of caimans along the edge of the lagoons. Caimans, or *lagartos*, are also visible during the day, and gave the place its name.

Guests at the lodge can go horseback riding along the edge of the forest ($10 for two hours) or take a boat down the San Carlos River to the San Juan ($18 for four hours). I longed for more time just to sit on the veranda and bird-watch. Local guides are available, but a trained naturalist guide can be arranged with prior notice. A three-day, two-night package includes lodging, meals, transportation, a boat trip to the San Juan River, and horseback riding. Languages spoken also include English, French, and German.

Twenty rooms are distributed in several buildings, all with private baths, six with hot water. Furnishings are simple. Each room has ceiling fans, and the newer ones have movable louvered shutters. Windows are screened, with reason. Bring your repellent.

Food, served in an open-air dining room, is an appetizing mix of Costa Rican and European. Pineapple, papaya, oranges, yucca, tiquisque, and pejibaye are grown near the lodge. The pejibaye also supply heart of palm—you can watch it being cut fresh for your meal. Black pepper is another crop.

The lodge is about 330 feet (100 m) above sea level, and temperatures range from 68°F (20°C) to 95°F (35°C). February to mid-May are the driest months, but for rainy times, boots and ponchos are available.

Transportation: La Laguna del Lagarto Lodge is 23 miles (37 km) of gravel road north of Pital, 4 miles (7 km) from Boca Tapada. There are buses from San José and Ciudad Quesada to Pital (taxi from Pital is $25), and a bus twice a day from Pital to Boca Tapada, with lodge pickup from there. The Pura Natura bus also goes from San José to the lodge (see Practical Extras). The lodge will pick up guests there for $10 per person.

Rates: A single is $73, a double $53 each, including meals and taxes. Credit cards are not accepted. Unguided trail walks and canoe rides are included in the price. Reservations are recommended.

Reservations: Telephone 289-8163, telephone/fax 289-5295.

La Selva Biological Station

La Selva Biological Station near Puerto Viejo de Sarapiquí offers a marvelous opportunity to see a variety of habitats: Besides the virgin tropical wet forest, there are swamps, creeks, rivers, pastures, agricultural lands, and secondary forests in various stages of growth. Dr. Leslie R. Holdridge, a tropical biologist, began La Selva as an experimental farm in the fifties and sold his plantation of peach palm (*pejibaye*), cacao, and laurel along with virgin forest to the Organization for Tropical Studies (OTS) in 1968. The primary use of La Selva is for biological research and education.

Vehicles for researchers at La Selva (Ree Strange Sheck)

Many of the leading tropical biologists in the hemisphere have studied or worked there.

Visitors are guaranteed to taste the area's diversity even if they never get farther than the main dining hall. The panorama from the porch may include flocks of parrots flying overhead or the red flash of a scarlet-rumped tanager. As you sway across the long suspension bridge over the Puerto Viejo River, look down. Machaca fish leap up to grab leaves floating down to the water's surface. You could be lucky enough to see a cayman or a river otter. La Selva is home to more than 100 species of mammals, including the howler, spider, and white-faced monkey, peccary, agouti, coati, sloth, jaguar, and tapir. There are more than 2,000 species of plants in this tropical rain forest, 410 species of birds, and thousands of species of insects.

The *bala*, or giant tropical ant, is one species it pays to look out for. Researchers tell tales of its powerful sting. It is the largest ant in Costa Rica—up to an inch (33 mm) long—and really looks big when you see it on a leaf next to you.

Brightly colored poison-dart frogs may jump in the leaf cover at the side of trail. Toxins secreted from their skin glands were used by Colombian Indians to poison blowgun darts—hence the name. Because of their toxic skin, these frogs have no need for drab coloration; in fact, their colors warn predators. As the life history of these tiny creatures is being discovered, we learn that they lay eggs on the ground, with adults transporting the tadpoles on their backs to water. Studies of one genus show that the female feeds the tadpoles unfertilized eggs.

Some 85 miles (56 km) of trails meander through the 3,077-acre (1,650-ha) reserve, all clearly marked every 50 meters. Sendero Tres Ríos is a 3.7-mile (6-km) paved path to western annexes of the forest. You'll see staff and researchers traveling it by bicycle. Don't miss the arboretum, where a keel-billed toucan perched patiently while a group of us drew near, admired his splendor, and photographed him. We spotted a purple-throated fruitcrow, collared aracari, crested owl, and yellow-billed cacique within a few yards. A large, pretty gazebo in the arboretum affords a pleasant place to pause and observe. Overnight guests, armed with a trail map and a delightful printed guide to the natural history trail, can set out for an experience in a tropical forest. Snakes do live in the tropics, however, and can appear as you make your foray into their world. As the trail guide suggests, watch where you walk, stay on the trail, and give any snake you see plenty of breathing room. The trail takes about an hour.

La Selva is open for day visits by reservations only. Guided walks at 8:00 a.m. and 1:30 p.m. daily offer natural history visitors high-quality educational experiences and a peek at research underway. Reservations are essential because the number of visitors per day is limited. Local naturalist guides have been trained in an intensive natural history course at the biological station.

Overnight facilities are open to natural history visitors as space permits. Accommodations are generally in four-person rooms (bunk beds), with a shared bath with shower-head hot water, between two rooms. There are reading lamps and ceiling fans. Since the rooms are primarily for researchers and students who may stay awhile, there is ample storage and closet space.

In the modern dining room, set up for cafeteria service, you may find yourself rubbing elbows with leading tropical scientists or student researchers. Mealtime conversations are fascinating, but don't expect these researchers to lead you on a tour; their time in the field is precious.

A small gift shop in the main building has a great selection of T-shirts and books, and there is also an information center with exhibits.

More than 4 inches (100 mm) of rain falls even in the drier months, from February to April, and the yearly total is about 152 inches (4 m). The average temperature is 75°F (24°C). Elevation ranges from 115 feet (35 m) to 656 feet (200 m). The reserve is adjacent to Braulio Carrillo National Park.

Transportation: La Selva has van transportation from San José on Monday, Wednesday, and Friday, but space is not always available. You can take the public bus from San José through Braulio Carrillo and Las

Horquetas to Puerto Viejo (tell the driver you want to get off at La Selva) or through Varablanca and Chilamate to Puerto Viejo, and then a taxi to La Selva.

The Pura Natura bus also goes by. (See Practical Extras.) If you are driving, the entrance to La Selva is less than 2 miles (3 km) on the road south from Puerto Viejo de Sarapiquí. A covered bus stop on the west side of the road says OET (the Spanish acronym), just past the Lapa Verde restaurant.

Rates and Reservations: Day visits are with prior reservation only, $20 per person for a half-day guided walk. Reserve with La Selva, telephone 710-1515, fax 710-1414. Area hotels also offer to tours to La Selva. For overnight visitors, the charge is $75 single, $60 each double occupancy, $45 per person extra, including lodging, meals, and guided walk. E-mail at La Selva is laselva@ns.ots.ac.cr. Overnight reservations should be made with the Organization for Tropical Studies office in San José, telephone 240-6696, fax 240-6783, e-mail reservas@ns.ots.ac.cr. VISA and MasterCard accepted.

Magil Forest Lodge

Tenorio Volcano looms behind. In front is an incredible panoramic view stretching from Arenal Volcano to the Caño Negro National Wildlife Refuge. Sometimes it is possible to see Lake Nicaragua from this mirador on the hills above the lodge at Magil.

In the 700 acres (283 ha) of rain forest in this private nature reserve live monkeys, ocelots, aracaris, raccoons, keel-billed toucans, three-toed sloths, tayras, and tapirs. There are orchids, heliconias, ferns, mushrooms, and tall, tall trees.

Once it was home to Maleku Indians, and the traces of their life here include strange rock formations, burial tombs, jade pieces, arrowheads, metates, and pottery fragments. Today it belongs to Dr. Manuel Emilio Montero, who has had it for more than 25 years and who developed the Magil Forest Lodge. The property also includes about 300 acres (120 ha) of ranchland for horses and cattle.

The rustic lodge contains 11 rooms with private baths but no hot water. Each room has single or bunk beds, a desk, a large mirror, and a porch off the back where a small creek rushes by. The sound of the water almost drowns out the hum of the hydroelectric generator. The porch is a good place for bird-watching in the early morning—there are lots of red-rumped tanagers.

Rooms open off the dining room, which has a long table fit for kings and made from a single log. There is a set menu, with cooking on a wood stove. You can look forward to fresh orange juice (trees on the property), cheese empañadas (the lodge makes its own cheese), gallo pinto, and other typical dishes. Food is tasty and plentiful.

Across a covered patio is a pleasant bar with a small television. A short walk away is a rancho with chairs and hammocks. There is even a telescope available for stargazing.

Guests have many activities to choose from. The $20 half-day tour to the 100-Waterfalls Trail is by horseback and foot, taking in the mirador and passing by an enormous, solitary ceiba believed to be 1,000 years old. It stands as sentinel over the pasture and surrounding forest. White-faced monkeys moved through the trees while I climbed along the river trail, and a blue morpho butterfly made my day.

A $35 full-day trip, also by horseback and foot, goes to the place where the waters turn blue in the Tenorio Forest Reserve. Waterfalls and hot springs are an added treat. With a minimum of six people, the lodge offers a full-day trip, at $35 each, to the Venado Caves, hot springs, and Arenal Volcano. With a minimum of four people, you can take a car and boat trip, for $35 each, to a farm where caimans are raised and see the gaspar fish and crocodiles. A boat trip to the Caño Negro Wildlife Refuge is $35 to $50 each, depending on group size.

On your own, you can walk down to the bridge you crossed coming in and bathe in clear pools in the river, play in small waterfalls in the good company of birds and butterflies, and soak up the healing green of the lush forest around you.

Magil Forest Lodge is 117 miles (189 km) from San José. It can be reached either from Ciudad Quesada, La Fortuna, Tilarán, or Upala heading for San Rafael de Guatuso. From San Rafael it is dirt road, with four-wheel-drive recommended. Turn left after crossing the suspension bridge and go 12 miles (19 km) to Río Celeste. From there, Magil is less than 2 miles (3 km).

Transportation: Magil offers transportation for a two-day minimum stay, $100 per person round-trip from San José.

Rates: A single is $70, a double $65 each, meals included. A two-day, one-night trip from San José is $190, including passing by Poás Volcano, Angel Waterfall, and La Marina zoo on the way in and Arenal Volcano and Venado Caves on the return. The tours leave San José every Wednesday and Saturday. Credit cards are accepted.

Reservations: Telephone 221-2825, 233-5991; fax 233-3713.

Rara Avis Rainforest Lodge and Reserve

Visiting the beautiful Waterfall Lodge for the first time, a local tour operator remarked to Amos Bien, founder of Rara Avis, "You know, Amos, most people would have put the road in first." But Amos Bien is not most people, and Rara Avis is not your ordinary country inn.

Now, a few years down the line, the road has progressed quite a lot; so much so that the famous three-hour ride in a tractor-driven cart, fording rivers and lurching in phenomenal mud, may become a thing of the past, at least as far as El Plástico, Rara Avis's hostel-like accommodations. What with bridges and gravel, a large jeep may one day make the trip in 45 minutes. But even if that dream becomes reality, for the final 1.9 miles (3 km) between El Plástico and the Waterfall Lodge, guests must still opt for the cart or hike in. Adventure is not dead.

Even in a jeep, the going will still be slow enough that there is a chance to see the great green macaw as you bump along, to hear about a nearby achiote plantation (the plants are grown in Costa Rica as both ornamentals and as a source of red dye), to observe the pasture lands clear-cut from tropical rain forest, and to see reforestation projects and secondary forest. If Amos is along, he spins tales; one about a horse who died along the way and the budding student of the tropical world who later lugged the bones for miles in the belief that they represented a giant tapir, another about the dog who wouldn't die—Pilingo.

Amos himself first came to Costa Rica in 1977 as a biology student. He returned to found Rara Avis, not only for nature/adventure tourism but also as a biological research center and a conservation proving ground to show his neighbors they can make more money by maintaining the forest than by clearing it for ranches or farms.

The road leads to Albergue El Plástico, a former prison-colony barracks rehabilitated into a rustic lodge with seven rooms containing bunk beds for thirty people and shared baths with hot-water showers. Guests sit at dining tables where the prisoners sent in to cut the forests once ate. Lighting is by kerosene lantern. There is good bird-watching from the upstairs porch/library, and a rushing stream down the open slope invites a dip on sunny days. At the edge of the clearing, forest beckons on all sides. A butterfly project is underway to export these beautiful tropical denizens to zoos and greenhouses in Europe and North America. Stop by to see it.

Two miles (3 km) farther into that forest is the impressive, two-story Waterfall Lodge, built of beautiful tropical hardwoods. Each of the eight spacious rooms is a corner unit with chairs and a hammock on a wraparound balcony and a private bath complete with both shower and tub (hot water). A longtime birder saw five birds he had never seen before from his balcony one afternoon. Rooms have a double and bunkbed down and a double in the sleeping loft, brightly colored blankets. Windows are screened; lighting is by kerosene lantern.

A delightful cabin up a forest trail about ten minutes from the lodge is also rented out. In a secluded, spectacular setting on the edge of a mountain, the cabin has two spacious rooms, each with its own hot-water bath, and a covered deck with a to-die-for view of forest above and below. Solar panels provide electricity. I recommend it for those who enjoy solitude and who are not reluctant to walk alone in the forest at night. Other, more rustic cabins may be available. Ask if interested.

Meals are served family style in a building steps away from the Waterfall Lodge. Flor and Alfredo outdo themselves—plenty of food, beautiful salads, a variety of meat dishes, and well-prepared local vegetables. The fried yuca is superb. Coffee and tea are always available. A reference corner has lots of good material and a small gift shop has T-shirts and other items. An extraordinary variety of hummingbirds feeds on flowers alongside the porch rail.

A short path leads to the spectacular 180-foot double waterfall that gave the lodge its name. Miles of marked trails go through the virgin rain forest, with emphasis on the rain. There is virtually no dry season at Rara Avis; rubber boots are essential. A fellow visitor, after an hour on the wet slippery trail between El Plástico and the Waterfall Lodge, commented, "This must be the only trail in the world with an undertow." In a four-day period, we explored Rara Avis in 4½ inches (114 mm) of rain. The annual rainfall is about 26 feet (8 m)!

A working biologist, bilingual in English and Spanish, guides visitors on the trails, spotting such exotic birds as the slaty-tailed trogon and the keel-billed and chestnut-mandibled toucans (more than 330 bird species have been identified), and the home of a tent-making bat, who cuts the leaf of a wild plantain on either side of the midrib and bends it to form a tent to sleep under in the daytime. Howler, white-faced capuchin, and spider monkeys are very common, as are pacas, coatis, vested anteaters, kinkajous, and brocket deer. Tapirs, jaguars, collared peccaries, agoutis, and three-toed sloths live here, but you probably will not see them. People from two to 86 years of age have found their way to this remote spot, but access and trails can be rough for those who are not in good physical condition. There are few mosquitoes. The elevation is from about 1,640 to 2,300 feet (500 to 700 m).

On a walk with Amos in the forest, you hear about the possibilities for sustainable production of forest plants that he hopes will convince his neighbors to harvest rather than destroy the forest, proving there is more profit in managing it than they could ever make by clearing the land for crops or cattle. An understory plant, the stained-glass-window palm, once thought to be extinct but found here, could provide seeds for export as an ornamental plant; the roots of a species of philodendron can be harvested for wicker products (the porch chairs are made of this); selective cutting of wood instead of clear-cutting can provide income while preserving rainforest habitat and biological diversity.

Rara Avis quietly extends its commitment to education beyond student researchers and natural history tourists. Local elementary school students and their families are invited to visit, school supplies find their way to the Las Horquetas school, and two sixth-grade students each year are sponsored to continue studies at the high school in Río Frío.

In addition to bird-watching, hiking, and river swimming, in high season guests can climb by rope and harness to two platforms: one at the foot of the waterfall is about 50 feet (15 m) high; the other, a ten-minute walk from the lodge, is 98 feet (30 m) up in the canopy. The platforms and a waterfall traverse are done in association with Don Perry Adventures.

Transportation: On a paved road from San José to Las Horquetas, it is 48 miles (77 km) by way of Braulio Carrillo National Park, taking about an hour, or some 120 miles (193 km) via Poás Volcano, taking about three hours. The Rara Avis office can advise you about buses or a taxi from San José. At Río Frío—about 25 minutes by taxi from Las Horquetas—there is an airstrip for charter planes. All visitors to Rara Avis leave from Las Horquetas, with the departure daily at 9:00 a.m. Guests may choose to ride in or out by horseback, $20 each way.

Rates: El Plástico Lodge is $45 per person per night. At Waterfall Lodge, a single is $85 per night, a double $75 per person, triple $65 per person. Prices include meals, guided tours with naturalist guides, and round-trip transportation from Las Horquetas to Rara Avis. Credit cards accepted. Youth hostel members should make El Plástico reservations at La Toruma in San José.

Reservations: Telephone/fax 253-0844.

Selva Verde Lodge

Dusk along the Sarapiquí behind the lodge at Selva Verde. The only sound is the rushing water; the green forest that gave Selva Verde its name guards the river. Brilliant blue morpho butterflies flutter along the forest's edge above the water. Dusk becomes darkness, the magic moment is gone, and yet it lives forever.

Images of time spent at Selva Verde Lodge near Chilamate, less than two hours north of San José, crowd in. The delightful day on a river trip down the Sarapiquí was arranged at the lodge. We saw river otter, crocodile, white-crowned parrot, kingfishers, keel-billed toucans, parakeets, blue herons, aracaris, a three-toed sloth, anhingas, egrets, flycatchers, a bananaquit, oropendolas, turtles, a scarlet-rumped tanager, trees full of vultures, and iguanas draped on limbs high above the water. We observed children playing along the river, women washing, men riding on horseback along a high bank. We passed ranches, farms, forests, and lush river vegetation.

Selva Verde has a reserve of its own across the Sarapiquí River, 529 acres (214 ha) with trails that reveal the wonder of a tropical lowland forest. You can go with Selva Verde's own bilingual guide ($15 per person for three hours) or follow a trail map. Well-marked trails offer walks ranging from easy to somewhat steep. Benches along the way provide a place to rest or a place to wait and see what the forest will reveal. It could be a coati, sloth, raccoon, kinkajou, brocket deer, anteater, river otter, monkey, or maybe a tiny lizard or frog. There are more than 2,000 species of plants, 700 species of butterflies, and 400 species of birds. The most commonly seen birds are tanagers, honeycreepers, oropendolas, trogons, toucans, and chachalacas. Wander on the trails behind the lodge to the river. Lots of birds and butterflies—take time to smell the heliotrope.

The Sarapiquí River boat trip is $25. At the tour desk, you can also arrange a horseback tour for $20, and canoeing or river rafting for $45.

The River Lodge consists of 40 rooms in a series of modules built on stilts and connected by walkways covered with thatch. One has the sensation of walking on a bridge through the forest. Construction is of beautiful tropical woods. Each double room has a small desk, reading lights at each bed, convenient closet space, lots of windows with louvered shutters, and large towels in the private baths with hot water—even washcloths! Five bungalows with fans and hot-water baths are across the road in the forest, more rustic than the River Lodge.

A large dining room that accommodates 100 people also has an outdoor deck on the river side, great for sitting and soaking up the beauty of the natural world. There is a set menu, served cafeteria style. Near the bar is a delightful outdoor area with an old-fashioned wood-fired bread oven where guests can help prepare *bocas* for happy hour if they wish. The dining room is open to the public with prior reservation.

The Botanical and Butterfly Garden is tucked among the trees on a forested hillside that both attracts butterflies and provides host plants for larvae. The butterfly enclosure is marvelous: colorful rattlesnake and hot-lips plants, dozens of butterflies, and benches to sit on; one section focuses on medicinal plants and endangered local species. A self-guiding booklet is in the works. The garden is open from dawn to dusk, free to guests at the lodge, $5 for others.

Selva Verde has a commitment to community involvement. The Sarapiquí Conservation Learning Center has been built on Selva Verde property for use by guests and members of the community. It has a library, auditorium, and work rooms where local people study English, attend natural history classes, or work on handcrafts for the hotel gift shop. The shop also has a nice selection of nature books at reasonable prices, as well as tropical forest posters, basketry, belts, primitive carvings, jewelry, and lots more—even slide film.

Transportation: You can take a public bus to Puerto Viejo through Braulio Carrillo and Las Horquetas (a taxi from Puerto Viejo to Selva Verde is less than $4) or a longer route toward Río Frío through Varablanca. Tell the driver to let you off at Selva Verde. The Pura Natura bus stops here.

Rates: In the River Lodge, singles are $73, doubles $63 each; in bungalows, doubles are $63 each, triples $53 each, including meals. VISA and MasterCard accepted.

Reservations: In the United States, call Holbrook Travel in Gainesville, Fla., at (800) 451-7111. In Costa Rica, call 766-6077 or 766-6277; or fax 766-6011. E-mail selvaver@sol.racsa.co.cr.

Villablanca Hotel and the Los Angeles Cloud Forest

As one approaches Villablanca, it appears to be a small village, and that is just what it was built to resemble: an 1800s colonial settlement centered on the *casa grande*, or big house, which would have belonged to the family that owned the land. The landowners in this case are former president of Costa Rica Rodrigo Carazo and his wife, Estrella, who bought the farm in 1989.

The individual *casitas* (little houses) where the workers would have lived serve as charming guest cottages. They have the look and feel of adobe, with rough white plaster and blue trim. Some are suites with separate sitting rooms. All have corner fireplaces with bancos extending out on each side, rocking chairs pulled up in front of the hearth, and writing desks. Colorful comforters on the beds and bright rugs lend a cozy look. Nights can be cool here, so the comforters and fireplaces are not merely decorative. Each private bathroom has both a shower and a tub, with a large, well-lit mirror in a small dressing area.

The big house contains the dining room, bar, small library, and sitting areas. Upstairs are five rooms, handy for those who prefer to be in the same building as the dining room. There is also a dormitory-style building with shared baths for student groups. To finish out the village, plans call for a small church that will offer Sunday mass for guests and nearby residents as well as a curate's house that can be used as a conference room or for parties.

Meals are buffet style, with breakfast at 7:30 ($6 plus tax), lunch at 12:30 ($11), and dinner at 7:00 ($11). Complimentary coffee and tea are available from early to late.

The 50 casitas have little gardens in front and a 2,000-acre (800-ha) forest out back. The Los Angeles Cloud Forest is wet, exuberant, and green.

331

There is a trail of a little more than a mile (2 km) and a shorter trail very near Villablanca. Walkways are wooden planks covered with wire to prevent slipping. It is home to more than 230 species of birds, including the bare-necked umbrella bird, hummingbirds, the tawny-capped euphonia, the black guan, the great curassow, and chachalacas. There are three species of monkeys, sloths, raccoons, squirrels, tepezcuintles, ocelots, and snakes, though you probably will not see a snake. The tree ferns are magnificent.

From a mirador about a mile from the main house one can see Arenal Volcano, Lake Nicaragua, and the Plains of San Carlos on a clear day. Though there are clear days, go prepared for rain, and for the clouds. The driest months are March to May according to Geovanni Bello, a resident biologist guide who leads guided walks into the cloud forest, which is about 3,600 feet (1,100 m) in elevation.

In addition to the nature reserve area, the farm has cultivated land with coffee, sugarcane, and vegetable crops, and pasture for dairy cows that provide milk and cheese for the dining room. Ask about availability of a guided agro-ecology tour for $22.

Horses, at $10 an hour, can be rented for exploring the farm. There is a two-hour horse trail in the forest. Villablanca can arrange car and driver to such area destinations as Tabacón, Poás, Arenal, and Sarchí. After dinner, free videos with ecological themes are shown in the library.

Transportation: Villablanca will bring you from San José for $30 or from San Ramón for $15. If you are driving, the turnoff is at the guard station just past the kilometer 8 marker from San Ramón.

Rates: Rooms in the main house are $53 for singles, $74 for doubles. In the casitas, singles are $68, doubles $89. There are special rates for student groups staying in the dormitories. Credit cards are accepted.

Reservations: Telephone 228-4603, fax 228-4004.

Northwest

Buena Vista Lodge
A rushing cold mountain stream, bubbling mud pots, steam escaping from open fissures in the earth and drifting up from pools of hot water to play hide-and-seek with the tall trees of the primary forest. Standing here one cannot help but think of the Earth in formation, of creation, of beauty, of the power of natural forces, of so much that we do not yet know or understand.

Here on the slopes of Rincón de la Vieja Volcano, next door to the national park that protects wonders such as these, Gerardo Ocampo and his wife, Amalia, and their four children share and conserve nature's bounty.

Buena Vista Lodge near Rincón de la Vieja Volcano (Ree Strange Sheck)

Buena Vista Lodge is both a private nature reserve and a working farm. Visitors are invited to hike forest trails, bird-watch, help ranch hands working with the cattle, bathe in thermal waters or mountain streams, and walk or go by horseback to waterfalls—with six large ones to choose from. All of this is on the 3,950-acre, (1,600-ha) farm, but there is also the option of a tour to Rincón de la Vieja National Park less than 2 miles (3 km) away. Day visitors are also welcome.

An intriguing sign points the way to a spa about 30 minutes by horseback from the lodge. A spa? Indeed it is. Enjoy the sauna, a simple wooden house built over one of the *pailas*, or mudpots. The steam flows up through the floor. A short distance away is a concrete and stone "hot tub" fed by a mix of hot mineral waters and cold water from the mountain stream alongside, set among the verdance of tropical rain forest. Along the trail, notice the rich pink fruit of the *pitaya*, a cactus-looking plant.

Trails in the forest just behind the lodge are well maintained and easy to walk. Five trails wind through the almost 100 acres (40 ha) of primary forest. A troop of white-faced capuchin monkeys fussed at me as I explored at dusk. You might see a paca, peccary, deer, river otter, macaw (either the scarlet or the rarer green), toucan, oropendola, or agouti. Perhaps you will hear a coyote concert or the sound of the howler monkey. One of the forest trails displays tree names.

The last time I was there, a pregnant peccary named Gerardina helped my sister hurry a bit between the dining room and our room. That night, a friendly skunk nosed around my jeep and waddled off. The resident scarlet macaw is always around, and now Pancho the monkey has joined the menagerie.

Keep a lookout on the drive up to the lodge. Just past a wooden bridge in magnificent forest, I have spotted a spider monkey in trees near the road, golden red hair shining on its back, while a motmot posed for pictures on the other side of the road. I have also seen quail, cuckoos, and morpho butterflies there.

Buena Vista now has 37 rooms, all but four with private baths, half with shower-head hot water. Rooms in the rustic main lodge are around a lush tropical patio. Others are grouped in cabins near the forest, in the landscaped gardens, and near a small lake. A creative mix of wood and river stone decorates some rooms, some have wooden ceilings, all have shared verandas or private porches. Perhaps you will sleep on a bed with a riverstone base.

A swimming pool should be finished by your arrival. On weekends, cowboys present some local customs of the Guanacaste sabanero for guests (maybe a barbecue, too); marimba music may accompany a nighttime meal in an open-air rancho/bar where buffet meals may be served in the evenings, especially when groups are present. Music or not, you are likely to see large frogs in the rancho. Breakfast continues to be served in the main house, where cooking is on a wood stove. Meals are ample, varied, delicious, and visually pleasing. Drinking water comes from a spring and electrical energy comes from a hydroelectric plant.

Buena Vista means "good view." There are quite a few: an almost touchable view of Rincón de la Vieja Volcano, a more distant look at Orosí Volcano, and the lights on a clear night of Bagaces and Liberia down below.

The rainy season from about May 15 to November 30 brings about 6½ feet (2 meters) of rainfall. The elevation at the farm ranges from 1,300 to 3,940 feet (400 to 1,200 m); at the lodge it is 2,592 feet (790 m). Gerardo says the best time to visit the crater at Rincón is March to May and July or August. The temperatures average 82°F to 86°F (28°C to 30°C), but in the early morning in December, it has gone down to 64°F (18°C).

Transportation: Buena Vista is 19 miles (31 km) northeast of Liberia. From the sign at kilometer 247 on the Inter-American Highway, it is about 12 miles (19 km), paved to Cañas Dulces, mainly gravel afterward. Round-trip transportation from Liberia can be provided by Buena Vista for $45 for up to four passengers, $60 for six. (Check Practical Extras for information about buses to Liberia.)

Rates: Rooms with two beds and shared bath are $20 per person; rooms with a double bed and private bath are $45. Bunk-bed rooms with private bath are $15. Breakfast is $6, lunch and dinner $8 each. Credit cards are accepted. Guided tours to the spa are $15 by horseback, $5 on foot. A half-day horseback trip to the waterfalls is $28; the horseback ranch tour is $15. An all-day visit to the park is $38, possible depending on weather. A day visit is $28, including a horseback ride, trail walk, and lunch. Readers take note: you get a 10 percent discount if you have this book and reserve directly with Buena Vista.

Reservations: Telephone/fax 695-5147.

Ecolodge San Luis & Biological Station

Ever dream of what it would be like to be a researcher in the tropical rain forest? Ever wish you could take part in village activities or meet local folks when you travel? Ever want to pick coffee or help reforest? Well, here's your chance to have a hands-on experience in a rain forest setting that mixes the research and education of a biological station and activities on a working tropical farm with natural history tourism.

Ecolodge San Luis was designed by tropical researchers Diane and Milton Lieberman to provide a rich mix among guests, scientists, students, staff, and members of the San Luis community, fostering interaction in as many ways as possible.

The rustic dining room is one place where this happens. Researchers and visitors sit elbow-to-elbow at long tables for meals, served family style. They run into neighbors who drop by for coffee and a bite to eat, and share the resources in the corner reference library.

According to interest, a guest can participate in a bird nesting study, help with research on living fence posts, work in the greenhouse with tree seedlings, plant trees, assist with a seed viability study, take daily weather data, or help with whatever research project is underway.

Perhaps you would just like the chance to sit in on lectures or slide shows when student groups are present. You are welcome. There's an orchid garden (help collect plants for it), a medicinal plant garden, and the organic garden, plus coffee fields and a small dairy operation.

And of course there's stupendous forest to hike in, either alone or accompanied by guides who are active researchers and trained biologists. The ecolodge property, 162 acres (66 ha), borders the Monteverde Cloud Forest Preserve and the International Children's Rain Forest, Bosque Eterno de los Niños. (San Luis is only about 30 minutes by car from Monteverde). More than 180 species of birds (still counting) have been seen here, along with mammals such as howler and white-faced monkeys, coatis, kinkajous, sloths, tayras, pumas, and agoutis. Station manager/naturalist Memo says there is a resident long-tailed weasel most often seen by the kitchen.

Night walks, bird-watching (Memo promises 60 species before break-fast), horseback riding, swimming in the San Luis River, hiking to a waterfall—all this and more are possible. And you really can pick coffee and even help take it by horseback to the local processing plant. Join cooks in the kitchen to learn how to make tamales and gallo pinto or, as I did, learn how to cook eggs on a banana leaf. Take part in local fiestas, soccer games, and dances.

Accommodations can be either in the research bunkhouse (formerly a milking barn) with bunk beds and shared baths, or in lovely cabins a short walk up the hill. Built of beautiful hardwood, two six-room wings share a big covered deck. High-ceilinged rooms have a double and single bed, closet, modern bath with hot water, and double glass doors onto a balcony with panoramic views of forest, mountains, and countryside. Coffee from the farm will be served at the rooms every morning. A glassed-in pavilion with ample areas for lounging and dancing will be finished by the time you arrive.

Transportation: By car, ask for the "travel notes" prepared by the Liebermans for a self-guided trip from San José that takes you right to the doorstep. By bus, take one of the direct buses for Monteverde and, with prior arrangement, you will be met at the San Luis turnoff. Escorted trips from San José either by car or public bus can be arranged.

Rates: The rooms with private baths are $80 per person, including meals, lodging, nature guides, access to trails, slide presentations, and lectures. The bunkhouse with bunk beds and shared bath is $50 per person. Horseback riding is $7 per hour with guide.

Reservations: Telephone/fax 645-5277. In the U.S. reserve through Americas Tours & Travel, telephone (206) 623-8850 or (800) 553-2513, fax (206) 467-0454.

La Pacífica

Pacífica means peaceful or tranquil, and indeed the traveler who pulls into La Pacífica senses a serenity to the place. Actually it was named for the wife of a former president of Costa Rica who once lived here, but why quibble? The name fits.

La Pacífica has been set up as a model for economic self-sufficiency and protection of natural resources, combining agricultural activities, tourism, and research.

Scientific researchers have been coming to "Finca La Pacífica" since the 1960s. The rich diversity of habitats that continues to draw researchers—tropical dry forest, river habitat, swampland, pastures—also makes the center attractive to today's natural history visitors.

Accommodations for visitors are in 33 pleasant rooms grouped in buildings among the trees on spacious grounds. Interiors in those nearer the swimming pool—what a treat that pool is on a hot Guanacaste day—reflect earth tones from the tile floor to striped woven bedspreads. Sliding wood and glass doors open onto small terraces, and rooms are cooled with ceiling fans. Private baths with central hot water have a glass opening onto a small patio. Older cabins have been completely redone, lots of light now and modern baths.

The restaurant has a pretty patio on one side and garden and fish pond on the other. It is open to the public also, from 6:15 a.m. to 10:00 p.m. Food is excellent. One wall is "art in pottery," from Nicoya.

Don't miss the small natural history center, with artistic use of monkey vine, seed pods, and tree trunks as decorative touches. Exhibits can change, but perhaps you will see seed pods, a tarantula, a small collection of snakes, or an explanation of uses of trees. Visitors are also welcome in the library that focuses on materials about the dry tropics.

Guests can follow the roads and trails on their own or go on hikes with a bilingual naturalist guide or on horseback rides. Two hiking trails are close by. The Las Garzas is a short walk in forest along the Corocibí, good for seeing water birds and birds such as turquoise-browed motmots, black-headed trogons, yellow-naped parrots, and orange-chinned parakeets. The 2-mile (3.5-km) Chocuaco Trail, named for the boat-billed heron—has both riparian and deciduous forest. The guide shares amazing facts about trees and plants. Did you know that the monkey ladder vine is used to treat diabetes? See the chewing gum tree, the water vine, and the *bejuco* (vine) used locally as sandpaper. You may see the long-tailed manakin, howler monkeys, Jesus Christ lizards, great egrets, and iguanas.

For history buffs, a visit to Doña Pacífica's house is a must, accessible by car or on horseback. Built in the early years of this century, it was remodeled in the 1930s and today is a museum. Several archaeological sites on the property have been excavated.

About 40 percent of the almost 5,000 acres (2,000 ha) of Hacienda La Pacífica is covered with natural forest, windbreaks, and reforested areas, including tree species such as the increasingly rare *cocobolo* (rosewood), the *caoba* (mahogany), and the spiny pochote. Bird life is abundant, with 26 percent of the species found in the country seen here; 68 species are migratory. The lagoon and rivers on the property lure water birds. La Pacífica has bird and tree lists available. Forest animals include armadillos, squirrels, tamandus (anteaters), deer, and monkeys. Studies on the howler monkey at Pacífica go back some 20 years.

Visitors are welcome to tour the agricultural operations, including a modern dairy and an organic garden. In addition to beef and milk products, the ranch produces mangoes, asparagus, corn, onions, squash, pepper, and garlic. Visitors can watch a reforestation project—using native species—as it develops.

The beautiful Corobicí River, popular with rafters, forms part of the center's boundary. Staff members can arrange rafting trips as well as river trips on the Bebedero to Palo Verde Park. Horseback riding and bicycling are also available.

If you happen to be at La Pacífica when a group is there, you may have a chance to hear typical Guanacaste marimba music in the large outdoor rancho used for cookouts.

The annual rainfall is about 66 inches (1,674 mm). the average high temperature is around 91°F (33°C), the average low 73°F (23°C).

Transportation: The center is about 3 miles (5 km) north of Cañas on the Inter-American Highway toward Liberia, 108 miles (173 km) from San José. You can take the bus for Liberia or buses going to La Cruz or Peñas Blancas. Ask the driver to let you off at La Pacífica, or get off in Cañas and take a taxi.

Rates: Singles are $55, doubles $67. Credit cards are accepted. Guided walks with the biologist and horseback tours with a local guide are $10 per hour.

Reservations: Telephone 669-0266 or 669-0050; fax 669-0555.

Los Inocentes

There's something special about waking at the dawn's early light to the bass-toned barks of the howler monkey. When you open the big windows of your south-facing room at Los Inocentes, Orosí Volcano looms big enough to touch. Teak floors, polished wood, wide L-shaped verandas both upstairs and down—the hacienda is so inviting that nothing less than those intriguing barks from the forest down by the river spur one to get dressed and leave it for an early morning horseback ride.

Los Inocentes is a working ranch as well as a naturalist lodge for travelers looking to experience a bit of life and nature in Guanacaste. Perhaps that accounts for horses that are a pleasure to ride. Don't worry if you are not an expert horse rider. Dennis Ortiz, your guide for the nature tour, will have you riding like a pro. We found the howlers and the white-faced monkeys. Dennis patiently tracked the shyer spider monkeys three times so I could get a perfect camera angle. He tried not to laugh when a tree and I got tangled up while I was juggling cameras, lenses, and binoculars. Another time he found not one but two sloths for me, and we saw deer, howler and spider monkeys, coatis, and—a highlight for me—a black-headed trogon. If horses are not your thing, manager Jaime Víquez has a tractor-driven trailer to take you to the forest (minimum of five people).

The forest generally follows the *quebradas* (ravines) and the riverbeds. Bird-watching is excellent in the open pastures. We heard the laughing falcon before we saw it. Both white-fronted and yellow-naped parrots are common, flying overhead in pairs or flocks. Even the elusive king vulture is among the 119 species of birds officially recorded on ranch property. Orange-fronted and orange-chinned parakeets, several species of hummingbirds, Montezuma oropendolas, and *pauraques* (nightjars) are among the birds seen regularly. Animals to watch for include white-tailed deer, coatis, raccoons, sloths, and peccaries. Los Inocentes is less than 1,000 feet (280 m) above sea level in premontane moist forest.

All nature tours are escorted. The guide knows not only where and what to look for in flora and fauna but also the boundaries of the ranch. Bird-watchers who want a solitary trip can go to the nearby river, and the veranda offers good viewing for those who cannot tear themselves away from the charm of the house. The hacienda was built in 1890 and remodeled in 1982 with an eye to maintaining the integrity of its architecture. Stone corrals, built by the same person who did those at Santa Rosa, also witness to the age of the property. A small swimming pool has been added, and guests can also swim in natural pools in the river.

On the south, Los Inocentes approaches Guanacaste National Park. Maybe you really do want to touch 4,879-foot (1,487-m) Orosí Volcano. You can visit one of the park's biological stations located on its slopes. Staff members can arrange transportation for a number of other day trips: to the beaches on the bays of Salinas and Santa Elena, to Murciélago (a section of Santa Rosa National Park), to Las Pailas and its bubbling mud at Rincón de la Vieja National Park, to Santa Rosa. Kayak tours can be arranged: $65 including lunch and transport. For a different kind of tour, with advance notice, you can visit the two-room school on the property that workers' children from the ranch and nearby farms attend. Local children perform traditional dances if requested beforehand. A guided night walk in the forest is another possibility. At night, turn your eyes to the heavens for a bit of stargazing; there may be new constellations for you in Guanacaste's vast sky. Day visitors are welcome.

Meals are something to look forward to, including fresh fish from a few miles away and fruit from trees near the house: limes, mangoes, guavas, nances, star fruit, and others.

The main house has 11 nicely decorated rooms with large closets. Each has its own bath—with solar hot water—but some of the baths do not adjoin the rooms, a necessary adjustment to preserve the original architecture. Five small houses that were used in earlier times by workers at the ranch have been redone for visitors, each with a private bath and solar hot water.

Transportation: By car, go north from Liberia to just south of La Cruz and turn right toward Santa Cecilia. Los Inocentes is almost 9 miles (14 km) on paved road from the Inter-American Highway. You can also approach it from the east through Upala. Bus service is available to La Cruz, taxis are available from La Cruz ($6) or Liberia, and there is a direct bus from San José to Santa Cecilia that passes in front. When making reservations, ask about transportation; ranch personnel can sometimes pick you up in La Cruz.

Rates: The cost for room and meals is $58 a day per person. The horse and guide service cost $18 for three hours. The day trip is $29, including lunch and a horseback tour. Credit cards are accepted.

Reservations: Telephone 679-9190 or 265-5484; fax 265-6431. In the U.S., telephone (504) 895-9822 (Jaime's sister).

Monteverde Cloud Forest Preserve

The flash of a resplendent quetzal above a waterfall made every bump on the road to the Monteverde cloud forest worthwhile. It was a rainy day, and the guide's search for the bird at familiar haunts had turned up nothing. Then suddenly, appearing almost a turquoise color against the rich, dark green of the forest behind, the red and emerald bird with its magnificent tail swooped across a picture-postcard setting. It took my breath away.

The desire to see what many consider the most beautiful bird in tropical America brings thousands of people every year to this biological reserve 113 miles (182 km) northwest of San José. But the Monteverde reserve is not just quetzals: There are more than 400 species of birds, 490 species of butterflies, 100 species of mammals, and 2,500 species of plants. It is the only known home of the golden toad, a 2-inch brilliantly colored amphibian: males are orange, females yellow and black with patches of scarlet. But none has been seen since 1989. Only time will tell if another species has disappeared. The preserve also is home to the tapir. (But there is a greater chance of seeing tracks than this wary, once-common, now-endangered animal itself.) From March to August, you are likely to hear the booming call of the three-wattled bellbird. At any time of year, the fantastic variety of epiphytes covering the trees in this cloud forest is dazzling: there are more than 395 identified species of orchids (though specialists believe the number can reach 450) and 200 of ferns. Gently press the moss covering a tree trunk to get an idea of how thick it is. There are checklists on birds and mammals and an informative nature trail guide. A map of the trails is also available at the visitor center. The preserve is open from 7:00 a.m. to 4:00 p.m. year-round.

Monteverde Cloud Forest Preserve is not a national park, but it is within the Arenal Conservation Area. It is managed by Costa Rica's Tropical

Casona and exhibit area at Monteverde Cloud Forest Preserve
(Ree Strange Sheck)

Science Center, a nonprofit scientific research and education organization based in San José. Founded in 1972, the reserve encompasses some 27,181 acres (11,000 ha) on the Continental Divide in the Tilarán Mountain Range, protecting both Atlantic and Pacific watersheds and containing eight ecological life zones.

The mean temperature at Monteverde is 56°F to 68°F (16°C–20°C). The average annual rainfall at the casona is about 118 inches (3,000 mm) but it can get up to 236 inches (6,000 mm) in the reserve. Bring your rain gear and rubber boots, or rent boots at the preserve; trails can be muddy. Though little rain falls from December through March, mist rolls in on strong trade winds from the Atlantic, and moisture forms on the abundant forest vegetation, dripping from the canopy to the ground. For the observant, this "indirect rain" is a striking demonstration of the importance of forest conservation. Without trees and forest plants to collect and disseminate this water, the mist would vaporize in the hot dry air to the west, and rivers that flow to the lowlands would carry less water. That is why the small group of dairy-farming Quakers from the United States who settled in this area in the 1950s set aside 1,369 acres (554 ha) to protect the watershed. That parcel is now part of the reserve, leased to the Tropical Science Center for management.

To protect habitat and ensure visitors a worthwhile experience, limits are placed on the number of people allowed on the trails. Priority is given to those coming for the preserve's guided natural history walks, led by bilingual naturalist guides. A slide show is part of the tour. Reservations for the walks can be made through hotels or directly with the preserve. In addition to public areas with marked trails and longer trails for backpackers, the preserve has areas where almost no use is allowed and others that are restricted to scientific investigation. The heaviest visitation is from December through May. Backpackers must make reservations for use of the shelters.

Overnight accommodations at the preserve's field station are limited to four rooms for about 35 people, with the space often filled by researchers and students. Baths, with hot water showers, are shared. However, hotels are available in the nearby towns of Monteverde and Santa Elena. Hotels can arrange transportation, or you can walk the 1.5 miles (2.5 km) from the cheese plant in Monteverde. Birds spotted along the roadside are your reward. The gift shop is worth a visit.

The cloud forest preserve has an environmental education program with 15 schools in the area, bringing them to the forest as well as working with the teachers. School groups from elsewhere in the country are received as well.

Volunteers assist with many activities at the preserve. A minimum of one week is required. Contact the preserve for more information.

Transportation: By car, you can reach the Monteverde Cloud Forest Preserve either from the Inter-American Highway, turning north at Sardinal or Lagarto, or from Arenal, coming south through Tilarían, Quebrada Grande, and Santa Elena. On either route the last portion is unpaved and rough. Express buses run between San José and Monteverde, but it is a good idea to buy your ticket in advance if you do not want to stand for the four-hour trip. (See Practical Extras.) There are also buses from Puntarenas and Tilarán to Santa Elena, with taxi service from Santa Elena. (See the description of the town of Monteverde in Chapter 9 for other transportation possibilities.)

Rates: The entrance fee for day visits is $8 per person, $4 for students with an identification card. Children under 12 are admitted free. Guided walks led by bilingual guides are $23 per person, including admission and slide show. The use of shelters on backpacking trips costs about $3 per night. A bed and meals in the rustic field station is $21 per person.

Reservations: For guided natural history walks, contact the preserve at 645-5112 or make arrangements through your hotel. For overnight accommodations, it is best to reserve in advance since space is limited. Telephone 645-5122, fax 645-5034.

Rincón de la Vieja Mountain Lodge

I almost did not get past the Colorado River at the entrance to Rincón de la Vieja Mountain Lodge. Cicadas were singing, a morpho floated above the river, shafts of sunlight sparkled on the rushing water, tall trees created a cathedral effect. Enchantment.

Enchantment might also be the best word to describe what awaits one here on the slopes of Rincón de la Vieja Volcano, just outside the national park that protects it. One can visit bubbling mudpots and geysers, hike to hidden waterfalls, bathe in mountain streams or hot springs, ride horseback through pristine forest, and visit a mountain lake. Some of these activities are in the national park, but lodge guests may explore 17 miles (27 km) of trails in the 740 acres (300 ha) of primary forest on the ranch. They can visit a hot spring, and return to the Río Colorado to watch for birds and butterflies, and soak up the energy and beauty of the place.

Guests at Rincón de la Vieja have an opportunity to traverse an exhilarating trail through the treetops, moving among 16 platforms via a strong steel cable. Top Tree Trails offers a four-hour forest canopy experience for $50, including the horseback ride to the platforms and lunch, or a full-day naturalist tour that adds bathing in thermal sulfur springs ($77). Horseback rides in the reserve are $28 for a half day, $50 for a full day. The full-day horseback and hiking tour to Rincón de la Vieja National Park is $45.

Owner Alvaro Wiessel is from a family with a history of more than 100 years in the area. The lodge was the family home. Today it contains a living area, dining room, kitchen, and rooms for guests. Alvaro has brought the number of rooms to 27 by adding guest cottages with private baths (five with hot water) and front porches with hammocks and chairs. Furnishings are simple but comfortable; some rooms have bunk beds. Beyond the lodge are groups of rooms built beside a small stream and in rich forest. The porch offers a comfortable place to sit and watch and wait for surprises from the natural world. A small swimming pool and rancho/bar are in front of the lodge.

Among the showier of the 257 species of birds spotted on the ranch are violaceous, elegant, and orange-bellied trogons; the crested caracara; red-lored, mealy, yellow-naped, and white-fronted parrots; toucans; motmots; and the three-wattled bellbird. Mammals include howler and white-faced monkeys, deer, coatis, peccaries, and pacas. Tapirs live here, but it is unlikely you will see one.

In addition to preserving the natural forest, Alvaro is reforesting other land. Guests may accompany ranch workers on their rounds, helping with the milking or herding cattle. The lodge has bicycles and horses for rent, and working cowboys can give riding instruction. These people who have grown up here are the local guides, though with advance notice a bilingual tour guide can be arranged.

Transportation: Rincón de la Vieja Lodge is about 16 miles (26 km) northeast of Liberia; take the road through Curubandé off the Inter-American. The lodge provides transportation from Liberia for $20 for up to five people.

Rates: Singles are $39, doubles $49. A camping area has latrines and showers, $5 per person. Meals are $9 for breakfast and $11 for lunch or dinner. A three-day package is $207 per person, double occupancy for lodging, meals, a horse tour to the mud pots, and a full canopy tour. Ask about other packages. Credit cards accepted.

Reservations: Telephone 225-1073 or 234-8835; fax 234-1676. At the lodge, telephone/fax 695-5553.

South

Albergue de Montaña Savegre (Cabinas Chacón)

At Cabinas Chacón, they do not talk about "if" you see a quetzal, they say "when." Roland Chacón, one of owner Efraín Chacon's 11 children, told me we would see one on our early morning tour, and we did. It was so easy. We drove up the mountain, and there it was, sitting in the tree he expected it to be in. The red, white, and green bird, so elusive in some places, seemed to appear as if on cue. Best months to see them are February through May.

The Chacóns' place in San Gerardo de Dota, between Cartago and San Isidro de El General in the Talamanca Mountains, is famous for quetzals and for hospitality. Efraín, who has lived here for 39 years, began a dairy farm. People started coming to fish for trout in the Savegre River that flows through his property, and sometimes they stayed late. At first, Efraín and his wife took the visitors into their home to spend the night. Eventually, they built a cabin for them, and then in 1980, ecotourists began to arrive in the hope of spotting a quetzal.

Cabinas Chacón now has 15 comfortable, simply furnished cabins, all with private baths (shower-head hot water), some with sitting rooms, and a spacious restaurant/bar to serve not only overnight but also day visitors and local folks. Be sure to bring your appetite; the food is good and plentiful, and fresh trout does appear on the menu. A lovely, bright lounge next to the dining room has lots of glass looking out to the river and to a dazzling display by hummingbirds who come to the feeders. Doors open to a narrow balcony. Most nights a fire blazes in the fireplace. Look at the guestbook in the lounge—entries since 1973. A small gift shop sells T-shirts, sweatshirts, photos of quetzals, and coffee, canned trout, and trout paté from the farm.

There is still a small dairy, and guests can visit the extensive apple orchards and packing plant on the property. All up and down the valley, apple, plum, and peach trees are replacing pastures on the steep slopes.

About half of the Chacón farm is in primary forest. There is a 5-mile (8-km) trail that takes two to three hours to hike (with fabulous views at times of the forest canopy), a 2.5-mile (4-km) trail, and a ½-mile (1-km) trail. For real hikers, a trail goes from the farm to Cerro de la Muerte. Roland suggests going there by car and walking back.

For those who just like gentle strolls, a walk along the country road in front affords a look at flowering trees, the rushing river that flows alongside, and a variety of birds. I watched a woodpecker gathering nuts. A good number of the more than 100 species of birds here can be seen from the cabin area. The quetzal is not the only flashy bird in the Dota Valley: trogons, emerald toucanets, and iridescent hummingbirds also lend color.

Animals that might be seen include porcupines, rabbits, white-faced monkeys, white-tailed deer, frogs, squirrels, and foxes. Local guides well versed in natural history can be hired for $12 per hour. Horseback riding is also $10 per hour.

Trout fishermen and ecotourists have been joined by scientists and students in this special place. The Quetzal Education Research Complex is Southern Nazarene University's tropical campus. A research laboratory is already in operation.

Cabinas Chacón is at 6,890 feet (2,100 m). The rainiest months are October and November, and there is generally little rain from December to June. Precipitation is 120–150 inches per year (3,046–3,807 mm) and temperatures rarely exceed 76°F (24°C). You may need insect repellent for hiking on the higher trails. The cabins are simple and comfortable. Bring a jacket for the cool evenings.

Transportation: The turnoff for San Gerardo de Dota and Cabinas Chacón is at kilometer 80 on the Inter-American Highway south of San José. Buses going to San Isidro can let you off here, and the Chacóns can pick you up. The $17 round-trip is on a 5.5-mile (9-km) attention-getting road with hairpin curves and beautiful views.

Rates: $63 per person including meals and taxes. VISA is accepted.

Reservations: Telephone 771-1732 or 284-1444; fax 551-0070.

Bosque del Cabo

If you like nighttime by candlelight, scarlet macaws flying overhead, a private outdoor shower with water heated only by the sun on the pipes, and the sound of the sea as you drop off to sleep, then Bosque del Cabo is for you.

Perched above Matapalo Beach on the tip of the Osa Peninsula, this small

Bosque del Cabo, above the sea (Ree Strange Sheck)

wilderness lodge has perhaps just the right amount of comfort and adventure. The naturalist in me thrilled at the continuous parade of tropical birds so easily seen. The explorer reveled in the horseback ride through a tropical storm, an encounter with a snake, and tracking howler monkeys on a forest trail. The romantic in me relished the thatched bungalows above the sea, mosquito netting draped gracefully over the beds, and a private outdoor shower with a forest for a backdrop. Four scarlet macaws flew over in perfect formation as I showered my first morning there.

I confess that I appreciated the modern bath with a flush toilet, the good food, and the comfortable beds. I enjoyed experiencing the bungalow at night with only candles or a kerosene lantern to warm the darkness. Doors fold back to open the front of each of the six bungalows to the sea and forest. The two deluxe bungalows have a king-size bed, wraparound deck, and big bathroom plus solar electricity, but you can still have the candlelight if you choose.

As I stood on my veranda, I counted a feeding flock of 15 chestnut-mandibled toucans while the sounds of howler monkeys mixed with the sounds of the surf and a hummingbird whispering by my ear. The scarlet macaws are regular visitors.

Owners Philip Spier and Barbara Odio make visitors feel like welcome house guests. Attentive to their needs, they also give guests the space they want.

If you can tear yourself away from bird-watching and ocean-gazing (whales sometimes pass by), you can take an hour's hike to the gulf side of the peninsula to swim in gentler waters, walk the trail down to the small river, or go on a horseback ride to the ocean side of the peninsula to visit the tide pools along a deserted beach and walk up to the 30-foot (9-m) waterfall. There also are other horseback tours. Philip and Barbara can secure a naturalist guide for tours and arrange for surfing, sea kayaking, deep-sea fishing, and sailing.

Dining room hours are fairly flexible to meet the needs of both bird-watchers and late sleepers. Local fruits and vegetables are incorporated in the meals which include both typical Costa Rican and North American dishes. Soft drinks and beer are available in the bar during the day. Special dietary needs can be met with advance notice. Solar power provides electricity in the dining room in the evenings.

The young owners have been so busy creating Bosque del Cabo that they have yet to compile bird and mammal lists. You can add to those lists while you are there if you wish. Philip and Barbara say they are beginners in natural history, but if so, they are avid students, and they like to share what they are discovering.

In addition to the bungalows, a two-bedroom, two-bath house with furnished kitchen is available on the property.

Transportation: You can take a direct bus from San José or fly on SANSA or Travelair to Puerto Jiménez. The taxi from Puerto Jiménez costs about $24 for the 10-mile (16-km) trip. If you choose the eight-hour drive from San José, you need four-wheel-drive for the road south of Puerto Jiménez, which can be slippery and muddy and crosses a few streams without bridges.

Rates: For standard bungalows, single occupancy is $90 per day and double is $70 per person, meals included. Deluxe bungalows are $100 for a single and $80 each for a double. The house rents for $500 a week for two, $750 for four. Credit cards discouraged.

Reservations: There is no phone at Bosque del Cabo, so make your reservations through the office in Puerto Jiménez: telephone/fax 735-5206.

Genesis II

Walking through the cloud forest at Genesis II is like moving through a hanging garden in the mist. Bromeliads crowd every inch of space on the stately oaks. Mosses and mushrooms abound. I counted four orchids blooming on the same tree branch. Fallen blossoms from the canopy high above decorate the forest floor.

This cloud forest in the Talamanca Mountains, more than 7,500 feet (2,286 m) high, has an air of eternity about it. It seems to call for hushed tones, for quiet observation. Bird songs echo through the trees. It seemed appropriate that a collared redstart, known as the "friend of man," followed as we walked on the trail. Five mixed feeding flocks passed by.

Birds bring many visitors to this 95-acre (38-ha) private reserve, located about 39 miles (62 km) south of San José. The current bird list has more than 153 species, and owners Steve and Paula Friedman expect it to grow to 200. The resplendent quetzal is no stranger here. It is easily seen from March to June. The Friedmans reported seeing nine quetzals one day from the balcony of their house.

The distinctive sounds of the three-wattled bellbird are sometimes heard here. There are collared trogons, black guans, emerald toucanets, silvery-fronted tapaculo, and hummingbirds—fiery-throated, magnificent, volcano, purple-throated, and gray-tailed mountain gems. Mammals are not as flashy but include sloths, armadillos, tayras, squirrels, and rabbits. The tracks of a tapir have been seen, probably visiting from the Río Macho Forest Reserve next door. One butterfly specialist told Steve that all the butterflies here are in the rare category. Twelve miles (20 km) of well-maintained trails and dirt roads let guests explore the area.

An optional side trip could include a visit to Dominical, or perhaps you can get in on a trip to Los Cusingos, the farm of Alexander Skutch, the well-known naturalist and ornithologist, near San Isidro.

Lodging in the main house, which is like an aerie itself, nestled in the trees, is in a five rooms that share two baths—hot-water showers. Facilities are humble, but the attention is first-class. Perhaps by your arrival, two separate cabins with private baths will be available near the lodge. Paula turns out marvelous meals served family-style, using many garden-fresh fruits and vegetables grown on the property. She uses many of the recipes published in her *Quetzal Cookbook*, everything from typical Costa Rican dishes to lemon chicken, lasagna, and corvina with a lemon, dill, and butter sauce.

Steve directs young people in a volunteer program helping him to re-create forest on a piece of cleared land. Activities include research on species as well as tree planting and follow-up. The program attracts people from around the world who pay to spend their vacations on conservation work in this cloud forest. In their spare time, they teach English to adults and children in a school down the road.

And the name, Genesis II? Steve explained that he and Paula chose it to signify a "second beginning," where they would attempt to live on the land in a more proper, peaceful way.

Transportation: Buses from San José to San Isidro de El General can drop you off at the Cañon church near kilometer 58, where the Friedmans will pick you up. Genesis II is 2.5 miles (4 km) farther. Packages include transportation. If you are driving, watch for probably the most beautifully decorated roadside bus stop in Costa Rica. The Genesis II sign—colorful quetzals and bromeliads—is painted on it.

Rates: Daily rate is $75 for lodging and meals and some guiding (no transportation). Packages include lodging, meals, and some guiding. For three days, singles are $380, doubles $530; for one week, singles $700, doubles $1,050.

Reservations: Telephone 381-0739, fax 225-6055. E-mail ctocsjo@racsa. sol.co.cr.

Hacienda Barú

Four young coatis had dashed across the trail and scampered up a tree, quickly disappearing in a leafy world hidden from our eyes. We had watched a blue-black grassquit doing rapid little song-jumps, seeming to somersault in the air as it fluttered up and down from the same low branch. What sounded like a giant crashing through the forest turned out to be monkeys feeding noisily, knocking down fruit and throwing branches to the ground in the process.

This is Jack Ewing's world. He became interested in ecology about 12 years ago, and he and his wife, Diane, eventually opened Hacienda Barú just north of Dominical on the Pacific Coast. It is a private nature reserve worth visiting.

We had already gone by horseback to see pre-Columbian petroglyphs scattered in a field high above the Barú River Valley. Now we were working our way down by foot on trails that lead to lowland forest and eventually to mangrove swamps and sandy beach along the Pacific.

Jack wanted me to see a giant ceibo tree. I found out for myself that the *jabillo* tree has spines, and he explained that its wood is good for boats because the outside is resistant to salt water and the inside is usually hollow. Jack is an untiring student of the natural world, enthusiastic about sharing what he has learned and dedicated to its conservation.

Some visitors arrive in the rain forest expecting boas to be hanging from the trees and jaguars to appear on the trails. Boas are on Barú's reptile list, but you are not likely to see one. And no jaguars have been spotted here, though there are pumas, jaguarundis, and ocelots. But visitors have plenty to see. More than 326 species of birds have been counted, 57 species of mammals (including bats), and reptiles and amphibians that run the gamut from caimans to red-eyed tree frogs and tiny, colorful, poison dart frogs. Humpback whales pass by offshore from December to April, and olive ridley and hawksbill sea turtles lay eggs on the beach from May through November. The hacienda helps with a nursery where about 2,500 baby turtles are

Exploring the canopy with Jack Ewing at Hacienda Barú
(Ree Strange Sheck)

hatched every year and released on the beach. Dolphins inhabit these warm waters.

About half of the 830-acre (336-ha) hacienda is forested, some in primary forest, some selectively logged a few years ago, and some regenerating on former pastureland.

Many visitors come to Hacienda Barú on day visits. There are a variety of hikes with naturalists or native guides: a three-hour lowland walk through mangrove, riverbank, and seashore habitat; the popular six-hour rainforest hike; and an all-day trek that goes from the beach to the petroglyphs. There also are guided horseback tours to the lowlands, to the petroglyphs, and to the highlands above the river valley. Some can be combined with hikes. Ask about self-guided tours.

An incredible experience awaits those who choose the ascend into the canopy by rope. Steve Stroud, who became a Barú partner in 1992, was instrumental in development of the platforms and canopy exploration and may be your guide. Harnessed and helmeted, the visitor is gently lifted more than 100 feet (30 meters) to an observation platform—fantastic views of canopy vegetation and surrounding forest guaranteed. Possibilities of wildlife to be seen are countless. I can practically guarantee you that you will not be ready to come down (minimum of 30 minutes on the platform). In addition, travelers can choose tree climbing, necessary though good physical condition is essential. The tour involves climbing two trees.

A night in the jungle is another option, camping in tents in the forest next to a shelter with flush toilets and shower. This may be your chance to see nocturnal animals, and bird-watching in the small clearing is excellent in the morning.

If your taste runs more to cabins, try Cabinas Hacienda Barú, six two- and three-bedroom units with kitchenette, bathroom with hot-water shower, and fans. A bamboo sofa with flowered cushions, security box, screened windows with shutters, and two double beds and a single are features. A complimentary continental breakfast is served in an open-air dining room. The cabins are near both forest and beach.

Before you start out on your tours, be sure to see Diane Ewing's orchid collection, 250 species and growing. She is responsible for riding herd on everybody's whereabouts. There are few phones in Dominical, so radio communication is a way of life.

Jack came to Costa Rica in 1970 to stay for four months, and the family followed shortly after. It looks as if they are going to stay. Stop by Hacienda Barú, and you will understand why.

Transportation: Bus and air service to Quepos and bus service to San Isidro de El General is a first step. Buses between Quepos and San Isidro pass by the entrance, just northwest of the Barú River. If you drive, stop by the El Ceibo gas station and information center on the road from Quepos. It is owned by the hacienda.

Rates: Per-person costs for activities include a lowland walk for $15; a rainforest experience for $30; an all-day trek for $35; a night in the jungle for $60 (with breakfast dinner, guides, and equipment); canopy exploration and tree-climbing for $45 with equipment, instruction, and lunch; and the canopy observation platform adventure is $35. These costs include a local guide; English-speaking naturalist guides are available at extra cost. Lodging in the cabins is $50 per person for double occupancy.

Reservations: Telephone/fax 771-4582. This is the office of Selva Mar in San Isidro. At Hacienda Barú, telephone 787-0003, fax 787-0004.

La Amistad Lodge

The bird list for this place tells the story—almost 400 species so far: 22 species of hummingbirds alone. On a short walk before breakfast with the resident naturalist, I saw a crimson-fronted parakeets, fiery-billed aracaris, acorn and lineated woodpeckers, a double-toothed kite, white-ruffed manakin, boat-billed flycatcher, green hermit, Vaux's swift, boat-billed flycatcher, blue-grey tanager, and a rufous-collared sparrow.

La Amistad Lodge is on Hacienda La Amistad, a private biological reserve on the Pacific slope of the Talamanca Mountains northeast of San

Joy of discovering new species—Belgian insect specialist shows find at La Amistad Lodge (Ree Strange Sheck)

Vito, bordering on Panama. It is within the Las Tablas Protected Area, which was declared part of the Amistad Biosphere Reserve by the United Nations and a World Heritage site by UNESCO for its incredibly rich biodiversity. Sixty percent of the flora and fauna in Costa Rica are thought to exist here.

I felt privileged to watch a quiet Belgian arthropod specialist practically in ecstasy as he collected tiny creatures from the forest floor that are not yet described in scientific literature. He confirmed the 3-inch (7.6-cm) grasshoppers on the balcony were not only the largest I have ever seen, they are the largest in existence.

To walk in this forest is to walk in a sacred place; and one of the trails even has a cathedral—an immense, awe-inspiring fig tree. More than 25 miles (40 km) of trails are suited to different energy levels and physical abilities in this 1,927-acre (780-ha) private, pristine rain forest. Watch for dead man's finger, one of the incredible variety of mushrooms along the paths. Howler monkeys, white-faced monkeys, and peccaries live here, among an estimated 215 mammal species in this area.

Owner Roberto Montero, whose grandfather owned this land, can tell you about the history of the area, how Las Tablas became a protected area, and how he believes conservation through sustainable development is the key to preserving our natural resources.

At La Amistad Lodge, guests get more than rain forest ecology; they also can see 1,038 acres (420 ha) of organic agriculture: coffee, vegetables, cardamom, sugar cane, fruit orchards. The La Amistad brand name is now on coffee, hot sauces, chips, refried beans, and other organic products for export. The fruit pulp from coffee is composted for organic fertilizer. Guests can see the coffee-processing plant from the lodge.

Radio, computer, and telephone operate on solar power, and a hydroelectric plant provides other electricity. Roberto smiles as he relates that the hacienda has had electricity for 40 years, while the nearby town of Las Mellizas waited until about two years ago for power.

The lodge itself is a three-story marvel of tropical woods. In the downstairs dining room, delicious buffet-style meals are served by friendly local people. Beautiful pre-Columbian pieces from the property are on exhibit (petroglyphs can be seen on some trails). The huge, high-ceilinged lounge area on the second floor has comfortable seating in front of the big stone fireplace and opens onto an ample balcony. Five rooms with shared baths also open onto the living area. Across a walkway in back are five additional rooms with ceiling fans and private baths. All have hot water and pleasant furnishings. An outdoor bar and barbecue area have a great view of the lodge, the forest, and the crops.

Guided tours include half-day and full-day natural history walks (from $20 to $45), horseback riding ($15), a night walk ($30), and bird-watching walks ($30 to $45). Though there is plenty to do at the hacienda, tours are offered to the Wilson Garden and over to Bambito in Panama.

The hacienda offers environmental education programs in three local schools.

Transportation: By car proceed to San Vito and continue on through Sabalito and Las Mellizas, following lodge signs—about seven hours from San José. La Amistad offers transportation to and from San José as well as to destinations such as San Vito, Tiskita, Golfito, and Jacó.

Rates: With private baths, singles are $40, doubles $50; with shared baths, $5 less, taxes included. Breakfasts are $7, lunch and dinner are $12, taxes included. A three-day package, double occupancy is $360 per person fully escorted or $288 with a local guide, including transportation, lodging, meals, and a full-day guided walk in Las Tablas. A four-day package adds the Wilson Garden.

Reservations: Make reservations through Tropical Rainbow Tours, telephone 290-3030, fax 232-1913. The lodge number is 773-3193.

Lapa Ríos

The brochure for Lapa Ríos asks "Who says wilderness and luxury can't mix?" The owners of this 1,000-acre (405-ha) private reserve, John and

Karen Lewis, thought it could be done, and set out to protect this piece of rain forest on the southeastern tip of the Osa Peninsula through a small, upscale ecotourism project that would have minimal impact on the environment while contributing to local development, education, and employment.

Located 10 miles (16 km) south of Puerto Jiménez where the Golfo Dulce meets the Pacific, Lapa Ríos is the result of their dream. The luxury wilderness resort has a spectacular main lodge that houses the reception area, restaurant, bar, and an outdoor terrace. Guests look up at the underside of the 50-foot (15-m) thatched palm roof. The intrepid can climb an open circular stairway that makes four complete turns to an observation walkway three stories high. A 360-degree view encompassing the forest and the sea 300 feet (92 m) below is the reward. The cliffside swimming pool next to the lodge has a dynamite view of the ocean.

Fourteen bungalows are built on three ridges below the main lodge. The first two are accessible to the lodge and pool by a wheelchair ramp, but the rest require walking. My bungalow was 100 steps down. Each has a peaked thatched roof and gleaming floors of tropical hardwood. One wall is white stucco and cane; the other three are largely open, low wooden walls with screens above, bamboo rollups for privacy. Double louvered doors open onto a large private deck and small patio garden with an outdoor shower. The tiled bathroom has two sinks set in tropical hardwood and a large shower, open to a view of the forest, with loads of solar hot water. Furnishings are primarily of bamboo. Each room contains two double beds with mosquito netting, desk, luggage racks, chairs with bright cushions, and ceiling fans. Battery chargers and razors can be used in the electrical outlets.

The Carbonara Beach down from the lodge is safe for swimming and has a number of tide pools. Surfers can find good waves nearby. Lapa Ríos uses local charter boat services for fishing, tours to Sirena Station at Corcovado and Caño Island, or a cruise on the Golfo Dulce.

A number of guided walks in the rain forest with a naturalist are available. A Coastal Wildlife Tour ($25) combines forest and beaches with a chance to see all four species of monkeys, and a four-hour Rainforest Ridge Walk ($25) along a fairly level mountain ridge is a nice introduction to the biodiversity of tropical rain forests. Among the species that live here are the small green-and-black poison-dart frogs, leaf beetles, army ants and the birds that follow their marches, howler monkeys, and boa constrictors. The $25, half-day Wild Waterfalls adventure will take you along the Carbonera River to a series of pristine waterfalls—this one is for the hardy.

Other options include an easy Medicinal Plant/Forest Walk ($25) or an Early Bird Tour to get a look at some of the more than 320 species of birds found here. Two bilingual guides, one a local shaman and one a biologist, lead tours. A $20 night walk reveals some of the forest secrets not visible during the day. Bring your flashlight to see the eyeshine of nocturnal creatures.

Horseback riding can be arranged, and guests can plant a tree on some of the 250 acres (100 ha) of regenerating forest on the property. The $25 fee goes into the Lapa Ríos reforestation program and the donor receives a certificate. Lapa Ríos is the proud recipient of the 1995 Tourism for Tomorrow Award for the Americas given by British Airways in recognition for responsible ecotourism and sustainable development.

Area tours include sea kayaking ($40), snorkeling in the Golfo Dulce (half-day for two persons $155), a visit to an orchid garden on the other side of the Golfo Dulce ($38), and a charter flight into the Sirena Station in Corcovado and hiking in the park is $600 for four persons. On Tuesday and Friday interested guests may accompany Karen to the local school to share songs, stories, photos, or readings with the children. Back at the lodge after all this activity, you can have a full or half-body massage in a private forest overlook.

Meals are a treat; they look and taste great. Though food is included in the rate, there is no fixed menu: guests choose from several selections. Desserts are scrumptious. Restaurant staff members are well-trained and friendly—introducing themselves politely at the tables they serve. The restaurant is open to the public.

Transportation: Lapa Ríos provides round-trip transportation from Puerto Jiménez for $20 per person. Visitors can reach Puerto Jiménez by either daily scheduled air service, charter flights, direct bus from San José, or charter boats or once-a-day launch service from Golfito.

Rates: Singles are $169, doubles $116 each, including meals and access to the private reserve. Off-season rates are lower. Credit cards accepted.

Reservations: Telephone 735-5281 or 735-5130; fax 735-5179.

Las Cruces Biological Station (Wilson Botanical Garden)

The Las Cruces Biological Station, 3.5 miles (5.6 km) south of San Vito near Panama, is owned and managed by the Organization for Tropical Studies (OTS) and is used as a field station for its graduate-level courses in tropical biology and agroecology. The station is in a rural agricultural setting, with the lofty peaks of Amistad National Park to the northwest, sometimes appearing above the clouds.

Even before you even arrive, you will be glad you came. The trip south from San José on the Inter-American Highway takes you through high mountain páramo, lowland pineapple plantations, and then, off the Inter-American, back up along a ridge that was the Indian route from Paso Real to Panama. If you come via Ciudad Neily, the views are equally spectacular.

The station's most famous connection for nature travelers is the Wilson Botanical Garden, founded by Robert and Catherine Wilson in 1962 and later turned over to OTS. The 25-acre (10-ha) garden contains an internationally known collection of tropical plants. Eighty percent of the tropical and subtropical genera of palms are grown here—the second largest collection in the world—and many can be seen on the delightful Tree Fern Hill Trail. More trails await you: Heliconia Loop Trail; Bromeliad Walk (where you may see bird drinking from the big bromeliads in dry season); Orchid Walk (with more than 200 native and exotic species); Fern Gully (Costa Rica has 800 species of ferns); Maranta Trail; Bamboo Walk. On the Natural History Loop, you will walk through Hummingbird Garden, with plants to attract this amazing creature. Costa Rica has 54 species of hummers; the garden has 24. A self-guided trail has 16 information stations. Another booklet describes uses of 75 species in the medicinal plant garden.

When you have had your fill of planted gardens, take off on trails that touch the adjacent 580-acre (235-ha) natural forest reserve area belonging to the Las Cruces station to see the orchids and palms and heliconias growing in their natural habitat. The River Trail offers excellent bird-watching.

Since 1983, the garden has been part of the Amistad Biosphere Reserve recognized by UNESCO. The garden and forest reserve contain about 3,000 native species of plants, 4,000 exotic species, more than 326 species of birds (including local aquatic species), 80 species of mammals, 71 species of reptiles and amphibians, and more than 3,000 kinds of moths and butterflies.

On Sunday especially, the garden is popular with area residents who come to spend the day. Local outreach and education is a prime component of a program being implemented by Director Luis Diego Gómez and associate director Gail Hewson de Gómez.

Having risen from the ashes of a devastating fire that destroyed lodge, library, and laboratories in November 1994, Las Cruces now offers 12 double rooms with private baths (shower-head hot water). The light-filled rooms have hardwood floors and a glass wall onto a balcony with garden and mountain views. They are furnished with a cushioned bamboo chair and bamboo night stands, a desk, and in-room telephone. Each is named for a flower; one is handicapped-accessible. You are practically guaranteed to see fiery-billed aracaris from your balcony. Four undamaged houses for researchers are also sometimes available to travelers. A new dining room with fantastic views may be finished by your arrival; until then guests eat in the house where the Wilson's lived, which has been remodeled for student groups and has rooms with shared baths that sometimes also are available to visitors for overnight stays.

A gift shop has marvelous publications about the garden and Las Cruces, pretty T-shirts, calendars, tropical playing cards, natural history books, and posters. The garden is open daily and the gift shop is open Monday through Friday from 7:15 to a.m. to 1:40 p.m., closed one hour for lunch; open on Saturday from 7:15 a.m. to noon.

The Wilson Garden is located in a mid-elevation tropical rainforest. There is little or no rainfall from January through March, but the rest of the year there is heavy fog and usually afternoon rains. Rainiest months are August through November. The annual rainfall is about 158 inches (4,000 mm). Year-round temperatures generally stay in the 70s (21°C–26°C) in the daytime and the 60s (15°C–21°C) at night.

Transportation: The road is paved from San José. By car, take the Inter-American Highway through San Isidro and Buenos Aires to 9.3 miles (15 km) past the El Brujo customs checkpoint. Turn left at the sign that says San Vito 45 km. If you are in Golfito, you can reach the Wilson Garden via Ciudad Neily, turning north on Route 16 to Agua Buena. The taxi fare from Golfito is about $40. An express bus from San José to San Vito takes about five hours; buy your tickets in advance. Taxis in San Vito can get you to the garden.

Rates: A day visit to the Las Cruces Biological Station is $8 for a full day or $16 including lunch and a guided walk; half day is $4. For overnight natural history visitors, lodging and meals are $58 for a single and $47 each for doubles in the Wilson Hall bunk rooms. In the private cabins, a single is $80 and doubles are $65 per person, including lodging, meals, and taxes.

Reservations: For overnight reservations or to reserve a lunch during a day visit, contact the Organization for Tropical Studies office in San José, telephone 240-6696, fax 240-6783. E-mail reservas@ ns.ots.ac.cr. The number at Las Cruces is telephone/fax 773-3278.

Las Esquinas Rainforest Lodge

As a steady rain fell in the Rainforest of the Austrians, a sector of Piedras Blancas National Park north of Golfito, I felt blessed to walk with guides Augustín and José Angel of La Gamba. They work for Las Esquinas Rainforest Lodge, part of a commendable project that involves park neighbors in ecotourism activities.

Together the three of us experienced the rain as well as the magic and mystery of this rich forest, letting the wet soak our hair and clothes and drip off our noses instead of hiding under umbrellas or ponchos. These two men, whose roots are here, showed me a tree that exudes a flammable liquid. They explained the medicinal qualities of trees and other plants, pointed out min-iature orchids and kingfishers and hummingbirds, and let me name two pristine waterfalls, each with its own spirit. My choices? Innocencia

(Innocence) and Vida (Life). Augustín named the trail between the two Innocencia de la Vida. I hope you get to name them, too.

The Esquinas Rainforest Lodge was built with the aid of the Government of Austria to offer people in the La Gamba Valley an alternative to destroying the forest. It provides employment, and a specified amount of profits from the lodge go to finance projects for the benefit of the community.

The main building of the lodge is spectacular, set in a former cattle pasture surrounded by forest. Its immense conical thatched roof covers kitchen, reception, gift shop, lounge area, and open dining room, with a second-level library and VCR/conference space tucked higher up under the roof. In the dining room Tiffany-style stained-glass hanging lampshades, tablecloths, and bamboo chairs with brightly colored cushions provide a pleasant setting for delicious meals served buffet style. Angela, the personable Brazilian chef, not only excels in the kitchen, she is becoming an expert on flora and fauna.

Ten rooms in five bungalows are a short distance away, upslope toward the forest's edge. Built of natural rock and wood, with curtained windows on three sides, the rooms have bamboo furniture, reading lamps, and ceiling fans. Private baths with shower-head hot water have blue fixtures—the shower is set off by a natural rock partition. Each room has its veranda with comfortable furniture (even a rocking chair) to lounge in. Be sure to watch in the landscaped gardens for golden-hooded tanagers (in Spanish called *siete colores*, seven colors); scarlet-rumped tanagers, and a variety of hummingbirds. Parrots and toucans abound. Perhaps you will see the flash of orange and blue as a Baird's trogon flies by. You will definitely hear the howler monkeys.

Guests can walk in the botanical garden next to the main building to find many tropical fruit trees—guanábana, cas, papaya, star fruit, three kinds of mamones, water apples; banana and cacao plantings are nearby. Augustín will probably cut one of the cacao pods so you can try the tasty pulp around the chocolate bean. Harvests find their way to the table. Perhaps you will be treated to fried yuca, to breadfruit, to tea made from lemongrass, or a heavenly chocolate dessert. A stream meanders through the grounds, flowing into a swimming pool, naturally filtered so there is no need for chlorine. A small pool by the dining room has fish and maybe a cayman or two.

Elevation at the lodge is about 787 feet (240 m), average temperature about 91°F (33°C). Manager Javier Salazar says this is one of the rainiest places in the country, but the sun does shine.

Marked trails, from three to five hours long, move through the park, which adjoins the lodge property; guided walks are $15. Guests can also choose from a variety of excursions: kayaking in the Golfo Dulce ($20), hiking in the Golfito wildlife refuge ($15), boating and snorkeling ($30), exploring the Río Coto mangroves by boat ($30), and visiting the Wilson Botanical Garden ($50). Horseback riding can be arranged. Packages are available.

In case you are wondering, the sector of the Piedras Blancas Park next to the lodge is called the Rainforest of the Austrians because of donations from the people of that country to purchase more than 3,000 acres (1,200 ha) of endangered forest, which was then turned over to Costa Rica to be included in the national park. Michael Schnitzler, an Austrian musician, spearheaded the campaign and was instrumental in the creation of Esquinas Rainforest Lodge. A biological station is also part of the project, open to biologists and students.

Transportation: By car, Las Esquinas Rainforest Lodge is about 4 miles (6 km) northwest of Golfito just past La Gamba. Coming from San José, turn right off the Inter-American at kilometer 37, and follow the signs, about 2.5 miles (4 km), four-wheel-drive not necessary. SANSA and Travelair have scheduled flights to Golfito, with free airport pickup for guests with reservations.

Rates: Single $95, double $130, including meals and taxes. A three-night package is $230, double occupancy, including lodging, meals, taxes, guided rain forest hike, tour of the Esquinas coast, and airport transfers. Ask about other packages. Some include additional nights at Punta Encanto Lodge on the Golfo Dulce. Credit cards are not accepted.

Reservations: Telephone 775-0131 or 284-7196; fax 775-0631.

Marenco

There are no roads to Marenco on the Osa Peninsula. You come in by boat or plane.

Remote, set in a hillside clearing amidst lush premontane wet forest, this tropical wilderness lodge and reserve is a center for natural history tourism. As you explore the miles of beach and forest trails on the reserve's 1,236 acres (500 ha), you can do some discovering of your own. In fact, you can sit on the balcony of your room and watch a parade of exotic birds—parrots, toucans with their outrageous beaks, scarlet macaws, brightly colored tanagers. At certain times of the year, humpback whales pass by in the ocean below.

On forest trails you may encounter a slow-moving sloth or catch the scent of white-lipped peccaries. The resident naturalist guide will advise you to climb a nearby tree and wait until they pass if you meet a herd of the piglike peccaries. There is a subspecies of squirrel monkey, called tití, that is endemic to southern Costa Rica and northern Panama. Watch for motion in the trees to spot them and the other three monkey species that live in Costa Rica: howler, white-faced capuchin, and spider.

You can rent one of the reserve's horses to go along the beach or forest trails, and you can walk to the cool waters of the Río Claro and take a dip beneath towering forest giants. If you are so inclined, you can walk on the beach and forest trails all the way to the tiny community of Drake Bay.

A nighttime visit to the tide pools reveals sea creatures you may never have seen before. Daytime snorkeling is good at coral gardens along Marenco's coastline, where you may see parrot fish, tangs, puffers, and angelfish. A boat tour to Caño Island, 11 miles (17 km) west of Marenco, opens up another underwater wonderland of octopuses, lobsters, moray eels, jacks, damselfish, and triggerfish. Near the island you will probably see dolphins, and you may be startled by a manta ray. The forested island holds the secrets of both a vanished Indian culture and fabled pirate treasure troves.

A highlight for most travelers to Marenco is a day trip to nearby Corcovado National Park, entering at San Pedrillo and hiking along the beach and into the forest. Plant and bird life is outstanding. A bilingual naturalist guide explains intricate biological relationships and points out what you often do not see. You know you are treading the turf of Corcovado's animal kingdom: the jaguar, giant anteater, tapir, agouti, ocelot, and kinkajou.

Marenco is a buffer zone that protects the park, employs local people, and offers the traveler a chance to taste the richness. A row of cozy rooms along the edge of the hillside have balconies open to a priceless view. Larger bungalows of wood and bamboo have shining hardwood floors, two double beds, and floor-to-ceiling screened windows that let in lots of light and forest colors. All have high ceilings and private baths. Meals are served buffet-style in high season in the large, open dining room.

The generator runs from 5:30 to 9:30 p.m.; bring a flashlight to complement the candle in your room after hours. The radio telephone is powered by solar energy. A small reference library with some preserved local flora and fauna is worth a visit. Crafts made by local people are also available in the Rain Forest Shop.

December through April are the busiest months at Marenco, which can house up to 50 guests. September and October are very rainy, but the off-season months can be pleasant, too.

Transportation: Package rates include round-trip transportation from San José. Non-package travelers should contact Marenco about land, sea, and air possibilities. Land/sea routes are usually through Sierpe.

Rates: A room and meals is $55 per person, while the bungalow and meals is $65. A half-day tour to the Río Claro is $35 and full-day tours are

$65 to Corcovado and $75 to Caño Island. All-inclusive packages include airfare, ground and boat transfers, meals, lodging, and specified tours. A two-night package with a trip to Corcovado is $390 per person, while the three-night is $540, including Corcovado and Caño Island. Credit cards are accepted.

Reservations: Telephone 221-1594, fax 255-1346. The office in San José is on the second floor of Edificio Cristal, Avenida 1, Calles 1/3.

Rainbow Adventures

Travelers take a 45-minute boat ride north of Golfito along shores where steep forest meets the sea, past small unpopulated beaches, to find a lodge with stained-glass windows and turn-of-the-century antiques. Pleasant surprises are the order of the day at Rainbow Adventures.

I no sooner arrived than I spotted a green honeycreeper moving through tree branches next to my room, my first glimpse of that gorgeous bird. During my stay I witnessed a continuing, stubborn battle between a red-lored parrot and a yellow-naped woodpecker over a hole in a nearby tree trunk. The brilliance of the scarlet-rumped tanager flashed in the landscaped gardens around the lodge and two cabins. Five chestnut-mandibled toucans perched in a single tree just off the trail during the free introductory jungle walk. Fellow guests swore that the live-in scarlet macaw (who decided to stay after being brought here injured) actually poses for photographers, changing positions after hearing the click of the camera.

Rainbow Adventures is in a small clearing between mile-long Cativo Beach on the Golfo Dulce and primary and secondary forest behind. The 1,200-acre (486-ha) private reserve abuts Piedras Blancas National Park. If you can tear yourself away from the activity near the lodge and the warm, usually gentle waters at the beach (85°F, 30°C), you can choose to fill your days with a wide variety of activities.

Hikes with a local guide include a two-hour trek to a 50-foot (15-m) waterfall, through the forest to the small hydro project that supplies electricity for Rainbow Adventures; a Jungle and Vanilla Grove tour; or customized jungle hikes—perhaps to a big swimming hole above the waterfalls. The cost is $4 per hour for guided tours, boots provided. Animals more commonly seen include the agouti, banded anteater, coati, kinkajou, raccoon, tayra, iguana, Jesus Christ lizard, armadillo, and howler, spider, and white-faced monkeys. More than 100 species of birds are on the lodge list. On my last visit, manager John Lovell and I saw the biggest, most beautiful fer-de-lance snake either of us had ever seen.

Boating activities include a birding trip on the Esquinas River through mangroves and primary and secondary forest (30 species counted on my tour, including a tree full of exotic king vultures), a dolphin tour, fishing, and snorkeling at a number of sites, where you may see parrotfish, angelfish, triggerfish, starfish, moray eels, octopus, sharks, sea turtles, or dolphins. Boat rental for these tours is $35 an hour, including guide, snorkeling gear, and safety equipment.

Another possibility is a $25 half-day boat trip to see the botanical gardens at Casa Orquídeas at San Josesito (Sunday to Wednesday only).

The lodge itself invites exploration. The first floor of the wooden structure has a lounge and dining room open to the gardens. The second has three double rooms that open onto a large veranda. The third, called the penthouse, is open on three sides, with stained-glass panels suspended between the waist-high wall and the roof. Antiques are scattered throughout, collected by owner Michael Medill of Oregon. All rooms have private baths with solar-heated or on-demand propane hot water and bidets, no less. The two secluded cabins have an open living area (with handwoven silk rugs) and two bedrooms and bath. The furnishings are handmade by resident craftspeople. You will probably find a tropical flower on your pillow when you arrive. A swimming pool is between the lodge and the palm-lined beach.

Delicious meals, including gourmet dishes are generally served buffet-style, with most herbs and vegetables coming from the organic garden. Staff provide some very nice touches, such as having a guanabana fruit on hand to show guests when a drink made of guanábana is served. The garden provides produce such as pineapples, papayas, bananas, plantains, water apples, avocados, star fruit, anona, *mamón chino*, chestnuts, and edible hibiscus. Guests, me included, rave about the food.

By the time you arrive, the new Buena Vista Jungle and Beach Lodge will be open about half a mile down the beach, also owned by Michael Medill, with the same standards and services as Rainbow Adventures. It has a single-story lodge with kitchen, dining, and lounge plus two two-story houses on the beach, each with four double rooms, private baths. A seven-minute video about Rainbow Adventures can be rented.

Transportation: SANSA and Travelair fly to Golfito. By the way, Travelair has a U.S. agent; see Practical Extras. Rates include round-trip Golfito airport to Rainbow Adventures or Buena Vista.

Rates: At Rainbow Adventures, singles in the lodge rooms are $170, doubles $210; in the penthouse $180 for single, $225 for doubles; in the beach cabins, single is $190, double $235. At Buena Vista, all rooms are $170 for a single, or $210 for doubles. Included is round-trip transport from Golfito, meals, snacks, snorkeling gear, jungle tour, nonalcoholic drinks, beer at meals, and taxes. A portion of the profits go to the local school.

Reservations: In the U.S., telephone (503) 690-7750, fax (503) 690-7735.

Tiskita Jungle Lodge dining room (Ree Strange Sheck)

Make your reservations there if possible. The Costa Rican number is in Golfito, where faxes are checked on trips in: telephone/fax 775-0220.

Tiskita Jungle Lodge

Two spectacular fiery-billed aracaris perched along the road, and small squirrel monkeys cavorting through tree branches introduced me to Tiskita Jungle Lodge on the Southern Pacific Coast before we even reached the main building. Guides can help you out with the name of the flashy bird if it is new to you, and explain that you will see this subspecies of tití monkey only in southern Costa Rica.

If you enjoy birds or nature photography, you can have a field day without leaving the landscaped grounds of the lodge. Hundreds of tropical fruit trees draw birds like a magnet. I watched three chestnut-mandibled toucans casually eat a fruit breakfast. In the same tree were blue-crowned manakins, a lineated woodpecker, and blue-gray and scarlet-rumped tanagers. A bird book is left handy to help you identify what you spot, and there is a bird list so you will know if anyone has seen it before you. So far the list includes more than 332 species. Ask for the illustrated booklet on tide pools and the printed guide for the nature trail.

Since 1980, Peter Aspinall, who owns the lodge with brother John, has been growing exotic tropical fruits gathered from around the world on about 62 acres (25 ha) of this almost 440-acre (180-ha) property. His experimental station has the most extensive collection of tropical rare and exotic fruits in the country. Birds and guests alike can have their fill of more than 100 varieties, tasting such delicacies as star fruit (*carambola* in Spanish), passionfruit (*maracuyá*), guava, guanábana, custard apple (*anona*), jackfruit, *araza, abiu,* and dozens of others that are not yet household words. Once, he reminds you, bananas and pineapples were considered rare and exotic fruits.

Animals also come out of a primary forest that covers more than 300 acres (120 ha) to savor the fruits. You may cross paths with all four species of monkeys found in Costa Rica; with the coati, paca, white-lipped peccary, anteater; or cats such as the ocelot, jaguarundi, and margay. Well-marked trails go through the farm, the forest, and to the beach at the bottom of the hill. Guests can choose a guided fruit walk through the orchards or the guided rain forest walk, A trail map facilitates exploration on your own. A short walk leads to a pristine waterfall whose waters flow into small, protected pools; bathe in the company of kingfishers and hummingbirds underneath a natural canopy of giant forest trees (don't mind the tickling by the fresh-water shrimp). Ocean swimming and snorkeling is best at low tide, which also reveals tide pools with colorful fish, anemones, and other sea creatures. Night walks and early-morning birding walks are also available, and horses can be rented.

Guests also can fish or surf. Nearby is the longest breaking left wave in the country, a 1,600-yard run at Punta Pavones. An Indian reserve borders Tiskita, which is the Guaymi name for fish eagle. A visit to the Indian settlement can be arranged. Dashing hats and attractive bags made by the Guaymis are for sale in the gift shop. Profits for sale of cards and T-shirts go to the Tiskita Foundation, which has purchased nearby endangered forest. Tiskita's work with the nearby community of Punta Banco has facilitated a local clinic; perhaps the new community center and library will be open by your visit.

Electricity has arrived at Tiskita. The cabins have fans, reading lamps, and an electric plug in bathrooms. Each of the cabins is a bit different. Construction is generally of wood and natural stone. Each cabin has an attractive bathroom (brightened by blue towels and washcloths), all but one semi-outdoor but very private, allowing bird-watching while you bathe. No hot water. The Aspinalls say Tiskita is five-star rustic. Support columns in the room are polished tree trunks, door handles are pieces of naturally sculptured wood. Screened windows and outdoor terraces are common features of the 14 cabins—some are individual, some share a common veranda. Smoking is not allowed in lodge facilities.

In a covered lookout at the edge of the hill, furnished with forest-green lounging chairs and surrounded by heliconias and palms, sounds of sea and land mix—lots of parakeets and hummingbirds. You can look out across the Pacific to the Osa Peninsula. It is a favorite spot for watching the sun slide into the ocean in the evenings.

The original farmhouse, built in 1979, has a small reference library, lounging chairs, and a dining room. Coffee, tea, and natural drinks are available throughout the day. Meals are served buffet style—delicious, varied, and generous. Mischievous Sam, the toucan, may join you. I watched him sneak a stack of napkins from the holder and proceed to scatter them about the yard (administrative manager Maryanne Aspinall, Peter's sister, has secret hopes he will find a mate and fly away).

Telephone has not yet arrived, but the lodge has radio contact with the outside. It is still remote, but it is possible to drive in. The 37 miles (60 km) from Golfito, 2½ hours, is a fascinating trip through farm and ranch lands into a frontier region, crossing the Río Coto by ferry and sometimes fording small steams. A bridge now stretches across the Río Claro. I am sorry, in a way, that you will miss the adventure of fording it, especially in the rainy season. That was something to write home about.

Though fireflies sparkle in the evening, you will need your own flashlight for nighttime walks. In the rainy season, you will want rubber boots. Tiskita is closed in October because of the heavy rain. Boots and umbrellas are available for guests.

Transportation: Most travelers arrive by air charter; round trip is included in package plans. Guests may come in by car, but it is always advisable to check with Tiskita first about road conditions. A daily bus between Golfito and Punta Banco passes by the entrance to Tiskita. It leaves Punta Banco at 5:00 a.m. and from Golfito at 2:00 p.m., about $2 for the three-hour trip (plus a pittance for the ferry). Check Practical Extras for San José–Golfito buses.

Rates: Daily rates are $65 for a single, $80 for a double, including a guided walk. Breakfast is $6, lunch and dinner $9, plus taxes. Packages have fixed departure days. The two-day, two-night package, which leaves on Monday and Saturday, is $495 per person (double occupancy) including meals, lodging, ground and air transportation from San José, and some guided walks. Ask about packages that combine Tiskita with other destinations such as Arenal, Monteverde, or Tortuguero. Credit cards accepted.

Reservations: Telephone 255-3418 or 221-0303; fax 255-4410; e-mail suntours@sol.racsa.co/cr. Reservations are handled by Sun Tours (owned by brother John Aspinall). The office is at Avenida 4, Calle 36.

Caribbean

Almonds and Corals Lodge Tent Camp

Distant lightning played across the night sky. Forest giants loomed in the foreground, fireflies among the dense foliage below. The sea and the cicadas harmonized into a constant melody. And I? I savored lying in a hammock in the middle of the jungle in the darkness.

Almonds and Corals Lodge Tent Camp helps make such fantasies come true. My hammock was suspended inside the platform enclosure that holds a tent, a bathroom, and a table and chairs in a corner sitting area. The walls are of netting, so the experience is one of being with the forest, not separated from it. My eyelids began to droop all too soon, and I resented missing a magic moment of this unusual opportunity.

Eighteen canvas-covered platforms on stilts are tucked into forest foliage under tall trees. The tent itself holds a double or two single beds with pretty quilted spreads, a floor fan, a nightstand, and lamps. Drawers in the base of the beds provide storage space. The tent flaps can be closed at night for privacy. The corner bathroom, set off by a partition, has a flush toilet, built-in sink, and a rounded metal shower—water at its natural temperature flows out of a pipe. There is even an electric plug, which is more than some hotel rooms have. No smoking in tents.

Some of you may be disappointed that you can glimpse other tents through the foliage; others, no doubt, will be grateful for near neighbors as darkness reveals the jungle in sounds and shadows.

Raised wooden walkways connect the clusters of cabins with the dining room/bar and on through the forest to the beach. At night, the walkways are lighted in a unique way—you will see for yourself. Meals in the open-air dining room are tasty, with a set menu each day, some options on main dishes. Staff is friendly and helpful—including delightful, refreshing owners Aurora and Marcos.

Guests are treated to good birding even from their lodging, but I recommend an early morning walk to the beach. You may see toucans, parrots, a slaty-tailed trogon. Howler monkeys seem to delight in leaving traces of their presence on the walkways, so watch your step.

The reserve right around Almonds and Corals, itself within the Gandoca-Manzanillo Wildlife Refuge, is small but beautiful. Tours to other parts of the refuge are led by excellent local guides, and sometimes by Marcos himself, who happens to be a physician. A hike starting at Manzanillo is a delight ($45). You can eat sea grapes when they're ripe, walk on secluded beaches, and explore a blowhole. You can climb to a mirador to look down through crystalline water to coral and look up to see all along the coast north to

Puerto Vargas. Finally, you can look in tide pools at sea urchins and tiny tropical fish, and learn something about medicinal plants and the history of the area.

An array of other tours offer a dugout wooden canoe trip to Punta Mona with a look at the Gandoca estuary ($65), biking to Punta Uva for snorkeling in the coral reef ($45), kayaking at Estero Negro ($65), and a visit to Volio Indian Ranch near Bribrí to visit an Indian woman and her clan, with an opportunity to buy handicrafts ($45). Just a few minutes from Volio is Chase, at the Panamanian border—if you like, the driver can take you there as well.

Aurora also owns Geo Expedicones, a travel agency that specializes in the Caribbean area. Tours to the Hitoy-Cerere reserve, Tortuguero, and Cahuita are easily arranged. Packages are available.

Transportation: Public buses can get you to Puerto Viejo de Limón or, via the Sixaola bus, to the Bribrí intersection, where Almonds & Corals can pick you up. A private shuttle goes directly to the tent camp from San José and intermediate Caribbean stops—price depending on distance and number of persons. Some packages offer an option of public or private transportation.

Rates: A single tent is $50, while a double is $70. Meals are $6 for breakfast, $9 for lunch, and $10 for dinner, plus taxes. A three-day package includes a visit in Braulio Carrillo National Park, a guided walk in Gandoca-Manzanillo refuge, and round-trip transportation from San José. Lodging and meals start at $276 per person double occupancy with private shuttle, and $192 with public bus (includes transfers between hotel and bus station in San José and between bus station and Almonds & Corals). Ask about other packages. One combines Almonds & Corals with charming La Quinta de Sarapiquí Lodge, owned by Aurora's sister and her husband. Credit cards accepted.

Reservations: Call Geo Expediciones, telephone 272-2024 or 272-4175; fax 272-2220.

Aviarios del Caribe

At night, a flashlight revealed the yellow eyes of caimans along the bank of the Estrella River. At midmorning, from the same spot, I saw a river otter playing in the water, a purple gallinule strutting his stuff, and a little blue heron foraging at the river's edge. All of this from the upstairs veranda of the lodge at Aviarios del Caribe, 19 miles (30 km) south of Limón.

Aviarios del Caribe is a labor of love for owners Luis and Judy Arroyo. Gracious hosts, they warmly share with guests their lives and their vision of humanity as caretaker of habitat and creatures. They have succeeded in having the island at the mouth of the Estrella River and the river delta declared a private wildlife refuge. Here there are freshwater canals and lagoons, humid tropical forest, sandy beaches, and marshland along with the forest and waterways. Its creatures are monkeys, sloths, river turtles, sea turtles, frogs, lizards, butterflies; aquatic, arboreal, migratory, and marine birds, plus birds of prey—299 species of birds so far. According to Luis, all six species of king-fishers found in Costa Rica are here, as well as the white-collared manakin, migrating orioles and warblers, collared aracaris, toucans, and even the black-crowned night-heron, which nests here but is uncommon in the Caribbean lowlands.

On a quiet canoe trip with Cali, a local guide who takes guests through the canals to the river's mouth and the Caribbean, we watched a boat-billed heron 15 feet (4.5 m) away as he watched us. I was almost within touching distance of a northern jacana, a pretty black and chestnut-col-ored bird with a striking yellow patch above its bill, before it took flight, revealing the yellow underside of its wing. When we got out of the canoe for a walk on the island, Cali deftly whacked off the top of a coconut with his machete. The liquid tasted marvelous in the morning heat. The three-hour trip is $30 per person.

On short, self-guided trails through forest next to the lodge, you will probably see a sloth. You are sure to see one upstairs in the lodge—Buttercup has a private tree there, though she seems to prefer a corner of the soft couch. Judy nursed the injured baby three-toed sloth back to health after her mother was killed on the highway; the sloth is now four years old. Judy has an album she refers to as "Friends of Buttercup"—filled with photos taken by former guests who have sent back pictures. People continue to bring injured animals to Aviarios, so there's no telling what you will find when you arrive.

The lodge has six bedrooms, all downstairs. The rooms are large with queen- or king-size beds, floor fans, and private baths with hot water. Fresh flowers say welcome. Laundry service is available, and there is a small gym.

Upstairs is both an indoor and outdoor dining area and an inviting living area with a library, television/VCR, and tables for a variety of games such as chess, dominoes, Scrabble, and checkers. Mystical seahorses live in a salt-water aquarium, along with anemones, shrimp, and other fantastic sea crea-tures. A few steps away on the outdoor deck, see colorful poison-dart frogs in glass tanks—the Arroyos are successfully breeding them. Benches at the deck's rail are ideal for bird-watching; if you forget your binoculars, there will be a pair there for you to use. Recently 51 species of birds were sighted from this vantage point in a two-hour period—just in the yard and forest edge, not including river birds.

Next to the river is another covered deck and benches. The first time I met the Arroyos, Judy was cooking in a makeshift kitchen on that deck after the 1991 Limón earthquake. It hit just as they were finishing the lodge the first time, so they started over.

Now, in addition to the main lodge, travelers can opt for a secluded stay in cabins at the mouth of the Estrella River. A launch will drop you off and pick you up, and the Arroyos will even do the food shopping for you if you wish. A rancho by the small pool has a comfortable lounge area, and there is a kitchen for guests' use. No electricity—though a generator runs four hours at night; radio communication links the lodge with this outpost. Each room has its own bath (no hot water here). The cabins, two individual and one with two bedrooms and two baths, have the river in front and are backed by a tropical flower farms planted among the trees.

If you want tours to other sites, talk to Brandon. He knows the Caribbean coast. He has a four-passenger vehicle or he can accompany you in your car for trips to Hitoy-Cerere ($40 per person), to Punta Uva, or to Bribrí and the iguana farm ($35). He will even transport you to Cahuita and back for dinner ($10). The Arroyos have headlamps for people to use on the night frog walk ($10).

Transportation: The entrance to Aviarios del Caribe is 19 miles (30 km) southeast of Limón and about 4 miles (7 km) before Cahuita. The San José–Sixaola bus passes, as do San José–Puerto Viejo buses and buses from Limón south (see Practical Extras for schedules). Taxi from Limón is about $16.

Rates: At the lodge, singles are $50; doubles $60, including a delicious, full breakfast. A cabin at the mouth of the Estrella River is $50, plus food if you want Aviarios to supply it.

Reservations: Telephone/fax 382-1335; this is a cellular phone at Aviarios. If you cannot get through, then fax to Aviarios del Caribe, 798-0374.

Casa Río Blanco

At Casa Río Blanco, you have a chance to walk with someone who falls in love with the forest all over again every time she enters it. Thea Gaudette is a naturalist with a gift for telling the rainforest story. She will have you stepping over spider webs in no time so as not to disturb them, and noticing the ways plants survive in the low-light conditions of the forest understory. A biologist, she spent ten years as a guide for Audubon in the U.S. before moving to Costa Rica.

Thea and husband Ron Deletetsky, owners of Casa Río Blanco, promise and deliver individualized attention. With their help, guests can explore this rich ecosystem, plan trips to other sites, or rest and recuperate.

From the comfortable lounge area on the back veranda of the main house, you can watch dozens of hummingbirds at feeders and flowering plants in a botanical garden. Plants are numbered, and a printed guide will lead you on your own walk of discovery. Where the garden stops, the steep forested drop to the river begins.

Resident birds include Oscar, a mealy Amazon parrot; and Felix, a red-lored parrot, brought here to heal. (Thea is also a registered nurse; is there a link?) Tuckie, a keel-billed toucan raised in captivity, is on loan from Zoo Ave, a wildlife rehabilitation center. Other wounded or captured birds who have found their way here include a spectacular golden-hooded tanager. The reception area also has an interesting exhibit of snakes (most brought by neighbors) and other forest creatures: wasps, tarantulas, leeches, bullet ants. At night Thea can show you the garden tarantula, a beauty. She can also show you the spider who hides in a dead leaf during the day to escape bird predators, leaving its marvelous web at work until it comes out at night to harvest the catch.

Each of the three wood cabins has a bench on a porch facing the forest for wildlife viewing. Actually, since the cabins have screened windows on all sides, some with shutters, others with curtains, you can enjoy the outdoors while inside. Polished light wood floors and rustic walls make a cozy room, each with a double bed and day bed. Private baths have individual propane units to heat the water, which results in a nice shower. When I visited, lighting was from fixed lanterns. Now Thea and Ron are in a quandary because electricity is arriving at Casa Río Blanco. Do they maintain the style they have created, or do they offer electric lights? You will find out for yourself. Two comfortable rooms are in the main house. No smoking in the rooms or cabins—there are designated smoking areas.

The river provides night music; during the day its pools are great for swimming, while the rushing white water provides a natural Jacuzzi. Your stay will include a complimentary rainforest tour on Casa Río Blanco's 12 acres (about 5 ha). By the time you arrive, a tree-climbing adventure into the forest canopy will be in operation.

If you can tear yourself away, other trips beckon. A day hike to a 275-foot (84-meter) waterfall on the Río Blanco requires good physical condition and advance notice ($25 each for up to three persons). A three-hour rain-forest and plantation hike is $15, with a chance to see sunbitterns, kingfishers, the rufescent tiger-heron, or the violaceous trogon. Ron and Thea can get you a discount on a tour of the Tortuguero canals: one day $57, two days and one night, $135, or three days and two nights $175, with pick up and drop off at the highway.

For $125 a week, you can be a volunteer at Casa Río Blanco, helping with bird, animal, or plant censuses, blazing and mapping trails, developing educational materials, or working in the organic garden. A one-month minimum stay is required.

About the personalized care: Every guest receives a list of suggested resources in Costa Rica in case of medical or dental emergencies while traveling.

Transportation: Casa Río Blanco is 36 miles (58 km) from San José through Braulio Carrillo park. The turnoff is to the right 300 meters after the Ponderosa Restaurant, just before the bridge over the Río Blanco. It is less than a mile (1.5 km) from the highway. To come by bus, take the Guápiles bus, which runs every half hour. Get off at the Ponderosa Restaurant, where a radio message brings someone to pick you up.

Rates: Single $40, double $55, including a full breakfast. No credit cards.

Reservations: Phone 382-0957 or 710-2652; fax 710-6161.

Cabinas Chimuri

For the traveler looking for adventure, a stay at Cabinas Chimuri outside Puerto Viejo de Limón may fit the bill. This 49-acre (20-ha) natural reserve offers an out-of-the-ordinary experience.

Traditional Bribrí structures house guests. Built on stilts, the buildings are of tropical wood and bamboo, the roofs thatched with cane. There are three doubles and one unit for four people, with shared baths and flush toilets a few steps away. You bring your own food and have use of a common kitchen. With advance notice, a cook can be arranged for breakfast and dinner. Bedding is furnished. The complex is in a clearing surrounded by forest. It is reached by a five-minute foot trail from the road below. The Caribbean is 600 yards (500 m) from Chimuri.

Managed by El Indio and Catherine, Chimuri always has a welcome-mat out. Owners Mauricio Salazar and his wife, Colocha, live not far away; Mauricio, a Bribrí, still guides here.

The reserve offers good birding and a multitude of butterflies—visit the butterfly nursery. An afternoon in inviting pools in the river is great after a morning on the trails. Right on the reserve you are likely to see sloths, porcupines, agoutis, armadillos, tayras, coatis, anteaters, kinkajous, bats, poison-dart frogs, boa constrictors, opossums, and iguanas. There are birds of prey, parrots, hummingbirds, trogons, motmots, jacamars, toucans, manakins, orioles, and tanagers. Just walking in on my latest visit, I saw oropendolas, keel-billed toucans, a black and green frog, and hummingbirds. You can go on the trail by yourself or walk with trained local guides for about three hours at $12 per person, leaving at 7:00 a.m. or 7:00 p.m.—very different experiences. Rubber boots may be borrowed. Bring repellent.

If you want to explore farther than the Chimuri reserve or the nearby

Cabinas Chimuri (Ree Strange Sheck)

Caribbean coast, there are optional tours. A one-day walking tour takes you through abandoned cacao plantations to traditional Bribrí stomping grounds in the KéköLdi Indian reserve, where you will learn about plants used by the indigenous peoples for medicinal, construction, and other purposes. Along the trails you are likely to see a sloth, a raccoon, a toucan, iguanas, and perhaps a snake. The group, limited to five people, will stop by a friend's home to eat a picnic lunch and get a glimpse of life on the Indian reserve. The return is by a different trail. It is a hard trip, intended for people in good physical condition. You can also visit the green iguana farm to have a typical dinner with a local black family.

Between the two of them, El Indio and Catherine speak English, Spanish, German, and French. Hospitality is warm. Perhaps Catherine will offer you a drink made of *arazá*, a peachlike fruit. *Chimuri*, by the way, means "ripe bananas" in Bribrí, and a stalk is always hanging at the main house, where any hungry hand may reach out and take some.

Transportation: As you enter Puerto Viejo from Limón, after turning off the highway to Sixaola, watch on the right for the Cabinas Chimuri sign with a banana-tree insignia on one side and a toucan on the other. From there, a short trail leads up to the cabins. Bus travelers should ask to be let off at the sign. (See Practical Extras for buses from San José or Limón.)

Rates: The double cabins cost $25 per day, the quadruple $35. The one-day tour is $25 per person, including a box lunch. Part of the tour fee is donated to the local Indian organization. No credit cards.

Reservations: Write to Cabinas Chimuri, Puerto Viejo de Limón, Talamanca, or send a fax to 798-1844.

14

Nature Tour Companies: What They Offer

Nature travel tours in Costa Rica run the gamut from two people with a guide to a microbus of travelers; from hiking, bicycling, sailing, rafting, or kayaking to the standard overland tour by horseback, car, or bus. Just as Costa Rica is small and friendly, so are the nature tours I have tried out—no herding people around like bodies that have to be moved. Chances are that by the time even a one-day tour is over, the guide will call you by name.

The companies included here specialize in nature travel. The listing begins with general nature travel, progressing to specializations: rafting/ kayaking tours, cruises, and ballooning. Finally, some of the companies outside Costa Rica that organize nature tours to the country are listed. Prices, of course, can change without notice. The listings of what each company offers are intended to give you an idea of the possibilities; they are not all-inclusive.

General Nature Travel

Two small companies that offer first-class nature travel are Geotur and Jungle Trails. Their bilingual guides are knowledgeable and personable.

Geotur is well known for its wildlife tour of Carara Biological Reserve. The one-day trip focuses on walks in the reserve but also includes a couple of hours at Jacó Beach for lunch, swimming, or a walk along the coast. At Carara, you see animals like monkeys, scarlet macaws, and crocodiles. Depending on the animal's cooperation, of course, you may also get a close-up look through a telescope the guide carries. The $75 tour includes transportation, guide, breakfast, and lunch. According to owner Sergio Volio, the population of scarlet macaws at Carara is now about 300 and seems stable. Thanks to the combined efforts of the reserve, scientists, and individuals concerned about the protection of this endangered species, the robbing of baby birds from the traditional nesting sites of Carara's macaws has been greatly reduced, and placement of artificial nests in protected areas helps secure their future.

A half-day tour goes to Braulio Carrillo. Features include waterfalls, cloud forest, trails through lush vegetation, and encounters with wildlife. Transportation, guide, and lunch are included. The price for custom tours varies. Telephone/fax 227-4029.

Jungle Trails, *Los Caminos de la Selva* in Spanish, has an impressive array of tours and will customize expeditions throughout the country. An intriguing trip is the Let's Plant a Tropical Endangered Tree, in which people visit a native tree nursery in the Central Pacific area (where humid and dry forests meet) to learn what each tree is good for. Each person chooses one to plant at a watershed project in cooperation with Arbofilia (the Association for the Protection of Trees), a grass-roots ecological organization. After the tree-planting, a visit to Carara Biological Reserve shows what virgin forest is like. Part of the $90 cost buys the tree and contributes to Arbofilia. The fees for other tours also include donations to Arbofilia.

Other one-day tours with Jungle Trails, at $90 each, include walking through cloud forest on Barva Volcano, bird-watching, or customized tours to any of the nearby parks or refuges—including an early departure for Poás to see the crater before clouds roll in. A $225, two-day trip combines either Barva and Poás or Braulio Carrillo, the Sarapiquí River area, and Poás, spending the night at Posada de Volcán Poás. (There is a minimum of four people.) A three-day trip explores Rincón de la Vieja on horseback. For $300, you can visit Cartago and nearby Lankester Gardens, go to Turrialba for a visit to CATIE, and then choose either a river trip or a visit to Turrialba Volcano or Guayabo National Monument—a three-day affair. Expeditions to Chirripó and Corcovado as well as to less-visited places such as Hitoy-Cerere, Caño Negro, and Barra Honda are available. Under a Trekking on Your Own program, Jungle Trails provides a hiking route with suggested campsites and information on necessary public transportation. It also will supply a guide if desired. On camping trips, all equipment is furnished except sleeping bags. The focus is on small groups. Telephone 255-3486, fax 255-2782. Jungle Trails' office is at Calle 38, Avenidas 5/7, near Centro Colón.

Costa Rica Expeditions, Horizontes Nature Adventures, and Costa Rica Sun Tours offer excellent nature-oriented tours of their own as well as booking a variety of tours offered by other companies.

Costa Rica Expeditions pioneered natural history travel in Costa Rica. A series of one-day trips under the heading of Tropical Forest Adventure offer travel with a professional naturalist for $79 to any of the following locations: Barva Volcano, El Tapir Private Reserve, Carara Biological Reserve, Cerro de la Muerte, Guayabo National Monument, Poás Volcano, Tapantí, or La Virgen del Socorro. A day tour to Irazú Volcano and the Orosí Valley, including lunch, is $63. A half-day Poás tour is $43.

The company also has multiday packages that combine several destinations: for example, an eight-day trip for $1,384 per person (double occupancy, high season). This Costa Rica Odyssey includes in-country travel, lodging, guide, taxes, and some meals. It includes visits to the Monteverde Cloud Forest Preserve and Butterfly Garden, and Poás and Corcovado National Parks. A ten-day Costa Rica Explorer offers the Monteverde Cloud Forest Preserve and Butterfly Garden, Arenal Volcano, Poás Volcano, Caño Negro and Tortuguero, plus white-water rafting. The high season (double occupancy) rate is $1,593. The company also offers white-water tours and Tortuguero packages (Chapter 11). Telephone 222-0333 or 257-0766, fax 257-1665. E-mail crexped@sol.racsa.co.cr; World Wide Web http://www.cool.co.cr/crexped.html. Costa Rica Expeditions owns the Monteverde Lodge, Tortuga Lodge, and Corcovado Lodge Tent Camp. Its office is at Avenida 3, Calles Central/2.

Horizontes Nature Adventures specializes in nature adventures and in personalized service, for both groups and individuals. It works to provide just the right itinerary for what travelers want to see or do, taking into account physical abilities, budget, length of visit, and time of year. The staff wants to make sure clients do not take off on a trip that is too long or too tough.

Basically, Horizontes acts as a reservation center, booking arrangements with private reserves, hotels, naturalist guides, and nature companies that it feels will give people an excellent experience. The company handles both one-day and multi-day tours. Its office is at Calle 28, Avenidas 1/3 (just north of the Pizza Hut on Paseo Colón). Telephone 222-2022, fax 255-4513.

Costa Rica Sun Tours operates two private nature reserves: Arenal Observatory Lodge and Tiskita Jungle Lodge. The Arenal Volcano Night Tour is $69, including stops at Zarcero for the topiary and at the hot springs at El Tabacón. Other one-day trips, $52 per person, include destinations such as Tapantí, Poás Volcano and Sarchí, Guayabo, and a combinations of Irazú Volcano, the Lankester Gardens, and the Orosí Valley.

Sun Tours has developed an interesting "Best of" set of tours. Here are two of them, seven-day trips, each for $1,095 per person (double occupancy): The Best of Arenal, Monteverde, and Guanacaste to the Arenal Volcano Observatory, Monteverde Cloud Forest, Palo Verde park, the beach at Tamarindo and, in turtle-nesting season, Las Baulas park. The Best of the South trip goes to Cerro de la Muerte, Los Cusingos (the farm of Alexander

Typical dances on island cruise tour (Ree Strange Sheck)

Skutch), Wilson Botanical Gardens, La Amistad park, and Tiskita Jungle Lodge. Others include white-water rafting, bicycling, and a cruise to Caño Island and Corcovado. See Chapter 13 for details on tours to Tiskita Jungle Lodge and Arenal Observatory Lodge.

The Sun Tours office is at Avenida 4, Calle 36. Telephone 255-3418 or 221-0303; fax 255-4410.

Tikal Tour Operators is a full-service travel agency that also specializes in nature travel. One-day tours include a city tour ($24), coffee tour ($19), Carara ($79), and the aerial tram ($70). Several eight-day Ecosafari series are $1,040 each, double occupancy. The Rainforest Ecosafari goes to Cerro de la Muerte, San Gerardo de Dota for quetzals, San Isidro and the Skutch farm at Los Cusingos; Dominical, Drake Bay, Caño Island, and Corcovado. The Ecoadventure tour goes to Las Baulas (including mountain biking), Culebra Bay (snorkeling), Coter Lake near Arenal, the Corobicí (a river float), and a Pacific dry forest (horseback riding). Telephone 223-2811, fax 223-1916. Internet address is advtikal@sol.racsa.co.cr. The office is at Avenida 2, Calles 7/9.

Camino Travel has a downtown office (Calle 1, Avenidas 1/Central) that offers travelers a "one-stop travel shop" to fit individual budgets and preferences. Services include hotel reservations, tour reservations, and purchase of bus tickets and domestic airline tickets, which can be delivered to any hotel in San Jose's metropolitan area. They also include car rental, with a driver or a private guide if you wish. You pay the same as if you book directly. What's more, if you go in with this book, you receive free an updated list of buses with station addresses and hours of service. Trip planning is a specialty, so travelers can contact Camino before arrival as well. Telephone 257-0107, fax 257-0243. Open Monday through Friday.

Camino Travel also offers a tour to Irazú volcano. The tour is followed by a visit to nearby Hacienda Retes in the Prusia Forest Reserve, for a horse-back ride with panoramic views from the 9,000-foot (2,700-m) vantage point. You'll see mountain springs and ancient oaks, and eat a lunch in the charming old log farmhouse, $77 per person. A three-day, two-night package to Chirripó is $357, including specialized guide, transportation, meals, and park fees. A seven-day, six-night Costa Rica Verde trip goes to Poás and Arenal volcanoes, Tabacón hot springs, Caño Negro wildlife refuge, Aban-garitos mangroves, and Monteverde. It includes a trained English-speaking guide, lodging, specified meals, entrance fees, and transportation. Fixed departures November through April, with other dates on request, $785 per person, double occupancy. Main office telephone 234-2530 or 225-0263; fax 225-6143.

Rafting/Kayaking

Some companies that offer river tours are Costaricaraft, Costa Rica Expeditions, and Ríos Tropicales. All have trained, bilingual guides and good equipment. If you have never rafted or kayaked before, this is a new way to experience the natural world. There are trips for beginners, and each company offers instruction. All offer one-day trips year-round on the Reventazón near Turrialba (rapids and calm stretches passing through spectacular land-scape) and the Coribicí near Cañas (a float trip good for wildlife viewing, especially birds and monkeys), both at around $70. The one-day Pacuare trip is about $90.

Costaricaraft has a $220, two-day Pacuare River rafting trip, which is great for seeing wildlife. Rafters hike to a nearby waterfall. A three-day trip on the Chirripó and General Rivers is $305. One-day Sarapiquí trips are also offered. A two-day trip combines the Pacuare River and a visit to the aerial tram, $250. Costaricaraft, which specializes in rafting, biking, and hiking tours, is affiliated with Aventuras Naturales, which also operates the Fleur De Lys Hotel in San José and Pacuare Lodge. Scheduled trips are from one to three days, but staff members also design custom packages. Telephone 225-3939 or 224-0505; fax 253-6934.

Costa Rica Expeditions offers a day-trip option on the Sarapiquí from

May to November for $69, plus runs for experienced rafters on the Reventazón, in addition to the easy-to-moderate Reventazón run. Scheduled trips from June 15 to December 15 include up to two days on the Pacuare and up to four on the Chirripó. Telephone 222-0333 or 257-0766; fax 257-1665. The office is at Avenida 3, Calles Central/2.

Ríos Tropicales has raft and kayak trips. A two-day Pacuare raft trip is $250, while the one-day Sarapiquí from July to January is $75. The company's four-day Río General trip runs from June to December only. A four-day kayaking trip to Curú is $600, and there is a nine-day Golfo Dulce tour. A ten-day rafting/kayaking adventure on the General, Reventazón, and Pacuare rivers is $1,375.

Trekking adventures are also offered for a minimum of four people by Dos Montañas, a division of Ríos Tropicales, either as part of a rafting or kayaking package or separately. Trips range from three to 15 days and can focus on a destination such as Chirripó or involve treks in the rainforest, some of which allow for interchange with the Indian culture. A five-day Corcovado adventure is $1,275, and there is a four-day trek near Cerro de la Muerte or a two-day near Tapantí. Telephone 233-6455, fax 255-4354. The office is at Avenida 2, Calle 32. Ríos Tropicales has a small outdoor store, Tienda de Aventura, with equipment for camping, hiking, climbing, and some water sports.

Cruises

Several companies offer day trips by yacht through the Gulf of Nicoya to Tortuga Island. Passengers are wined and dined during the day-long outing, with time for swimming, snorkeling, or just relaxing.

One that goes to Tortuga Island is **Bay Island Cruise**. The trip includes transportation from San José in an air-conditioned bus to Puntarenas, and the cruise on the Bay Princess along with snacks, cocktails, and lunch. The cost is $70. Telephone 296-5551, fax 296-5095. Another is **Calypso Tours**, which offers a trip by a catamaran with two Jacuzzi pools on deck; $99 including air-conditioned bus, continental breakfast, and lunch (with wine).

Calypso Tours has other $99 cruises to choose from. One is by yacht to Punta Coral, a private reserve on the Nicoya Peninsula in front of Negritos Island Biological Reserve. You can walk nature trails, see monkeys and parrots, or you can kayak, snorkel, or swim. Chilled white wine accompanies lunch. Another tour, leaving in late afternoon from San José, takes you on a tropical sky cruise with an astronomer. You'll stargaze on the waters of the Gulf of Nicoya, have dinner and use a star-finder telescope at Punta Coral,

Cruising the Pacific coast on the Temptress (Ree Strange Sheck)

and return to San José about 1:00 a.m. Telephone 256-2727, fax 233-0401. E-mail calypso@sol.racsa.co.cr.

Temptress Cruises offers three- and six-night cruises in a 99-passenger, 185-foot boat. All outside cabins with windows, private bath, and air conditioning. The voyages include morning natural history walks with naturalist guides and afternoons for snorkeling, scuba diving, sea kayaking, water skiing, or swimming. The three-night Curú voyage embarks from Puntarenas. It includes time at Curú wildlife refuge, Tortuga Island, Drake Bay and Corcovado park, and Golfito, flying back to San José. The three-night Caño voyage begins with a flight from San José to Golfito, visiting Corcovado, Caño Island, and Manuel Antonio. Each of these is $895 per person, double occupancy. A six-night Pacific voyage combines the two previous itineraries, $1,695, double occupancy. These rates are November to May; June to September rates are lower. The naturalist guides are excellent and food is superb. Telephone 220-1679, fax 220-2130. In U.S. (800) 336-8423.

Ballooning

Serendipity Costa Rica offers another way to experience the country—by hot-air balloon. The Naranjo option includes ballooning, transportation, breakfast, lunch, and visits to Poás Volcano and Sarchí, $235. The flight-only fare is $185, including breakfast and transportation. You can see Arenal at sunset for $220 per person or turn it into a two-day trip with a visit to Tabacón hot springs, and horseback riding or caving, for $435. Another trip features the Turrialba Valley. Serendipity also has a seven-day trip that combines balloon, horseback, plane, and raft. It takes you to Arenal, Tabacón, Los Angeles cloud forest, Caño Negro, Irazú Volcano, Lankester Garden, and rafting on the Reventazón and Pacuare or Pejibaye Rivers, $2,500 per person. Telephone/fax 450-0328. In U.S. (800) 635-2325.

U.S. Companies with Nature Tours to Costa Rica

Many tour companies offer trips to Costa Rica. Here are a few of those that specialize in nature travel.

Costa Rica Connection has a nine-day, eight-night national parks tour that begins at $1,479 from Los Angeles or $1,255 from Miami, with visits to Tortuguero and Manuel Antonio parks. Specialty tours focus on beaches, adventure, language and culture, and a family tour. The eight-day, seven-night Costa Rica Odyssey tour combines the Monteverde Cloud Forest Preserve, Sarchí, Manuel Antonio, a Pacific island cruise, and sightseeing in San José. Ask about a flydrive package or a sea-turtle conservation expedition at Ostional. Send for a brochure. Telephone (805) 543-8823, fax (805) 543-3626. The address is 975 Osos Street, San Luis Obispo, CA 93401.

Geo Expeditions has a ten-day natural history tour, Costa Rica Explorer, led by first-class naturalist guides. It focuses on Poás and Tortuguero National Parks, Monteverde Cloud Forest Preserve, Arenal Volcano, and Caño Negro and includes rafting on the Reventazón. The high-season cost is $1,516. The eight-day Best of Costa Rica Tour takes in Tiskita, Arenal Volcano, and Monteverde for $1,195. Costs do not include international airfare. Custom-designed tours also available. Telephone (800) 351-5041 or (209) 532-0152; fax (209) 532-1979. Or write to Box 3656, Sonora, CA 95370. E-mail geoexped@mlode.com.

The biologists and ecologists of **Geostar Travel** design bird-watching, botanical, and natural history tours. Naturalists lead the ten-day Costa Rica Explorer to Monteverde Cloud Forest Preserve, Poás, Arenal Volcano, Caño Negro, and Tortuguero, plus a trip on the Reventazón River. The cost during the high season is $1,546. The ten-day Odyssey tour visits Monteverde, Poás, and Corcovado. It also includes visits to a butterfly garden. It costs $1,349 in the high season. Birding and botanical tours are also offered. These rates do not include international airfare. New are Rainforest Educational

Workshops held in conjunction with the Organization for Tropical Studies, where you interact with scientists at either the Wilson Botanical Garden or La Selva Biological Station. Telephone (800) 624-6633 or (707) 579-2420; fax (707) 579-2704. The address is 1240 Century Court, Santa Rosa, CA 95403.

Wildland Adventures offers tours as well as an individual trip planner that lets you build your own program. The eight-day Tropical Trails Odyssey travels to Monteverde and the Osa Peninsula. A ten-day Family Odyssey takes in the aerial tram Selva Verde, Arenal Volcano, Caño Negro, Tamarindo Beach, and the Fun Park in San José. A six-day adventure-wellness vacation at Nosara Yoga and Retreat Center offers travelers hatha yoga classes, hikes, beach outings, massages, aromatherapy, horseback riding, and meditation. For prices, brochure, or travel planner, telephone (800) 345-4453 or (206) 365-0686, fax (206) 363-6615. The address is 3516 NE 155th, Seattle, WA 98155.

Preferred Adventures does customized individual travel as well as tours for birders, horticulturists, and natural history travelers. A Tropical Birding and Discovery Journey to the Rainforests of Costa Rica is led by Dr. Noble Proctor, author of *A Manual of Ornithology*. The 11-day trip goes to top birding destinations around the country, $2,395 per person, double occupancy. New are Rain Forest Ecology Workshops in collaboration with the Organization for Tropical Studies: one at Las Cruces Biological Station and Corcovado, the other at the La Selva Station and Tortuguero. Contact Preferred Adventures (800)840-8687 or (612) 222-8131; fax (612) 222-4221. E-mail paltours@aol.com. One West Water Street, Suite 300, St. Paul, MN 55107.

Americas Tours and Travel offers individual itineraries emphasizing Costa Rica as a nature destination. It encourages travel to the private reserves and to less-visited parks and reserves, as well as the more popular ones. Discounted air fares available, including student and youth fares. Telephone (800) 553-2513 or (206) 623-8850, fax (206) 467-0454; 1402 Third Avenue # 1019, Seattle, WA 98101-2110.

Holbrook Travel has an array of all-inclusive natural history tours, some with fixed departures. Birding, photography, and biodiversity and national parks tours are available, generally led by individuals noted in their fields, as well as naturalist tours. Telephone (904) 377-7111, fax (904) 371-3710. E-mail travel@holbrook.usa.com and World Wide Web http://www.gorp.com/holbrook.htm.

Practical Extras

International Airline Information

In San José

Airline	Address	Reservations	Airport
Aero Costa Rica	2 blocks south of Hospital México	296-1111	446-2682
American	Across from Hotel Corobicí, Avenida 56, Calle 42	257-1266 441-0841	442-8800
Continental	From U.S. Embassy, 200 meters south, 300 east, 50 north	296-4611	442-1904
LACSA	Calle 1, Avenida 5	296-0909	443-3555
Mexicana	Calle 5, Avenidas 7/9	257-6334	441-9377
TACA	Avenida 3, Calle 40	222-1790	442-3606
United	La Sabana, Edificio Oficentro	220-4844	441-8025

Reservation Numbers—United States and Canada

Aero Costa Rica	(800) 871-9096, (800) 825-2377, United States
American	(800) 433-7300, United States and Canada
Continental	(800) 231-0856, United States
LACSA	(800) 225-2272, United States and Canada
Mexicana	(800) 531-7921, United States and Canada
TACA	(800) 535-8780, United States
United	(800) 426-5560, (800) 468-1808, United States

Domestic Airline Scheduled Service

SANSA

San José office at Calle 24, Paseó Colón/Avenida 1, Telephone 233-0397 or
233-3258; fax 255-2176.

Daily flights to Coto 47, Golfito, Palmar Sur, Puerto Jiménez, Quepos,
Tamarindo, Tambor.

To Barra del Colorado on Tuesday, Thursday, and Saturday.

To Sámara (Carrillo) and Nosara on Monday, Wednesday, Friday, and
  Sunday.
To Liberia on Monday, Wednesday, and Friday.

Travelair
San José office at Tobias Bolaños Airport in Pavas, Telephone 220-3054, fax
220-0413.
Daily flights to Barra del Colorado, Carrillo, Golfito, Liberia, Nosara,
Palmar Sur, Puerto Jiménez, Punta Islita, Quepos, Tamarindo, Tambor,
Tortuguero.

Costa Rican Tourism Institute
San José
Plaza de la Cultura
Calle 5, Avenidas Central/2
Telephone 222-1090
442-1820 (airport office)
Fax 223-5452
In United States (800) 343-6332 (8:00 a.m. to 5:00 p.m. Central Time)

Private Information Services
INFOtur: U.S. telephone (800) 807-TICO, except California (800)
901-TICO. Fax (805) 929-7006
Via Computer:
Costa Rica's TravelWEB, http://www.magicom/crica/
    or e-mail iiclayton@magi.com
TravelNet, http://www.centralamerica.com
    or e-mail calypso@centralamerica.com
Tico Times, http://magi.com/crica/ttimes.html
    or e-mail ttimes@sol.racsa.co.cr
National Chamber of Tourism (CANATUR), http://www.costarica.
tourism.co.cr

Embassies in San José

United States
Rohrmoser, road to Pavas
  in front of Centro Comercial
  (any taxi driver can take you)
Telephone 220-3939
Consulate: 220-3050

Canada
Oficentro Ejecutivo La Sabana,
  Sabana Sur, (Building 5,
  3rd floor)
Telephone 296-4149
Fax: 231-4783

France
Road to Curridabat,
    200 meters south,
    25 east of Indoor Club
Telephone 225-0733, 225-0933

Germany
Rohrmoser
Telephone 232-5533, 232-5450

Great Britain
Edificio Centro Colón, 11th floor
    Avenida Colón, Calle 38
Telephone 221-5566, 221-5816

Holland
Oficentro Ejecutivo
    La Sabana, Sabana Sur
    (Building 3, 3rd floor)
Telephone 296-1490

Italy
Los Yoses, Avenida 10,
    Calles 33/35
Telephone 224-6574, 234-2326

Japan
Residencial Rohrmoser,
    400 meters west,
    100 north of La Nunciatura
Telephone 232-1255

Spain
Calle 32, Paseo Colon/Avenida 2
Telephone 222-1933, 222-5745

Switzerland
Centro Colon, 10th floor
    Paseo Colón, Calle 38
Telephone 221-4829

Transportation Tidbits

Ferries
Puntarenas ferry (Puntarenas–Playa Naranjo on Nicoya Peninsula) Telephone
661-1069, car fee plus driver is $10.50, passengers $1.50 each.
    Leaves Puntarenas 3:15 a.m., 7:00 a.m., 10:50 a.m., 2:50 p.m.,
    7:00 p.m.
    Leaves Playa Naranjo 5:10 a.m., 8:50 a.m., 12:50 p.m., 5:00 p.m.,
    9:00 p.m.
Tempisque ferry (across mouth of Tempisque River) Telephone 685-5295, car
and driver about $3, passengers less than 25 cents each.
    Leaves Puerto Níspero (mainland side) at 5 a.m. and Puerto Moreno
    (on the peninsula) at 5:30 a.m., continuous service until 7 p.m.
Puntarenas–Paquera ferry (Puntarenas to Paquera on Nicoya Peninsula)
Telephone 661-2084, $2.75, passengers $2 each or $4.25 first class.
    Leaves Puntarenas 4:15 a.m., 8:45 a.m., 12:30 p.m., 5:30 p.m.
    Leaves Paquera 6:00 a.m., 10:30 a.m., 2:30 p.m., 7:15 p.m.

Paquera Launch (Puntarenas to Paquera on Nicoya Peninsula)
Telephone 661-2830, fax 641-0241, passengers only, less than $2 each.
    Leaves Puntarenas from behind market 6:15 a.m., 11:00 a.m., and
    3:15 p.m.
    Leaves Paquera 8:00 a.m., 12:30 p.m., 5:00 p.m.

Taxis
If you have access to a phone directory, you can look in the yellow pages for
taxis, or your hotel can call one for you. Here are a few in San José, since
public phones do not have phone books.
Coopeguaria—226-1366
Coopeirazu—254-3211
Coopetaxi—235-9966
Coopetico—253-5838, 253-5691
Coopeuno—254-6667
Taxis San Jorge—222-0025, 221-3434, 221-3535
Taxis Unidos—221-6865, 441-0333 (airport)

Intercity Buses
Regular intercity bus service provided by different companies covers practically the entire country, with varying frequency and levels of service.
Departure locations are listed below alphabetically by town or destination,
along with phone numbers and length of trip. Most are buses from San José;
ones from other cities are so indicated. Sometimes there is a terminal, but
sometimes there is only a sign alongside the street indicating the bus stop.
Bus stops sometimes move; check with the ICT information office if you
have trouble.
Airport (Juan Santamaría): Avenida 2, Calles 12/14 (24-hour
    service, leaving every five minutes from 5:00 a.m. to 8:00 p.m., then less
    frequently), 222-5325, 30 minutes
Alajuela: Avenida 2, Calles 12/14 (same as above), 222-5325
Arenal from Ciudad Quesada: Municipal Terminal, twice a day
    (this is the bus to Tilarán)
Barva Volcano–Braulio Carrillo: From central market in Heredia
    bus to Paso Llano), three times daily except twice on Sunday, then walk
    to park
Braulio Carrillo National Park: Calle 12, Avenidas 7/9 (every half
    hour from 5:30 a.m. to 7:00 p.m.), 257-8129 (this is the Guapiles
    bus; get off at the ranger station), 35 minutes
Cahuita: Calle Central, Avenidas 9/11, three times daily (this is the bus for
    Sixaola), 257-8129, 4 hours

Cahuita from Limón: 75 meters north of Radio Casino, six times a day, 758-1572

Cañas: Calle 16, Avenidas 3/5 (buy ticket in advance), five times daily, 222-3006, 3 hours

Cartago: Avenidas 18/20, Calle 5 (every ten minutes from 5:00 a.m. to 7:00 p.m., then less frequently), 233-5350, 35 minutes

Ciudad Quesada (San Carlos): Calle 16, Avenidas 1/3 (every hour from 5:00 a.m. to 7:30 p.m.), 255-4318, 2½ hours

Ciudad Quesada–La Fortuna: Municipal bus station in Ciudad Quesada (take bus for El Tanque), 460-0326, 1 hour

Ciudad Quesada–Arenal–Tilarán: Municipal bus station in Ciudad Quesada (goes through Fortuna and around Lake Arenal and Volcano), 4 hours

Dominical: Calle 12, Avenidas 7/9, twice a day, 771-1384

Flamingo Beach: Calle 20, Avenida 3, twice a day, 222-7202

Fortuna: Calle 16, Avenidas 1/3, 255-4318, 3½ hours

Fortuna from Ciudad Quesada: Parada Municipal (Municipal Terminal), twice a day (this is the bus to Tilarán)

Golfito: express bus, (buy ticket in advance), three times a day, 221-4214, 8 hours

Guayabo National Monument from Turrialba: twice daily

Heredia: Calle 1, Avenidas 7/9, (every 10 minutes from 5:00 a.m. to 10:00 p.m.), 233-8392, 25 minutes; or microbuses from Avenida 2, Calles 10/12

Jacó Beach: Calles 16/18, Avenida 1, three buses daily, 233-1109, 2½ hours

Junquillal: Calle 20, Avenida 3 (daily express), several buses daily, 221-7202, 5 hours

La Cruz or Peñas Blancas: Calle 16, Avenidas 3/5, two buses daily, 222-3006, 6 hours

Lankester Garden from Cartago: south side of Central Park, every 30 minutes, 574-6127, 15 minutes

Liberia: Calle 14, Avenidas 1/3 (several express buses daily, ticket in advance), 222-1650, 4 hours

Limón: Avenida 3, Calles 19/21 (hourly from 5:00 a.m. to 7:00 p.m., through Braulio Carrillo), 223-7811, 2½ hours

Manuel Antonio: see Quepos

Monteverde: Calle 14, Avenidas 9/11 (tickets in advance), 222-3854, also at La Toruma Youth Hostel, Avenida Central, Calles 29/31, 224-4085, 645-5051 (in Monteverde), several buses daily, 4 hours

Monteverde from Tilarán: from Santa Elena (3 km from Monteverde), 3 hours

Nicoya: Calle 14, Avenidas 3/5 (buy tickets in advance), 222-2750, 6 hours
Nosara (Garza and Guiones): Calle 14, Avenidas 3/5, 222-2750, 5 hours
Nosara from Nicoya: Main terminal, once a day, 685-5352, 1½ hours
Playa del Coco: Calle 14, Avenidas 1/3, 222-1650, 5 hours
Puerto Jiménez (for Corcovado): Calle 12, Avenidas, 7/9 (twice daily), 771-2550, 8 hours
Puerto Viejo de Limón: Calle Central, Avenidas 9/11, 257-8129, 4½ hours
Puerto Viejo de Sarapiquí: Avenida 11, Calles Central/1, several daily, 4 hours
Puerto Viejo de Sarapiquí from Ciudad Quesada: Municipal Terminal, three times daily, 460-0638, 3 hours
Puntarenas: Calle 16, Avenidas 10/12 (every 40 minutes from 5:00 a.m. to 7:00 p.m), 233-2610, 2 hours
Quepos and Manuel Antonio: Calle 16, Avenidas 1/3, express from lot beside Hotel Musoc (advance tickets in adjacent market), 223-5567, 3½ hours
Quepos from Puntarenas: Next to Puntarenas Terminal, three times daily, 643-3135
Quepos from San Isidro: Municipal market in Quepos (twice daily), 771-1384, 3½ hours
Sámara and Carrillo beaches: Calle 14, Avenidas 3/5 (daily express), 222-2750, 6 hours
San Isidro de El General: Calle 16, Avenidas 1/3 (every hour from 5:30 a.m. to 5:00 p.m., advance tickets), 222-2422, 3 hours; in San Isidro get bus for San Gerardo de Rivas (233-4160) for Chirripó
San Vito: Avenida 5, Calles 14/16 (advance tickets), 222-2750, 5 hours
Santa Cruz: Calle 20, Avenidas 1/3, 221-7202, 5 hours
Sarchí: Calle 16, Avenidas 1/3, express, 1½ hours
Sarchí from Alajuela: from Avenidas 1/3, Calle 8, in Alajuela; 441-3781
Tamarindo: Calle 14, Avenidas 3/5, 222-2750, 223-8229, 5½ hours
Tilarán: Calle 14, Avenidas 9/11, four times daily, 222-3854, 4 hours
Turrialba: Calle 13, Avenidas 6/8 (hourly express from 5:00 a.m. to 10:00 p.m.), 556-0073, 1½ hours
Zarcero: Calle 16, Avenidas 1/3 (hourly bus from 5:00 a.m. to 7:30 p.m.— Ciudad Quesada bus), 255-4318, 1½ hours
Another Option: The Pura Natura bus company offers seven interlinked routes; travelers choose where they want to stay along these routes and move to another destination with a day's notice. Telephone 233-9709, fax 223-9200. Fares for this door-to-door service are considerably higher than regular bus service.

Route 1: San José–Las Horquetas–Sarapiquí, La Fortuna, San José
Route 2: San José–San Ramón–La Fortuna–Sarapiquí–San José

Route 3: San José–Puntarenas–Jacó–Manuel Antonio–San José
Route 4: San José–Liberia–Flamingo–Tamarindo–San José
Route 5: San José–Braulio Carrillo–Limón–Cahuita–San José
Route 6: La Fortuna–Lake Arenal–Cañas–Liberia–La Fortuna
Route 7: San José–Monteverde; La Fortuna–Monteverde

Metric Conversion Tables

To change	to	Multiply by
Hectares	Acres	2.471
Meters	Feet	3.2808
Meters	Yards	1.094
Kilometers	Miles	.6214
Millimeters	Inches	.0394
Centimeters	Inches	.3937
Square kilometers	Square miles	.3861
Liters	Gallons (U.S.)	.2642
Liters	Pints	2.113
Kilograms	Pounds	2.205
Grams	Ounces	.0353

Temperature Conversion

Celsius to Fahrenheit: multiply by 9/5 (or 1.8) and add 32.
Fahrenheit to Celsius: subtract 32 and multiply by 5/9 (or .56).
Here are some reference points to save some of the math:

Celsius	Fahrenheit
0°	32°
10°	50°
20°	68°
30°	86°
35°	95°
40°	104°

Fauna: English and Spanish Names

English	Spanish
agouti	guatusa
armadillo	cusuco
bat	murciélago
bird	pájaro, ave
brocket deer	cabra de monte

English	Spanish
butterfly	mariposa
caiman	caimán, lagarto
coati	pizote
collared peccary	saíno
cougar, mountain lion	puma, león
crocodile	cocodrilo
frog	rana
gopher	taltusa
howler monkey	mono congo
jaguar	jaguar, tigre
jaguarundi	león breñero
kinkajou	martilla
lesser anteater, tamandua	oso hormiguero
margay	caucel, tigrillo
ocelot	manigordo
opossum	zorro
paca	tepezcuintle
parrot	loro
raccoon	mapachín
river otter	nutria, perro de agua
scarlet macaw	lapa
silky anteater	serafín
skunk	zorro hediondo
sloth	perezoso, perica
snake	serpiente, culebra
spider monkey	mono colorado, mono araña
squirrel	ardilla, chisa
squirrel monkey	mono tití, mono ardilla
tapir	danta
tayra	tolomuco
toad	sapo
turtle	tortuga
white-faced capuchin monkey	mono cara blanca
white-lipped peccary	cariblanco
white-tailed deer	venado cola blanca

Recommended Reading

A Naturalist in Costa Rica, Alexander F. Skutch. Gainesville, Fla.: University of Florida Press, 1971.

The Costa Ricans, Richard Biesanz, Karen Zubris Biesanz, and Mavis Hiltunen Biesanz. Englewood Cliffs, N.J.: Prentice-Hall, 1982.

Costa Rican Natural History, edited by Daniel H. Janzen. Chicago: University of Chicago Press, 1983.

The Butterflies of Costa Rica and Their Natural History, Philip J. DeVries. Princeton, N.J.: Princeton University Press, 1987.

Costa Rica National Parks, Mario A. Boza. Madrid: Incafo (for Fundación Neotrópica de Costa Rica), 1996.

The Rivers of Costa Rica: A Canoeing, Kayaking, and Rafting Guide, Michael W. Mayfield and Rafael E. Gallo. Birmingham, Ala.: Menasha Ridge Press, 1988.

Journey through a Tropical Jungle, Adrian Forsyth. Toronto: Greey de Pencier Books, 1988.

A Guide to the Birds of Costa Rica, F. Gary Stiles and Alexander F. Skutch. Ithaca, N.Y.: Cornell University Press, 1989.

The New Key to Costa Rica, Beatrice Blake. San José: Publications in English, 1991.

The Quetzal and the Macaw: The Story of Costa Rica's National Parks, David Rains Wallace. San Francisco: Sierra Book Club, 1992.

The Biodiversity of Costa Rica, Zaldett Barrientos and Julián Monge-Nájera (eds.). Instituto Nacional de Biodiversidad, 1995.

Index

Index

Braulio Carrillo National Park, 94, 129, 265–69; tours to, 94, 375

Buena Vista Lodge, 150, 332–35

Buses: intercity, 45–48; city, 47–48; schedules, 386–89

Business hours. See Stores

Butterfly gardens: near Arenal, 119; near Braulio Carrillo, 130; at La Guacima, 68; in Monteverde, 155–56; near Muelle, 112; at Puerto Viejo de Sarapiquí, 126, 330; at San Joaquín de Flores, 68–69; in San José, 69; at Tortuguero, 242; near Turrialba, 104

Butterfly museum, 69

C

Cabinas Chacón, 189, 344–45

Cabinas Chimuri, 250, 371–73

Cabo Blanco Strict Nature Reserve, 140–42, 269–70; tours to, 140, 142

Cacao, 245; overview of, 237

Cacao Biological Station, 278, 280

Cahuita, 244–49

Cahuita National Park, 244, 245, 249, 270–71; tours to, 236, 245, 271

Calypso Tours, 379–80

Camino Travel, 377–78

Canal, dry, 203

Canals, Tortuguero, 238, 241, 242, 243, 244

Cañas, 143

Caño Island National Biological Reserve, 271–72; tours to, 198–99, 200, 201, 202, 360–61

Caño Negro National Wildlife Refuge, 113, 304–5; tours to, 111, 112, 113

Canopy tours: near Braulio Carrillo, 130–31; Casa Río Blanco, 370; Dominical, 351; near Liberia, 344; Monteverde, 155, 157; near Orotina, 204; Parrita, 213; Rara Avis, 329

Car rental, 50–51; at airport, 38

Carara National Biological Reserve, 206, 272–74; tours to, 206, 213, 374–76

Caribbean Conservation Corporation, 240–43

Caribbean region, 230–56; map, 231; national biological reserves in, 284–85 (Hitoy Cerere); national parks in, 270–71 (Cahuita), 300–302 (Tortuguero); national wildlife refuges in, 302 (Barra del Colorado), 307–8 (Gandoca-Manzanillo); private nature reserves in, 366–73

Cartago, 97–100

Casa Río Blanco, 232, 369–71

CATIE, 101, 102–3; tours to, 101

Caverns: at Barra Honda, 264–65; tours to Venado, 112, 118, 119, 122, 123

Cecropia tree, 268

Central Valley, 16–17, 314–15

Central region, 87–104; map, 88; national parks in, 265–69 (Braulio Carrillo), 281, 283 (Guayabo), 285, 287 (Irazú), 292–94 (Poás), 299–300 (Tapantí); private nature reserves in, 314–15

Cerro de la Muerte, 187, 190; tours to, 376, 377, 379

Chachagua Rain Forest Hotel, 108, 318–19

Chiggers, 55

Children's Museum, 66

Children's rainforest, 14, 107, 153

Chirripó Mountain, 16, 274–75

Chirripó National Park, 192, 274–75; tours to, 192

Cholera, 29

Ciudad Quesada (San Carlos), 109–11

Climate, 18, 20–23

Clodomiro Picado Institute, 67–68

Clothing, 31–34

Coastline, lengths, 18

Cocos Island, 275–76

Coffee, 25; overview of, 96

Colón, 39

Columbus, Christopher, 5, 235

Conservation, 14–15, 24–25, 257

Conservation areas, national, 258

Conservation organizations, 14, 153

Corcovado National Park, 197, 198, 276–78; tours to, 198, 199, 200, 201, 202, 278, 360–61, 379

Corobicí River, 144; tours to, 144, 378

Costa Rica Connection, 381

Costa Rica Expeditions, 378–79

Costaricaraft, 378

Costa Rica Sun Tours, 376–77

Coter Lake, 320

Credit cards, 40–41, 42

Cruises. See boats

Currency, 38, 39

Curú National Wildlife Refuge, 138, 305–7; tours to, 138, 380

D

Debt-for-nature swaps, 12, 14

Democracy, 6–7

Dengue, 29

Departure tax, 29

Diving: at Bahia Gigante, 138; at

393

Index

Other Books from John Muir Publications

Rick Steves' Books

Asia Through the Back Door, 400 pp., $17.95

Europe 101: History and Art for the Traveler, 352 pp., $17.95

Mona Winks: Self-Guided Tours of Europe's Top Museums, 432 pp., $18.95

Rick Steves' Baltics & Russia, 144 pp., $9.95

Rick Steves' Europe, 528 pp., $17.95

Rick Steves' France, Belgium & the Netherlands, 256 pp., $13.95

Rick Steves' Germany, Austria & Switzerland, 256 pp., $13.95

Rick Steves' Great Britain, 240 pp., $13.95

Rick Steves' Italy, 224 pp., $13.95

Rick Steves' Scandinavia, 192 pp., $13.95

Rick Steves' Spain & Portugal, 208 pp., $13.95

Rick Steves' Europe Through the Back Door, 480 pp., $18.95

Rick Steves' French Phrase Book, 176 pp., $5.95

Rick Steves' German Phrase Book, 176 pp., $5.95

Rick Steves' Italian Phrase Book, 176 pp., $5.95

Rick Steves' Spanish & Portuguese Phrase Book, 304 pp., $6.95

Rick Steves' French/German/Italian Phrase Book, 320 pp., $7.95

A Natural Destination Series

Belize: A Natural Destination, 344 pp., $16.95

Costa Rica: A Natural Destination, 380 pp., $18.95

Guatemala: A Natural Destination, 360 pp., $16.95

City·Smart™ Guidebook Series

All are 240–256 pages and $14.95 paperback.

City·Smart Guidebook: Cleveland (avail.2/97)

City·Smart Guidebook: Denver

City·Smart Guidebook: Minneapolis/St. Paul

City·Smart Guidebook: Nashville (avail.1/97)

City·Smart Guidebook: Portland

City·Smart Guidebook: Tampa/ St. Petersburg (avail.12/96)

For Birding Enthusiasts

The Birder's Guide to Bed and Breakfasts: U.S. and Canada, 416 pp., $17.95

The Visitor's Guide to the Birds of the Central National Parks: U.S. and Canada, 400 pp., $15.95

The Visitor's Guide to the Birds of the Eastern National Parks: U.S. and Canada, 400 pp., $15.95

The Visitor's Guide to the Birds of the Rocky Mountain National Parks: U.S. and Canada, 432 pp., $15.95

Unique Travel Series

All are 112 pages and $10.95 paperback, except Georgia and Oregon.

Unique Arizona

Unique California

Unique Colorado

Unique Florida

Unique Georgia ($11.95)

Unique New England

Unique New Mexico

Unique Oregon ($9.95)
Unique Texas
Unique Washington

Travel+Smart™
Trip Planners

All are 240–256 pages and $14.95
paperback.
**American Southwest
Travel+Smart Trip Planner**
**Colorado Travel+Smart
Trip Planner**
**Eastern Canada Travel+Smart
Trip Planner**
**Florida Gulf Travel+Smart
Trip Planner** (avail. 12/96)
**Hawaii Travel+Smart
Trip Planner**
**Kentucky/Tennessee
Travel+Smart Trip Planner**
**Minnesota/Wisconsin
Travel+Smart**™ **Trip Planner**
**New England Travel+Smart
Trip Planner**
**Northern California Travel+Smart
Trip Planner** (avail. 8/96)
**Pacific Northwest Travel+Smart
Trip Planner** (avail. 8/96)

*Other Terrific
Travel Titles*

**The 100 Best Small Art Towns in
America**, 256 pp., $15.95
**The Big Book of Adventure
Travel**, 384 pp., $17.95
**Indian America: A Traveler's
Companion**, 480 pp., $18.95
The People's Guide to Mexico,
608 pp., $19.95
**Ranch Vacations: The Complete
Guide to Guest and Resort,
Fly-Fishing, and Cross-Country
Skiing Ranches**, 528 pp., $19.95
Understanding Europeans,
272 pp., $14.95
**Undiscovered Islands of the
Caribbean**, 336 pp., $16.95

**Watch It Made in the U.S.A.:
A Visitor's Guide to the
Companies that Make Your
Favorite Products**, 328 pp.,
$16.95
The World Awaits, 280 pp., $16.95

Automotive Titles

**The Greaseless Guide to Car
Care**, 272 pp., $19.95
How to Keep Your Subaru Alive,
480 pp., $21.95
**How to Keep Your Toyota Pickup
Alive**, 392 pp., $21.95
How to Keep Your VW Alive,
464 pp., $25

Ordering Information

Please check your local bookstore
or call **1-800-888-7504** to order
direct and to receive a complete
catalog. A shipping charge will be
added to your order total.

Send all inquiries to:
John Muir Publications
P.O. Box 613
Santa Fe, NM 87504